Introduction to American Studies

Introduction to
American Studies

Edited by
Malcolm Bradbury and Howard Temperley

Longman
London and New York

Longman Group Limited

Longman House, Burnt Mill, Harlow Essex, UK

Published in the United States of America
by Longman Inc., New York

First Published 1981

British Library Cataloguing in Publication Data

Introduction to American studies.
  1. United States – Study and teaching
  I. Bradbury, Malcolm II. Temperley,
  Howard
  973'.07'2 E175.8 79–42620

  ISBN 0–582–48903–2
  ISBN 0–582–48904–0 Pbk

Printed in Singapore by Kyodo Shing Loong Printing Industries Pte Ltd

Contents

Chronology

1733	Founding of Georgia
1744–48	King George's War against French
1754	Beginning of French and Indian War
1760	French surrender Canada to British
1763	Peace of Paris
1765	Stamp Act
1767	Townshend Duties
1773	Boston Tea Party
1774	Coercive Acts
1775	Fighting at Lexington and Concord; Second Continental Congress assembles
1776	Thomas Paine, *Common Sense*; Declaration of Independence
1778	Franco-American alliance
1781	Articles of Confederation proclaimed; defeat of British at Yorktown
1782	H St John de Crèvecoeur, *Letters from an American Farmer*
1783	Articles of Peace ratified (Treaty of Paris); Noah Webster, *American Spelling Book*
1785	Ordinance passed for sale of western lands
1787	Constitutional Convention meets in Philadelphia; Northwest Ordinance provides for govenment of national domain
1787–88	Alexander Hamilton *et al.*, *The Federalist*
1788	Constitution ratified
1789	George Washington elected first US President
1790	First US Census shows population of 3.9 million
1791–96	Hamilton–Jefferson feud leads to emergence of first American party system (Federalists versus Democratic-Republicans)
1793	Eli Whitney invents cotton gin
1800	Thomas Jefferson (Democratic-Republican) elected third US President
1803	Louisiana Purchase extends US border to Rockies
1807	African slave trade to US abolished; Joel Barlow, *The Columbiad*
1812–14	War of 1812
1815–17	Collapse of Federalist Party

1852	Harriet Beecher Stowe, *Uncle Tom's Cabin*
1854	Kansas–Nebraska Act repeals Missouri Compromise; emergence of Republican Party; Henry David Thoreau, *Walden*
1855	First edition of Walt Whitman's *Leaves of Grass*
1857	Supreme Court's Dred Scott decision denies citizenship to US blacks and right of Congress to exclude slavery from territories
1859	John Brown's raid on arsenal at Harper's Ferry, Virginia
1860	Abraham Lincoln (Republican) elected sixteenth US President
1861	Secession of Southern states leads to outbreak of Civil War; Morrill Tariff inaugurates new high-tariff policy
1862	Homestead Act
1863	Emancipation Proclamation frees slaves in areas with rebel control
1865	Surrender of Confederate forces; slavery abolished by 13th Amendment; assassination of President Lincoln
1867	First Reconstruction Act; purchase of Alaska from Russia; Horatio Alger, *Ragged Dick*
1869	Mark Twain, *Innocents Abroad*; completion of first transcontinental railroad
1870	Bret Harte, *The Luck of Roaring Camp*
1875	Mary Baker Eddy, *Science and Health*
1875–76	Second Sioux War; defeat of Custer's cavalry in Battle of the Little Big Horn
1876	Invention of the telephone by Alexander Graham Bell
1877	Withdrawal of Federal troops from the South marks end of Reconstruction
1881	John D Rockefeller's Standard Oil Trust established; Henry James, *Portrait of a Lady*
1885	Mark Twain, *The Adventures of Huckleberry Finn*; William Dean Howells, *The Rise of Silas Lapham*
1887	Dawes Severalty Act provides for the settlement of Indians on homesteads
1888	Edward Bellamy, *Looking Backward*

1890	Sherman Antitrust Act; Eleventh US Census declares frontier closed
1891	Formation of the People's (Populist) Party
1893	Chicago World's Columbian Exposition
1895	J P Morgan and Co established; Stephen Crane, *The Red Badge of Courage*
1896	Supreme Court upholds legality of 'separate but equal' facilities for blacks
1898	Spanish-American War; annexation of Hawaii and Philippines
1899	Thornstein Veblen, *The Theory of the Leisure Class*; Frank Norris, *McTeague*
1900	Theodore Dreiser, *Sister Carrie*; Twelfth US Census shows population of 76 million
1901	US Steel Corporation established
1903	Henry James, *The Ambassadors*; Jack London, *Call of the Wild*; W E B Du Bois, *The Souls of Black Folk*
1906	Upton Sinclair, *The Jungle*
1907	Peak immigration year: 1,285,000 immigrants enter US; Henry Adams, *Education of Henry Adams*; William James, *Pragmatism*
1909	First Model T Ford; Gertrude Stein, *Three Lives*
1913	Armory Show exhibits modern art
1914	Eight-hour day with five dollar minimum wage introduced in all Ford plants; President Wilson proclaims US neutrality
1915	British steamer *Lusitania* torpedoed with loss of over a hundred American lives; Germany restricts submarine warfare; D W Griffiths, *The Birth of a Nation*; Edgar Lee Masters, *Spoon River Anthology*
1917	German resumption of unrestricted submarine warfare; US declaration of war; T S Eliot, 'The Love Song of J Alfred Prufrock'
1918	Wilson outlines his 14 points to Congress; Armistice ends war in Europe
1919	Prohibition Amendment ratified; Sherwood Anderson, *Winesburg, Ohio*; Senate votes down US membership of League of Nations
1920	Red Scare leads to mass arrests of labour agitators; Sinclair Lewis, *Main Street*; Ezra Pound, *Hugh*

	Selwyn Mauberley; Fourteenth US Census shows urban population exceeds rural
1921–24	Quota laws restrict immigration
1922	T S Eliot, *The Waste Land*; Eugene O'Neill, *Anna Christie*
1923	Henry R Luce launches *Time*; D H Lawrence, *Studies in Classic American Literature*; Wallace Stevens, *Harmonium*
1925	F Scott Fitzgerald, *The Great Gatsby*; Gertrude Stein, *The Making of Americans*; Scopes (evolution) trial in Dayton Tennessee; Harold Ross launches *The New Yorker*
1926	Ernest Hemingway, *The Sun Also Rises*
1927	Execution of Sacco and Vanzetti; Charles Lindbergh flies Atlantic
1928	First full-length sound film; 26 million cars and 13 million radios in use in US
1929	William Faulkner, *The Sound and the Fury*; Ernest Hemingway, *A Farewell to Arms*; stock-market crash
1930	Hart Crane, *The Bridge*; Ezra Pound, *A Draft of XXX Cantos*
1932	William Faulkner, *Light in August*
1933	Inauguration of Franklin D Roosevelt; beginning of New Deal; end of prohibition
1934	Scott Fitzgerald, *Tender is the Night*; William Carlos Williams, *Collected Poems, 1921–31*
1935–37	Neutrality legislation passed in order to prevent US being drawn into future foreign wars
1936	John Dos Passos, *U.S.A*
1939	John Steinbeck, *The Grapes of Wrath*; Nathanael West, *The Day of the Locust*; Britain and France declare war on Germany
1940	Richard Wright, *Native Son*
1941	Lend-Lease Act; Orson Welles's *Citizen Kane*; Japanese attack on Pearl Harbor leads to American entry into war
1942	American troops fighting in Pacific and North Africa; UN Declaration signed in Washington
1943	Rogers and Hammerstein, *Oklahoma*

1944	Allied invasion of Normandy; advance of Russian forces into Czechoslovakia, Hungary and Poland
1945	German capitulation; surrender of Japan following dropping of atomic bombs on Hiroshima and Nagasaki; UN Conference in San Francisco
1946	Robert Penn Warren, *All the King's Men*; William Carlos Williams, *Paterson, Book One*
1947	Truman Doctrine and Marshall Plan designed to counteract Soviet expansionism and provide for European reconstruction; Taft-Hartley Act restricts trade union power; Tennessee Williams, *A Streetcar Named Desire*
1948	Norman Mailer, *The Naked and the Dead*
1948–49	Berlin blockade and airlift
1949	NATO established; Arthur Miller, *Death of a Salesman*
1950–53	Korean War
1950	Alger Hiss convicted of perjury; McCarthy launches anticommunist crusade; Seventeenth US Census shows population of 151 million
1950–60	Advent of mass television
1951	J D Salinger, *The Catcher in the Rye*
1952	Ralph Ellison, *Invisible Man*
1953	James Baldwin, *Go Tell it on the Mountain*; execution of Rosenbergs for atomic espionage
1954	J Robert Oppenheimer denied security clearance; Senate censures McCarthy; Supreme Court rules against school segregation, Wallace Stevens, *Collected Poems*
1956	Suez crisis; Soviet invasion of Hungary; Eugene O'Neill, *Long Day's Journey into Night*
1957	Jack Kerouac, *On the Road*; Federal troops enforce school desegregation in Little Rock, Arkansas
1958	John Kenneth Galbraith, *The Affluent Society*
1959	Saul Bellow, *Henderson the Rain King*; Robert Lowell, *Life Studies*
1961	Inauguration of President Kennedy who calls for a 'New Frontier'; Bay of Pigs (Cuban invasion) fiasco
1961–68	Birth control pill comes into general use
1962	Cuban missile crisis; international live telecasts by

satellite; Rachel Carson, *Silent Spring*; Edward Albee, *Who's Afraid of Virginia Woolf?*

1963   Assassination of President Kennedy

1964   President Johnson calls for a Great Society; Saul Bellow, *Herzog*; Gulf of Tonkin Resolution leads to build-up of US ground forces in South Vietnam

1965–67   Race riots in Los Angeles, Cleveland, Chicago, Newark, Detroit and other major cities

1968–72   Student protest on US campuses

1968   Assassination of Robert Kennedy and Martin Luther King; Norman Mailer, *Armies of the Night*; John Updike, *Couples*

1969   US astronauts land on moon

1970   US forces invade Cambodia; National Guard fire on students at Kent State University, Ohio; Saul Bellow, *Mr Sammler's Planet*

1971   Severing of historic link between the dollar and gold marks the end of the post-war international monetary system

1972   President Nixon visits China; SALT agreement with Soviet Union

1973   US ground troops withdraw from Vietnam; Allende Government of Chile overthrown; October War between Egypt and Israel; OPEC quadruples price of oil; Thomas Pynchon, *Gravity's Rainbow*

1974   Watergate scandals lead to resignation of President Nixon

1975   South Vietnam and Cambodia surrender to Communist forces

1978   Egypt and Israel sign peace agreement at Camp David; President Carter launches national campaign to conserve energy

1979   Revolution in Iran; starvation in Cambodia; Soviet invasion of Afghanistan

1980   Japan overtakes US in steel and automobile prodution

Introduction

Howard Temperley and Malcolm Bradbury

I

Ever since its discovery, America – and especially that part of North America that eventually became, after the War of Independence, the United States – has been an object of perpetual fascination to outside observers. Initially this may be attributed to the wonder of its discovery; later it can be seen as a result of the sheer speed of its growth. What first presented itself to the Renaissance European gaze as a geographical wilderness, untouched by civilization, though settled by aboriginals, became, in course of time, a burgeoning democracy and then, as a result of the new nation's massive territorial expansion, a technological wonderland and a superpower, presiding over the affairs of half mankind. It is hardly surprising that these images and developments should stimulate the imagination, not just of those who settled in America, but of those who observed it from elsewhere. But what has made these images – and the underlying realities of American development which, with various degrees of accuracy, they have reflected – so peculiarly compelling is the way in which they have been used, over the years, to throw light on the past, present and future of other societies. For, whatever observers made of this new phenomenon in the West, it was hard for men not to draw parallels and comparisons between what was happening there and what they hoped or feared would one day happen to their own societies. Since Sir Thomas More and before, America has been both Utopia and Dystopia for those in other lands. From its finding and founding, and even before that, America has been a point of refraction – less an objective reality than a mirror, in which observers have seen their own reflections, sometimes curiously diminished, sometimes immensely enlarged.

This varied, multi-faceted view of America has also been shared by those who settled in America. For many Americans, America has been a semi-mythical place, to which they or their ancestors were drawn from elsewhere, which has been open to multiple definition and interpretation. To be sure, simply by living there Americans were freed of many of the more simplistic preconceptions held by those who never visited the country or the hemisphere. But 'there' in the case of America is apt to mean only one part of what is, after all, a very large continent, a geographically and ethnically varied land-mass. In any case, there were always apt to be discrepancies between what America stood for in image or concept – the City on the Hill, the Land of the New Start, Democracy, Equality, Liberty, Freedom of Opportunity – and the explicit realities Americans actually encountered in their everyday lives. It came to be conventional to note, in American life, a space between ideal and real, between dream and fact. A recognizable spirit of idealism in constant contention with material fact pervades much of American writing. Foreign visitors, immigrants and minorities have particularly noticed or experienced these discrepancies, which arise, in part, because all that is America – nationality, society, character, ideals, ideology – has had to be invented. But what has been invented has spread its meanings back through the world. Similarly, Americans have also had to define the world beyond their shores, and just as the views of outside observers have always been influenced by what they wanted or needed to believe about America, so the beliefs of Americans about other parts of the world have often been based on what they, too, wanted or needed to believe about other countries.

Defining America, in short, has been as much an American as it has been a foreign preoccupation; and it is part of a triangulation process by means of which individuals and societies locate themselves, geographically, politically and culturally. This is a universal phenomenon, examples of which occurred long before the discovery of America. Aristotle attributed the peculiar virtues of the Greeks to the geographical chance which placed them between the energetic but anarchic tribes of Europe and the ingenious but servile nations of Asia. In the same way, other peoples over the centuries have attempted to define their identities by referring to the characteristics, real or imagined, of neighbouring societies. There are, however, clear historical reasons why, in more recent times, America should have featured so prominently in this process. One is that, as a new nation, which had deliberately severed its political ties with the Old World (from which, nonetheless, it necessarily continued to draw much of its culture), Americans were indeed particularly inclined to speculate on the nature of their nation's identity. And such doubts as they had on this score were exacerbated by the continuing influx of new and increasingly diverse groups of immigrants, as well as by the rapid expansion of the United States itself, and the geographical mobility of its own native-born population. Thus Americans have been inclined to engage in such acts of triangulation more often than most other peoples. At the same time, for outsiders, the primitiveness of the original state of the continent, the fascination of its novelties and wonders, the rapidity of its settlement, the distinctiveness of the cultures which developed there, and the nature of the causes which, over the years, the United States has espoused, made her, for those who deprecated as well as those who welcomed these developments, a necessary point of reference for their own acts of triangulation – a potent image in the modern world.

For these reasons it is easy to see why America should have so fascinated men of the sixteenth century. Since Classical times, the sum of the world's known parts had remained much the same. Great migrations had occurred, empires had risen and fallen, beliefs had waxed and waned, but the boundaries in which these events had occurred had remained virtually unaltered. To the north lay the Arctic circle, to the south, Africa, to the east, India, China and the legendary spice islands, and to the west, the Atlantic. Thus the effect of the voyages of Columbus and his successors was to add a wholly new element to the equation. Here was a continent, enormous in area, rich in resources, peopled by men of exotic and diverse cultures, whose very existence up to that time had been unknown. But above all – and this was what made it so peculiarly fascinating – it was a New World in the sense that it had developed in its own way, untouched by Christianity or indeed any other outside influences. All the wars, controversies and other perturbations of Europe had simply passed it by.

Yet although America had been unknown, it would not be true to say that it had been undreamt of; it existed in the European imagination long before the news of Columbus's discoveries in 1492. Since ancient times men had speculated about Atlantis and other mythical lands beyond the western horizon – much as people today imagine life on other planets. In a sense, as historians have argued, America was invented before it was discovered. This was, of course, one aspect of that process of mental trigonometry already mentioned, for when concrete examples are lacking there is a natural propensity to invent them. But the presence of a *terra incognita* provoked the imagination to fantasy and speculation about every kind of alternative to familiar history and existence; and this element of invention has remained a fundamental part of the perception of America, leading, for example, to the many 'imaginary Americas' of the arts that have existed from before discovery to the present day – hence books like Franz Kafka's *Amerika* (1927), written without a visit. One reason why the discoveries amazed and transformed the Renaissance world was that they raised the principle of alternative, while at the same time invoking the need to relate fact to fantasy, to compare the reports of what life was indeed like there with beliefs about what it theoretically ought to have been. It this sense, the discoveries constituted a profound challenge to existing ideas and assumptions. Did the people of America constitute a separate creation? If so, did they have souls like other men? Were they susceptible to Christian conversion or were they, as some suspected, enthralled to the Devil? Answering questions such as these was not easy, particularly when the cultures of the native

Americans proved to be so diverse, and reports about them were often wildly inaccurate. Did they even have arms, legs and heads like other men? Most did; but others, it was widely rumoured, did not.

In other words, the initial response to the discovery of the Americas was not simply to collect and catalogue information, although there was also a good deal of that. Mariners needed maps and were not prepared to depend on vague theories about where islands were situated or how the various coastlines ran. So innovation was stimulated. Explorers were instructed to collect examples of the local flora and fauna; settlers were told to experiment with various crops; and artists were despatched to draw pictures of the new land and its inhabitants. One consequence of the discoveries, therefore, was to encourage the development of a more scientific view of the world. At the same time, however, the discoveries inevitably gave rise to a great deal of speculation, as observers attempted to square what they saw, or were told, with what they previously believed, or now wished to believe, or which they felt they ought in faith to believe.

In a sense, the situation has not changed: for, though we no longer believe that there are races of men in the New World whose heads grow out of the middle of their chests, we are aware that life there differs from life in other parts of the world, and we are prone to regard these differences as constituting in some way a challenge to our own societies and systems of belief. For it was not long before the wonderment inspired by the American Indians was transferred to those who took America as a place to settle. To be sure, they were not as exotic as the natives, but they were generating new institutions in a new world, and it soon became evident that the ways of life in the New World differed in some important respects to those of the Old. There was even speculation that this was the result of some form of geographical determinism, so that in due course the Europeans would revert to the condition of the Indians. Indeed, there was no lack of evidence that in many cases something very like this was happening. But, whatever the nature of the forces at work, it was plain that when men and their institutions crossed the Atlantic they suffered a sea-change, and that, whatever their plans, and however determined they might be to preserve European practices, they invariably ended up with something different.

These changes were particularly marked in the case of the English settlements in North America, and above all by those that became in time the United States. There had been an indigenous culture in the Americas from prehistory, a major pre-Columbian culture many aspects of which continue to survive in some parts of the Americas: the explorers and settlers found not a pure virgin land but a populated one, yet in a sense they brought history with them. They came to the New World with European issues in their heads, and these issues, values and historical awarenesses came to be projected on to America. They brought Europe's ideologies and technologies: the Bible, the Church, the city, the school, the seminary, the printing press. They thus linked America's history to the general development of the Western world; and they carried with them Europe's ways of writing, recording, ordering and celebrating the world they found. Even if they came in repudiation or dissent, they still depended on the language, commerce and thought of England or, increasingly, of other parts of Europe. Yet they became in some real sense indigenous. That process may in part be put down to the constraints which Parliament placed on the Royal Prerogative at home in England, and to the fact that the early settlements were initially so unsuccessful, economically speaking, that it was scarcely worth anyone's while governing them. Thus the English colonies escaped those tight controls which other European settlers found imposed on them by their home governments. There were, of course, Royal Governors, and, from the middle of the seventeenth century on, carefully regulated patterns of trade. But each colony had its own assembly, responsible for raising taxes and framing laws; so that, to a remarkable degree, they were free to go their own ways.

One consequence of this was that Britain's colonists enjoyed an unusual degree of liberty as compared with their fellow countrymen at home – or, for that matter, with other settlers elsewhere in the New World. This meant, in turn, that they tended to be more flexible in their responses to their environment than would have been the case had they been continually required to regulate their behaviour in accordance with instructions from overseas. A further consequence was that, when eventually they did become more wealthy, the wealth they generated was remarkably evenly distributed throughout the population at large. There were exceptions: the Indians were largely excluded, Negro slaves, of whom there were a great many in the southern colonies, were systematically denied the enjoyment of the fruits of their labour. There were rich men, mostly planters and merchants, whose wealth and prestige placed them well above the average. But there was no counterpart to the aristocracy of the mother country, and social distinctions, though they plainly existed, were in general less marked. Most settlers were in fact farmers, and, as such, were as rich or poor as their own and their families' labour made them. This was not what the first settlers – many of whom had arrived with thoughts either of precious metals or else of Bible Commonwealths – had intended. Nor was it what the English Government had had in mind when it helped sponsor the early expeditions. In a sense, no one had *planned* it at all. It had simply grown up as a result of a laissez-faire policy, a superfluity of cultivable land, and a lack of more immediately attractive alternatives such as those which had drawn Spaniards to the mines and the more readily exploitable indigenous populations of Mexico and Peru. But, for all that, it represented a new variant of Western culture, and as such it excited a good deal of interest overseas, even before the Revolution brought it so dramatically to the world's attention.

Curiously enough, what most impressed observers of the British North American settlements, before the Revolution and after, had much in common with what had previously drawn their attention to the American Indians: freedom from the constraints of European society. Of course, the colonists were by no means as free from such constraints as the Indians had been; history had indeed not passed them by, and they had brought European ideas, institutions and processes along with them and set them to work. Yet many of their achievements could be seen as the working out of processes which, first initiated in Europe, had, for historical reasons, failed to reach fruition there. To this extent, the societies of North America were, in a sense, *more* in touch with history, or at least with recent historical trends, than those from which they had broken away, and they evolved a historiography deriving from this perception. To an age in which an increasing number of Western thinkers were becoming converted to the idea of Progress, and to the belief that necessary changes were being thwarted by the dominant powers of church and state, it was of no small significance that societies should exist which, European in origin, and committed to the realization of European ideals, had nevertheless begun to develop in circumstances which rendered them largely immune from such influences. These were post-Gutenburg societies, preoccupied with self definition; a world with a ministry of learned men, where writing, the arts, science, law and philosophy had established themselves; communities engaged in formulating modern historical ideas and institutions. It was hence gratifying to progressive minds that these societies were more committed to rational ideas of liberty and equality than those from which they had detached themselves, since these were the ideals the powers of Europe were most concerned to suppress. Here, then, was a test case, a laboratory experiment, showing how men in general, European as well as American, might order their affairs if only they were given the chance. The American Revolution was implicitly a transformation of Europe; it was more than an American event. And among other effects it transformed the image of America from a static, paradisial Brave New World to an historically active power, a 'Beacon of Freedom' which, by the end of the eighteenth century and throughout the nineteenth, was to be a continuing source of inspiration to men elsewhere.

II

Needless to say, the reality was a good deal more complicated, as became evident when the French Revolutionaries set themselves the task of achieving similar ideals on European soil. Freedom from political constraints, it soon appeared, was not the only factor that made North America distinctive. There was a great difference between the immense and still largely unexplored continent across the

Atlantic and the small, densely populated, historically rooted nations of Europe, with all their traditions and antagonisms. This also became apparent to the new Americans themselves, now concerned to define the distinctiveness of American experience, and fulfil the aims of a romantic liberal nationalism. The problems of national cultural formation and innovation were great. If politicians, writers and artists sought a declaration of intellectual, artistic and cultural independence as potent as the political one, they immediately found the traces of their dependence on Europe. Lexicographers like Noah Webster sought after the Revolution to define a separate American language, distinct from British. Yet, though from the start books had appeared, historical records kept, and faith and experience registered in works of historical interpretation, theology, philosophy, politics and poetry, many of these modes of thought and structures of feeling remained largely imitative. America had developed a literary and artistic class, yet the main cultural capitals and institutions stayed in Europe, whither many of those artists and writers expatriated themselves: the issue of the basic provincialism of American culture now became central.'Who reads an American book?' asked Sydney Smith in *The Edinburgh Review* in 1820; Melville later prophesied that in the future everyone would, and the prophesy is now largely true. But it took much time, and it raised the essential problems of American identity: the theme, in fact, with which so much American writing and art is concerned. The problem of inventing America still continued; without an indigenous historical past of sufficient strength to sustain a rooted folk tradition or a distinct language, or to create distinct artistic genres, with only a sense of mission, often combined with a sense of cultural deprivation, and in a democratic social order suspicious of artistic elitism, the arts of the new nation seemed profoundly hard to originate, and their very existence an ambiguity. Thus Americans found themselves mythologizing Europe in reverse: as past to America's future, as stasis to America's dynamic movement, but as culture to America's bare, democratic space. In fact, the arts had flourished in the American colonies, in travel-writing, sermons, theology, poetry; and after the Revolution, in the atmosphere of Romanticism, they soon enriched themselves. By the 1840s there were signs of a remarkable achievement, and what we call the 'American Renaissance' of the arts – the work of Poe, Emerson, Hawthorne, Melville, Whitman and others – gave a firm foundation to American literature. Yet a mixture of nationalism and uprooted uncertainty lay behind this achievement. The reverse triangulation process became evident in American culture and the arts: looking to the world outside, it expressed hunger for self-definition.

At the same time, the United States became, and to a degree remained, a romantic ideal in itself, to which reformers in other parts of the world looked for guidance and inspiration. To generations of British radicals, fed by the spirit of nineteenth-century liberalism,

America was not only standing proof that the reforms they called for were practical; it also represented in rough outline the kind of society they wished to see in Britain itself. By the same token, the United States was also a potent, threatening symbol to those who felt that any shift towards a more democratic policy would threaten their positions in society, or otherwise jeopardize what they held to be the nation's best interests. But in practice, most observers, on the Continent as well as in Britain, fell into neither category. They saw in a rapidly developing United States a mixture of elements, some of which invited emulation, others of which did not. Liberals, for example, could applaud America's democratic political system but at the same time deplore the fact that the system was used to uphold a slave regime which, even to European conservatives, appeared unjust and anachronistic. European travellers reported on America: Chateaubriand, Tocqueville, Charles Dickens, Harriet Martineau. Theirs were reports not unlike those that came from Russia after the Revolution: often they represented shock and disappointment, as in the case of Charles Dickens. Tocqueville's book *Democracy in America* (1835–40), looked beyond America to a sociological view of the workings of democracy; he noted the benefits, and the price, which included the problems of evolving a democratic art and literature. And Americans, too, explored their own contradictions, especially in literature: in the novels of James Fenimore Cooper, the gothic and agonized stories of Poe, the transcendental essays of Emerson, the novel-romances of Hawthorne and Melville, we can sense a prevailing tension, a split between idealism and realism, individual and society, artist and culture, European heritage and American, between what Lionel Trilling has called the 'yes' and the 'no' of the culture. It is there as a culture stress, and as a formal anxiety. 'Two bodies of modern literature seem to me to have come to the real verge: the Russian and the American...,' wrote DH Lawrence in *Studies in Classic American Literature* (1923), a book that helped bring home to twentieth-century American writers, still concerned about the distinctiveness of American writing and culture, the usable past behind them; 'The furthest frenzies of French modernism or futurism have not yet reached the pitch of extreme consciousness that Poe, Melville, Hawthorne, and Whitman reached.'

Thus as the nineteenth century developed, the images represented by the United States, both internal and external, became more complex. For those abroad, this was partly because, thanks to newspapers and easier travel, people were becoming better informed: it was no longer so easy to confuse the idea with the reality. But it also reflected the fact that America itself was becoming more diverse, and finally, with the Civil War, divided against itself. Even those radicals in England who had supported the North in the Civil War, and rejoiced in the overthrow of slavery, were far from sure they liked the post-war society of massive corporations, home-grown plutocrats and downtrodden immigrant workers they saw emerging. Its elements were too much like those they objected to in their own societies, yet manifested on a more massive and terrifying scale. Many began to wonder whether, after all, freedom and equality went together, as they had appeared to in the past. If freedom meant the freedom of capitalists to exploit workers, it was hardly worth having. Of course there were aspects of American society that liberals still found attractive – its relative open-endedness, and its capacity to accommodate change. But if what they were looking for was a way of reconciling change with the interests of society at large, and in particular with those of its less advantaged members, it was plain that they would have to look not to a diminution in the power of the state, one of the things which American Government up to that time had symbolized, but to its increase.

The same complication of image was felt by Americans themselves. They saw the Jeffersonian America of the yeoman farmer giving way before industrial and corporate growth, and a whole rationale and image of Americanness fading with it. Writers grew realist, concerned with the detail and often the unpleasantness of American life: they responded to a sense of the fundamental transformation of American images; they allied themselves with reform and naturalism. In this, of course, they were, as always, close to the movements of Europe – even though realism had as one of its aims the reporting of the local and the distinctively American. For now many Americans were beginning to see in the growth of capitalism the development of an irresponsible power, perhaps only to be contained by the intervention of government. Yet, with the tradition of governmental non-intervention, it was often more difficult for them to achieve effective reforms than it was for Europeans, who, although they had often regretted it in the past, at least had governments capable of intervening, and shaping social and economic affairs. On the whole, indeed, Europeans were quicker than Americans to recognize the problems of industrial society, and less inhibited by libertarian traditions in advancing proposals for dealing with them. In fact, by the late nineteenth century, European radical thought, taken as a whole, was a good deal more trenchant and thorough-going than its American counterpart, with the result that Americans were as apt to look to Europeans for inspiration as vice versa.

III

This rebalancing of the refracting images of America and other nations has continued into the twentieth century, when, as a result of wars and revolutions or simply the problems of the modernizing process, governments all round the globe have been turning to radical expedients. Most of these purport to be, and many in fact are, a good deal more thorough-going than anything attempted in the United States. This is not, though, to say that America has ceased to serve as a political model. Indeed, much of the political reconstruction which occurred after the Second World War was undertaken with the American example specifically in mind; and even the most drastic of left-wing expedients have, on occasion, been justified on the grounds that they were necessary to catch up with or overtake the United States, And, of course, it can be argued that, for all its defects, the American system of government reflects the wishes, and to that extent serves the needs, of the American people more effectively than those purportedly democratic governments which do not consult the opinions of those they govern but presume to act on their behalf. Nonetheless, in the world's political spectrum the United States is not now regarded, as for so long she was, as pre-eminently the country of the left. Whatever her rightful place, or for that matter the position of those countries whose rulers merely claim exercise their authority on behalf of the ruled, it is plain that there are now many nations whose democratic credentials, though more recent, are equally valid.

Yet while America was ceasing to be the land of the future in one sense, she was rapidly acquiring a new kind of claim to that title. She had, of course, for long been regarded as a land of opportunity – largely because of the relative open-endedness of society there and the possibilities it afforded for individual advancement. But until the mid-nineteenth century the United States was, economically speaking, an underdeveloped country. The dramatic rise of American industry in the latter half of the century, however, fundamentally transformed the nation, upset its inward image, and also opened up exciting new possibilities. By 1890, the United States had achieved primacy as an industrial producer, just as the frontier line was closing; by 1900 her manufacturing output exceeded that of her two principal rivals, Britain and Germany, combined. This astonishing achievement, together with the associated growth of massive cities and new transportation systems, owed much to factors of scale, the immense natural resources of the continent, to labour problems leading to capital-intensive industrialization, and to the tradition of practical know-how and invention for which Americans had long been famous. Much of the basic technology was European: Americans had not invented machine technology any more than they had invented democracy. But their wholesale and skilful application of it, their willingness to innovate and invest, and the sheer speed of their rise to economic and industrial pre-eminence combined to capture the world's attention, just as surely as their early commitment to democratic values had done a century earlier. In fact, by the beginning of the twentieth century, the image America presented to the world, and to Americans themselves, had become more or less what it is today: an image of modernization and modernity.

Thus the United States came to be seen, in writing, painting, and thought generally, as a modern technological and urban wonderland. There were those who remained haunted by the older American images – of the West, the Big Country, the land of New Starts – but these were in many ways receding into nostalgia, a nostalgia that nonetheless retained, and still retains, power in American politics and iconography. American cities, with their skyscrapers and drug stores, seemed modern in a way cities elsewhere were not. So did American roads, built to accommodate an automobile-owning citizenry at a time when few people elsewhere had cars. American life-styles and American cultural expressions came to seem no longer provincial but urbanely advanced. The new mass media, such as radio and cinema, seemed themselves American technological marvels, and they spread American images and influences internationally: images that bore testimony to the fact that in America ordinary people behaved in novel ways, and took for granted privileges – such as owning telephones or taking annual holidays – which in other countries were the prerogative of the rich and powerful. In the arts, Gertrude Stein, settled in experimental Paris, looked on European modernism in writing and painting and declared it an American possession, appropriate to the new 'space-time continuum' only really to be found in the United States.

But, as always, what fascinated observers was not just these phenomena in themselves, however remarkable they were; it was what they portended for their own societies, in which similar tendencies were also evident. Often it was hard to distinguish what was specifically American from what was simply modern; usually the two went together, and Americanization and modernization appeared much the same thing. Nonetheless, it seemed to many that by looking at America it was possible to discern the shape of the future, and, again, many Americans shared this futurist confidence. In matters of art and culture, Van Wyck Brooks in 1915 declared America's 'coming of age', and with justice, for an extraordinary creative generation in the arts, paralleling the energy and achievement of the 'American Renaissance' (Ezra Pound called it the 'American Risorgimento'), made its claims apparent with such power that it became possible to suspect, especially after the cultural collapses of Europe during and after the First World War, that the centre of the arts was shifting westward across the Atlantic — a view further encouraged by the westward flight of refugee European intellectuals and artists in the 1930s. The American arts had always been cosmopolitan, fed by European influence and by immigrant and expatriate elements; they evoked both the images and anxieties of a modernizing world. Increasingly, everyone began to read an American book, watch an American movie, or listen to American music, a reflection both of increased power and of the engaging yet ambiguous attraction of modern American mythologies.

After the Second World War, these notions and images became

even more complicated as, with the new balance of nations and power, the United States found herself one of the two great 'superpowers', counterposing the essential principle of modernization and development through individualism and capitalism against the communist way of economic planning and the ideologically single state. Atomically armed and strategically powerful, the United States radiated her political and economic influence round the world. In business operations and merchandizing patterns, on television and movie screens, in speech, clothes and life-styles, its international role and its capacity to offer an image of a modern, freewheeling life, especially to young people, became increasingly evident. The superpower had evolved a superculture. And if one reason for the claim of the United States on the world's attention came from its history, politics and power, another came from its cultural achievements at their best, and their evident contemporary importance. Even if, as Gore Vidal, the American novelist, once remarked, writers in powerful countries win more attention than they deserve, the fact remains that some of the best modern writers, painters and musicians, are American, and that America is a capital of the contemporary arts. Another part of their significance, though, is that they represent not so much the ideology as the persisting complexity of American culture: its tensions, its stresses, its wry and often traumatic insight into modern experience. They also represent the internationalism of at least one essential part of modern American culture – a culture that has increasingly opened out to the fundamental ethnic and ideological variety of American life, assimilated many modern thought-movements, and shown remarkable qualities of eclecticism. The relationship between any society and its artistic achievements is never absolutely direct, nor easy to analyse (as we shall see in this book). But one of the deductions we may make from contemporary American writing is that it articulates the functional complexity of American culture, the enormous refractability of its images, and an eclectic variousness drawn in part from the American social order.

As for the present day, the issue has grown even more difficult, as the view that America represents the way the world is going has lost some of its plausibility. Partly this is a matter of other nations catching up – a process that would doubtless have occurred sooner had it not been for the ravages of two world wars. The United States, thanks to its size, is still the richest country in the world, but its productivity relative to that of other countries is declining and her citizens are no longer necessarily the best paid. Since 1948 the United States has become a net importer of oil, upon which, it is now clear, her economic achievements considerably depend – and this oil that sooner or later will run out. America has also been the loser in a long and costly war which has not only cost it its reputation for military invincibility but led many of its citizens to wonder whether the dream of endless progress and prosperity based on hard work and moral rectitude, on a politics based on the notion of being 'the world's policeman', had not been an illusion, the product of a period of history which is now ending. American culture still has a radiating and fundamental influence. However, much of the interest in America in the years ahead will inevitably focus on the way in which it copes with modern change. Perhaps it will become an ordinary country, larger than most, but in other respects unremarkable. Alternatively, it is possible to imagine it repeating the experience of other nations which once enjoyed pre-eminence. In the Revolutionary period, Americans were drawn to theories of the cycle of Empire, the curve of rise and fall that explained the declension of Europe, the rising glory of America. Possibly such a cycle has been run in America, and it will become a vast network of highways, petrol stations, franchise restaurants and suburbs, all grown rather shabby, dreaming nostalgically of the days of former greatness. This has certainly been feared by many Americans, who are aware that the United States is no longer quite the political and economic giant she once was, and who seek to recapture the earlier sense of achievement and mission that once made their country so distinctive.

Yet it would be unwise to see this as the end of a cycle, to assume that the preoccupations of the present reflect the shape that will be taken by the future, or to underestimate the capacity of America and Americans to adapt to changing circumstances. The jeremiad has been written in America from the earliest days of settlement; many previous generations of Americans have felt deep doubt about the nation's destiny; the rhythms of dream and nightmare, boom and crash, have played a significant part in the national self-awareness. Despite the remarkable consistency of American ideals, and the remarkable stability of the American political system, extraordinary changes of role and situation have indeed occurred throughout American history. There is no reason to suppose that this process will not continue. It is equally reasonable to suppose that whatever America will come to represent in the next century will be as different from its present aspect as that aspect now is from the images and facts of America two hundred years ago. But whatever it is, America doubtless will remain – not simply for Americans, but for the rest of the world as well – an object of compelling interest.

IV

This book is an introduction to American Studies, and one way of explaining American Studies is to say that it is both a product of and the study of this significant history of images and facts, of massive internal development and external influence. The term 'American Studies' can mean many things. It does no more than mark out a geographical area – itself not clear, for do we mean to speak only of the United States, or the Northern American hemisphere, or the entire American land mass? – and claim it as an object for analytical attention. Yet that attention can be of many kinds, and it can come from many different intellectual disciplines. It can mean the study of America by its own citizens; it can be the study given to America by those who observe it from outside with exterior standpoints and ideologies. It can be an inclusive description laid over the work of many people who attempt, separately, to look using the independent methods of history, political science, sociology, literary and cultural study, at aspects of American life; or it can designate a more inclusive and inter-disciplinary emphasis, the attempt of people from those many disciplines to come together, unite their methods and interests, and seek to move, either eclectically or according to one single theory, toward a multi-disciplinary analysis of American history, life and culture. But the term certainly does not say how this is to be done, nor does it explain what methods, approaches, disciplines of study, in what order of precedence, might be most useful for doing it. If one of the deductions we may make from the history of America is that nations and societies are not-clear cut entities, but mythical powers, posing problems of definition, difficulties will carry over into the enterprise of analytical study. Indeed the images and myths we have talked of must become themselves part *of* the study – partly because such images are themselves potent in history, and partly because they help instruct us that there is no clear line between a fact and a fiction, or an historical event and the beliefs that interpret and define it.

'American Studies', then, is a vague term, and it calls up many of the difficulties we always have when we attempt to define and explore any geographical, historical, political and cultural entity. But what has been striking about the study of America, and especially of the United States, is the way in which it has drawn many scholars and analysts toward the search for an overview – for what one writer has called an 'holistic' or systematically comprehensive approach toward the American 'cultural gestalt'.[1] In many ways this inclusive approach itself seems American, a derivative of Emerson's ideal for the American scholar, who would 'distil all the systems', or of Whitman's poetic aim which was, he said, to 'contain multitudes'. We could well identify this disposition or tendency as a remarkable consequence of the relative lack of ideological division and contention in American thought, and of its tendency to abstract and idealize the national concept. But we should also notice that the desire to develop inter-disciplinary study has been marked in a good deal of modern intellectual thought generally; we live in the times when the desire to overcome the progressive balkanization of the disciplines consequent on the modern explosion of knowledge and the profes-sionalization of academic subjects has been strong. During the 1950s and 1960s, there was evidence of a very spirited tendency to move away from subject specialism toward more inclusive views of study.

People from a variety of disciplines – history, sociology, psychology, economics, politics, geography, law, literature, music, art and popular culture – found themselves coming together in inter-connected enterprises. The problems of method were great and they were certainly not solved; but we may see, in the cultural-studies movement in Britain, or the development of structuralism in France, a hunger for intellectual cross-fertilization which affected work in many areas. But – perhaps because America was at that time a superpower with a wide cultural radiation, perhaps because the inclusive aim was already present in an America historically preoccupied with self-definition, with trying to interpret American experience, American culture, American identity – American Studies became a central version of this enterprise.

It is as well to say from the start that no single method, no overriding synthesis, has really emerged from this enterprise to solve the problem of how we analyse the fundamental interrelationships of a society: how we discern the governing themes of a culture, how we relate ideals and myths to hard facts, connect artistic expression to historical events or forces, or reconcile the classical divide between superstructure and substructure. But what did promise much in the 1950s was the appearance of a number of major books which aspired to get away from narrow types of historical and artistic study, to reach across disciplines, and to create a movement towards an inclusive view of cultural studies. Some of the most important of these were Henry Nash Smith's *Virgin Land: The American West as Symbol and Myth* (Cambridge, Mass., 1950); David M Potter's *People of Plenty: Economic Abundance and American Character* (Chicago, 1954); R W B Lewis's *The American Adam: Innocence, Tragedy and Tradition in the Nineteenth Century* (Chicago, 1955); and, a little later, Leo Marx's *The Machine in the Garden: Technology and the Pastoral Ideal in America* (New York, 1964). They were all books of wide-ranging intention, written by scholars based primarily either in history or in literature, but aspiring to draw together many aspects of American experience and to generate explanatory theses of it. They were examples of modern cultural studies, relating historical, sociological, economic, literary and artistic materials to large cultural themes and tendencies, and they remain central; anyone seriously interested in the ideas of American Studies will need to read them. They generally share the view that national cultures are distinctive, that all forms of expression and action share certain governing principles or common ground, that there are dominant myths that embody national ideals and lead us toward a notion of the basic governing style of a culture. They attempt to unify disciplines and see the connections between different realms of human activity; thus, in *Virgin Land*, Henry Nash Smith turns to literature to find there embodied 'collective representations', symbols and myths that express the 'assumptions and aspirations of a whole society'.

All these books, and many that have followed on from them, represent a remarkable broadening of the intellectual study of America. Nonetheless, they do not attempt to assert that there is one fundamental method in American Studies, nor, for that matter, do they fix any clearly defined mixture of disciplines on which cultural studies might be based. In a famous article of 1957, called 'Can "American Studies" Develop a Method', Henry Nash Smith argued that the focus of attention for American Studies should, indeed, be 'culture' – the expressive, ideological, creative life of a nation.[2] He argued that this could be examined through approaches based on history, sociology and literary study, and remarked: 'Why may we not say quite simply that the problem of method in American Studies can be solved by presupposing a value implicit in culture which includes and reconciles the apparently disparate values assumed in the disciplines of, say, literature and sociology?' But he acknowledged that such reconciliations are never easy – for example, literature is not best served if it is regarded simply as a manifestation of society, taking the form of a report on its nature or events, or as an innocent expression of its ideologies – and he recognized that disciplines need to sustain their own methods and insights rather than merge totally with other disciplines. He therefore proposed a method of 'principled opportunism' for American Studies, as indeed for cultural studies generally. Since the 1950s, there have been many more ambitious attempts to find a 'total' method for cultural study, based in Marxist theory, or in structuralism, or in cultural anthropology. Most of these have attempted to define systematically the relation between literary, artistic or popular expression and social structure, between superstructure and substructure. A good deal of this work has been of theoretical value, and has changed our perception of the way in which the elements of culture interconnect one with another. Yet nothing like a final solution has been arrived at, and there can be no doubt that what survives is still a 'principled opportunism', based on some changes of emphasis, yet making of American Studies (and cultural studies generally) an open-ended and various area of enquiry, valuable because of the kind of questions it asks rather than because of the solutions it offers.

This is hardly to be deplored: we can scarcely expect totalistic descriptions of the entire life of a people, or of human life in general. American Studies is many things; but what it principally is is a form of cultural studies in which the essential problems of analysing the complex nature of a modern technetronic, ideologically plural, ethnically mixed, artistically vigorous society arise. And hence much of the best work done in it has not come from the application of a single meta-discipline, with clearly defined rules and resources, but from the efforts of individuals, variously trained, to obtain insights by relating aspects of various fields of study: history, sociology, cultural anthropology, social psychology, political science, law and institutions, economics, literary and artistic studies. It has spawned several localized progeny: Black Studies, Women's Studies, Popular Culture Studies. The spectrum of dominant subjects may vary very widely, and there is, perhaps, no particular reason why the linkage proposed by Henry Nash Smith – literature and sociology, finding a common ground in a species of history – should dominate. But in practice it largely has: history, literature and sociology still tend to provide much of the central common ground. This may be because of an anxious sense of incompleteness often found within those disciplines themselves; it has also something to do with the expressive richness of American culture. It is hard to study literature without some apprehension of the significant processes of society; it is hard to study society without attending to the complex conditions underlying creative expression, and then recognizing the remarkable laws *of* that expression. Thus many of the emphases raised in the 1950s remain our emphases. Perhaps what has most changed since the 1950s is the view that America, the United States, is to be studied as an 'exceptional' society, one that differs radically from others in its historical and cultural experience, in its structures of myth and its definitions of human identity. For the fact is that the United States has, in many respects, always been deeply in interaction with other societies. It has followed comparable patterns and processes of development; in some ways it typifies the rhythms of modern development and technological evolution, and its 'mythic' character is not solely a product of its internal progress but of those refractive and potent images that have kept it a central force in the world, especially the Western world. For these reasons it is often best seen not 'holistically' but comparatively, from outside as well as from inside, if its complex images and meanings are to be discerned, its historical significance pursued.

But, in that case, why should we concentrate particularly on America? We have tried in what has gone before to suggest an answer to this question: in its historical evolution, the United States has been, as Tocqueville suggested, more than America, and it has revealed or can reveal to us much that we need to consider about modern thought and modern experience. It has been through the fundamental rhythms of modernizing change: from agrarian, utopian democracy to post-technetronic society. It has persistently emblemized developments, potential or real, elsewhere. It is a society that has not been solely itself: it is a society of radiating influences. Its historical boundaries are relatively clear; it was born in historical daylight, as a self-concious social experiment derived in part at least from European religious, social and intellectual principles, and so it began in a condition of developed modernity. Yet, cut off as it was from these roots by a one-month sea voyage, its experiences have been in many ways distinct, and it came to regard itself as an 'exceptionalist' society, divorced from the bleakness and depravity of history elsewhere. Nonetheless, such became its position and power that it has constantly affected and been affected by that history. Its territorial boundaries were always far less clear, and yet, by comparison with many middle-European countries, they have become remarkably distinct. The new Americans entered a land where pre-Columbian indigenous cultures in great variety existed, yet these had only a small impact on the settlers. During the nineteenth century the nation spread massively from the Atlantic seaboard to become a transcontinental power, reaching from coast to coast, from temperate to semi-tropical zones. Yet what is superimposed on that remarkably varied terrain is a pattern of relative social and cultural unity. Visitors to the United States persistently remark on the 'sameness' of America, from coast to coast, from Maine to New Mexico; and, though this may be exaggerated, it is indeed a sign of a remarkable degree of socio-cultural coherence, a spread of essentially East Coast ideas through what was often seen, in the nineteenth century, as essentially 'empty' continent. The fact is that a nation profoundly mixed ethnically and geographically is remarkably unified culturally and ideologically, having to all intents and purposes a single language, a clear concept of 'Americanness' (and indeed of 'un-Americanness') and a sense of having been 'chosen' by its citizens. Yet that Americanness has never been a single, stable entity; and America is, as a result of its geographical expansion, and its role as a lure to immigrants, a nation remarkably mixed ethnically, culturally plural, and socially various.

This mixture of cohesion and separation is another reason for the central interest of America. We can define a clear object of attention – in this book we have made it, firmly, the America of the United States – and therein find many of those central themes of modern experience, of modernizing, technologizing, urbanizing development, of material prosperity and social doubt, which everywhere deserve our serious concern. It is not for nothing that the image of the United States persists in obsessing us, for it contains many of those problems of modern development, economic stress, and psychic uncertainty that we regard now as world-wide issues. The United States is a recognizable parable of modern development, a society that focuses both social expectations and social unease. It is a culture which, precisely because of the speed of its historical development, its technological and geographical growth, and its multi-ethnic structure derived from immigration and expansion, represents to us many contemporary problems of social cohesion and social segmentation. It is a society that has encouraged mobility, psychological reformation, existential rediscovery, generational change; it has thus experienced many of the problems of modern rootlessness and alienation. In the 1950s much concern was expressed in Europe and other parts of the world about the process of Americanization – the growing influence of American goods, cultural objects, and styles of living which were displacing older, customary *mores*. Today we perhaps more readily recognize that it was not so much Americanization but modernizing change that was reshaping experience – but America was a symbol of that change, and its influence came as a means for producing habits and styles which fitted new structures of social organization coming from modern economic and psychic restructuring.

But there is a further reason for the study of America, and that is the remarkable fullness of its expressive culture. One result of America's late settlement and its preoccupation with its national and personal identity is that it has been a culture with a remarkable degree of articulacy, of discourse about itself. The pattern of settlement, the act of revolution, the emblematic role of beacon of freedom in the nineteenth century, the assertively modern role it has acquired in the twentieth: all of these things have encouraged an intensity of recording, an articulation of principles and intentions, a hunger for self-definition. It has been a nation that has needed to assert, to itself and the world, aims and principles, dedications and intents, doctrines and destinies, myths and dreams. This has much to do with its rich level of expression in cultural matters, its high level of activity as a nation talking to itself and to others. As a result, the workings of American culture over time have been laid out very visibly before us. We can see, therefore, a modern nation in development, articulating both its processes and the very problems of articulation itself. For modern American literature began amid many of the difficulties and anxieties that underlie the existence of artistic forms in modern history, the complex relations between the uneasy and often alienated modern artist and the society that calls upon him to express its best meanings. As in American history, where historians like Frederick Jackson Turner, Henry Adams, Charles A Beard and Vernon Parrington have sought to express large and inclusive explanations of American history, character and intent, but have also analysed the paradoxes and doubts of the nation, so in American literature there has been both an inclusive mythologizing propensity and a deep self-questioning. The mythic intent is clear in many of the classic works – James Fenimore Cooper's 'Leatherstocking' novels and Herman Melville's *Moby-Dick,* Joel Barlow's *Vision of Columbus* and Walt Whitman's *Song of Myself,* Ezra Pound's *Cantos* and William Carlos Williams's *Paterson,* Hart Crane's *The Bridge* and Charles Olson's *Maximus Poems,* Gertrude Stein's *The Making of Americans* and John Dos Passos's *USA.* Yet behind that inclusive enterprise we can observe the more difficult aspects of a modern expressive culture in process of formation; we can see the coming of a major modern literature, one that, because of those uncertainties and the complex forms they call into being, seems an exemplary literature for our age.

It is the centrality of this modern development, and the equal centrality of the expressive and artistic record, that make the United States both a significant field for contemporary attention and a fascinating test-case for modern cultural studies. And this is what we have set out to explore in this book. It is indeed an *Introduction* to American Studies; we are, as editors, highly conscious of all that might have been included yet has not been. But we have deliberately chosen to concentrate on the relation between American historical development and the expressive culture, to focus, that is, on history and literature – as so many American Studies programmes have. Beyond that, we have not attempted to promote any single 'method' of American Studies, nor to bind our contributors to any single mode of approach. We have asked our contributors, usually one historian and one literary or cultural critic, to collaborate together on inter-disciplinary essays. The plan of the book is essentially chronological, but we have singled out a number of important themes and areas central to the discussion of American culture: the black experience, the immigrant experience, the significance of regions and sections like the frontier and the South. Our aim is to suggest the richness of the subject and some of the possible areas of effective inter-disciplinary study. Evidently much could be added: on American geography, American political and legal institutions, American painting, music, film, the Indian, the city, the machine, the role of women. These matters are not entirely overlooked, but the student interested in such subjects would need to take them further. We have also given an especial weight to the modern period, and in the later part of the book have concentrated attention on the decades. As more than one of our contributors suggests, this is not necessarily the best means for observing the deeper processes of development that work through modern history, or shape the complex relations between social organization and artistic expression. But it does attend to the fact that one essential feature of modern American development has been its pace, the speed of its transaction with history; indeed a sense of historical pace is a significant part of modern American sensibility, and part of the meaning of that sensibility as a psychology, responding to and interpreting life in a modernizing world.

The contributors are largely from American Studies programmes in Britain, and they might be said to reflect contemporary British interests. But they have, as we wished, taken our brief variously, and in different ways come to a definition of the significant issues, and the problems of relationship between the historical and social order and the arts which arise from it, and in complex ways express it. All of them would no doubt want us to say that we have been very active editors, making many suggestions and some changes, in the interests of making the book both broad in coverage and reasonably coherent as a survey – a book that can be read through continuously as well as consulted for an approach to a particular theme, issue or period. The aim has been to try to help the reader toward an intellectual idea of what it means to be or have been American, but also of what it means now to see America, her role, meaning, and symbolic purport, past and present in the world. It is itself an act of triangulation, and we hope it will lead the reader on to other aspects of American Studies. Hence there is a general bibliography at the end of the book giving a booklist of important works many in areas of American Studies not covered here. There is also a bibliography related to each of the essays, and suggesting further reading in each area. We have also provided maps and a chronology of major historical and artistic events. While indeed an introduction, we hope the book will be found useful by readers in many different disciplines or fields, and by the general reader. And we hope it will lead those who read it to ask many further questions, not just about the historical and artistic experience of the United States, but about the problems of studying culture itself.

Norwich 1979

References

1. Cecil F Tate, *The Search for a Method in American Studies,* University of Minnesota Press, Minneapolis, 1973.
2. Henry Nash Smith, 'Can "American Studies" Develop a Method?', *American Quarterly,* IX (Summer, 1957), 197–208; reprinted in J J Kwiat and Mary C Turpie, *Studies in American Culture,* University of Minnesota Press, Minneapolis, 1960.

Chapter One
New Founde Land

Ellman Crasnow and Philip Haffenden

The New Founde Land

Most objects of academic enquiry are synthetic. Scholars, that is, in defining any area of study, impose upon it a certain unity, in order to make it coherent. We should certainly learn to question these syntheses and definitions, as Michel Foucault has encouraged us to do.[1] American Studies is a synthesis of this sort; and so, within it, is the content of the present chapter. But the very idea of America is also a synthesis: the problem of defining America is indeed an old one, even older than America itself. Hence the study of the 'New Founde Land' is highly instructive for those who heed Foucault's advice. For ready-made syntheses are a common feature of all cultures, as well as being a means toward their study. Cultures are probably knowable only through their own encoded identities and definitions. Many cultures, especially those which are primitive or without systematic social records, accept that their beliefs and activities are an unquestioned feature of the way things are. Other cultures, more sophisticated, self-conscious, or less firmly rooted in inherited practice, make these syntheses a good deal more explicit, so that it is possible to trace their creation and the rules which govern them. America was, it has been said, not so much discovered as invented, and came into existence very much as a result of ideas already attached to it by men elsewhere. This 'New Founde Land', then, is obviously not natural and given. And the student rediscovering the presuppositions of its identity is thus well placed to examine the experience of a culture in which the problem of definition is, right up to the present, a continuing preoccupation.

Inventing America

America existed in the European imagination long before its official discovery by Columbus in 1492. The unknown world located at 'the end of the east' was a focus for Edenic and Utopian legend from classical times on. Plato speculated that the land outside of the

Oikumene – the world known to the Greeks – contained Atlantis, a lost continent. In early Christian times, interest revived through the story of St Brendan, the Irish monk who journeyed among enchanted islands to the west of Ireland; closely related to this fable was the legend of the seven Bishops who fled boldly into the Atlantic from Moorish Spain, to discover the beautiful island of Antilia, upon which they built seven cities. All these tales influenced the explorations of the fifteenth century, which brought legend into closer contact with fact. Columbus himself believed in the Antilia legend. The idea of the 'paradise terrestrial' was further developed by the *Travels of Sir John Mandeville,* a late medieval fantastic work which had immense appeal in Western Europe. Sir John placed the location of this paradise east of the fabulous land of Prester John, which itself was held to contain the fountain of Youth and rivers that ran gold, silver and jewels; again, Columbus looked for many of these details on his voyage to 'Cathay', and so did the other early voyagers who transformed late medieval Europe with the impact of their discoveries.

To the late medieval idea of the paradise at 'the end of the east' there came to be added another fundamental myth: the Renaissance myth of Utopia, given form in the imaginative work of that title by Sir Thomas More, first printed in 1516. Ideal climate was an essential element: the air 'soft, gentle and temperate'. The urban environment – planned and aesthetically pleasing – was in accord with nature. Society was guided by free, compulsory education for the young, in adulthood extended to daily lectures. Free minds were exercised at town meetings, through which government took place. It has been said that every group of English pioneers from Maine to Georgia was influenced by More's ideas. Thus men's eyes were raised to an unattainable peak; whatever bounties the land had to offer, whatever opportunities there were to reform the Old World, had to fall short of the Utopian ideal. But the idea of an alternative world was crucial in the Renaissance imagination, charged as it was with the notion of freedom from existing institutions. It is important to note that these sanguine expectations were founded, in one important respect, on absence. They are an account of what is *not there.* Indeed they almost rely on a *lack* of empirical evidence to use the New World as a vehicle for the projective imagination. This 'imaginary America' has been an important meaning of the land. Writing about it preceded knowing it. And, despite the disconfirming experiences of history, this ambition has evolved in the mythopoeic attitude of many later writers, for example Barlow and Whitman in the nineteenth century, Hart Crane and Charles Olson in the twentieth.

During the sixteenth century, encouraged by such ideas, explorers from every part of Western Europe probed the New World. Fishing prospects drew Englishmen into the North Atlantic, perhaps initially in the 1480s through voyages from Bristol in search of the mythical island of Hy-Brasil. The discovery of the 'New Founde Land' off present Canada by the Genoese John Cabot in 1497 focused English interest on the exploitation of its rich fishery, but the northern coasts lacked the drama of the Indies; it was not really until the search for a north-west passage to Cathay, in the second part of the sixteenth century, coincided with contentions with Spain over religion and trade that the British shared the broader Renaissance vision of 'the New World'. The major explorers were, of course, the Spanish and Portuguese. By 1550 Spain had extended its empire over Central and vast areas of South America. However, she showed less interest in the land north of Florida, where the rewards in gold and possessions were fewer. Portugal was over extended in Asia as well as Africa and Brazil. In 1524 the Florentine Giovanni da Verrazzano, with royal backing from France, had sought a passage between Spanish Florida and Newfoundland to put France in contact with Asia. His landfall was at Cape Fear, North Carolina, and he then explored the coast northwards, visiting the Hudson estuary, stopping for two weeks in Narragansett Bay (Rhode Island), and making contact with the Indians of Casco Bay (Maine). Myths thus began to build up around the more northerly explorations, and there were hopes of finding a northerly empire as rich as that of the Aztecs and Incas. English taverns heard of 'the Glorious Kingdom of Norumbega' (on the Penobscot) from David Ingram, a silver-tongued English sailor who claimed to have walked there from the Gulf of Mexico, and to have found a huge city with gold-clad women.[2]

However, for many years from 1550 the main preoccupation of the English propagandists with North America was the quest for a passage to the East. In 1566, Sir Humphrey Gilbert, half-brother of Sir Walter Raleigh and close acquaintance of the influential cartographer John Dee, produced the important *Discourse of a Discoverie for a New Passage to Cataia*, which circulated in manuscript for a decade before being printed. Like Verrazzano, he was concerned with finding the northern passage to Cathay, but, swayed, probably, by More's *Utopia*, he added further ideas, seeing America as a place of refuge for religious dissidents and the poor of England, with learning, lectures and scholars. Yet all the colonizing ventures of the Elizabethans were underwritten by a complex web of exploitative aims, brought together by Richard Hakluyt in his *Discourse Concerning Westerne Planting* (1584), which elaborates the colonial ideal, though very much in the interests of what was later to be called mercantilism. Colonies – plantations – were intended to serve the purposes of the state, not to create an earthly paradise. The colonist's prime function was to improve the quality of life for those who remained behind in England. By emigrating, they reduced the numbers of unemployed and, if soldiers, reduced the dangers from demobilization. As planters, they could produce essential commodities for England's economy, and in due course offer markets for her goods. They could provide bases from which to counter the nation's enemies, especially Spain, and check the dangerous spread of Catholicism among the Indians. Colonists, whether in Ireland or North America, were considered servants of the nation, their interests regarded as subordinate. Not that they were to be victims; the expectation from the enterprise was private profit, at least for the leaders, and compensation for the rank and file in generous acres of land protected from European annexation by the might of the mother country.

Yet in nearly all these reports, practical as they were, the projective imagination exists; fantasy and fact shade together. America still retained mythical associations. Thus John Seelye offers us the apt phrase 'geophantasy' to describe how, for instance, Verrazzano's supposed glimpse of an inland sea persisted as a graphic illusion in successive maps.[3] In the South, of course, the Spaniards remained explicitly romantic. Ponce de Leon died searching for a fountain of eternal youth; the ill-fated expedition of Hernando de Soto was recounted as a tale of chivalric adventure. For the northern experience, the hard facts seemed more relevant, but Michael Drayton's 'Ode to the Virginian Voyage' (*c* 1605), based on an expedition sponsored by Raleigh, freely celebrates 'Earth's onely Paradise' and seeks to fire the 'heroic minds' of Englishmen with romantic ambitions:

> And cheerfully at sea,
> Success you still entice,
> To get the pearl and gold,
> And ours to hold,
> Virginia,
> Earth's onely paradise.

Drayton in fact transfers the tradition of Arcadian pastoral across the seas, as many other poets soon would, as Shakespeare indeed would in *The Tempest*. And this naturally resulted in a degree of conflict between fact and fiction, all too clear in Captain John Smith's *General History of Virginia* (1624),where William Simmons comments on the actuality of the foundation of Virginia after 1607:

Nay, so great was our famine, that a Savage we slew and buried, the poorer sort took him up again and eat him; and so did divers one another boiled and stewed with roots and herbs: And one among the rest did kill his wife, powdered her, and had eaten part of her before it was known; for which he was executed, as he well deserved: now whether she was better roasted, boiled or carbonado'ed, I know not; but such a dish as powdered wife I never heard of. (pp. 34–5)[4a]

Yet Smith's promotional – indeed self-promotional – work nonetheless shows expectations of the land of plenty persisting, even in this 'starving time':

it were too vile to say, and scarce to be believed, what we endured: but the occasion was our own, for want of providence, industry, and government, and not the barrenness and defect of the Country, as is generally supposed. (p. 35)[4a]

But despite such travails, Britain's colonies survived. In Virginia there arose a society of tobacco cultivators; in New England small townships dotted the sea coast; and in due course other colonies were founded: Maryland in 1634, Rhode Island in 1636, and New York (formerly a Dutch possession) and New Jersey in 1664. Gradually the British were taking possession. Yet America did not cease to be a place of wonders. It had to be promoted, and its life listed and recorded. Much of the writing now employed a device to become prominent in later American writing, notably in Whitman – the catalogue. William Wood's *New Englands Prospect* (1634), following on from further settlement, thus lists the land's resources, down to its shellfish, in prose and verse:

> The luscious Lobster, with the Crabfish raw,
> The Brinish Oister, Muscle, Periwigge,
> And Tortoise sought for by the Indian Squaw,
> Which to the flats daunce many a winters Jigge,
> To dive for Cocles, and to digge for Clamms,
> Whereby her lazie husbands gut shee cramms. (p. 402)[4c]

Indeed, as the New England colonies developed, the device of the catalogue became a complex Puritan form. Samuel Sewell (1652 – 1730), who held high office in Massachusetts, was author of a remarkable *Diary* recording his experiences, and writer of America's first anti-slavery pamphlet. He also produced various biblical and apocalyptic studies; one of these, the *Phaenomena* (1697), surveys the plenty of New England, mentioning Smith's *History,* and proceeds:

As long as *Plum Island* shall faithfully keep the commanded Post; Notwithstanding all the hectoring Words, and hard Blows of the proud and boisterous Ocean; as long as any Salmon, or Sturgeon shall swim in the streams of Merrimack; or any Perch, or Pickeril, in *Crane-Pond.* . .

But this is indeed a *Puritan* catalogue, a catalogue with a difference. The conditional clauses gesture forward through their syntax to the religious end:

. . . So long shall Christians be born there; and being first made meet, shall from thence be Translated, to be made partakers of the Inheritance of the Saints in Light. (p. 377)[4a]

The catalogue has, in short, now been transformed into a religious plot. For now, with the advent of settlement, a new type of mythification was taking place. Legend and report alike gave way to the ascription of an intentional pattern that was attached to America – a pattern more complex and more purposeful than the earlier, more fantastic imaginative projections.

Settling the colonies

This is logical enough; it was only with the establishment of permanent settlements in the seventeenth century that the assertion of American purposes and an American cultural identity could really begin. In our comments, we emphasize the role of the Puritan colonies; this reflects the greater complexity and tension of Puritan culture, and its inescapable significance for later American history. For, with the Puritans, many of the essential 'American' themes emerge. Their culture was of course derived from Europe, but it is best seen and understood through the workings of its internal dynamics, an interplay of forces grouped in opposing functional categories, working as a 'doctrine of contraries', as in the logic of the French Protestant martyr Peter Ramus, who was so highly influential in Puritan America. The central categories for observing Puritan New England are those of location and dislocation, for this was a culture in which the sense of place was literally and figuratively crucial. Indeed, for the Puritans the primary experience was that of dislocation – doctrinal dislocation for many, geographical dislocation for all.

In fact the Reformation had necessitated for all the English nation a dislocation with consequences both diverse and profound. The creation through Henry VIII of the Anglican Church encouraged questioning of the doctrine of apostolic succession; for some, this led to repudiation of the entire ecclesiastic hierarchy. God's will could be interpreted through Scriptures alone. The search for Purity brought forth a radical element under Robert Browne (the Brownists or Independents), for whom an autonomous church was a solitary congregation of 'visible saints'. The text came from St Paul 2: Corinthians 6:17: 'Therefore come out from among them, and be ye separate, saith the Lord, and touch not the unclean *thing*'. The unclean thing was the Church of England. However, though a congregation of Independents from Scrooby, Nottinghamshire, fled first to Holland and then ultimately in 1620 to Plymouth in the 'New World', the members did not aim to separate from the English nation as such, to which they were bonded by culture and economic interest. Nevertheless, their experience as an independent religious community, the tempering effect of the harsh New England environment, and the sense of fulfilling God's providence, had, by the spring of 1621, created in them a distinctive spirit. As one of them wrote: 'It is not with us as with other men whom small things can discourage'. Ten years later, New England settlers contrasted their ruddy vigour with the pallor of visiting Virginians: 'When they come trading in our part . . . we know them by their faces'.

But the intent behind the large-scale migration of Puritans to New England at the end of the 1620s is less easily defined. Their leaders disclaimed desire to separate from the Anglican Church (a stand maintained by Cotton Mather in the early eighteenth century); but Englishmen were unconvinced. And the relationship with the English state was equally equivocal. The General Court of Massachusetts – the colony's governing body – demanded an oath of allegiance which ignored Charles I. When Archbishop Laud tried to take away the charter of 1629, they erected fortifications and began military drill to defend the New England way. In fact their resolution was not tested – England was preoccupied with Scottish affairs and then the Civil War – but the defiance was evident enough. Prolonged civil strife in England in the 1640s further strengthened self-consciousness; and, in the absence of English protection against Catholic France or Spain (or their colonies), a Confederation of New England was formed, also to serve as a hedge against English interference, whether from King or Parliament. Large-scale migration also speeded the maturing of the Bay Colony, and congregations gathered to form churches first at Salem, then later at Boston, Roxbury and other coastal centres. Now the fear grew that complete religious autonomy would create discord and endanger the state: in 1637 a synod defined heresy, and introduced the principle of 'Brotherly counsel', and in 1648 another synod produced the Cambridge Platform of Church Discipline, explicitly granting the state power to enforce obedience 'in matters of godliness'. Thus location and state organization grew. Church attendance – for saints and sinners alike – was made compulsory in the early 1630s, and the upkeep of ministers put on the rates.

These steps likened New to Old England, though in some respects New differed from Old in being more systematic. Novelty was not to be seen in the curriculum of Harvard College, though the speed of its creation indicated the urgent need to provide a native ministry independent of England's influence. The rapid spread of grammar schools, and the obligation by law (1647) that towns over a certain size should create them, had echoes of More's *Utopia;* it also helped created the 'bookishness' of New England culture, which in turn led to New England's predominance in the creation of an American literature. These policies reflected New England's desire to create a better England on the American shore, and to use education to combat Satan, the old Deluder who roamed the Edenic paradise. It was Massachusetts that established in 1639 the first printing press in the colonies, producing the famous *Bay Psalm Book* (1640). In one respect, however, Massachusetts did differ from England in that it extended the franchise only to 'visible saints': a contrariety that provoked opposition from the excluded on the grounds that it constituted a denial of English rights. Important critics of these theocratic tendencies were those merchants who supported Ann Hutchinson, who questioned the validity of the procedures used to identify visible saints, in the Antinomian crisis of 1636, though, ten years later, reconciled to church membership as the qualification for voting, they urged that it be broadened, not abolished. In general, the leaders of the Bay Colony, of whom John Winthrop – author of one of the two notable journals recording its foundation, the other being by William Bradford – was outstanding, sought to preserve their churches through strict and widespread regulation. Political dissent was tolerated no more readily than religious. However, after the boom years of the 1630s had ended, attempts to regulate economic life by fixing prices and wages failed. But the social structure inherited from England was substantially preserved, though the range of ranks and classes was less various than in Old England.

The settlers' initial fears of interference from the authorities at home were not realized but, disappointingly, the successful Puritans in Old England did not move in the direction hoped for by those who had emigrated. During the Cromwellian period some eminent settlers, such as Hugh Peter and Sir George Downing, did return to serve the English state in high office. Meanwhile New England, like most of the colonial world, was largely left alone to mature on its own and at its own pace. However, under a restored Stuart monarchy, England, guided by Lord Clarendon, moved with cautious deliberation to impose the restraints of a purposeful economic policy on its New World settlements. The Navigation Laws of 1660 and 1663 sought the increase of English shipping and English seamen by regulating the export of all important colonial commodities and the import of European goods. Many of these restrictions benefited New England commerce, but those which did not were regarded as an intrusion. The tendency to ignore unpalatable imperial rules convinced Restoration statesmen that New England in general, and Massachusetts in particular, must be brought to a proper state of obedience. By 1684 Massachusetts had lost its venerated charter of 1629, annulled by the English courts, and was about to be merged in a new and vast administrative domain, the Dominion of New England, stretching from the Delaware to the St Croix. Under the all-but vice-regal powers of a General Governor, Sir Edmund Andros, old landmarks such as the legislative assembly of the General Court disappeared, and others – for example, land titles, one of the major pillars of society – were threatened, as was the power of the Puritan theocracy. Other internal dislocations grew. After the Restoration, sights had to be lowered, and the disasters and uncertainties encountered raised doubts as to whether the Puritan experiment even in New England could succeed. By 1660 many young adults were failing to become church members, and in many churches the 'visible saints' were in the minority. What should be the fate of the children of those not full members of the church? To deny baptism would break the 'chain of godliness'; to admit children of unregenerate parents would flout the basic purposes of New England. A synod in 1662 compromised with the Half Way Covenant, permitting baptism but not communion or voting in church matters. Opposition to this in individual churches burdened New England with controversy and doubt.

The seeds of dislocation were many, among them growth of commercial and economic wealth, through the West Indies trade. Merchants found membership of the British Empire important and were opposed to restrictive practices in the theocracy. But in theory

Puritan culture could cope with all this. Indeed, it was so structured as to cope with any dislocation. Its strategy came from that ascription of intentional pattern to which we have referred; the Calvinist belief in the doctrine of Predestination, and the ubiquity and omnipotence of Providence, made everything meaningful. Urian Oakes, in a 1677 sermon on 'The Sovereign Efficacy of Divine Providence', could claim that, properly understood, chance does not exist: 'Truth is, Chance is something that falls out beside the Scope, Intention and foresight of *man*, the Reason and cause whereof may be hid from him; and so it excludes the counsel of *Men;* but it doth not exclude the Counsel and Providence of *God*; but is ordered and governed thereby' (p. 362)[4a]. For William Bradford – the leader and historian of the Plymouth Migration of 1620 – even the fact that 'sodomie and bugerie (things fearfull to name), have broak forth in this land' could be coped with and explained through the cosmic drama: 'One reason may be, that the Divell may carrie a greater spite against the churches of Christ and the gospell hear, by how much the more they indeaour to preserve holynes and puritie amongst them. . .'. (p.112)[4a] So the negative is turned into a positive; impurity is the evidence of purity, and the contingent a working of God's providence. In Puritan historiography there is the frequent device of the interpolated incident, as narratives break off to recount an apparently trivial happening that is in fact not trivial at all but an instance of divine intent. Bradford, recording the famous *Mayflower* voyage, writes of the first fatality on board not merely as an instance of 'greevous disease', but as 'a spetiall worke of Gods providence'. It is 'a proud and very profane yonge man' who dies: 'his curses light upon his own head; and it was an astonishment to all his fellows, for they noted it to be the just hand of God upon him'. (p. 98)[4a]

Puritan typology

So stated, the providential order may seem to afford no more than an abstract, general sense of comfort and orientation. But its function was larger; it was brought to bear specifically on Puritan experience through the system of typology. Typology originated in early Christian times, a response to the problem of incorporating the Hebrew scriptures into a new biblical canon. A solution was found whereby 'types' – persons, places, events, institutions – in the Old Testament were seen as foreshadowing 'antitypes' in the New Testament. Thus Matthew 12:40 (NT) refers to Jonah 1:17 (OT); 'For as Jonas was three days and three nights in the whale's belly; so shall the Son of man be three days and three nights in the heart of the earth'. Jonah is no longer significant simply as Jonah, but as a type of Christ. Typology was extended to include not only correspondences between the Testaments but between sacred and secular history as well. So the great Puritan divine John Cotton, preaching a farewell sermon to the passengers of the *Arbella* in 1630, used 2 Samuel, 7:10: 'Moreover I will appoint a place for my people Israel, and will plant them, that they may dwell in a place of their own, and and move no more. . .'. Here God's intent is explained with reference to the community: and a key American myth stated. The settlers are the new chosen people, their land (New England) is divinely appointed, as was Israel's. The powerful sense of location in time and space, the establishment of identity and value, are obvious. The community is to enact an ordained destiny; 'a great hope and inward zeall they had' writes Bradford, 'of laying some good foundation. . . for the propagating and advancing the gospell of the kingdom of Christ in those remote parts of the world'. (p. 96)[4a] Later generations emphasized this destiny; hence the title of an election sermon preached by Samuel Danforth in 1670: 'A Brief Recognition of New England's Errand into the Wilderness.' The sense of errand was to become a powerful prop for cultural identity, but it was not without its dangers. The first was ideological; the endorsement of national destiny could (and on occasion arguably has) become automatic, dissociated from its original context. The second was psychological; to act as a type is to act as an example, and the community may not maintain its standard. This anxiety was definitively conveyed to the *Arbella's* passengers in the famous lay sermon preached during the voyage by their leader, John Winthrop:

for wee must Consider that wee shall be as a Citty vpon a Hill, the eies of all people are vppon us; soe that if wee shall deale falsely with our god in this worke wee haue vndertaken and soe cause him to withdrawe his present help from vs, wee shall be made a story and a by-word through the world . . . (p. 199)[4a]

The City upon a Hill, as a type of Zion (and of the heavenly city), is positive; but, as an index of exposure to possible censure, it is negative. Sinners in the Puritan church were placed on the mourner's bench for public admonition, and the backsliding community, whether a single congregation or entire New England, was always potentially in this role.

Yet backsliding itself could serve a purpose. It fitted into the typological pattern: Israel was a notorious backslider, attracting divine vengeance. Untoward events in the colonies could thus be made into vengeances and turned to good effect for both explanation and remonstrance. The expressive form for such occasions was the jeremiad, an address which reviewed society's errand, stigmatized its declension, threatened (or identified) its punishments, and promised renewal for the repentant. Michael Wigglesworth took advantage of a drought in 1662 to produce a rhymed jeremiad, 'God's Controversy with New-England', which displayed 'New England planted, prospered, declining, threatened, punished'. (p. 43)[4c] The closing stanzas, however, are typically positive; God speaks in pentameter:

Ah dear New-England! dearest land to me;
Which unto God hath hitherto been dear,
And mayst still be more dear than formerlie,
If to his voice thou wilt incline thine ear . . . (p. 54)[4c]

The Puritans rested their strategies of location on the assimilation of human affairs to a total order, providential and predestined: the visible was located by reference to the invisible. Understandably, the linkage between these two worlds preoccupied them greatly. The scriptural figure of linkage is the covenant; and Puritan writing abounds accordingly with covenantal examples. But the degree of assurance with which linkage is asserted may vary. The most confident typological identifications are made: (*a*) communally – when the fortunes of a group can be made to accord with scriptural or apocalyptic patterns; or (*b*) after the event – when, in elegy, funeral address or biography, notables can be typified as Moses leading the people out of Egypt, or Nehemiah rebuilding the wall of Jerusalem. It is in the present and future fortunes of the individual that least confidence can be shown. Thomas Shepard (1605–49), one of the ablest and most widely read of the first generation of Puritan preachers, offers 'exhortation to all confident people, that think they believe and say, they doubt not but to be saved, and hence do not much fear death,' telling them that, on the contrary, they must learn 'to suspect and fear . . .' . (p. 101)[4b] Here we meet the problem of Puritan soteriology – its doctrine of salvation. If everything is predestined, so is salvation. And, as Shepard remarks in the same sermon, 'those that are saved are very few; and . . . those that are saved, are saved with very much difficuty'. (p. 98)[4b] Add to this the view that no mere human activity can obtain salvation; it rests entirely on divine grace, and as Increase Mather (1639–1723) writes: 'God is not bound to give Sinners Grace: He is an absolute Sovereign, and may give Grace or deny Grace to whom he pleaseth'. (p. 335)[4a] So at the core of Puritan culture there is the crucial problem of identifying which individuals belong with the group of those who are to be saved, God's Elect. The problem is, strictly, insoluble. But one could accumulate evidence that must, in the nature of things, remain inconclusive; and an immense energy is poured into this accumulation. Journals, biographies and autobiographies sift individual lives for signs of 'justification', alert for symbolic moments. The problem of interpreting these signs is expressed in a prevailing rhetoric of vision, of proper 'seeing': the desire, as Shepard writes, 'that no man's Spectacles may deceive him'. (p. 71)[4a] But visible and behavioural signs are deceptive; as Samuel Willard (1640–1707) preached, 'Saints [are] not known by Externals'. (p. 369)[4a] The rhetoric of vision is accordingly introspective, as in Edward Taylor's adaptation of Shepard's spectacles:

You want Cleare Spectacles: your eyes are dim:
Turn inside out: and turn your Eyes within. (p. 205)[4b]

But even if it could never quite succeed in locating the individual within a predestined pattern, this habit of introspection left a rich heritage. For one thing, it occasioned the period's most moving human documents: its journals, memoirs, histories, apologetics and poetry. Thomas Shepard left an autobiography for the instruction of his son; at one point he traces the shifts in his attempted submission to providence on the death of his wife:

this affliction was very heauy to me, for in it the Lord seemed to withdraw his tender care for me & mine, which he graciously manifested by my dear wife; . . . but I am the Lords, & he may doe with me what he will, he did teach me to prize a little grace gained by a crosse as a sufficient recompense for all outward losses; but this losse was very great . . . when her feuer first began (by taking some cold) shee told me soe, that we should loue exceedingly together because we should not liue long together . . . I haue euer found it a difficult thing to profit euer but a little by the sorest & sharpest afflictions. (p. 474–5)[4a]

Introspection also left its mark on the secularized 'New England mind' of later centuries, and greatly affected later literature; characterization and symbolism in American fiction, in the line that runs through Hawthorne, is profoundly indebted to this Puritan habit. But it is important, especially from our post-Romantic standpoint, to realize that this subjective and in a sense symbolic experience is not valued for its own sake. It was to be *used* for evidence or instruction. The private often becomes public, and the individual is located in relation to the community as an exemplar; notably, in the public avowal of conversion which determined church membership (and in Massachusetts, enfranchisement). Conversion as regeneration was taken very literally as a cohesive device, a re-birthing, the taking on of a new identity as a visible saint, who (not without doubts) could join the Visible Church.

Colonial Culture

The antitheses of Puritan culture were never quite resolved. We cannot speak of synthesis when the individual cannot finally locate herself or himself in the total pattern, and when individual action is finally useless in establishing such location. As if in reaction to this irresolution, social and cultural structures tended to aspire towards order at all costs, as if to restore what Thomas Hooker (1586–1647) called 'the beautiful frame, and that sweet correspondence and orderly usefulness the Lord first implanted in the order of things'. (p. 296)[4a] The result was a hierarchically rigid social order in which toleration and democracy were excluded. The gulf between a tolerant and an intolerant colony was illustrated by the controversy between Roger Williams (1604–83), the radical Protestant who founded the settlement of Providence, in Rhode Island, and John Cotton of Massachusetts. Williams argued in *The Bloudy Tenent of Persecution for the Cause of Conscience* (1684) that peace in the church and peace in the city were separate, that schism in the former need not affect the latter (p. 220–1).[4a] Such an opinion was impossible in the Puritan theocracy.

Historically (and perhaps partly because of the portrait of Puritan Boston in Nathaniel Hawthorne's evocation, *The Scarlet Letter*, (1850)), the Puritans have become associated with intolerance, sexual control, witch-hunts. Intolerance was clearly present and functional, as a device of social cohesion: a means of asserting identity by postulating an 'other' as the not-self, and so defining one's self against it. The 'other' in this period was sometimes savagely persecuted, sometimes strangely ignored, as if not there. Winthrop's *Journal* records a violent gale in 1643: 'It darkened the air with dust, yet through God's great mercy it did no hurt, but only killed one Indian with the fall of a tree' (p. 138–9).[4a] (Mark Twain uses a like episode ironically in *Huckleberry Finn*: "We blowed out a cylinder-head". "Good gracious! anybody hurt?" "No'm. Killed a nigger".) Dehumanization of the Indian was neither immediate nor indiscriminate. In the early years of Massachusetts, the Indian's role was less crucial than it had been in Virginia or Plymouth, because of the experience gained. The relationship of natives to settlers at Jamestown in Virginia had been an uncertain one: white strength inclined them to generosity, while weakness encouraged attack. In the early days, Englishmen imprudent enough to venture unarmed from the stockade risked sudden or slow death. But the advantages of political alignment with settlers against local enemies was evident to the Indians. And, though lacking a Pocahontas to show the way, the New England experiences were generally not dissimilar. A formal alliance between the English and King Massasoit of the Wampanoags lasted fifty years; and social contacts were often genial ('we use them kindly: they come to our houses sometimes by half a dozen or half a score at a time when we are at victuals'). In the 'strawberry time', as observers of the early process of settlement described it, the natives were treated as near-equals by many, and Indians were still regarded as white.

In Providence, Roger Williams's 'strange opinions' included friendship with the Indians, and a conviction that the Bay charter was worthless because the King could not give away land belonging to the natives. His enlightened relationship with those already indigenous in America (foreshadowing the policy of Quaker Pennsylvania in the eighteenth century) highlighted a fundamental issue facing all settlements in the New World. What should be the attitude to the native population? After the discoveries, Indians, like the New World itself, had been a thing of wonder. When Columbus visited Lisbon in 1492, the population flocked to see Indians as much as Columbus himself; and their physique, sexual behaviour, eating habits and warfare were exposed to inquiry and exaggeration. Yet the 'noble savage' became celebrated, while the marriage of Princess Pocohontas and John Rolfe overcame the hurdle of mixed marriages. After 1700, however, Massachusetts would forbid this by law. For in New England, as elsewhere, the idyllic relation ceased with the first major conflict: here the Pequot War of 1637, when an entire tribe was virtually destroyed. The impact of this savage struggle was, however, lessened by the alliance of whites with Indian neighbours anxious to see the Pequot destroyed; and, though New Englanders acted often without mercy or compassion, they remained concerned with Christianizing the Indian. During the next forty years, aided by the missionary work of John Eliot and the views of Roger Williams and others, some 4,000 converts – 'praying Indians' – chose a European way of life and lived in or close to Puritan settlements. Not until King Philip's War in 1675–76 did New England experience the horrors of large-scale Indian massacres, such as had shattered confidence in Virginia in 1622. In the conflict, frontier posts were abandoned and battle came close to the doorstep of some of the larger seaboard communities. In time the unconverted Indians came to be seen as dogs to be hunted down, 'because they did not manage their war fairly'.[5] And such were the dimensions of King Philip's War that it was seen as indicative of New England's declension, a focal point for jeremiad.

A more subtle, equally enduring and no less influential shock was administered by the Quakers, tolerated by Rhode Island, but regarded by Massachusetts as a threat. In the 1650s whipping preceded expulsion, and those who returned suffered extreme hardship and barbaric punishment. Finally, in 1658, in an unsuccessful endeavour to keep out these intruders who threatened 'the mission of Zion in the wilderness', the death penalty was made the punishment for re-entry. Next year two young men were hanged; in 1661 Mary Dyer received the martyrdom she so resolutely sought. Quaker sufferings did not pass unnoticed in England; the influence of Quaker leaders, especially Admiral Sir William Penn, Charles II and James, Duke of York, helped sharpen the resolve of the Lords of Trade after 1675 to bring Massachusetts to heel. And, even after the Glorious Revolution of 1688, the Quakers – like the Abnaki Indians, who in war destroyed frontier settlements such as Wells, in Maine, and Deerfield, in the Connecticut Valley – long continued as a thorn in the Bay Colony's side. Indeed, a generation of almost continuous war after 1675 inhibited the growth of any firm sense of security. There was also the problem of New France, which grew, after successive campaigns against Quebec, to almost obsessive proportions (and was not stilled until the French citadel fell in 1759). The last major shudder of the seventeenth century for Massachusetts came with the Salem witches of 1692. It was a complex social and intellectual issue.

Witches, too, were the 'others'. The first enemy of the godly Commonwealth was, always, Satan. Unconverted Indians roaming the howling wilderness were his agents, as were those of other faiths. Women were identified with his worship – an indication of their weakness and inferiority. The witchcraft scandals, trials and hangings that struck Salem village came in time to disturb the entire province, evidence of Puritan unease and the terrifying power of Satan. But they were, as Perry Miller has noted,[6] as much to be anticipated among the afflictions of New England as the Indian raids, and were equally intelligible to everyone concerned within the logic of the covenant, in a world where what Max Weber has called 'acting in accordance with God's pattern' was extended throughout all social, economic and political life.[7]

How much, then, had Puritan Massachusetts in common with the other eleven colonies in being by 1713? (Georgia, the last of the thirteen colonies which were ultimately to break away from Britain, was not founded until 1733.) Excluding Connecticut, an early offshoot, Massachusetts presented in organization and structure a striking contrast with all her neighbours. The orderly creation of townships, the physical area in which a congregation resided (normally a village with attached lands) and the supporting educational system, had no parallel outside of New England save where New Englanders may have settled. Virginians aimed to recreate England – at least rural England – and operated with the minimum of institutional aids. Where precedents were unsuitable – as was the case with the regulation of Anglican clergy – old forms, such as the vestry, were adapted to suit the needs of an emergent planter class. But contrasts with Massachusetts are easier to find than parallels; Virginia was an economy based upon tobacco and a society increasingly dependent upon slavery. Nearer to Massachusetts in the dimensions of its conception, if not in its material purpose, were the ambitious social and political structures designed for the Carolinas by the political theorist John Locke and Anthony Ashley Cooper, later Earl of Shaftesbury. The Fundamental Constitutions influenced by James Harrington, author of the *Commonwealth of Oceana*, endeavoured to create a semi-feudal hierarchy with political and social influence determined by land-holding. The power of the nobility was to be restrained by that of the Commons or democratic element. The scheme for the Carolinas was utopian, while Virginia just grew. In neither was religion the driving force. But it was in Pennsylvania, the last of the seventeenth-century colonies to be formed. In many respects, the Quaker way in Pennsylvania contrasted sharply with that of godly Massachusetts; Quakerism was known for its contempt for forms and hierarchies, and for its hostility to dogma. Yet, just like the New England theocrats, the Quaker leaders found that the commercial life was not only a potent source of prosperity, but that it was also responsible for a shift in values which could discomfort them and undermine their ideals (though the practical religion of Benjamin Franklin was in due course to constitute a form of reconciliation). What is clear is that the priestly power achieved by the Congregational ministers in the seventeenth century was nowhere equalled outside of

New England. And, though it declined thereafter, it remained a formidable force, and a power in the New England spirit.

The Puritan arts

One consequence of Puritanism and its powerful ministry is often thought to be hostility to the arts. Yet the paradox is that New England was perhaps the most significant centre of artistic creation in the colonial period. In the end, this is not surprising, given the bookishness of the Puritan colonies, the strength of an educated ministry, and the preoccupation with typology and with writing the providential record. Puritanism, certainly, had been a protest against elaboration in English Protestantism, and it maintained a similar standard in the matter of cultural expression: the important issue was 'use', the social and religious value of artistic expression. Yet this could be resolved: indeed, the typologizing disposition, and the concern with conscience and self-knowledge, led to a serious exploration of written forms. Indeed, even the criterion of 'use' sometimes seems perfunctory. It was a common Puritan practice to anagrammatize names, the intent being didactic and moral, an eliciting of providential meanings. But the anagrams were clearly enjoyed with a metaphysical and cryptogrammatic satisfaction. Similarly, Nathaniel Ward (1578–1652), the author of *The Simple Cobler of Aggawam* (1647), condemned, in the Puritan fashion, frivolous elaboration in women's dress, by which ladies 'disfigure themselves with such exotick garbes, as not only dismantles their native lovely lustre, but transclouts them into gant bar-geese, ill-shapen shotten shell-fish, Egyptian Hieroglyphicks, or at the best into French flurts of the pastery, which a proper Englishwoman should scorn with her heels . . .'. This sounds strict, but Ward evidently enjoys the elaboration of his own language. In an age of wit, he is conscious of wit, and he continues, charmingly: 'We have about five or six of them in our Colony: if I see any of them accidentally, I cannot cleanse my phansie of them for a month after. I have been a solitary widdower almost twelve years . . .'. (p. 233)[4a] The Puritan imagination could generate many of the riches it seemed to condemn.

Thus aesthetic satisfactions apparently denied in one area could freely emerge elsewhere. The theatre was proscribed; but theatricality is rife throughout Puritan expression. Edward Johnson (1598–1672) produced his *Wonder-Working Providence of Sion's Saviour in New England* during the 1650s; it is sometimes known as *A History of New England*, and it was meant to be, and was, a primary record of the founding of Plymouth, with a firm didactic intent to elicit God's marvellous purposes. But it is in fact an elaborately dramatized epic, in which the emigrants are directly addressed by Christ's voice, and the reader is specifically alerted to the symmetrical tableaux of the departure from England:

> Passe on and attend with teares, if thou hast any, the following discourse ... both of them had their farther speech strangled from the depth of their inward dolor, with breast-breaking sobs, till leaning their heads on each others shoulders, they let fall the salt dropping dews of vehement affections, striving to exceede one another.... (p. 147)[4a]

And another kind of theatricality surely accounts for part of the success of New England's best-selling poem, Michael Wigglesworth's *The Day of Doom* (1662):

> So at the last, whilst Men sleep fast in their security
> Surpriz'd they are in such a snare as cometh suddenly.
> For at midnight brake forth a Light, which turn'd the night to day,
> And speedily an hideous cry did all the world dismay... (p.56)[4c]

The affective power that many puritan writers display was not cultivated for its own sake, though it may have been appreciated as such. Its 'use' lay in the affect on an audience – particularly, the audience of that key form of puritan expression, the sermon. Edward Johnson describes Thomas Shepard, with obvious approval, as a 'soule ravishing Minister' (p.151).[4a] The best sermons combine this eloquence with a highly determinate structure of doctrine and propositions, uses and applications. The experience intended by these preachers can be defined by contrast with their English contemporary Sir Thomas Browne, writing in *Religio Medici*: 'I love to lose myself in a mystery, to pursue my reason to an *O altitudo*!' The Puritan would not indulge the sublime, would not seek to lose himself. On the contrary, within the articulated form of the sermon, and the process of its argument, he was always placed. The animus against elaboration indeed shows in comments on early Puritan writing. Cotton Mather (1663–1728) looked back to a sermon by John Cotton,

> wherein sinning more to preach *Self* than *Christ*, he used such Florid Strains, as extremely recommended him unto the *most*, who relished the *Wisdom of Words* above the *Words of Wisdom*; Though the pompous Eloquence of that Sermon, afterwards gave such a distaste unto his own *Reverend Soul*, that with a Sacred Indignation he threw his Notes into the Fire.... (p.73)[4a]

But by the time this was written (1695) such a reaction was out of date. Cotton Mather himself used a far more 'florid' style than his father Increase or grandfather Richard.

Verse was subject to much the same criteria as prose. It attracted no special odium, but was widely practised as one among other forms of expression. Edward Johnson, celebrating the death of a Puritan worthy, can break into verse as a kind of mnemonic: 'For future Remembrance of him mind this *Meeter*' (p. 150).[4a] The major poets, Anne Bradstreet (*c*.1612–72) and Edward Taylor (*c*.1642–1729), turned the procedures we have described to their own advantage. Both attempted extended forms that correspond with the rationally systematic structure of the sermons (and ultimately, by analogy, with the providential order): Bradstreet's 'Contemplations', or Taylor's 'Gods Determinations touching his Elect'. Bradstreet wrote charming personal poems on her husband or family which nevertheless manage the exemplary transformation of private feeling into public type. Taylor, too, could typify an intimate or trivial stuation, as here, through the rhetoric of vision:

> Lord cleare my misted sight that I
> May hence view thy Divinity.
> Some sparkes whereof thou up dost hasp
> Within this little downy Wasp.... (p. 220)[4b]

Leaving England after the Restoration, Taylor continued the witty and meditative tradition of English Metaphysical poetry in a Puritan context. The Preface to 'Gods Determinations' shows some of his range, from typically curious and intricate detail:

> Who Lac'd and Fillitted the earth so fine,
> With Rivers like green Ribbons Smaragdine? [emerald]
> Who made the Sea's its Selvedge [border], and it locks
> Like a Quilt Ball within a Silver Box?
> Who spread its Canopy? Or Curtains Spun?
> Who in this Bowling Alley bowld the Sun?

– to close verbal play on just two words, making it 'all' out of nearly 'nothing':

> Oh! what a might is this! Whose single frown
> Doth shake the world as it would shake it down?
> Which All from Nothing [fetched], from Nothing, All:
> Hath All on Nothing set, lets Nothing fall.
> Gave All to nothing Man indeed, whereby
> Through nothing man all might him Glorify. (p.137–8)[4c]

The complexity of the Puritan mind led, in fact, not to a denial of art, but to a set of complex typological, symbolistic and metaphysical usages which passed on into the American literature of later times.

The waning of Puritanism

But in the event New England Puritanism could not stay pure amid the dislocations of American circumstances. It never recovered fully from the loss of power occasioned by the creation of the Dominion of New England. The accession of William III in 1689 gave the empire a constitutional monarchy and a firm Protestant commitment, acceptable even to New Englanders, though for most of their colonial history they were suspected of republican tendencies. The colonial charters, most of them revoked by James II, were restored by his successor, reassuring the colonists that their political rights were secure. But there was one exception, and that was Massachusetts. In 1691 it received a *new* charter; not only was the governor now appointed by the Crown, but the franchise was divorced from church membership and related to property, as in England and the other colonies. Puritanism was threatened, but it remained a potent force, still capable of passing restrictive legislation. Indeed, as in the 1720s, Baptists, Quakers and Anglicans paid taxes, under protest, to support Congregational ministers. The erosion of theocratic power was thus a slow one; so was the transition from Puritan to Yankee. By the end of the seventeenth century, latitudinarian forces, which were strong at Harvard, the very citadel of Puritanism, had initiated, with the support of influential elements among the commercial classes, an abandonment of the old covenant ideal. Church membership widened, then declined numerically; control of the churches by the General Court progressively weakened.

However, the principal mark of change was the 'Great Awakening', the mass Evangelical movement which between 1720 and 1750 brought a religious revival throughout the colonies. The new mood was represented by Jonathan Edwards (1703–58), the last of the great Puritan preachers, as gifted as any of his predecessors, and as concerned to search for evidences, for 'distinguishing signs of truly gracious and holy affections'; but these are now located in 'influences and operates on the heart' (p.517).[4b] There is an increased subjective stress on his work, when compared with that of the previous century. Edwards learned from Locke to 'exalt experience over reason'; he incorporated some of Newton's beliefs into Calvinist thought;[8] his account of consciousness in *Freedom of the Will* is the first major contribution to American philosophy; his *Images or Shadows of Divine Things* offers 'a new inward perception' that has some affinities with Transcendental symbolism in the nineteenth century. As the Great Awakening brought a revival of Calvinist vitality, a diminution of sectarian differences, and an increase in the millenial tendency of American religion, along with a weakening of authority and a declining respect for intellect, so the 'Moderate Enlightenment' and the 'Skeptical Enlightenment' of 1750 to 1789 opened the way to the spread of deism and the freeing of the individual from social constraints.

So, as the eighteenth century progressed, Massachusetts moved into the broader historical currents – political, ideological, intellectual, religious – that diminished the distinctions between colonies, and, in some respects, between colony and mother country. The Glorious Revolution of 1688 underwrote representative government; each settlement possessed a general assembly. The similarities between Parliament and the colonial assemblies encouraged that imitative process which, Jack Greene has shown, was powerful in shaping colonial attitudes and aspirations.[9] Certainly neither the instruments nor the situation were identical: colonial governors were not monarchs and, whether elected, appointed by proprietor or by the Crown, their influence was less than the King's in some spheres, greater in others. But the drive for greater Parliamentary powers came, with some provinces like Virginia and Massachusetts having an early start, and others like Pennsylvania, and New York (acquired by conquest), rapidly forging to the front. The model of New England town government fed the quest towards political autonomy. And, though sometimes exaggerated, the influence of the frontier as a democratizing force was significant. It promoted some social changes, for instance in the role of women. It fostered the evangelical movement by preferring emotional over intellectual religion, and encouraged the rejection of the European-trained ministry. Often back-country areas most of which were, thanks to population growth, under-represented in colonial assemblies, demanded the same privileges as the communities to the east, appealing to the rights of Englishmen. But, also drawn from England, a more radical ideology was emerging that transcended provincial boundaries. Colonists, alarmed at the spread of absolutism in Europe, sought a bulwark against political corruption and decay in republican ideas, the ideas of the 'commonwealthmen' popularized by John Trenchard and Thomas Gordon in the *Independent Whig* and *Cato's Letters*. In Massachusetts a Country Party, committed to local political rights lost in the charter of 1691, grew up; and three generations down to the Revolution (the mantle finally descended on Sam Adams) fought the 'Court' executive and its powerful instrument, patronage. Similar patterns appeared in other provinces like Pennsylvania and West Jersey. But in general colonial divisions had to do with local circumstances, and the ebb and flow of provincial politics did not before 1760 encourage a full-throttled drive for autonomy. As Governor Fauquier observed of the Virginia burgesses: 'Whoever charges them with acting upon a premeditated plan, don't know them, for they mean honestly, but are Expedient mongers in the highest degree.'[10]

The dialectic of location and dislocation evolved into new forms. Whig ideology, leavened in the colonies by Commonwealth radicalism owing something to European historians such as Paul de Rapin-Thoyras, the Huguenot exile, helped to create an American as distinct from an English identity. But American-born historians in the eighteenth century tended to strengthen rather a provincial than a wider identity. Robert Beverly's *History and Present State of Virginia* (1705) reflected a growing self-consciousness in the old dominion. Virginia had found other important writers in William Byrd, the Reverend Hugh Jones and later William Smith, and their often filiopietistic writing helped to generate self-esteem. William Smith's *History of New York* (1757), an important work, was designed to promote a better understanding of the colony in England. But, as

Louis B Wright has observed, it was New England that produced more histories and other narratives than all the rest of British America combined. Much of this reflects the very powerful sense of identity which had created in Massachusetts at an early stage 'a nation within a nation'. But part of it pointed forward to an identity as yet unformed, neither English or New English. The vision preserved in Cotton Mather's *Magnalia Christi Americana* or the *Ecclesiastical History of New England* (1702) emerged in the nineteenth century. To Harriet Beecher Stowe and her generation, 'God's mercies to New England foreshadowed the glorious future of the United States of America... commissioned to bear the light of liberty and religion through all the earth and to bring in the great millenial day...The New England clergy...were children of the morning.'[11]

Notes and references

1. Michel Foucault, *The Archaeology of Knowledge*, trans. by A M Sheridan, Tavistock, London, 1972, p. 22: 'We must question those ready-made syntheses, those groupings we normally accept before any examination, those links whose validity is recognized from the outset.'

2. S E Morison, *The European Discovery of America: The Northern Voyages, A.D. 500–1600,* Oxford U.P., New York, 1971, pp. 467–8.

3. John Seelye, *Prophetic Waters: The River in Early American Life and Literature,* Oxford, U.P., New York, 1977, p. 89. Also see Edmundo O'Gorman, *The Invention of America,* Indiana U.P., Bloomington, 1961; Hugh Honour, *The New Golden Land,* Allen Lane, London, 1975, which superbly illustrates the iconography of the Americas, and has an excellent text; and Sigmund Skard, *The American Myth and the European Mind,* University of Pennsylvania Press, Philadelphia, 1961.

4a-c. References in the text are to three basic paperback anthologies, to which the reader is directed:
    a. Perry Miller and Thomas H Johnson (eds), *The Puritans: A Sourcebook of Their Writings,* 1938 (reissued by Harper Torchbooks, 1963).
    b. George F Horner and Robert A Bain (eds), *Colonial and Federalist American Writing,* Odyssey Press, New York, 1966.
    c. Harrison T Meserole (ed), *Seventeenth-century American Poetry,* Norton, New York, 1972.

5. Perry Miller, *The New England Mind from Colony to Province,* Harvard U.P., Cambridge, Mass., 1953, p. 229

6. Perry Miller, *ibid.,* p. 192.

7. Max Weber, *The Sociology of Religion* (1922), trans. by E Fischoff, Methuen, London, 1966, p. 203: 'The belief in predestination, although it

might logically be expected to result in fatalism, produced in its most consistent followers the strongest possible motives for acting in accordance with God's pattern.'

8.   On this see D Hawke, *The Colonial Experience*, Bobbs-Merrill, New York, 1966, p. 436.

9. J.P.Greene, 'Political mimesis: A consideration of the historical and cultural roles of legislative behaviour in the British colonies in the eighteenth century', *American Historical Review*, **75**, 2 (1969), pp. 337—67.

10. J P Greene, *The Quest for Power: The Lower House of Assembly in the Southern Royal Colonies, 1689–1776*, University of North Carolina Press, Chapel Hill, 1963, p. 9.

11. Sacvan Bercovitch, *The Puritan Origins of the American Self*, Yale U.P., New Haven/London, 1975, p. 88.

Chapter 2

The first new nation

Peter Marshall and Ian Walker

The making of the new Canaan

Until quite recently the colonial period accounted, chronologically
speaking, for more than half of American history. Between the
establishment of the first permanent settlement at Jamestown in 1607
and the Declaration of Independence of 1776, 169 years elapsed. This
was quite long enough, as the previous chapter has shown, for new
variants of Western culture to develop. Britain's colonists might, and
in practice frequently did, insist on their rights as Englishmen, but they
were also aware that their own histories and traditions set them apart
from Englishmen at home. In particular, they cherished their right to
regulate their own affairs, through their elected assemblies, and not to
have laws and taxes thrust on them by the mother country.

Viewed in this way, it is easy to assume that the colonies were
naturally and automatically destined to break away. Yet up to 1763
there is little evidence that the colonists were eager for, or even
prepared to contemplate, such a development. What altered the
situation, and ultimately provoked the colonists into taking up arms,
was the British government's determination, following the defeat of
the French in the French and Indian War, to impose closer controls
over its imperial possessions. As the colonists saw it, this meant
depriving them of their cherished liberties. To the British, on the other
hand, these so-called liberties were without constitutional foundation;
if the colonists had hitherto been left to regulate their own affairs as
they saw fit, it was merely because the government in Britain had
allowed them to do so, not because it lacked constitutional authority.
Faced with continued British intransigence, the colonists' sense of
righteousness was reinforced by the conviction that it was not they but
the British who were the aggressors in the conflict. Thus as the struggle
escalated they resorted first to boycotts and protests, later to armed
resistance and ultimately to a military alliance with their former
enemies the French as a means of preserving what they saw as their
rightful liberties.

In a sense, then, the American Revolution was fundamentally
conservative. It began as a colonial response to British policy. In

retrospect it is plain that the colonists had misjudged Britain's aims no less than the British had misunderstood the concerns of the colonists. Yet once the fighting was over, Americans, as in the past, were quick the detect the hand of Providence in these events. On 8 May 1783, Dr Ezra Stiles, President of Yale College, preached an Election Sermon before the Governor and General Assembly of Connecticut, reflecting on what had happened. Later published under the title of *The United States elevated to Glory and Honour*,[1] his address traced, with mingled awe, pride and astonishment, the process of American separation from the British Empire and the establishment of an independent nation distinguished, by the aid of divine guidance, for its unique civic virtue; it also faced the problem of giving an explanation *of* these events.

How utopian it would have been [Stiles asserted] to have predicted at the battle of Lexington, that in less than eight years the independence and sovereignty of the United States should be acknowledged by four European sovereignties, one of which would be Britain herself. How wonderful the revolutions, the events of Providence! We live in an age of wonders; we have lived an age in a few years; we have seen more wonders accomplished in eight years than are usually unfolded in a century.

The liberty that Americans had secured for themselves would, before long, be extended throughout the world as their example became widely known:

We shall have a communication with all nations in commerce, manners, and science, beyond anything heretofore known in the world...all the arts may be transplanted from Europe and Asia, and flourish in America with an augmented lustre, not to mention the augment of the sciences from American inventions and discoveries, of which there have been as capital ones here, the last century, as in all Europe.

The rough sonorous diction of the English language may here take its Athenian polish, and receive its attic urbanity, as it will probably become the vernacular tongue of more numerous millions than ever yet spake one language on earth. . . .

A nation, Stiles concluded, whose Revolution had achieved so much so openly, was particularly committed to maintaining a purity of purpose: 'the United States are under peculiar obligations to become a holy people unto the Lord our God, on account of the late eminent deliverance, salvation, peace and glory with which he hath now crowned our new sovereignty.'

Stiles, not for the first time, had displayed an ability to develop, at a particularly apposite moment, a theme of both general and fundamental significance for Americans seeking to define their nation's purpose and progress. Precedents for his claims had been established in both literature and life: so, earlier in the century, Bishop Berkeley's 'Verses on the prospect of Planting Arts and Learning in America' had contrasted the decay of Europe with the promise of the New World as

Westward the course of empire takes its way;
The four first acts already past,
A fifth shall close the drama with the day;
Time's noblest offspring is the last.

Half a century later, travellers encountered the sense of the poetry as popular belief. Andrew Burnaby reported from Virginia in 1759–60 that

An idea, strange as it is visionary, has entered into the minds of the generality of mankind, that empire is travelling westward; and every one is looking forward with eager and impatient expectation to that destined moment when America is to give law to the rest of the world.

Views differed on the form in which this was to be achieved. John Adams, expressing in his *Dissertation on the Canon and Feudal Law* (1765) beliefs whose sources in both secular political philosophy and the Book of Revelation have been declared by Ernest Lee Tuveson to constitute 'apocalyptic Whiggism',[2] saw America as forming the centre of resistance to 'a wicked confederacy' between the two systems of tyranny – ecclesiastical and civil – that had subjected Europe to total ignorance until the Reformation, and had 'obscured true learning for long afterwards.' Youthful opinions were no less emphatic: for the Commencement exercises of the College of New Jersey in 1771, two of the graduating class, Philip Freneau and Hugh Henry Brackenridge, offered Princetonians *A Poem on the Rising Glory of America*. The derivative quality of their verse did not lessen its religious and visionary quality:

And when a train of rolling years are past
(so sung the exil'd seer in Patmos isle)
A new Jerusalem, sent down from heaven,
Shall grace our happy earth – perhaps this land,
Whose ample breast shall then receive, tho' late,
Myriads of saints, with their immortal king,
To live and reign on earth a thousand years.
Thence called Millennium. Paradise anew
Shall flourish, by no second Adam lost.
No dangerous tree with deadly fruit shall grow,
No tempting serpent to allure the soul
From native innocence. – A Canaan here,
Another *Canaan* shall excel the old,
And from a fairer Pisgah's top be seen.

The idea of America as the new Canaan was examined at length by another author of much more exalted academic standing but perhaps even less poetic talent. Timothy Dwight (1752–1817), the 'Connecticut Wit' who became President of Yale, devoted fourteen years to the composition of *The Conquest of Canaan*, producing in 1785 an extraordinarily dull and noisy eleven-book epic in heroic couplets on the subject of Joshua's battles and entry into the Promised Land. The patriotic analogy intended was evident enough: Joshua was modelled on George Washington, while other American heroes were but lightly disguised. The Promised Land of Canaan was, of course, the United States:

> Far o'er yon azure main thy view extend,
> Where seas and skies in blue confusion blend:
> Lo, there a mighty realm, by Heaven design'd
> The last retreat for poor oppress'd mankind;
> Form'd with that pomp which marks the land divine,
> And clothes yon vault where worlds unnumber'd shine.
> Here spacious plains in solemn grandeur spread,
> Here cloudy forests cast eternal shade;
> Rich valleys wind, the sky-tall mountains brave,
> And inland seas for commerce spread the wave,
> With nobler floods the sea-like rivers roll,
> And fairer lustre purples round the pole.

Claims and expectations of this magnitude may have reflected individuals' optimism, but also gave rise to consequential difficulties: if America was so evidently superior to all other regions of the world, it had no cause to remain inferior in any respect. The achievement of political independence formed but a part of the whole acknowledgment of cultural distinctiveness, for as Noah Webster (1758–1843) proclaimed, in the 1783 preface to his 'Speller', 'America must be as independent in *literature* as she is in *politics.*' How this would be achieved was less clear, but authors and critics united to establish a national literature produced by worthy successors to the greatest authors of past civilizations. Freneau's view of the future was typical of these hopes:

> I see a Homer and a Milton rise
> In all the pomp and majesty of song,.....
> A second Pope, like that Arabian bird
> Of which no age can boast but one, may yet
> Awake the muse by Schuylkill's silent stream,...
> And Susquehanna's rocky stream unsung,...
> Shall yet remurmer to the magic sound
> Of song heroic.

So widely spread was this ambition that even as prosaic a figure as a John Adams permitted himself the hope that he should 'live to see our young America in Possession of an Heroic Poem, equal to those most esteemed in any Country'. Unfortunately, these eager expectations found all too little satisfaction in the first outpouring of national literature, no matter how idealistic the authors' intentions may have been.

In his preface to the *Vision of Columbus* (1787) – revised and reissued as *The Columbiad* (1807) – Joel Barlow (1754–1812) was at pains to stress his extra-literary purposes:

My object is altogether of a moral and political nature. I wish to encourage and strengthen, in the rising generation, a sense of the importance of republican institutions; as being the great foundations of public and private happiness, the necessary aliment of future and permanent ameliorations in the condition of human nature.

Cast in the form of an imitative sub-Miltonic 'epic,' the poem describes how Columbus, now imprisoned, is visited by Hesper, the guardian Angel of the New World, who reveals to him the future awaiting the land he has discovered. The colonial years, the coming of the Revolution, the creation of the federal system, are unfolded in a visionary panorama, and Columbus's prison despair turns to joy as he is shown the future glories of a land where:

> Courageous Probity, with brow serene,
> And Temperance calm presents her placid mein,
> Contentment, Moderation, Labour, Art,
> Mould the new man and humanize his heart;
> To public plenty private ease dilates,
> Domestic peace to harmony of states,
> Protected industry, careening far,
> Detects the cause and curses the rage of war,
> And sweeps, with forceful arm, to their last graves,
> Kings from the earth and pirates from the waves.

Barlow's enterprise is a national republican epic, and a search for the mythology of the new nation; such epic intentions would persist through much subsequent American writing. Yet it is noticeable that Barlow's revolutionary poem is cast in the forms of neo-classical eighteenth-century English poetry; the spirit but not the form of romanticism which was sweeping Europe, and which to some extent the American Revolution itself released, is visible. Behind idealist themes and the conviction of a vast historical transition there lie hard facts of cultural dependence; in writing as in social and political institutions, the struggle into nationhood was still just beginning.

The growth of party

Literary figures might proclaim the presence of a faultless society, and the coming of a new imperial cycle; the political leaders of the new nation, proud as they were to have achieved independence, were more aware of the practical problems of its preservation than of the imminent attainment of some idealistic goal. Political realism invoked an altogether more prudent assessment of progress than that claimed by the authors of a national literature whose existence was hailed more frequently than it could be perceived. Many were alarmed by the growth of parties, a development not anticipated by the nation's founders. During the Revolutionary years much emphasis had been given to the need for solidarity. Yet once the war was over, it soon became clear that Americans were not all of one mind. This was evident during the period of the Articles of Confederation (1777–87) when, for a time, it looked as if the United States was not a nation at all but a collection of states each intent on going its own way. These tendencies were arrested by the adoption (1787–88) of the new Constitution. Nevertheless, problems remained. In particular, the divisions in Washington's own cabinet between the Hamiltonians and the Jeffersonians, and their uninhibited use of rhetoric to castigate one another's policies, seemed to threaten the very foundations of the new state. It was out of these divisions that the first American party system arose, the Federalists (until their demise following the War of 1812) stressing the need for economic diversification, a governing elite and a strong central authority; and the Jeffersonian Republicans urging the need to protect the existing agrarian order and encourage a broad diffusion of wealth while viewing with distrust any growth in the powers of the central government. To a degree these same divisions are also evident in the struggles between Whigs and Democrats in the 1830s and 1840s.

Yet with the benefit of hindsight it can be concluded that there was little immediate likelihood of the destruction of the United States by either internal conflict or external attack in the decades after 1783, even though there is ample evidence to indicate that contemporaries thought otherwise. There were particular economic and political problems attributed to the aftermath of war and the Articles of Confederation; there were general doubts as to the possibility of preserving stability in a state whose size far exceeded that considered compatible with the working of popular government; there were fears that the empires of the Old World, so recently deposed from the rule of North America, would not accept the outcome of the Revolution as a final decision. Although some of these alarms were reduced by the composition and ratification of the Constitution, the unanticipated emergence of political parties was viewed with disquiet. It has been suggested that those who chose to support parties did so out of uncertainty rather than from subscription to political beliefs. Richard Buel, Jr, holds that 'Federalism was the choice of those who felt insecure as leaders because of changes wrought by the Revolution', and concludes of their opponents that until the War of 1812 seemed to prove otherwise:

Many Republicans had defended the nation's unique institutions less because they were assured that this form of government was stable than because the alternatives were unacceptable. For most of the revolutionary generation, despite their brave words at the time of trial, republicanism had remained a faith still unproved by experience.[3]

A political system so imperfectly defined might well seem unable to confront external dangers and liable to magnify their threats: to Federalists, the Revolution in France presaged universal upheaval and chaos, while to Republicans the fear of Britain's return as an imperial authority over North America could not be dispelled. Each party saw its adversary as a willing accomplice in the advancement of the aims of its alleged European ally. In these circumstances there was ample ground for many to maintain the belief that held, as Paul C Nagel has put it, that 'The political party from the start was considered the serpent in America's Garden.'[4]

Despite the undoubted partisan bitterness that distinguished Federalist from Republican, it is possible to attach too much significance to their differences: the two parties were not absolutely opposed and chose not to engage in mortal conflict on matters of fundamental importance. Thus, both accepted without question the fact of the Revolution and the emergence of the American nation: the form and purpose these events involved were grounds for deep disagreement, but any return to British rule was beyond consideration. Loyalism and Loyalists had no part to play in the politics of the United States. The first generation of American party leaders, no matter how greatly at variance, remained constant in their adhesion to a system whose novelty was compounded by its uncertain prospects.

Party arguments often turned on differing views of the purpose and limits of the Revolution. To a Federalist as vehement as Fisher Ames, 'The American Revolution was in fact, after 1776, a resistance to foreign government', and had no ground to engage in domestic change. The presence of democracy rendered this a constant danger, since the people were liable to fall under the sway of demagogues. 'To make the nation free', Ames declared, 'the crafty must be kept in awe, and the violent in restraint . . . it is only by the due restraint of others, that I am free'. Political turbulence sounded the alarm to others of a previously sanguine outlook: at the Constitutional Convention of 1787 Elbridge Gerry of Massachusetts gave vent to his fears. 'The evils we experience flow from the excess of democracy', he declared. 'The people do not want virtue, but are the dupes of pretended patriots . . .' 'He had', he said, 'been too republican heretofore; he was still however, republican, but had been taught by experience the danger of the leveling spirit . . .' Federalists were continually exercised by the need to combat these tendencies and to maintain popular deference to their betters. Stephen Higginson insisted that 'The people must be *taught* to confide in and reverence their rulers', and it was generally agreed that restraint, obedience and subordination were popular qualities essential to the preservation of public order. Their Republican adversaries were certainly rendered more radical by Federalist description than by party intent: New England's fear, mistrust, and assertion of Southern, and particularly Virginian, political aims confirmed party differences throughout the quarter-century between the framing of the Constitution and the War of 1812. John Adams expressed a typical opinion when he asserted in 1805 that:

The Southern Men have been actuated by an absolute hatred of New England. Nothing but their fears ever restrained them from discarding Us from their Union. Those Fears, as their population increases so much faster than ours, diminish every day; and were they not restrained by their Negroes they would reject us from their Union, within a year.

The threat of men rendered powerful and arrogant by the profits of slavery weighed heavily upon Federalists, to assume personal shape in their depiction of the malevolent character and purposes of Thomas Jefferson. Few Federalists seemed to have taken seriously the President's Inaugural assertion that all Americans were of both parties. As he left office in 1809, the precocious William Cullen Bryant could bid farewell to a 'wretch' whose intellectual pretensions, alleged sexual relations with a slave, and futile policies, had disgraced 'the presidential chair':

Disclose thy secret measures, foul or fair,
Go, search with curious eye, for horned frogs,
Mid the wild wastes of Louisianan bogs;
Or, where Ohio rolls his turbid stream,
Dig for huge bones, thy glory and thy theme.
Go, scan, Philosophist, thy Sally's charms,
And sink supinely in her sable arms;
But quit to abler hands the helm of state,
Nor image ruin on they country's fate!

If the violence of political conflicts was limited to words – Alexander Hamilton constituted the only untimely casualty of the revolutionary generation, and his death occurred on the duelling ground, not on the scaffold or the barricades – the uncertainty generated by the particular nature of the break with Britain would be very slow to disappear. It left, as Linda Kerber has pointed out, an 'ambiguous legacy' to later generations, with the consequence that:

In the years after the Revolution, the American walked a strange tightrope between optimism and pessimism. The Revolution had been both a radical break with the past and a conservative affirmation of it; that ambivalence persisted through the early years of the national experience. The Federalist characteristically searched the American social order to find the stability that would justify the Revolution; for the same purpose the Democrat searched it to find flexibility.[5]

In the long run, the fact that the search was being undertaken within an American, not a colonial, social order would uncover a new national political and cultural structure, as Tocqueville was so sharply to see in the 1830s. But, for the moment, efforts to achieve change appeared much more obvious than its successful provision.

Declarations of Literary Independence?

There were some among the Founding Fathers who saw the development of the arts and cultural expression as a matter of small importance, given the practical problems; others looked with gravity at the task of proclaiming and defining the purposes of the new nation in the arts and culture. The proof of independence demanded not merely a distinctive literature; but also, according to some, a separate language in which it could be written: Noah Webster, the nation's first grammarian and lexicographer, was well aware of the implications of his interests. In 1807, looking back at over twenty years' work, he assured Joel Barlow that he had always:

had it in view to detach this country as much as possible from its dependence on the parent country. . . . Our people look to English books as the standard of truth on all subjects and this confidence in English opinions puts *an end to inquiry*.

Although, as he himself came to recognize, Webster's intentions of change always remained far larger than his achievements, his was a crucial contribution towards establishing the educational basis of the American nation.

Others shared the task. Webster believed that the creation of a common national loyalty could be fostered by the teaching of American history in the schools. Support in this endeavour was provided by the first generation of American historians, for whom the Revolution was the central episode of their accounts and to whom colonial differences were of far less significance than the national achievement of independence. Objectivity did not distinguish their narratives and if, to them, history was past politics, they themselves were present politicians. Despite this, however, partisan views were subordinate to common agreement on the national purpose. Although Mrs Warren's *History of the American Revolution* (1805) was a product of Republican sympathies and John Marshall's *Life of Washington* (1804 – 07) was a justification of Federalism rather than a biography, Arthur H Shaffer has concluded that:

The division between Warren and Marshall was predominantly over specific policies and individual motives . . . these differences are minor compared to a common bias in favor of the national government as the expression of American nationality . . . If Marshall had not been a prominent Federalist and Warren a known Republican, or if neither had dealt with the years after 1789, it would have heen difficult to discover marked differences between them. In this they were characteristic of their fellow scholars; allegiance to national unity tended to minimize differences even among the most partisan of the historians.[6]

The use of the Revolution as a principal source for an historical literature of national unity was fully and rapidly introduced: the story of Independence confirmed, rather than confused, the sense of communal identity.

Other forms of literature proved less suited to this purpose, though hopes and encouragement were continually being expressed. In part, as even those sympathetic to the new society had to admit, failure represented the inevitable absence of necessary elements, without which the achievements of Europe could not be matched. So, after his visit in 1793 and prior to his emigration to America, Thomas Cooper, Manchester radical and political admirer of the United States, had to admit that:

> With respect to literary men, it is to be observed that in America there is not as yet what may be called a *class* of society, to whom that denomination will apply; such, for instance, as is to be found in Great Britain, and indeed in most of the old countries of Europe. A class, whose profession is literature; and among whom the branches of knowledge are divided and subdivided with great minuteness, each individual taking and pursuing his separate department as regularly as the respective fabricators of a watch or a pin. Literature in America is an amusement only – collateral to the occupation of the person who attends (and but occasionally attends) to it. In Europe it is a trade – a means of livelihood.

Cooper did not believe that Americans were condemned to a permanent state of literary inferiority but acknowledged that, lacking libraries and limited almost entirely to modern books, with a land impoverished by war and where attention was naturally turned toward economic improvement, it would take time for an American literature to equal that of Europe. But Thomas Cooper's observations were scarcely original; indeed they were confirmed and elaborated many times over, then and for years into the future, by commentators on American culture (or the lack of it) from both sides of the Atlantic. For example, Cooper's eminent namesake, James Fenimore Cooper (1789 – 1851) complained bluntly in his *Notions of the Americans* (1828) of the many obstacles hindering the American writer, not least of which was the democratic dullness of the land:

> There is scarcely an ore which contributes to the wealth of the author that is found here in veins as rich as in Europe. There are no annals for the historian; no follies (beyond the most vulgar and commonplace) for the satirist; no manners for the dramatist; no obscure fictions for the writer of romance; no gross and hardy offences against decorum for the moralist; nor any of the rich artificial auxiliaries of poetry. The weakest hand can extract a spark from the flint, but it would baffle the strength of a giant to attempt kindling a flame with a pudding-stone.

This complaint about the absence of literary materials in the new land and the new nation would last on, up to Hawthorne and Henry James. It helps explain why early American writing is touched with a sense of displacement and doubt, even sometimes a sense of artistic alienation. This is clear in Washington Irving (1783–1859), usually taken as America's first professional writer. One of the New York

'Knickerbocker School', Irving tried to establish a native subject
matter; yet his famous *Sketch-Book of Geoffrey Crayon, Gent.* (2 vols,
1819, 1820), containing, among other things, 'Rip Van Winkle' and
'The Legend of Sleepy Hollow', was written just after the war of 1812
and in England, and aimed at an Anglo-American audience. To win
the way to an American romanticism, cultural dependence was
inevitable: even the famous folk-tales are adaptations of German
sources on to American ground. Other essays dwell on the problems of
establishing writing as an institution in the new nation – problems
illustrated by the career and concerns of Hugh Henry Brackenridge
(1748–1816), a generation older than Irving, who was a child of the
Revolution. Brackenridge's composition, with Philip Freneau, of *The
Rising Glory of America* initiated a commitment to patriotic literature
that led him to the composition of verse dramas on *The Battle of
Bunker's Hill* (1776) and *The Death of General Montgomery* (1777). In
1778 he established in Philadelphia the *United States Magazine,* from
the belief that Americans 'are able to cultivate the *belles lettres,* even
disconnected from Great Britain; and that liberty is of so noble and
energetic a quality, as even from the bosom of war to call forth the
powers of human genius'. He was unable, however, to prove his point,
for the magazine failed within the year. Brackenridge, his savings lost,
turned to law and politics in the frontier town of Pittsburgh.

In 1792 Brackenridge published in Philadelphia the first two
volumes of *Modern Chivalry;* further volumes appeared at intervals
and the edition was not complete until 1815. Although he had in the
meantime pursued a successful judicial career, setbacks had also been
encountered: *Modern Chivalry* may have been initially provoked by a
failure to secure election to the Constitutional Convention in 1787 and
defeat by an Irishman Brackenridge considered unfit to hold public
office. The work may be fiction but it is hardly a novel in the modern
sense; character development is set aside and for plot is substituted an
account of the wanderings and adventures of Captain Farrago, a
sympathetic caricature of a Jeffersonian landed gentleman (perhaps of
Brackenridge himself), well-mannered, well-read, sensible, kindly,
conservative, always ready to lecture and instruct the populace, and
his 'bog-trotter', 'redemptioner' servant, Teague O'Regan. Their
Quixotic adventures are designed to reveal the stupidities, crudities,
and absurdities of their world through humour and satire, though
Brackenridge, too, enters directly into the book in inter-chapters of
'Reflections'. His early idealism had been modified by experience:
while seeing himself as a confirmed democrat, he now recognized that
liberty was a matter of curtailment as well as expression, and had
become fearful – as James Fenimore Cooper would – of populist
control and a consequent diminution of standards. Here Captain
Farrago encounters an election: he is horrified to discover the
populace about to elect one Traddle, an illiterate weaver, as their
representative, and even more horrified when they turn their attention

towards the stupid Teague:

While they were thus discoursing, a bustle had taken place among the crowd. Teague hearing so much about elections, and serving the government, took it into his head, that he could be a legislator himself. The thing was not displeasing to the people, who seemed to favor his pretensions; owing, in some degree, to there being several of his countrymen among the crowd; but more especially to the fluctuation of the popular mind, and a disposition to what is new and ignoble. For though the weaver was not the most elevated object of choice, yet he was still preferable to this tatterdemalion, who was but a menial servant, and had so much of what is called the brogue on his tongue, as to fall far short of an elegant speaker.

The Captain coming up, and finding what was on the carpet, was greatly chagrined at not having been able to give the multitude a better idea of the importance of a legislative trust; alarmed also, from an apprehension of the loss of his servant. Under these impressions he resumed his address to the multitude. Said he, 'This is making the matter still worse, gentlemen; this servant of mine is but a bog-trotter; who can scarcely speak the dialect in which your laws ought to be written; but certainly has never read a single treatise on any political subject; for the truth is, he cannot read at all. . .he is totally ignorant of the great principles of legislation; and more especially, the particular interests of the government.

'A free government is a noble possession to a people: and its freedom consists in an equal right to make laws, and to have the benefit of the laws when made. Though doubtless, in such a government, the lowest citizen may become chief magistrate; yet it is sufficient to possess the right; not absolutely necessary to exercise it. . .You are surely carrying the matter too far, in thinking to make a senator of this hostler; to take him away from an employment to which he has been bred, and put him to another, to which he has served no apprenticeship; to set those hands which have been lately employed in currying my horse, to the draughting-bills, and preparing business for the house.'

The people were tenacious of their choice, and insisted in giving Teague their suffrages; and by the frown upon their brows, seemed to indicate resentment at what had been said; as indirectly charging them with want of judgement; or calling in question their privilege to do what they thought proper. (Ch.3)

Problems of democracy

Brackenridge's unease resounds through early American writing; Americans were torn between stressing the promise or the problems created by a democratic society. If Federalists, with their more elitist view of government, had reached Brackenridge's view of popular elections with much greater speed and certainty, they possessed no clear alternative means of management. 'One of the central dilemmas of Federalism', James M Banner, Jr, has pointed out, 'lay in the fact that the party never had any alternative but to accommodate itself to the ascendant democratic political mode'.[7] Fearing the worst, Federalists strove assiduously to secure superiority within a constitutional system they could claim to have devised, no matter how alarming its political operation may have proved. In stark contrast, Jefferson declared himself happy to accept the people's choice: 'In general', he told John Adams in 1813, 'they will elect the real good and wise. In some instances, wealth may corrupt, and birth blind them, but not in sufficient degree to endanger the society. . . .' No Federalist could have subscribed to this belief.

For all his singular lack of moderation, Fisher Ames probably declared what many others thought when he asserted that:

The people, as a body, cannot deliberate. Nevertheless, they will feel an irresistible impulse to act, and their resolutions will be dictated to them by their demagogues. The consciousness, or the opinion, that they possess the supreme power, will inspire inordinate passions; and the violent men, who are the most forward to gratify those passions, will be their favourites. What is called the government of the people is in fact too often the arbitrary power of such men. Here, then, we have the faithful portrait of democracy.

Political fears were a consequence of beliefs in the inevitability of social degeneration. John Adams, for instance, held that the fruits of virtue would be vices. 'Will you tell me', he asked Jefferson in 1819:

how to prevent riches from becoming the effects of temperance and industry? Will you tell me how to prevent riches from producing luxury? Will you tell me how to prevent luxury from producing effeminacy, intoxication, extravagance, vice and folly?

For his part, Jefferson's hopes for the future were far less bleak. In a letter to DuPont de Nemours in 1816 he pinned his faith to popular education:

Altho' I do not, with some enthusiasts, believe that the human condition will ever advance to such a state of perfection as that there shall no longer be pain or vice in the world, yet I believe it susceptible of much improvement, and, most of all, in matters of government and religion; and that the diffusion of knowledge among the people is to be the instrument by which it is to be effected.

Neither proofs of progress nor of decay were to gain unqualified assent. If, after 1815, the cause of growth might seem to have prevailed, there were those who continued to offer criticisms in terms to which John Adams could have wholeheartedly subscribed. Lawyers in particular saw little but disaster in prospect: Chancellor Kent of New York assembled in 1836 a formidable array of social evils:

The rapidly increasing appetite for wealth; the inordinate taste for luxury which it engenders; the vehement spirit of speculation, and the selfish emulation which it creates; the contempt for slow and moderate gains; the ardent thirst for pleasure and amusement; the diminishing reverence for the wisdom of the past; the disregard of the lessons of experience, the authority of magistrates, and the venerable institutions of ancestral policy.

Differences on the question of the state of the nation were not, however, aligned after 1815 with party allegiance. The outcome of the War of 1812 appeared to have obliterated or relegated to permanent obscurity the issues, whether internal or external, that had sustained the Federalists. In political terms the optimism of Republicanism had prevailed decisively over the pessimism of their opponents after a war in which, or so Republicans liked to think, both the people and their symbolic representation, the nation, had demonstrated qualities of strength and certainty.

If a considered judgement on the military aspects of the War of 1812 might have reduced sharply the scale of American success, it would in no way have diminished the stature gained by the nation's first post-revolutionary hero, Andrew Jackson (1767–1845), who in 1815 had defeated the British at New Orleans. In many ways Jackson represented the same things Jefferson had stood for a generation earlier, but he was cast in a cruder mould. Jefferson, for all his democratic sympathies, had been a Virginian aristocrat. Jackson came from Tennessee, still a frontier area, and in his personal style as well as his politics he played up his frontier origins. In 1828 he decisively defeated John Quincy Adams in the election for the Presidency, thus ending the period of single party rule which had effectively existed since 1816. In contrast to Adams (the son of President John Adams), Jackson was able to present himself as a representative of the common people and, in particular, of the settlers in the growing and increasingly influential new states of the West. Thus in manner, as well as in fact, Jackson served notice that a new type of American had come to embody national characteristics. The Jacksonian epoch, characterized at the political level by its struggles between the Jacksonian Democrats and their Whig opponents, brought to the forefront of American awareness those problems of liberal evolution that were also preoccupying European radicals. With the 1830s, the sense of American direction grows stronger; but the sense of American conflict sharpens, especially in the realm of the imagination, where the ambiguous image of a self that either expresses the potential of society or transcends it altogether acquires a force in a period of intensified artistic creation.

The path to the new arts

The decisive shifting of emphasis in Jacksonian America presented writers with new prospects and new problems. It offered the opportunity to new themes, yet it offered little likelihood that the new social exemplars would hold 'gentlemanly' authorship in high regard. These were the contrasts particularly felt by James Fenimore Cooper, America's first major novelist and fictional mythologist. Cooper's background in upper New York State gave him familiarity both with frontier conditions and the problems of landed ownership, with the idylls of freedom in the wilderness and the harsh specifics of agrarian conflict, apparent from the 1760s. It is not surprising that throughout Cooper's fiction there runs both a pastoral romantic myth and a fear of anarchy, mob-rule, and the consequent breakdown both of law and order and civilized standards of behaviour. Cooper was the novelist both of American pastoral and of underlying and deep-rooted social tension. Thus, in his first successful novel, *The Spy* (1821), the 'neutral ground' between the revolutionary forces and the British army is threatened by groups of irregulars and mercenaries known as 'Skinners' and 'Cow Boys': the 'Skinners' were republican 'gangs of marauders who infested the country with a semblance of patriotism, and were guilty of every grade of offence, from simple theft up to murder'. These 'fellows whose mouths are filled with liberty and equality, and whose hearts are overflowing with cupidity and gall' are in direct contrast to the heroic spy, Harvey Birch, solitary and dignified, motivated only by patriotic ardour and his honour as a gentleman. In *The Prairie* (1827), order and civilization on the frontier are threatened by the lawless Bush tribe led by the terrible Ishmael:

At some little distance in front of the whole, marched the individual, who, by his position and air, appeared to be the leader of the band. He was a tall, sunburnt man, past the middle-age, of a dull countenance and listless manner. His frame appeared loose and flexible; but it was vast, and in reality of prodigious power. It was only at moments, however, as some slight impediment opposed itself to his loitering progress, that his person, which, in its ordinary gait, seemed so lounging and nerveless, displayed any of those energies which lay latent in his system, like the slumbering and unwieldy, but terrible, strength of the elephant. The inferior lineaments of his countenance were coarse, extended, and vacant; while the superior, or those nobler parts which are thought to affect the intellectual being, were low, receding, and mean.

   The dress of this individual was a mixture of the coarsest vestments of a husbandman, with the leathern garments that fashion, as well as use, had in some degree rendered necessary to one engaged in his present pursuits. There was, however, a singular and wild display of prodigal and ill-judged ornaments blended with his motley attire. In place of the usual deerskin belt, he wore around his body a tarnished silken sash of the most gaudy colors; the buck-horn haft of his knife was profusely decorated with plates of silver; the martin's fur of his cap was of a fineness and shadowing that a queen might covet; the buttons of his rude and soiled blanket-coat were of the glittering coinage of Mexico; the stock of his rifle was of beautiful mahogany, riveted and banded with the same precious metal; and the trinkets of no less than three worthless watches dangled from different parts of his person. In addition to the pack and the rifle which were slung at his back, together with the well-filled and carefully guarded pouch and horn, he had carelessly cast a keen and bright wood axe across his shoulder, sustaining the weight of the whole with as much apparent ease as if he moved unfettered in limb, and free from incumbrance. (Ch. 1)

Would the frontier be settled by brutish, uncivilized, disordered, landless people like Ishmael? Cooper certainly recognized, feared and was fascinated by his power and persistence; and though at the end of the fiction he and his band wander away leaving the stage and country to the gentry – Capt. Middleton and Inez – the solution is arbitrary and unconvincing, and the landless with sharp axes and few scruples would surely return. What Cooper realized was that in any society there must be firm laws governing relations between man and man and his environment, and in a frontier society these laws were often non-existent. Thus in *The Pioneers* (1823), Natty Bumppo and the Indian John obeyed natural law before the settlements came: they killed only what they needed and ate only when they were hungry; but the new settlers have no relationship with the land and kill indiscriminately: for example, they slaughter great quantities of passenger pigeons (now extinct!) with anything they can lay their hands on, from long poles to artillery, until the ground is covered in bodies. Ironically, it is Natty (who later breaks the 'law' by killing a deer out of season) who points out to Judge Temple, the embodiment of Cooper's conservative, benevolent paternal democrat, the need to restrain human greed and weakness:

'It's much better to kill only such as you want, without wasting your powder and lead, than to be firing into God's creaters in such a wicked manner. But I come out for a bird, and you know the reason why I like small game, Mr. Oliver, and now I have got one I will go home, for I don't like to see these wasty ways that you are all practysing, as if the least thing was not made for use, and not to destroy'.

'Thou sayest well, Leather-stocking', cried Marmaduke, 'and I begin to think it time to put an end to this work of destruction'.

'Put an end, Judge, to your clearings. An't the woods his work as well as the pigeons? Use, but don't waste. Wasn't the woods made for the beasts and birds to harbour in? and when man wanted their flesh, their skins, or their feathers, there's the place to seek them. But I'll go to the hut with my own game, for I wouldn't touch one of the harmless things that kiver the ground here, looking up with their eyes at me, as if they only wanted tongues to say their thoughts'.

With this sentiment in his mouth, Leather-stocking threw his rifle over his arm, and, followed by his dogs, stepped across the clearing with great caution, taking care not to tread on one of the hundreds of the wounded birds that lay in his path. He soon entered the bushes on the margin of the lake, and was hid from view. (Vol. 2, Ch. 10)

Cooper's criticisms of American society, when coupled with lengthy residence in Europe, from 1826 to 1833, led to his being attacked as lacking in patriotic attitudes. he responded with *The American Democrat* (1838) as a definition of his stand:

The writer believes himself to be as good a democrat as there is in America. But his democracy is not of the impracticable school. He prefers a democracy to any other system, on account of its comparative advantages, and not on account of its perfection. He knows it has evils; great and increasing evils, and evils peculiar to itself; but he believes that monarchy and aristocracy have more. It will be very apparent to all who read this book, that he is not a believer in the scheme of raising men very far above their natural propensities.

It was not that doubters of the democratic system were so few but that alternatives were quite absent. Even those whose mistrust of democracy proved habitual believed that the destiny of the United States involved unparalleled growth and expansion: as conservative a figure as Gouverneur Morris could, in 1801, announce that 'The proudest empire in Europe is but a bauble, compared to what the United States *will* be, *must* be, in the course of two centuries; perhaps one!'.

Proclamations of political power and significance, projects to create a national literature, bore little relationship to American achievements in the first decades of independence. Reviewing the condition of the United States in 1820, Sydney Smith, writing in the *Edinburgh Review*, damned the nation's qualities with the faintest of praises:

The Americans are a brave, industrious, and acute people; but they have hitherto given no indications of genius, and made no approaches to the heroic, either in their morality or character. . . .During the thirty or forty years of their independence, they have done absolutely nothing for the Sciences, for the Arts, for Literature, or even for the statesman-like studies of Politics or Political Economy. . . .In the four quarters of the globe, who reads an American book? or goes to an American play? or looks at an American picture or statue? What does the world yet owe to American physicians or surgeons? What new substances have their chemists discovered? or what old ones have they analyzed? What new constellations have been discovered by the telescopes of Americans? – what have they done in the mathematics? Who drinks out of American glasses? or eats from American plates? or wears American coats or gowns? or sleeps in American blankets?. . . .

If such an estimate was unfair at the time of writing and totally inaccurate as a prediction of the future, it served to point the distinction between the ambitions of Americans and their actual realization. Recognition abroad, whether of the nation's political standing or of its artistic and literary contributions, was to be long delayed. The withholding of any acknowledgments proved dispiriting to many who had so enthusiastically greeted the appearance of specifically American qualities and then found their expectations dispelled. Yet some always persisted in the search, pursuing the task in a fashion which, for all the changes that had occurred in the meantime, Ezra Stiles would have found familiar. The Sermon of 1783 and Herman Melville's *White Jacket* of 1850 are linked by a common belief in the special mission of the United States; a process which, by mid-century, had begun to be defined and described in the nation's history and literature. It had much further to travel and to change in the process, but the society which could elicit Melville's description had developed in ways that would ensure a sense of uniqueness for at least a century to come:

We Americans are the peculiar, chosen people – the Israel of our time; we bear the ark of the liberties of the world. Seventy years ago we escaped from thrall; and, besides our first birthright – embracing one continent of earth – God has given to us, for a future inheritance, the broad domains of the political pagans, that shall yet come and lie down under the shade of our ark, without bloody hands being lifted. God has predestined, mankind expects, great things from our race; and great things we feel in our souls. The rest of the nations must soon be in our rear. We are the pioneers of the world; the advance-guard, sent on through the wilderness of untried things, to break a new path in the New World that is ours. In our youth is our strength, in our inexperience, our wisdom. At a period when other nations have but lisped, our deep voice is heard afar. Long enough have we been sceptics with regard to ourselves, and doubted whether, indeed, the political Messiah had come. But he has come in *us*, if we would but give utterance to his promptings. And let us always remember that with ourselves, almost for the first time in the history of earth, national selfishness is unbounded philanthropy; for we cannot do a good to America, but we give alms to the world. (Ch. 36)

By 1850, in literature as in politics, the great themes of the American experience had been assembled. Yet we cannot miss in the range of Melville's work something of that sense of alienation and disturbance that tests and questions the note of American idealism which he also speaks to: expectation meshes with an anarchic doubt. Tempered through change, the hopes and fears of the revolutionary generation were now embodied in a distinctive national identity.

Notes and references

1. Included in John Wingate Thornton, *The Pulpit of the American Revolution*, Da Capo Press, New York, reprint 1970, pp. 401–70.
2. Ernest Lee Tuvesen, *Redeemer Nation,* Chicago U.P., Chicago, 1968, p. 24.
3. Richard Buel Jr, *Securing the Revolution,* Cornell U.P., Ithaca 1972. pp. 85, 292.
4. Paul C Nagel, *This Sacred Trust*. . .Oxford U.P., New York, 1971, p. 27.
5. Linda K Kerber, *Federalists in Dissent,* Cornell U.P., Ithaca, 1970, p. 212.
6. Arthur H Shaffer, *The Politics of History,* Precedent Press, Chicago, 1975, p. 159.
7. James M Banner, Jr, *To the Hartford Convention,* Knopf, New York, 1970, p. 266.

Chapter Three
New England in the nation

Christine Bolt and A Robert Lee

Seeing 'New Englandly'

What has it meant to see – as Emily Dickinson said she did – 'New Englandly'? Probably more than any other region in American culture, New England evokes a body of quite specific associations – in founding intention and ideas. It calls to mind a landscape of settlement, of religious utopias, of stern 'theocracies', and also a later world of abolitionists and reformers, writers, thinkers and sages, men who, like Henry David Thoreau, 'travelled much in Concord' and explored the potentials of a significant part of American sensibility. In philosophy, religion, literature, it offers a starting place for perceiving a particular, and an American, way of regarding the mind and exerience. It has been the focus of a number of key ideas – Puritanism, Zeal, Mission, Reform, Transcendentalism – that have fed the American sense of 'exceptional' personal and national destiny. New England ideas shaped national ideas in the deepest ways, and there has always been in the New England mind a patrician bent, a confidence that New England's leading voices had a high and destined role to play in all the major debates and movements of their times: politics, humanitarianism, culture. There were, of course, many New Englanders whose lives were very different, but we can also sense in their less obvious and less patrician records something of the New England confidence. New Englanders were always fiercely self-aware and yet conscious of the need to look outside themselves for survival. The cultural symbol of their duality and their success is Boston, Massachusetts, that rich, central city receiving and dispatching the world's people, goods, ideas, and dominating not only the region but America in the first century of settlement. But to see 'New Englandly' is also to see in interrelated ways, to seek to ride, as Emerson would have it, several horses: of self and society, commerce and religion, science and imagination, realism and idealism. We too have an obligation to take, of New England, and the elements of its culture, the wider interpretive view.

The Puritan mind

The most important single fact about New England was that it was settled in the seventeenth century by Puritans: its leaders clearly shaped the history of their section, and Puritanism was the most important formative influence on American culture. This influence came neither from the success with which the colonists realized their founding objective, nor from the welcoming climate and topography of New England. Despite celebration of the new promised land, the landscape the pilgrims found was daunting and its hardships severe. New England was cut off by the Green and White Mountains; there were few navigable rivers other than the Connecticut; the land was hilly and stony, winters prolonged and hard. The Puritans were thankful to find a country 'fruitful and fit for habitation', but, as Richard Slotkin has argued, Puritan pioneers were involved essentially in a 'psychological and spiritual quest', so that 'Actual landscapes are less important than the landscape of the mind'. Accordingly, they stamped their influence on a difficult land by zealous devotion to the details of social and religious organization. Even so, within thirty years of the Plymouth Landing in 1620, Puritanism was being challenged by forces of religious dissent and economic change. The former questioned Puritan respect for traditional authority and dislike of spiritual enthusiasm; the latter undermined the old distinction between the honest pursuit of a personal calling and what Cotton Mather denounced as 'the *Cursed Hunger of Riches* [which] will make men *break through* all the Laws of God'.

The legacy of Puritanism was paradoxical, but it was potent. The seventeenth-century Puritans had struggled to re-establish English ideas and social forms in the New World; in the process they opposed much that would later be regarded as quintessentially American – religious toleration, the separation of Church and State, 'progressive' education, rugged individualism. However, as James Henretta reminds us, Puritanism unconsciously represented a 'transitional phase in the long and slow evolution from a traditional to a modern conception of life, authority, and personality'. Puritan education and child-rearing were designed to produce conformity, veneration for law and society, a strong moral code; yet the 'ultimate effect of the Puritan emphasis on self-examination, self-knowledge, and self-mastery was to replace institutions external to the individual by an inner conscience as the arbiter of moral decisions'.[2] The Puritan Fathers favoured a stratified and regimented commonwealth, but in their autonomous congregations, with the considerable participation they allowed, there was a democratic tendency that would exert a powerful influence on nineteenth-century attitudes. Puritanism began with the absolute sovereignty of God and the institutionalization of religious enthusiasm; but its elements eventually encouraged sectarian fragmentation and anarchic religious revivalism. Its emphasis on law was matched by a high respect for education: there was a lower level of illiteracy in New England than anywhere else in America, a system of elementary and grammar schools was established, and the region had more colleges than any other, a superiority it boasts to the present day. The static society that Puritans hoped to secure was undermined by the vigorous individual pursuit of 'calling', the stress on the moral dignity of work and profits, and the displacement of religious zeal into other realms. The social energies thus unleashed helped to transform the New England Puritan into the Yankee – that thrifty, pertinacious, ambitious, acquisitive, versatile and ingenious type whose commercial enterprise was to have its impact not only in America but around the world, and whose name would ultimately be applied by foreigners to Americans generally.

This ingenuity was not simply one of the unexpected consequences of Puritan teaching; it was essential for survival. Although New England quickly became the colonies' major shipping centre, most of its people remained dependent on agriculture. Diversification was hampered by a dearth of local markets, good river transport and commercial towns, while the Revolution destroyed the old triangular trade between New England, Europe and the West Indies. Fortunately, from the 1790s onwards, the credit of the New England states was improved by the federal assumption of state debts, the establishment of banks facilitated speculation of every kind, and shipping was assisted by bounties and protection. New trading opportunities were subsequently discovered throughout the world and new fortunes founded.

And yet there was much that was happening in the country that caused New Englanders disquiet. Rightly fearing that the rapid admission of new states would undermine their power in the Union, many successively opposed the purchase of Louisiana from France in 1803, Texas annexation and the Mexican war in the 1840s. Having constituted just over half the American population in 1650, they were reduced to a quarter in 1790, a fifth in 1810, a seventh in 1830, and a tenth in 1860. Whereas 4 of the original 13 states were New England states (Vermont declared its independence in 1777 and Maine, which was initially part of Massachusetts, in 1820), New England comprised 6 out of a total of 23 by 1820, and by 1860, 6 out of 33. The political consequences of minority status were felt both in the Senate, where individual states were equally represented, and in the House, where the size of a state's delegation depended on the size of its population, estimated by a decennial census.

This would not have mattered so much if New England had always seen eye to eye with other states on matters of importance. But such was far from being the case. Its leading citizens found difficulty in coming to terms with the rise of partisan politics after the Revolution and with the protection for its interests, including slavery, which the South managed to win under the new party system. New Englanders then supported the Federalists for their helpful economic programme, pro-British stance and respect for elitist government, voting solidly for that party in 1800 when most of the rest of the country favoured

Jefferson and the Republicans. The election marked the beginning of the great Virginia Republican dynasty of Jefferson, Madison and Monroe, yet New Englanders clung contrarily to the Federalists, despite the party's inability to change as society changed, thereby confirming their position as a minority section. The War of 1812, 'Mr Madison's War', was strongly opposed in New England, where trade and shipping suffered, and secession from the nation was briefly considered. But in the end economic counter-pressures prevailed and New Englanders proved to be no more unanimous in outlook than citizens of other regions, or than they had ever been.

New England's hostility to the Union anticipated without matching the bitter sectionalism which developed in the South from the 1830s. The second party system which replaced the Virginia dynasty was much more to its liking, and the election of John Quincy Adams of Massachusetts as President in 1824 presented the New Englander as nationalist, not localist, and seemed to promise much. The promise did not last. By contrast with the emergent popular style of politics carefully personified by his opponent Andrew Jackson, Adams was presented by his critics as an over-refined aristocrat. Between the election of Adams in 1824 and the succession of Calvin Coolidge in 1923, only one New Englander, Franklin Pierce in 1853, became President of the United States. Of course the region continued to produce national leaders – Daniel Webster in the 1830s and 1840s and Charles Sumner in the 1850s and 1860s. But political power now lay elsewhere.

The influx of Irish immigrants into New England was another cause for concern. While the most enterprising of the native-born felt impelled to seek their fortunes in New York, the Ohio Valley and the Mid-West, hungry refugees from the potato famine crowded into the region to take their places. By 1860 a third of Boston's 168,000 inhabitants were Irish. The newcomers were poor, obliged to take any work they could get, and allegedly willing to sell their votes for favours even before they were eligible to cast them. They placed a strain on housing resources, social welfare and New England tolerance. Coming out of necessity rather than inclination into an ethnically homogenous part of America, they were soon disliked by the old stock as clannish, Catholic and an unhealthy element in 'the mass of ignorance and intemperance which disgraces our cities'. Such antipathies were emphatically mutual. Attempts to exclude them failed but, whatever their early impact on Democratic politics, the Irish remained before the Civil War an apparently unassimilable element in the population, at odds with both native whites and the small, still more despised black community.

Surmounting these sources of unease, New England succeeded in making its distinctive voice heard in the nation. Often it was necessary to be content with cultural instead of economic influence, although as usual Yankee versatility made its mark. This was evident in the swift acceptance of technological innovation and the factory system. At first the operatives in such factories were mainly farm girls, as in the famous textile mill in Waltham, Massachusetts, which was remarked on by admiring foreign visitors alike for its cultivated workforce and employer paternalism. Spinning and weaving had always been household industries in New England, and with the development of new machines, together with the decline of farming due to competition from the Mid-West, it was natural for the women to move out to the factories. Later their places were taken by Irish immigrants, and conditions of employment generally declined. Without a tradition of collective action, workers could offer little resistance, despite the legalization of union activities by the Massachusetts Supreme Court in 1842. But when formal association failed, there was always the threat or reality of mass violence to alarm politicians and reformers, a tradition which was particularly strong in New England, with its long history of civic activism.

Reform and New England

Reform, as a way of bridging political, religious and economic problems, became a central preoccupation of New England society in the nineteenth century. In the political realm, matters were greatly affected by the rise of the new party system from the 1820s, when Federalists and Republicans were superseded by Whigs and Democrats. New England proved to be the Whig stronghold, and the party recruited many former Federalist leaders and voters, notwithstanding the attractions of the Democrats. For Whiggery appeared to offer a distinctive antidote to what seemed the worst features of the administration of Andrew Jackson, the first Democratic President: limited government, ironically ensured through executive 'despotism', strident partisanship, demagogic appeals to the masses, and the replacement of enlightened political elites by second-rate professional placemen. Of course the two parties had similarities: both looked to the past as well as the future for inspiration – just as, according to the New England sage Ralph Waldo Emerson, each individual was affected by the 'opposition of Past and Future, of Memory and Hope'. Many Whigs, like the Federalists before them, supported a variety of benevolent organizations – the Bible Society, the American Temperance Society, the Sunday School Union, the Home Missionary Society – which aimed at 'keeping society godly and orderly, stable and quiet'.[3] On the other hand, in the changing world of urbanization and industrialization, they took up new issues: the building of art galleries and libraries, educational and prison reform, campaigns for less acquisitive policies towards the Indians, improved provision for care of the handicapped and insane, women's rights, and, above all, anti-slavery and abolition. In all these enterprises the emphasis on individual liberation and humanitarianism was important. Yet there were Whigs, notably in Massachusetts, who advocated harmony with the South and close ties with the Southern cotton producers (who provided business for the state's manufacturers and merchants, and who sent their sons to Harvard); there were, on the other hand, the 'Conscience' Whigs who distrusted this alliance with the Southern 'Cotton' Whigs, and some of them defected to the uncompromisingly abolitionist Liberty Party during the 1840s. Moreover, the Democratic party also managed to exert considerable influence on Massachusetts politics, and was indeed popularly regarded as the party of progress, free-thinking and innovation; which may account for its attraction, in Harriet Martineau's judgement, to 'the men of genius'. And elsewhere, as in New Hampshire, where urbanization and industrialization were not so well advanced, the Democrats dominated.

There was thus no simple connection between politics and reform, and there were many who thought that reform should transcend politics altogether. Men of letters were repelled by the ultimate and deliberate blurring of party differences by party leaders, with a view to attracting the largest possible vote, while moral reformers often felt that efforts to improve American society should not be restrained by caution or the other imperfections of such institutions as political parties, believing that the individual's responsibilities were to God and his own conscience – an oblique derivation of Puritan principles. It is equally difficult to disentangle the religious roots of New England reform. Not only New England but the whole nation was affected by the religious revivals of the first half of the nineteenth century, in the course of which many sects came to place a fresh emphasis on the importance of religious enthusiasm, free will, and the immediate release of the individual from guilt through repentance and good works. However, New England did evolve its own distinctive forms of reaction against Calvinist doctrine, in the two great movements of Unitarianism and Transcendentalism. Transcendentalism, as we shall see later, was an essential part of the great intellectual 'flowering of New England', and its implications in philosophy and in literature are crucial. But it is also important to note that for many of its upper-class adherents the philosophy was essentially a spur towards reform, both individual and collective. Emerson reported that in the 1840s every reading man had the draft of a new community in his waistcoat pocket, and Transcendentalism united many prevailing reform interests, from feminism to socialism on the Fourierist model and to anxiety about the mechanical industrialism evolving in American life.

There are historians who believe that the Transcendentalists were primarily held together by 'the wide range of reform movements they so freely and publicly discussed' in pursuit of 'an ethical way of life', and that theirs became the 'popular reform philosophy of the day'.[4] This is to exaggerate their distinctiveness and practical significance. A belief in the perfectibility of man was central to the entire religious renaissance of these years, and was not confined to Transcendentalists. Like other Americans, Transcendentalists disagreed about the merits and methods, the appropriate pace and scope, of reform. They were more frequently the publicists than the organisers of reform efforts, and few found formal association appealing, even in the famous idealistic Massachusetts communes of Brook Farm, Hopedale and Fruitlands. These had a Transcendentalist involvement, but Emerson and Thoreau avoided them, preferring Concord and the path of Emerson's 'first-person singular'. To doubters, including Nathaniel Hawthorne, who went to Brook Farm but wrote ironically of it in *The Blithedale Romance* (1852), contrasting its pastoral images with the facts of the city, these foundations represented the extreme or eccentric wing of the new philosophies, though there was much that was admirable in Brook Farm's educational experiments and its attempts to reduce the division between manual and intellectual work. Communities with a religious and socialistic inspiration were certainly not confined to New England, although there were more there than elsewhere. Brook Farm was probably the best known, if one of the least enduring. As a contributor to *Harper's Monthly* noted: 'there were never such witty potato-patches and such sparkling cornfields before or since. The weeds were scratched out of the ground to the music of Tennyson and Browning, and the nooning was an hour as bright as any brilliant moonlight at Ambrose's'. But where the Transcendentalists did voice a widespread unease was in condemning the materialism of their day. Their faith in unfettered individualism was in accord with the ideology of the Democratic party and of the contemporary entrepreneur, and they were the voice of as well as the critics of their age. Their dissatisfaction with existing institutions, among them the political parties, was the consequence rather than the cause of the weakness of these institutions as vehicles for reform, in times when old suspicions of organized parties had not entirely vanished, and in a country where the federal political system seemed to frustrate responsible government. Clearly Transcendentalism's attempt to look beyond the social order into a larger wholeness had its ideological roots.

The impetus given by New England to ante-bellum reform is striking. The South was restrained by distrust of modernizing forces which might undermine its defence of slavery, by the 1830s confined to that section. Pennsylvania and New York rivalled New England in enterprise, but New England's role was supported by its economic, demographic and cultural characteristics. A good transport network, a relatively dense population, a sound church and lyceum organization and a high level of literacy aided the work of protest's itinerant publicists. Equally, the large profits of the new industrial order and what Charles Francis Adams later called 'the terrible New England Conscience' demanded and facilitated the use of surplus wealth for public good. For such reasons, the efforts for anti-slavery, peace, educational improvement, women's rights and temperance were extremely strong there, and even though the section's political and economic power was weakening, the consequent threat to the influence of reformers in and beyond their own communities was not great before the Civil War. All these movements, and especially abolitionism, were national in scope and found vigorous support in the Middle States and the Mid-West. Yet, along with Philadelphia and New York, Boston was the key forum for the discussion and dissemination of reform, as indeed for the radiation of all important cultural trends.

Boston as cultural capital

Although there never was in the United States an undisputed cultural capital comparable to Paris or London, nineteenth-century Boston rejoiced in its nickname 'the Athens of America'. Its citizens saw history made manifest in fine colonial buildings and all the prosperous vistas of Beacon Hill, and took pride not only in their city's thriving economy but also in its vast concentration of clubs, societies and improving establishments. In fact it was not until the 1880s, when William Dean Howells – the Ohio writer who had come East to continue the apostolic succession of Longfellow, Lowell and Holmes, and to edit *The Atlantic Monthly* – decided to move from Boston to New York, that the cultural pre-eminence of Boston in the nation seemed in dispute. From the Puritan period onwards, Boston was active in education and ideas. Harvard College had been founded in 1636, only six years after the first settlement; by the mid-seventeenth century Boston had a flourishing book-trade and numerous booksellers. From Independence onwards, the region had produced a high proportion of the republic's writers and artists; and from the 1820s Boston led the way with a lyceum movement that aimed to improve educational facilities both in schools and society at large. During the winter of 1837–38, some twenty-six courses of lectures were mounted in Boston alone. Where the Puritan sermon had been the chief entertainment, now the public lecture and the political speech became prime attractions for godly audiences who feared the saloon but lacked alternative respectable forms of recreation. Reformers and evangelists, quick to see how converts might be made, wooed these audiences with a judicious blend of emotionalism, simplification, repetition and piety. 'The impassioned utterance of a common exhorter will often move a congregation beyond anything that. . .splendid exhibitions of rhetoric can effect', recollected the popular preacher Charles Grandison Finney. In William Channing, Lyman Beecher and Theodore Parker, Boston claimed the services of the three best preachers of the day, who between them represented the transition towards a more liberal theology. Nor was the printed work neglected in Boston: it produced the nation's best literary periodical, the *North American Review,* the transient but impressive *Boston Quarterly Review,* and innumerable pamphlets, newspapers, reviews and reform journals, as well as many of the nation's books.

In addition Boston was the centre for historical scholarship, the most distinctive contribution of New England to the republic before the 'New England Renaissance' in poetry and fiction from the 1840s to the 1850s. Among the historians who at various times lived there, we should note George Bancroft, Francis Parkman, William Prescott, Richard Hildreth, John Lothrop Motley, John Palfrey, Jared Sparks, George Ticknor and Samuel Eliot. Indeed, the great majority of eighteenth- and nineteenth-century American historians were New Englanders, and their work reflects the continuing Puritan preoccupation with the concrete and instructive, with glorifying the work of God in every aspect of men's lives, and with reaffirming the Puritan's sense of a special destiny in the New World. The bulk of the authors of local and school-book histories and many more eminent practitioners of the discipline were themselves clergymen, so that their biases were professional as well as regional. It was in Boston that the first American historical society was established (in 1791) and New England as a whole was notable for the number of town chronicles and other historical works it produced and which served as models for scholars in different parts of the country. Yet if pride in their forebears' formative role in the making of the country inspired New England historians, they were seldom parochial in outlook, seeing it as a patriotic as much as a religious duty to distil the essence of the unique national culture which was allegedly developing. In the process, they attached an importance the Puritans would not have appreciated to individual liberty and the idea of progress, and Francis Parkman, the aristocratic Bostonian, even delighted – in *The Oregon Trail* (1849) – in a Western movement which filled many New Englanders with jealous dread.

The reformers who made their homes in Boston were similarly influenced by a combination of local pride and large vision, an awareness of the heritage of the past and the exciting prospects for future change. Feminism and abolitionism in particular seemed to encourage the 'terrible propensities' which conservatives feared were being released as America approached democracy. It was in Boston that, in 1831, William Lloyd Garrison launched his *Liberator* with the intention of overcoming the apathy he found all around him on the questions of slavery and prejudice towards black people. If he was reassuringly pious and Whiggish in his politics, the relentless urgency of Garrison's message was alarming to many sections of New England opinion. 'I shall', he declared, 'strenuously contend for the immmediate enfranchisement of our slave population. . .I *will be* as harsh as truth, and as uncompromising as justice. On this subject I do not wish to write, or speak, or think, with moderation. . .AND I WILL BE HEARD'. Although Garrison's main concern was slavery, his catholic approach to reform attracted many women to his banner and caused them, when they encountered hostility to their full participation in abolition activities, even from male co-workers, to consider the similarities between sexual and racial oppression and, by the 1840s, to begin organizing on their own account. Divided in ideas and aims, the women's movement nonetheless produced such genuine radicals as Margaret Fuller, the Boston Transcendentalist who declared that every woman should have the freedom 'as a nature to grow, as an intellect to discern, as a soul to live freely and unimpeded to unfold such powers as were given'. Not surprisingly, the contemporary press took a very jaundiced view of feminist endeavours, describing one Massachusetts women's rights convention as an 'Awful Combination of Socialism, Abolitionism, and infidelity'.

There was likewise some substance to the contemporary feeling that whereas the agitators of the middle and western states generally displayed a practical approach to reform, whether this meant retaining good relations with the clergy or entertaining political compromise, the New England mind, however quick to see and seize new opportunities by the nineteenth century, still displayed a Puritan intolerance of opposition, compromise and popular opinion, which frequently doomed the region's zealots to disappointment, or at best to the psychic satisfaction of belonging to an elect group whose features their quarrels helped to define. [5] New Englanders undoubtedly contributed to the break-up of the Whig coalition, the increasingly intransigent defence of slavery by Southern Democrats and thus, eventually, to the dissolution of the second party system and the rise of the Republicans, a party with an overtly sectional appeal. But that party, which owed so much to New England support and ideals, representing what Eric Foner has described as a 'profoundly successful fusion of value and interest,' ironically secured the triumph of anti-slavery, the major cause of ante-bellum reformers, albeit only with the appalling sacrifices of war and of radical hopes that racial equality would be secured along with abolition.[6] Moreover while the influence of New England 'ultras' might be diminished after the Civil War in the more cautious atmosphere of Reconstruction politics, many of its reformers turned their attention then and in the years that followed to the challenges posed by mistreatment of the Indians and black freedmen, and by the maturing industrial revolution. Something remarkable was indeed apparent, as the abolitionist Stephen Foster remarked, in 'the productions of this barren soil.'

New England and the 'American Renaissance'

One consequence of New England's cultural hegemony was that when, between the 1830s and the Civil War, that extraordinary efflorescence of literature, art and ideas that we now call the American

Renaissance occurred, New England was its clear centre. From the Revolution onwards Americans had been hungering for a declaration of literary and cultural independence as potent as their political one. By the 1820s, with the works of Washington Irving (1783–1859), turning European folklore into American fable, with James Fenimore Cooper's (1789–1851) massive body of fiction, a vivid pageant of pioneer experience, and with the dark, interiorized writings of Edgar Allan Poe (1809–1849), the stock of achievement had been accumulating. But it was over a few stunning years at mid-century, when American literature could suddenly count among its major achievements Melville's *Moby-Dick* (1851) and 'Benito Cereno' (1855), Hawthorne's *The Scarlet Letter* (1850) and *The House of the Seven Gables* (1851), Whitman's *Leaves of Grass* (first edition, 1855), Henry David Thoreau's *Walden* (1854), the 'hidden' poems of the Amherst genius Emily Dickinson, now brought into the light, and the poetry and essays of Ralph Waldo Emerson, that the high moment arose. Not all the figures of the Renaissance were Transcendentalists; Poe's inner landscape is a bleak and quite un-Emersonian world, and Hawthorne and Melville deeply questioned, with their 'No! in Thunder,' its note of Adamic optimism. Not all were New Englanders: Poe was from the South, Melville from New York, Whitman from Long Island. Yet, for all of them, Transcendentalist New England was a stimulus and a centre: it was, said Emerson, from New England's 'bar-rooms, Lyceums, committee rooms' that 'many words leap out alive' and 'fill the world with their thunder.' And it was Emerson's essay 'The American Scholar' (1837), which called for a specific American national culture ('We have listened too long to the courtly muses of Europe') shaped by American history, American democracy and American optimism, that was the starting cry of the Renaissance. A fellow Brahmin and Boston man of letters judged it precisely 'our intellectual Declaration of Independence.'

If the high culture of America sounded its aspirations through any one spokesman, it was indeed Ralph Waldo Emerson (1803–82). His was the oracular voice of Transcendentalism, the shifting and often ethereal philosophy of human perfectibility and the belief in Nature as the ideal and outward show of benign Divinity that dominated the 'optative' spirit of American culture. He expressed the note of a time when the nation in general was on the move, when resources and space seemed vast, the bonds of the past no longer held the present, the virtues of individualism and self-reliance seemed proven, untried possibilities were being made real, and America itself seemed imbued with spiritual and moral meanings. There was a New England legacy in Emerson's expression of this: none knew that legacy better, for his roots lay deep in the region's past, ministers to one side, astute Yankee businessmen to the other. For him, as for like-minded spirits throughout New England, in Boston and townships like Cambridge and Concord, the original theology of Election and Special Grace, in

fact the whole Puritan vision of a punitive Gŏd and of Man as heir to a
fallen and guilty human realm, was long defunct. Beliefs which
compelled earlier New England luminaries like John Winthrop,
Cotton and Increase Mather, and the redoubtable Jonathan Edwards,
now seemed a body of irrelevant Post-Reformation doctrine and
liturgy. Indeed, by the 1830s, when Emerson was making his public
bow, even Unitarianism, that liberal and humanist body of Christian
ethics which had replaced Puritanism in the New England mind, and in
which Emerson and many fellow-Transcendentalists had first trained,
would itself no longer do. Emerson saw a new time, and found in an
America caught up in the westering impulse and the settlement of the
continent, the prospect of a fresh liberation of self, an inward and
exemplary regeneration of the human spirit. Nowhere did he
enunciate this more loftily than in 'Nature,' a tract published
anonymously in 1836, where he first struck his epochal note:

Our age is retrospective. It builds the sepulchres of the fathers. It writes
biographies, histories, and criticism. The foregoing generations beheld God
and Nature face to face; we, through their eyes. Why should not we also enjoy
an original relationship to the universe? Why should we not have a poetry and
philosophy of insight, and not of tradition, and a religion by revelation to us,
and not the history of theirs?... There are new lands, new men, new thoughts.
Let us demand our own works and laws and worship.

By Transcendentalism, Emerson looked to the essence behind any
one single cause – Abolition, Temperance, Reform – and sought to lay
seige, as he said in his essay 'The Transcendentalist' (1842), to 'the
whole connection of spiritual doctrine.' The world's essential
meanings, he held, derived from spiritual 'laws' which 'transcended'
all received dogma and institutions, and came to men through their
intuitive faculties. Godhead lay within. So radical a confidence in the
powers of individual vision, which Emerson called 'self-reliance,' and
in the benevolent God-principle he called the 'The Over-Soul,' struck
the orthodox as 'the latest form of infidelity.' And yet, paradoxically,
Transcendentalist arguments owed much to older Puritan culture – the
interpretation of Nature as 'God's hieroglyph,' the commitment to the
self's inner drama as part of a larger, 'exceptional' American destiny,
the view of reality as the emblematic garment of the spirit. In one way,
'Nature' and the addresses and essays Transcendentalists subsequently sponsored belonged to a parochial New England debate: a dissident
minister and his adherents repudiating the faith of their forefathers.
But from a wider perspective, Emerson served notice of far deeper
currents in his age and place – the belief in a hitherto unrecognized
'American' self and a new American way of seeing the world. What
was affected, and reinvigorated, was a whole cultural vision. And this
included a reconsideration of the place of the artist in American life,
and of the very language and forms by which this 'American'
perception of reality might be transposed into art.

But if Emerson knew himself by heritage to be a New Englander, he also belonged to the wider movement of nineteenth-century Romanticism. His affinities lay with Plato and the neo-Platonists, and of his nearer philosophical contempories, with Kant (to whom he credited the term 'transcendental'), Berkeley, Hume and Locke, Swedenborg and his theories of 'correspondence.' He read closely in Coleridge, Wordsworth and Goethe, indeed in all the main figures of European Romanticism; he conducted a lifelong correspondence with his fellow sage and metaphysician Thomas Carlyle; he also looked East, to the Vedas and the *Bhagavadgita*. This eclectic reading had a deprovincializing aspect both for Emerson and those around him, and if sceptics like Hawthorne and Melville judged Transcendentalism facile, a doctrine of American good cheer which ignored the human capacity for evil, or the place of war and pain in human affairs, they could not deny that it drew on reputable sources. Nor could it be denied that in seeking within the sovereign self rather than in society or tradition a sanction for individual vision, Emerson represented something fundamentally American, which Melville or Hawthorne would express in their own writing, and Thoreau in the literal conduct of a life. As he looked on the America before him, a culture of business, and frontier and aggressive materialist expansion, Emerson recognized that Puritanism had come to mean the Protestant ethic, that manifestation of 'grace' as entrepreneurial energy which Benjamin Franklin had cannily set forth in his *Autobiography* and *Poor Richard's Almanack*. 'Things' were too much in the saddle; he pitched his appeal to the idealist element in American experience, writing in 1844, in *The Young American*, 'I call upon you, young men, to obey your heart, and be the nobility of this land.' He re-evoked the image of the American as an Adam and a 'new man' that Crèvecoeur had fashioned in *Letters from an American Farmer* (1782), the note of an age of optimistic, pioneer individualism.

Above all, Emerson spoke to the need for poetic imagination, writing enticingly in 'The Poet' of the creative challenge offered by the New World:

Our log-rollings, our stumps and their politics, our fisheries, our Negroes and Indians, our boats and our repudiations, the wrath of rogues and the pusillanimity of honest men, the northern trade, the southern planting, the western clearing, Oregon and Texas, are yet unsung. Yet America is a poem in our eyes; its ample geography dazzles the imagination, and it will not wait long for metres.

Indeed he was a major poet himself, and the power of his imagination is bared in the work-pages of his *Journals*, a rich quarry of aphorisms and notations on the awakening of his mind. To see the first draft of his central preoccupations – his trust in Nature's 'sanitive' powers, his regard for individual vision, his belief in a balanced and generous universal order – is to glimpse a spacious intelligence at work as it moves toward the dialectics of the major writings – 'Self-Reliance,'

'The Over-Soul,' the Harvard 'Divinity School Address' which, together with his other *Essays* (first and second series, 1841 and 1844), his *Representative Men* (1850), his *English Traits* (1856) and his poems, represent him at his best. His larger work in the culture is represented by his part in *The Dial* (1840–44), which he edited from 1842. For Transcendentalism was more than one voice. Most of the review's contributors belonged to the Transcendentalist Club, a forum for debate and the exchange of ideas. *The Dial*'s founding editor was Margaret Fuller (1810–50), a controversial *prima donna* and feminist – as she revealed in her *Woman in the Nineteenth Century* (1845) – on whom Hawthorne would model Zenobia in *The Blithedale Romance*. Others of the club's diverse lights included George Ripley (1802–80), the Unitarian minister who was main begetter of Brook Farm; Bronson Alcott (1799–88), a key influence on American pedagogy and child education; Orestes Brownson (1803–76), an obsessive son of the Puritans who converted to Catholicism, flirted with socialism, and whose autobiographies reveal the eccentric rim of self-reliance; the caricaturist Christopher Pearse Cranch (1813–92), whose line-drawings depict the main presence of Transcendentalism in a wry, irreverent light; Jones Very (1813–80), poet and ex-Unitarian minister, whose mystical sonnets deserve their recent revival; William Ellery Channing (1818–1901), poet and essayist, and nephew of the great Unitarian minister; and Elizabeth Peabody (1804–94), whose Boston bookshop served as a Transcendentalist meeting place, who provided America with its first kindergarten, whose sister Sophia married Hawthorne, and who is usually thought the model for Miss Birdseye in Henry James's retrospective look at New Englandism, *The Bostonians* (1886).

Among the Transcendentalist group themselves, there were signs that Emerson's plea for a literature of 'our own works' was being answered. Emerson, Thoreau and Very were important poets. Around them, in New England, were others: John Greenleaf Whittier (1807–92), the author of powerful anti-slavery and pastoral verse; Henry Wadsworth Longfellow (1807–82), with his massive transatlantic popularity; and James Russell Lowell (1819–91), Longfellow's successor in the Smith Chair of Modern Languages at Harvard. In Oliver Wendell Holmes (1809–94), another Harvard professor, but no admirer of Transcendentalism, New England vaunted a witty belle-lettrist *(The Autocrat At The Breakfast Table*, 1858, etc.). His medicated novels, as he called them, include his minor *tour de force*, *Elsie Venner* (1861), which in tackling the decidedly modern subject of schizophrenia attacked fundamental Calvinist assumptions about human behaviour. A New Englander more palpably responsive to Mission was Harriet Beecher Stowe (1811-96), born of Calvinist stock in Connecticut, internationally known for her *Uncle Tom's Cabin* (1851–52), a richer achievement than its reputation usually admits, for it sucessfully blended purpose into art in creating the most famous of all abolitionist works. But she also deserves to be known for her other fiction, especially *Dred: A Tale of the Great Dismal Swamp* (1856) and *The Minister's Wooing* (1859). For Emily Dickinson (1830–86), a reclusive, inward New England imagination, fame came posthumously. Of the nearly 2,000 poems which made up her collected *oeuvre*, only a handful saw print in her lifetime. 'Tell all the truth but tell it slant', begins one of her important lyrics, a typically staccato turn of voice which points up the almost metaphysical strategies of her poetry. The intense local power of her Nature poems and her unsettling and epigrammatic accounts of Faith and of dying and the ancestral New England concern with sin and redemption reveal a wonderfully alive sceptical temper – and a major American poet.

Transcendentalist inheritors: Thoreau and Whitman

But of the major writers who answered Emerson's call to the creative-Transcendentalist spirit, the nearest to hand was Henry David Thoreau (1817–62), Transcendentalism's most practical disciple, and a spirit almost martial in his emphatic individualism. When, after Harvard and a spell as handyman in Emerson's house and his editorial assistant on *The Dial*, Thoreau moved to a hut at Walden Pond, near Concord, on 4 July 1845 – truly his Independence Day – he began a process which gave us, in his classic diary-narrative, *Walden* (1854), a deep mid-century account of a life lived inwardly to its existential limits. 'I went to the woods', Thoreau explained,

> because I wished to live deliberately, to front only the essential facts of life, and to see if I could not learn what it had to teach, and not, when I came to die, discover that I had not lived. I did not wish to live what was not life, living is so dear; nor did I wish to practise resignation, unless it was quite necessary. I wanted to live deep and to put to rout all that was not life...to drive life into a corner and reduce it to its lowest terms.

The economy of Thoreau's prose speaks perfectly for the economy of his purpose, the need to corner life, and to arrest its overwhelming essence. That same fierce, independent energy animates nearly all his writing, and certainly the biographical pattern of his life. When he observes 'I have travelled much in Concord,' he is speaking of Transcendental 'travel,' the kind of 'home-cosmography' he alludes to in *Walden*'s concluding chapter. Few American writers pursued essence more tenaciously than Thoreau ('I love to come at my bearings' he confides at one point), or wrote a more engaging metaphoric idiom (his use of 'economy,' 'expense,' the 'cost' of things). More than any contemporary, Thoreau held Nature in the regard Emerson had described in *The Young American*:

> The land is the appointed remedy for whatever is false and fantastic in our culture. The continent we inhabit is to be physic and food for our mind, as well as our body.

In plumbing the depths of Walden Pond, Thoreau sought no less than the terms of his own innermost being, a Transcendentalist enquiry into his manifestly separate self and into Nature's subtler currents and significations. In observing with so responsive a curiosity each seasonal shift and turn, Nature's freezings and thaws, Thoreau detected a clue to the whole ecology of human personality, its resistances and higher possibilities. His attacks on the 'costs' of much contemporary capitalism, and of false wars and unacceptable taxes, he offers in the name of an utter commitment to the potential of his own, and every, sovereign self. As the Pond expresses Nature's 'eye' so Thoreau seeks to adapt his own 'eye,' both to the natural surface of things and to a comprehension of their inward and shaping powers. With the arguable exception of John James Audubon (1785–1851), whose graphics gave to the world a magnificent view of American fauna and wildlife, nineteenth century America knew no busier naturalist than Thoreau. But his was always a vision which sought to run deeper, the testimony of a radical New England seer and anarch.

This expansive spirit of 'exploration' marks Thoreau's other writings: *A Week On The Concord And Merrimack Rivers* (1849), composed while he lived in his pondside hut, and like *Walden* a journey (this time 'up-river') into self-illumination; 'Civil Disobedience' (1849), a widely influential testament of conscience against slavery and the State; his 'Plea for Captain John Brown' (1859), made in the name of the absolute claims of human liberty; and the journey pieces – *Excursions* (1863), *The Maine Woods* (1864), *Cape Cod* (1865) and *A Yankee in Canada* (1866) – collected after his premature death. More than any other Transcendentalist, Thoreau tried in life to make reality of precept. His insistence on the need to awaken buried consciousness and reach through to Nature's vital 'physic' led to a reputation still not entirely clear of eccentricity; but he saw with discomforting clarity, and his work shows an author who refused all complacency and unearned truth.

But the most full-blooded of all responses to Emerson's appeal came from a Long Islander who read his message at a certain distance. Born of a radical Jacksonian father and a Quaker mother, Walt Whitman (1819–92) began with several false starts – as journeyman printer, carpenter, real-estate dealer, journalist, bohemian – before he established his true *métier*. In 1855, in a slim and anonymous green volume, its type partly set by himself, he published his first version of *Leaves of Grass*, a verse sequence of twelve 'chants,' which includes the earliest version of 'Song Of Myself.' The book would grow, over nine editions, by accretion and revision, into the Death-Bed Edition of 1891–92, an epic of more than 400 pages, working and re-working a lifetime's preoccupation with the 'single self' and Man 'en masse' and with Nature and the uniqueness of American destiny. From the outset, Whitman appropriated for himself the *persona* of 'Walt' – the bardic voice of democracy speaking at once for the quotidian and the 'divine afflatus.' It was an extravagant, bold, androgynous posture, 'unpoetic' in that it apparently offered catalogues and paragraphs of incantatory prose; but it represented a profound commitment to America as the theatre of the common man, a polity and geography in which all experience might be democratically confronted and declared. The poet, for Whitman, is no Shelleyian 'legislator'; rather he writes on behalf of, and to reveal the transcendent purpose of, the democratic human norm, as the custodian and mouthpiece of Emerson's 'each and all' (the text is from the 1891–92 edition):

> I am the poet of the Body and I am the poet of the Soul,
> The pleasures of heaven are with me and the pains of hell are with me,
> The first I graft and increase upon myself, the latter I translate into a new tongue.

The stance allows Whitman to speak also as the poet of Love ('a kelson of the creation is love'), of Orphic and natural sexual energy ('Urge and urge and urge, Always the procreant urge of the world'), of War ('I am the old artillerist, I tell of my fort's bombardment'), of Death and pain ('I am the man, I suffer'd, I was there'), and above all, of the 'divine' eternal purpose behind human existence which, at the close of 'Song Of Myself,' he calls the 'form, union, plan.' Whitman's assumed *persona* is nothing if not confident, at once voluptuous and exploratory:

> I know perfectly well my own egotism,
> Know my own omniverous lines and must not write any less,
> And would fetch you whoever you are flush with myself.

In naming himself, he names a brother democrat, a Christly reconciler of warring opposites, assuming a voice of caress which, for all its Emersonian affinities, speaks out unhampered by any New England reserve:

> Walt Whitman, of Manhattan the son,
> Turbulent, fleshy, sensual, eating, drinking, and breeding,
> No sentimentalist, no stander above men and women or apart from them,
> No more modest than immodest.

On occasion, Whitman's rhetoric risks sounding operatic, intoxicated with its own ambition, a fault which has exposed him to harsh rebuke. But when read as an ordered and overall sequence, his poetry remains something wholly special. It draws on striking links of image and motif, a sureness of voice. Poems as fine as 'Crossing Brooklyn Ferry' or 'There was A Child Went Forth' amply confirm his lyric powers of language. And the force of his commitment to his 'democratic' vision never flags:

I speak the pass-word primeval, I give the sign of democracy,
By God! I will accept nothing which all cannot have their counterpart of on
the same terms.

To read *Leaves of Grass* in its subsequent incarnations is to watch a
poem – like Pound's later *Cantos*, or William Carlos Williams's
Paterson – building on its own momentum. The 1856 edition, for
instance, strikes a bolder sexual note than the first, and it reprints the
letter Emerson sent privately to Whitman ('I greet you at the
beginning of a great career'). In 1860, Whitman added his 'Children Of
Adam' and 'Calamus' poems, sequences deeply taken up with sexual
confession and observation. In 1867, he included *Drum Taps* (first
published as a pamphlet), his sensitive and healing response to the
Civil War and to Lincoln's murder, together with the exquisite 'When
Lilacs Last In The Dooryard Bloom'd.' The sixth edition (1876)
included his most explicit 'transcendentalist' poem, 'Passage To
India,' and his major prose essay *Democratic Vistas*. Finally, in 1892,
now the 'good grey poet' of national and international acclaim,
Whitman offered his last edition of the 'book' ('who touches this
touches a man') begun so inauspiciously thirty-five years earlier.
Whitman's creation of the new audience ('you whoever you are'), the
scale of his interpretation of Emerson's vision of man, and his role as a
radical experimentalist in idiom and syntax, place him unambiguously
at the centre of American literature. To a subsequent and central line
of American poets – Carl Sandburg, William Carlos Williams, Hart
Crane, Ezra Pound and Allen Ginsberg – his linear collage and
self-appointed oracular role ('I am large, I contain multitudes')
offered decisive imaginative points of departure. Whitman, if anyone,
serves as Emerson's Arch-Transcendentalist, the sacramental and
visionary poet-philosopher.

The nay-sayers: Hawthorne and Melville

In the account he gave of Nathaniel Hawthorne (1804–64), in 1879, for
the English Men of Letters Series, Henry James judged him 'subtle
and slender and unpretending,' a nature 'strongest and keenest' when
'the dark Puritan tinge showed…most richly.' He also believed
Hawthorne (and most American writers of prose narrative) to be
dispossessed of the novelist's authentic subject – society, the play of
manners. America could claim only a provincial social tradition, small
pockets of consciousness which left the creative temper isolated and
obliged to turn in on itself: only in Europe, where consciousness drew
on infinitely richer grain, and society knew itself intricate, self-aware,
old in institutions and habit, could the novelist find his best occasions.
But to Herman Melville, Hawthorne had no need of a European stage.
Deep amid the imagining of *Moby-Dick*, his own 'wicked book,' as he

once described it, Melville responded to Hawthorne with the deepest 'shock of recognition.' Here was no provincial New Englander, but 'the Portuguese diamond in our American literature,' an immense and passionate imagination, in whom the world was 'mistaken' if it thought him less than the complete man of letters, a contemporary American master. And, above all, Melville confessed himself drawn by Hawthorne's 'blackness', his belief in a blighted and Calvinist fate to men's affairs, and to artifice whose subtleties called to mind the Shakespeare of the great problem plays and the tragedies:

For spite of all the Indian-Summer sunlight on the hither side of Hawthorne's soul, the other side – like the dark half of the physical sphere – is shrouded in a blackness, ten times black...this great power of blackness in him derives its force from its appeals to that Calvinistic sense of Innate Depravity and Original Sin, from whose visitations, in some shape or other, no deeply thinking mind is always and wholly free. For, in certain moods, no man can weigh this world, without throwing in something, somehow like Original Sin, to strike the uneven balance. At all events, perhaps no writer has ever wielded this terrific thought with greater terror than this same harmless Hawthorne.... You may be witched by his sunlight, transported by the bright guildings in the skies he builds over you, but there is the blackness of darkness beyond.... In one word, the world is mistaken in this Nathaniel Hawthorne.

Melville's response undoubtedly tells as much about the axes of his own thought as of Hawthorne's, but the generosity of his esteem, and his insight into the duplicitous surfaces of Hawthorne's art, make his account as momentous a declaration as any in the history of American literary relationships.

Whether or not Hawthorne was truly the Promethean Melville believed, or more a great miniaturist of human foible and a fallen world, he assuredly wrote fiction different in texture from the great works of European realism. Hawthorne rightly defined his longer narratives as 'romances,' a mode whose imaginative ground he describes in the Custom House sketch introducing *The Scarlet Letter* (1850) as 'neutral territory, somewhere between the real world and fairy land, where the Actual and the Imaginary may meet, and each imbue itself with the nature of the other.' Of all his fiction, *The Scarlet Letter* best brings his major themes to imaginative order, especially his play of emblem, allegory, figurative and perceptual ambiguity. Its ostensible tale of a Puritan adultery, and of a wronged husband's abuse of his intellectual powers to secure revenge, masks far wider enquiries. The book dramatizes the fundamental moral conflict between self-duty ('What we did had a consecration of its own' says Hester Prynne) and the community standard. Its other dialectics explore the conflict of 'science' and the values of the 'heart,' the forest domain of sexual and creative energy as against the ordered world of society, daytime reality as against its night-time counterface. Both in 'The Custom House,' an astute allegory of the American author's search for his subject and an appropriate form, and in the text proper,

Hawthorne's equivocations are everywhere evident. He writes in a voice full of shades and hints, allowing the burden of interpretation to fall wholly, and unfailingly, upon his reader. As each object or person is defined, so equally is the definer: the scarlet 'A' itself, the triangle of Hester, Roger and Arthur, the elfin child Pearl, the forest realm, the scaffold and prison world of the Puritans. His seventeenth-century materials mask a nineteenth-century body of doubts, a brooding relativism. Behind this New England 'usable past,' Hawthorne sought to project the perennial drama of human need and the will-to-power.

His other romances give further gloss to his aims. In *The House Of The Seven Gables* (1851), an emblematic dynastic legend, he purports to seek 'a certain latitude' for his 'atmospherical medium.' In *The Blithedale Romance* (1852), re-working his Brook Farm experience, he rather coyly declares his tale to be 'a little removed from the highway of ordinary travel,' and given over to 'an atmosphere of strange enchantments.' His last full-length work, *The Marble Faun* (1860), a fable of expatriate New Englanders faced with pagan and Catholic Italy, barely prevents his typical play of ambiguities from collapsing into mystification. Hawthorne sought his antecedents not in Fielding and realist literary convention, but essentially in Puritan typology and in the pictorial allegories of Spenser and Bunyan. Others helped to shape the American romance (James Fenimore Cooper, Charles Brockden Brown and William Gilmore Sims notably); but it was Hawthorne who first gave the form its distinctive identity.

The local effects of the romance equally mark out his principal collections of stories, *Twice Told Tales* (1837), *Mosses From An Old Manse* (1846), *The Snow-Image And Other Twice Told Tales* (1852). His touch is delicate, often genial, even if he himself thought them no more than 'attempts and very imperfectly successful ones, to open an intercourse with the world.' They are, in effect, 'story-mosses' meant to take root in the reader's gathering response; close-woven episodes which come at human experience obliquely. In 'Ethan Brand' and 'The Birthmark' two tales which depict 'The Unpardonable Sin,' Hawthorne's phrase for the cool tyranny of egotism, he uses the Puritan emblematic language of wizardry and the fiery furnace to explore the contemporary spectacle of one human being exploiting great individual power over another, an iniquity that he calls in his *American Notebooks* 'the separation of the intellect from the heart.' In 'Young Goodman Brown,' he makes his subject Puritanism itself, or rather its tyrannical and darker side, the process whereby a Puritan view of mankind can make sexual felicity a source of guilt and thus inhibit the creative energies of the human personality. This conflict of natural energy with authority, an old Puritan conflict, he dwells upon brilliantly in 'The Maypole of Merry Mount,' a story appropriately set out as a confrontation between Elizabethan rout and Pilgrim law. And his characteristic doubts about Transcendentalism shape 'The Celestial Omnibus,' a lively Bunyanesque parody.

In 1856 Hawthorne, now American consul in Liverpool, strolled with Herman Melville (1819–91) on the Southport sands, renewing their earlier encounters in the Berkshire hills of New England half a dozen years earlier. Hawthorne's entry in his *English Notebooks* yields a marvellous estimate of Melville's general disposition.:

Melville, as he always does, began to reason of Providence and futurity, and of everything that lies beyond human ken....He can neither believe nor be comfortable in his unbelief; and he is too honest and courageous not to try to do one or the other.

The very qualities Melville had been drawn to in Hawthorne – his 'blackness,' his covert disclosure of truth, his 'contemplative humor' – on this judgement, might equally have been his own. Similarly, the view Melville once gave out of Emerson – 'I love all men who *dive*' – testifies to the appetite for Truth he shared with the New Englander, for all that he doubted the Emersonian ethos, indeed pilloried it in *The Confidence Man* (1857), as dark a portrait of American ruling illusions as any in the national literature. Unlike Emerson, Melville's searches led him to 'armed neutrality,' a defensive scepticism in the face of an unknowable universe and man's inability, as he saw it, to resist evil. More than any of his contemporaries. Melville believed himself embattled, a seeker and 'diver' for whom almost all quests for Truth ended in circles and solipsism. The ground condition of his philosophy he expressed perfectly in 'Hawthorne And His Mosses':

For in this world of lies, Truth is forced to fly like a scared white doe in the woodlands; and only by cunning glimpses will she reveal herself, as in Shakespeare and other masters of the great Art of Telling the Truth – even though it be covertly, and by snatches.

This impulsion to locate, and name, Truth, runs right through Melville's fiction, and indeed into his later, and still largely unread poetry, especially *Battle Pieces* (1866), his Civil War poems, and *Clarel* (1876), a formidable late-Victorian poem of religious doubt. Though not born in New England, Melville's whole inclination leant towards a transcendent and final view of Truth. The fiction he wrote, accordingly, is cast almost always in the form of the journey, as an impending *rendez-vous* with the true nature of things. He bequeathed a major body of writing, 'inside narratives' in the half title of *Billy Budd*, whose depths, as Hawthorne observed of Melville's third book, *Mardi*, 'compel a man to swim for his life.'

Melville's first journey-fictions, *Typee* (1846), *Omoo* (1847) and *Mardi* (1849), which derive intimately from his ship and South Seas adventures as a common sailor, and *Redburn* (1849) and *White Jacket* (1850), based on two other sea-journeys (to Liverpool and back when he was eighteen and aboard a returning man-of-war in 1844), culminate in the imperial achievement of *Moby-Dick* (1851). Each is told in the *persona* of a Melvilleian 'isolato'. In *Moby-Dick* it is Ishmael, the classic wanderer and man of doubts. The *Pequod's* 'journey-out,' a quest after ultimate 'transcendent' truths, and made as an apparently literal quest for whale oil, or 'light,' Ishmael takes with Ahab, an emblematic captain of American industry and a crew-of-all-nations; the journey is profoundly mythic in dimension. Melville uses the *Pequod*'s endeavour to confront and to catch the white whale, as a way of repudiating the illusion that any single register of truth can fix the world's ambiguous meanings – whether in language, systems of religious belief, folklore, categories of cetology, or simple naming of parts. The epic and adventurely scope of his story justifiably seizes the imagination; but so, too, should Melville's inventive topography, the playful and skilled doubleness of his telling.

With *Pierre, Or The Ambiguities* (1852), his imagination turned inland, to the spectacle of a heroic 'fool of truth' literally as well as morally incarcerated by the labyrinths of his quest. Melville's tales of the 1850s, five of which he selected as *The Piazza Tales* (1856), reveal his powers in closer focus. In 'Bartleby, The Scrivener' (1853), he wrote a parable of Wall Street, a diagram of liberal capitalism's deathly grip on the spirit. 'Benito Cereno' (1855) makes of a slave insurrection an enquiry into the metaphysics of evil and human blindness. In 'The Encantadas' (1854), sketches of the Galápagos Islands where Darwin found his inspiration for the theory of natural selection, Melville drew a map of earthly hell, a portrait of loss and unremitting human desolation. With the exception of *Israel Potter* (1855), an ironic fable about American national types and first published as a nine-part serial in *Harper's New Monthly Magazine* (1854–5) and the posthumous *Billy Budd* (1885–91), his last mythic tale of slaughtered innocence, Melville's only other full-length composition was *The Confidence Man* (1857), a satire which gives no quarter to the gods of Progress and optimistic New World panaceas and which (in Chapters 14, 33 and 44) gives important bearings on his theories of fiction. As he grew older, Melville's fiction became increasingly knottier, but his ambiguous and testing visions were hard-won and made in the face of an inattentive, and often uncomprehending, readership. He stood in uneasy relationship with the professed Transcendentalist good faith of the age, yet shared the taste for a view of man, and of America, which was at once cosmic and deeply sacramental. Melville's fiction thus represents a dissenting imagination, a conviction that far older and blacker forces than America commonly acknowledged gave shape to human destiny. It perhaps took Melville, a New Yorker and one time Pacific whalerman, to 'see' most 'New Englandly' of all.

'This great allegory the world': Melville's phrase goes to the essence of the imaginative temperament of nineteenth-century New England. To the makers of the American Renaissance, the world was a realm to be decoded, unravelled. In this they were true heirs of their Puritan ancestors. The same preoccupations are also to be found in the work of many later New England writers, among whom the habit has persisted, though to different effect as, for instance, in the poems of Robert Frost or Robert Lowell. The central phase of American literary culture, that remarkable efflorescence which occurred about the middle of the nineteenth century, is appropriately thought 'transcendental,' a view of reality as but the show of the inward energies of the spirit. For many of their immediate successors, however, the faith in themselves and in their unique destiny was eroded as the long maturing forces of change – westward expansion, industrialization, immigration – convincingly augmented the power of the rest of America. Accordingly the Puritan conscience, though still active, lost something of its cutting edge, producing a merely genteel reform tradition. And for many New Englanders, self-confidence gave place to a defensive Anglo-Saxonism, mourning the loss of racial purity, the foreign threat to liberty, and the passing of the ancestral ways.

Notes and references

1. R Slotkin, *Regeneration Through Violence: The Mythology of the American Frontier, 1600–1860,* Wesleyan U.P., Middletown, Conn., 1973, pp. 38–9.
2. J A Henretta, *The Evolution of American Society, 1700–1815: An Interdisciplinary Analysis,* D C Heath, Lexington, Mass., 1973, pp. 99–100.
3. C S Griffin, 'Religious Benevolence as Social Control, 1815–1860,' in D B Davis (ed), *Ante-Bellum Reform,* Harper and Row, New York, 1967, especially pp. 84–5.
4. C S Griffin, *The Ferment of Reform, 1830–1860,* Thomas Y Crowell, New York, 1967, p. 22; and A F Tyler, *Freedom's Ferment: Phases of American Social History From the Colonial Period to the Outbreak of the Civil War,* Harper Torchbooks, New York, 1962, pp. 47, 67.
5. For this view of abolitionist disputes see R G Walters, *The Antislavery Appeal: Abolitionism After 1830,* John Hopkins Press, Baltimore, 1976, Chapter 1.
6. E Foner, *Free Soil, Free Labor, Free Men: The Ideology of the Republican Party Before the Civil War,* Oxford U.P., New York, 1970, pp. 10, 104, 106–8.

Chapter Four

The Old South

Edward Ranson and Andrew Hook

Defining the South

We begin by assuming that there existed in the past, and that there still exists, a region of the United States known as 'The South', which, having undergone a peculiar historical experience, has evolved a variety of political, economic, social, religious, cultural, and even psychological characteristics distinguishing it from the rest of the country. Visitors to the South today, whether American or foreign, carry with them similar expectations of difference, distinctiveness, otherness. And they are rarely disappointed. The South does appear different. Nevertheless, problems arise as soon as one tries to explain this difference either by analysing the experiences of the past, or by enumerating distinguishing characteristics, or even by trying to establish a definition of the South. The same difficulties emerge, perhaps even in heightened form, if the focus of one's attention is not the present-day South but the South of before the Civil War – what we know as the Old or Ante-Bellum South.

Even these names create problems. Both are oddly attractive and appealing, in a way that, say, the 'Slave South' would not be. The 'Old South' contains a hint of sentiment and nostalgia, a regret for a world that is lost; the 'ante-bellum South' is redolent of that classical civilization so proudly claimed by the Old South as its model, not only for much of its architecture, but for its way of life. In fact, both names have clinging to them something of the South's enduring mythology. Promoted and promulgated by an enormous range of novels, plays, films, histories and pseudo-histories (the single best-known example is of course the novel and film *Gone With the Wind*), the image of the heroic, romantic, legendary South continues to exercise a fascination which no reference to the complex realities of history seems able to dispel. Not even the counter-image, which probably has its source in Harriet Beecher Stowe's portrayal of Simon Legree in *Uncle Tom's Cabin* (1852), of the debauched and degenerate Southerner brutalized by his association with slavery, has been strong enough to drive out the romantic myth of an Old South populated by aristocratic, chivalrous planters and their beautiful, elegant womenfolk, living in serene white mansions, amid the fragrance of moonlit gardens, with slave gangs singing in the cotton fields. This romantic and glamorized vision can be traced fairly precisely to the 1830s and 1840s, as we shall see, and was given an enormous boost by the Southern defeat in the Civil War; it was then to be embellished in the popular culture of the late nineteenth and twentieth centuries. But it is now a major dimension of what the Old South has come to mean, and for the historian the mythology has become almost as important as the reality.

The historian's problem, though, is not just the relatively simple one of seeking to determine what degree of truth is contained in this elaborate, romantic stereotype. For, like nearly all stereotypes, it contains a limited or partial truth, but distorts much and leaves a great deal out of account. For example, it tells us little about the actual social, political, and ideological conservatism of the Old South; about the degree to which the region was in fact class and caste-ridden, xenophobic, racist, and introverted; about the way in which a professed commitment to romantic and chivalrous ideals of honour and courage could, and did, coexist with a barely suppressed current of individual and collective violence. It is hoped that in the course of this essay a more accurate picture of the Old South will emerge than that provided by a set of popular images. But a useful beginning is to suggest how it was, in historical terms, that the romantic myth of the Old South came to be created, and why it has proved so enduring.

The truth of the matter, perhaps, is that the mythology of the South is so powerful and tenacious because, deprived of it, the South would seem like the emperor without his clothes: that is, no longer clearly identifiable. In other words, at some specific point in its history, the Old South created and diffused a particular self-image in order to persuade itself, and the world outside, of its own distinct identity. Historical necessity required that the Old South should be seen to be different. Paradoxically, then, through the creation of images and myths, the Old South became an historical reality. Is it any wonder that the images and myths should have subsequently proved more tenacious and enduring than the reality?

Was the South unique?

The Old South needed to create an identity for itself because, historically, it lacked any simple or straightforward means of self-definition. When, in the 1760s, two English surveyors named Mason and Dixon ran a line between Maryland and Pennsylvania in an effort to settle a boundary dispute, no one imagined that the states to the north and south of that line had thereby any more or less in common with each other. Until as late as the early nineteenth century, the Southern states had in fact undergone much the same historical experience as the rest of the United States: fairly rapid geographical expansion, as new territories were acquired in the west and south, a moving frontier, and contact with European rivals and hostile Indians. As it grew in size, the South inevitably became increasingly diverse in topography, climate, soil and vegetation. There was no mountain range, no great river, no physical obstacle nor natural boundary separating it from the rest of the country. The South has therefore never been a single, monolithic region, easy to distinguish and describe. Rather it has always remained an ill-assorted collection of subregions, collectively known as 'The South' not because they were geographically similar, but despite the fact that they were geographically different. Nor is it geography alone that fails to provide a satisfactory definition of the South. In terms of its origins, language, law and religion, the South hardly differed from the rest of the nation; and those broad patterns of economic, political, and social change which affected the other regions of the United States produced parallel developments in the South. In the area of cultural history the story is the same. Even in the decades immediately prior to the Civil War, Northerners and Southerners by and large read the same books, responded to the same ideas, discussed and debated the same issues. Scott and Byron, Dickens and Bulwer Lytton were immensely popular writers in all sections of the United States. As thinkers, Emerson, Carlyle, and Macaulay were scorned or admired in both North and South. It is difficult to argue, therefore, that the cultural experience of North / and South differed in any fundamental way, or that any Southern 'world view' had emerged even by 1860 that was wholly alien to that of the North. (It has often been noted that, when the Southern states finally seceded, the constitution adopted by the Confederacy bore a marked resemblance to that of the Federal Union from which they were withdrawing).

Attempts to find factors common to the Southern states but absent elsewhere, which might therefore be seen as creating a distinctive Southern identity, have not on the whole proved any more successful. The rural and agricultural nature of the South, its one-crop system, even the widespread use of slave labour, the lack of urban and industrial development, its pre-bourgeois or pre-modern society, its poverty, its sense of failure, defeat or guilt: at different times all of these have been offered as explanations of the South's uniqueness. But none of them have commanded general agreement, and all have been subject to serious objection or qualification. Part of the problem is that few of these characteristics were peculiar to the American South; and most of them can be used to differentiate between the regions or sections of various countries other than America. Not all of these countries, however, have had to endure the trauma of civil war, and, at least in the American context, the Civil War is the crucial factor. While it may be possible to demonstrate the extraordinary difficulty of discovering any set of facts, circumstances or characteristics which give the South a clear, separate and identifiable existence, while it may be possible, as it were, to argue the South out of existence, the fact of the American Civil War in the end makes all such arguments academic. By 1861 the Old South not only existed, but was ready and willing to fight a long, bitter, and bloody war in a vain attempt to preserve its separate existence. The question then is how and why it was done. What were the forces or factors which created the Old South, and how did they do so?

In the period before the American Revolution, the settlers in the Southern colonies – Virginia, Maryland, the Carolinas, and Georgia– did not think of themselves as 'Southerners': indeed, it is highly unlikely that many of them even regarded themselves as Americans. A sense of American nationality only began to grow in that period of unrest, discontent, and increasingly violent political argument and debate which preceded the outbreak of the Revolution itself, and in which the Southern states played a full part. The unity achieved by the opponents of the British administration in the different colonies, in fact, surprised the British and contributed to their defeat. The absence, during these years, of inter-colonial or sectional rivalries may be partly attributable to the skill with which the Southern political elite, particularly in Virginia, not unaware of the consequences of allowing Massachusetts and New York to dominate the revolutionary movement, used their position to lead and guide it. Nonetheless, the Revolutionary War itself, while forging an American identity, did nothing to create a peculiarly Southern one. Military campaigns were fought out in both Northern and Southern states; North and South both contributed to the patriotic army; and both sections contained sizeable Loyalist groups. The creation of the United States of America was thus in no way a sectional achievement.

In the political world of the new nation in the years after the Revolution, it is still difficult to identify any distinctive Southern point of view. It is clear that Virginia-born presidents like Washington, Jefferson, Madison and Monroe did not think of themselves as 'Southerners' in the way that politicians born in Virginia or elsewhere in the South a generation or so later were almost bound to do. Over such a major political issue as the ratification of the new Federal Constitution, support and opposition did not divide along clear sectional lines. It is true that in the Federalist era from 1789 to 1801 the argument over the interpretation of the new Constitution did begin to assume a more sectionalist form. The North was inclined to favour a stronger form of central (Federal) government, while the South preferred a more restricted role for the central authority, with residual rights reserved to each individual state. As a result, in his Farewell Address of 1796, George Washington felt impelled to warn his countrymen of the dangers of sectionalism and partisanship. However, such subsequent developments as Jefferson's defeat of the Federalists in the 1800 presidential election, and the nationalistic enthusiasm with which the South supported the War of 1812 against

Great Britain, seem once again to have worked against the emergence of any clearly recognizable group identity among the Southern states. Even as late as the second decade of the nineteenth century, there is no clear evidence that a Southern consciousness, an awareness by the South of its own difference and distinctiveness, had in any general sense developed. The South that some fifty years later was to fight the Civil War was still waiting to be born. But however late it may have been in emerging, a Southern consciousness and a Southern identity had been potentially present from the early years of the colonial period. Despite all the varied arguments that have been adduced, attempting to assimilate the South into the rest of America, denying it any distinct or special status, the possibility of a South radically and decisively unassimilated had always existed. It had existed in the form of the crucial figure in the history of the Old South: the Negro slave. It is only in terms of the slave and slavery, we believe, that the creation, existence, and demise of the Old South are finally to be understood. It was the very existence of the black slave in the tobacco and cotton-growing states of the South which provided the one bond, the one shared interest, that could in time unify the South and create its identity. As a way of differentiating between one group of states and another, the presence or absence of Negro slaves was always liable to be a crucial consideration.

The South and slavery

Slavery in the South was of course a legacy of British rule; it had existed since the early seventeenth century, but had not occasioned a great deal of comment until the nineteenth. Many of the leaders of the American Revolution, including Washington and Jefferson, were slave-owners, and some at least were not unaware of the incongruity of their position: slavery was hardly compatible with the 'life, liberty and pursuit of happiness' that the new America promised its people. Although Southern touchiness on the subject made it necessary to omit any direct reference to slavery in the Declaration of Independence, the existence of slavery was recognized and accepted by the new American Constitution. On the other hand, one should not assume too readily that America's Founding Fathers were either blind or cynical in the way they tried to deal with the slavery issue; towards the end of the eighteenth century it was widely believed that slavery would gradually die out, and that the problem would thus solve itself. It was Eli Whitney's invention of the cotton gin in 1793 which put an end to such hopes; the new efficient method of separating cotton lint from cotton seed made possible a vast expansion in the production of cotton. As a result, the economics of slavery were transformed and, rather than declining, the number of slaves in the South began rapidly to increase. Around 1820, there were 1½ million slaves in America; in 1860, the figure was just under 4 million. Just how profitable the slave system was for the individual owner, for the South, and for the United States as a whole, remains a question of historical dispute. It does appear, however, that slavery was profitable in the 1850s and promised to remain so in the 1860s and beyond. It is also worth remembering that, on the eve of the Civil War, three-quarters of the cotton crop went for export, accounting for 60 per cent of the United States' foreign earnings. Thus, in strictly material terms, it is easy to understand why for much of the nineteenth century the South, rather than seeking out ways to bring an end to the institution of slavery, was committed to its rapid extension into the new territories that America was acquiring in the west and south-west.

The material benefits of slavery, whether real or imagined, were not enough in themselves to subdue doubts and misgivings in other directions. The enormous contradiction involved in the tolerance of a slave system by a nation whose whole political and social philosophy–indeed, whose very existence–centred on the concepts of freedom, self-determination and the rights of the individual, did not go unnoticed. From the earliest days of the republic, this paradox was picked on, in particular by those foreign observers (Charles Dickens, for example) who believed it questioned the entire libertarian principle, or else were anxious that the American experiment in freedom and democracy should fail. Many Europeans saw in the continued existence of slavery within American society a potentially explosive issue which, as upholders of the traditional European power structures, they hoped and predicted would in the end bring America's democratic institutions crashing down.

The first major indication that these dire forebodings could in fact be fulfilled came with the bitter controversy surrounding the Missouri Compromise of 1820–21. Missouri territory had reached a stage in its development when it was in a position to apply for admission to the Union as a state; the point at issue was whether or not slavery should be permitted in the new state. The Southern states favoured the extension of slavery into that area; the Northern states opposed it. After a two-year struggle, a compromise was arrived at whereby Missouri was admitted as a slave state at the same time as Maine was admitted as a free one; thus the balance of power between free and slave states in the United States Senate was preserved. At the same time, in the vast territory west of the Mississippi acquired from France in 1803 as the Louisiana Purchase, slavery was prohibited north of latitude 36° 30', but permitted south of it. But, though a compromise had been agreed, the political and moral passions which had been roused were not easily subdued. The Missouri debates made it clear that anti-slavery sentiment was growing in the North. So the need to defend their interests produced a new sense of unity among the Southern slaveholding states: the slavery issue was at last shaping Southern sectionalism into a clear and definable form. To the ageing

Thomas Jefferson, the whole affair was deeply alarming; the sectional nature of the struggle over Missouri was an ominous portent. 'This momentous question,' he wrote, 'like a fire bell in the night, awakened and filled me with terror. I considered it at once the knell of the Union.' The compromise he saw as 'a reprieve only, not a final sentence'; the end could only be an 'irrepressible conflict.'[1]

As we shall see, during the 1820s and 1830s the Old South's sense of its own distinctiveness, and of its separation from the rest of America, gradually increased. But in cementing Southern group identity, the catalyst was always the Negro slave. In January 1831 came the publication of the first number of William Lloyd Garrison's *Liberator* – a New England newspaper dedicated to the abolition of slavery. A few months later the South was horrified, and terrified, by the outbreak of the most serious slave insurrection it had ever faced: sixty whites had died before Nat Turner's revolt in Southampton County, Virginia, was finally suppressed. These two events electrified the South, and they did much to ensure that the spirit of sectional unity would continue to grow. In the face of enemies both without and within, what was needed was unity of purpose and attitude. The last open discussion of the merits of slavery, and the possibility of emancipation, took place in the South in the Virginia legislature in the 1831–32 session. When, by a surprisingly narrow margin, Virginia decided to retain slavery, the time for discussion was over: in the view of the South, the issue was now settled. Hard on the heels of these events came the Nullification Crisis of 1832–33 when, in protest at alleged Northern economic exploitation of the South, South Carolina threatened to 'nullify' – or declare invalid – a contentious tariff act of the Federal Government. Admittedly the crisis over the tariff was primarily an economic one, but it centrally involved the issue of states' rights, and thus indirectly a crucial argument in the defense of slavery. It is in the 1830s, then, that the Old South enters history as an undeniable reality, called into being by the need of the Southern states to unite in defense of the 'peculiar institution' – slavery.

Before the 1830s, Southern spokesmen had tended to apologize for the existence of slavery as a necessary evil. Under the pressure of Northern abolitionist propaganda, however, the South, as the 1830s went on, ceased to apologize. Rather, having allowed the abolitionists the great advantage of determining the nature and scope of the debate, it sought increasingly for ways of justifying slavery. From this period up to the outbreak of the Civil War, a great deal of the South's intellectual energy was expended in a fruitless attempt to win this debate. Pseudo-scientific arguments were produced to prove that Negroes were racially inferior, or specially suited for agricultural work. The sanction for slavery to be found both in the Bible and the Federal Constitution was constantly cited. History was searched for examples of civilizations that had made use of slaves; it was argued that paternalism was the guiding principle of Southern slaveholders, and that as a result slaves were better off and enjoyed better conditions that would have been the case had they remained in Africa. More aggressively, Southerners argued that there was little to choose between the chattel system of slavery in the South and the wage slavery that operated in the North. If anything, the oppressed and exploited workers in the mills and factories of the North were worse off than the plantation slaves in the South.

Of course, the picture of slavery created by the Northern abolitionists was a very different one. Driven by the humanitarian or religious zeal which swept America in the 1820s and 1830s, the abolitionists were a heterogeneous group united only by the idealistic fervour with which they assailed slavery and the South. High-principled, as for the most part they were, there is no doubt that their crusading zeal exacerbated North–South feeling, encouraged the South to turn defensively upon itself, and so materially contributed to the coming of the Civil War. The abolitionists argued that slavery was working against the economic development of the South, and that non-slaveholders in particular were disadvantaged by the system. More pointedly, they insisted that the existence of slavery was morally degrading in its effects upon those who owned slaves. But of course the main thrust of their onslaught came from the account they provided of the effects of the system on the slaves themselves: theirs was a life of degradation and brutal ill-treatment, of economic, physical and sexual exploitation. Much emphasis was laid on the denial to the slave of the right to a stable family life: it was repeatedly insisted that not only were children taken away and sold at an early age, but that husbands and wives lived in constant fear of being sold to separate masters. Slaves were also denied both proper religious instruction and education of even the most rudimentary kind. Defending slavery, the South was defending a monstrous social crime. At first the abolitionists believed that this great wrong could be righted by moral persuasion, but by 1840 many saw the exercise of political pressure on the South as a more likely answer; and in the end some did not shrink from violence as the only means of attaining the ideals they pursued.

Few historians today would accept as an accurate account either the abolitionists' nightmare vision, or the South's version of slavery as an early form of social security for the underpriviledged. Equally, few would agree on what would constitute an accurate and truthful account. Perhaps there is no single truth about slavery. Certainly the fact that there were 4 million slaves and some 400,000 slave-owners on the eve of the Civil War should make us suspicious of broad generalizations. Such figures allow us to question, for example, how far the Old South should even be described as a slaveholding society. There were some 1¼ million white families living in the Old South; thus only a minority of whites owned any slaves at all. And it is undoubtedly true that the large yeoman class of small farmers – who owned few if any slaves, but who constituted numerically the largest single group in Southern society – has traditionally been largely neglected by commentators and historians. Again, of the 400,000 Southerners who did own slaves, only a minority owned more than twenty and the great majority fewer than five. The image of an Old South wholly composed of vast plantations with slave gangs toiling on their broad acres thus has no basis in reality. Some 50,000 slave-holders owned 20 slaves or more; 10,000 owned 50 or more; 2,300 owned 100 or more; and a mere handful owned something approaching 500 slaves.

The conditions under which slaves were held must clearly have varied enormously from situation to situation, depending on such factors as the attitude of the owner or overseer, the size of the plantation, the number of slaves, the geographical location, and the nature of the crop. At worst, slaves could be regarded as renewable capital goods to be exploited to their maximum and then replaced; on the other hand, they could be seen as highly valuable investments to be prized accordingly. Certainly, slavery did not have the effect of making all slaves equal. Slave society was strictly hierarchical, running from the field hand at the bottom of the scale to the house servant or skilled blacksmith, wheelwright, or carpenter at the top. Slaves who lived in towns could form an even more privileged group; sometimes they were allowed to ply their own trades and simply remit a percentage of their earnings to their owners. Thus it is true that the day-by-day slave experience of several million human beings in the Old South was by no means a uniform one; the condition of slavery could and did vary enormously. And yet every slave, whatever his material situation, was still a slave. In a sense that the Old South could not or would not understand, slavery as an institution could not survive. Attempts to justify it were attempts to justify the unjustifi-able. By the middle of the nineteenth century, at least in the Western world, slavery could only be an offence to every idea of progress and the growth of civilization. In attempting to cling on to its 'peculiar institution', the Old South was ultimately defying the movement of history itself.

The South and Secession

In the 1820s and 1830s the Old South's consciousness of its own existence continued to grow and began to assume highly significant new forms. It was under the pressure of the knowledge that the United States was fundamentally and fatally divided by the slave economy of the Southern states that the South had at last become aware of its own existence as an historical entity. But this knowledge in turn demanded that the South become aware of itself in areas remote from the institution of slavery. It had above all to recognize in itself a culture and a way of life that gave it both identity and a redeeming value. It was not enough that the Old South should define itself by its hatred of the Northern abolitionist; it needed to be seen to embody a positive social good that was worth preserving and maintaining at whatever cost. Precisely here it is possible to identify the source of what was to become the over-arching mythology of the South – it was the need to believe in itself, to identify its own value, that produced the most potent and enduring images of the South.

The mode of life possible on a handful of large plantations provided the basis for the self-identification the South needed and sought. Around the existence of such plantations there thus developed a whole set of theoretical assumptions about the South's way of life – and its absolute contrast with that of the North – which soon passed into general circulation. The South had created an aristocratic, agrarian civilization; the North, a democratic, commercial one. Totally different sets of attitudes and values animated the two sections. Essentially the North was a materialistic society given over to the pursuit of money; Southern society gave its allegiance to such values as honour and personal integrity. Hence, where Northern society was an aggregate of competing individuals, the South was an aggregate of communities. Southern society was conservative, upholding the values of a traditional way of life; Northern society was rootless, changing, fluid, dominated by money-minded Yankees. In the end, the South found for itself even a satisfying myth of its historical origins: Southerners were descended from the stock of gallant, carefree, seventeenth-century Cavaliers, while Northerners derived from austere and frowning Puritan Roundheads. From the 1830s, what the South was defending was no longer simply the institution of slavery; it was an entire social structure, with a culture and way of life it passionately believed to be in every sense superior to those of the North.

So, as the opposition between North and South came to be seen not only as a collision of sectional interests, but as a confrontation between different cultures, the area of common political ground declined. After the Nullification Crisis in South Carolina it came to seem that inter-sectional conflict was a permanent condition. From the mid-1840s it was no longer the case that one area of tension was followed by another; it was rather that a permanent crisis moved on from one phase to the next. The annexation of Texas (1845), the Mexican War (1846–48), the Compromise of 1850, the Kansas–Nebraska problem (1854–56), the Supreme Court's Dred Scott decision (1857), John Brown's raid on the Federal Arsenal at Harper's Ferry, Virginia (1859) and the Presidential Election of 1860: these were no more than high points in a continuing crisis in North–South relations. There were, of course, many in North and South who refused to believe that the differences between the two sections of the United States were beyond resolution, and more who held that any attempt to break up the Union could lead only to disaster. Even as late as 1860, when the southern states saw in Lincoln's presidential victory their own final

defeat in the national political arena, the movement for secession –
though in most southern states now too powerful to be denied – still
encountered considerable opposition. Had the issues been debated
purely on their political merits, the outcome might have been
different, but extremists in both North and South had succeeded in
raising the political temperature to so high a level that emotion rather
than reason determined the actual course of action. Slavery excited the
strongest emotions: for several decades it had been the flashpoint in
North–South relations, and it provided the ultimate occasion for all
the major crises – from the annexation of Texas to John Brown's raid.
Slavery, its precise status, its right to expand, had become the centre of
every confrontation and the ghost at every political feast. The need to
preserve and defend slavery may have brought the Old South into
existence. But, as we have seen, to believe in itself the Old South
needed to be persuaded that it possessed a society, culture and way of
life crucially different from and superior to that of the Yankee North.
And this in the end it did believe. In 1860, on the edge of the conflict
that would bring the 'Old South' to an end and in the long run create it
as a necessary memory, Mary Chesnut, a Southerner, wrote in her
diary: 'We separated because of incompatibility of temper; we are
divorced, North from South, because we have hated each other so'.[2]

Thus for Mary Chesnut, writing in the dangerously exciting
atmosphere of 1860, what we have been calling 'myth' was now
incontestable reality. (We need here to remind ourselves that history is
made just as much by what people *believe* as by what is actually the
case.) So what North and South may or may not have had in common
was now largely irrelevant: what mattered was the immense gulf of
bitterness that now divided them. How far Mary Chesnut was right to
believe that by 1860 North and South had in fact become two different
worlds, two incompatible societies and cultures, is a question which
modern historians and sociologists still debate. And there are those
who argue that, even if the question of slavery is set aside, the society
of the Old South can be seen as reflecting an awareness of traditional
human values that indeed differentiates it from the progressive,
thrusting, materialist society of the North. Honour, courage,
generosity, amiability, courtesy may not be the kind of values to
ensure success in the world of capitalistic economic competition; but
they do provide the basis for an attractive way of life. The long conflict
and the Southern defeat perpetuated the dichotomy, arresting and
perpetuating the myth, and turning it into a governing idea. In the later
1920s and the 1930s, when there was much talk of a New South,
urbanized and industrialized in the manner of the rest of the United
States, these were exactly the kind of civilized, humane values that
that group of major American writers who produced the Southern
Literary Renaissance saw embodied in the culture of the Old South.
Believing, like so many other modern artists and writers, that the most
powerful forces at work in twentieth-century society were hostile to

human dignity and integrity, these modern Southern writers felt that the order and stability and sense of community traditionally present in Southern society provided a positive alternative to the 'waste-land' vision of the modern world, so powerfully projected in a great deal of twentieth-century writing.

Writing in the Old South

However, even for the Southern writer most alienated from the modern industrialized life around him in America, and most eager to admire those dimensions of the society of the Old South which preserved the values he prized, there was, apart from slavery, another significant problem about the Old South which demanded recognition. Most mature cultures are preserved in the great works of the mind and imagination they produce. But the enduring creative achievements of nineteenth-century America were produced, not in the Old South, but in the New England heartland of the Yankee. As Allen Tate, writing in 1935 on 'The Profession of Letters in the South', put it: 'we had no Hawthorne, no Melville, no Emily Dickinson. We had William Gilmore Simms. We made it impossible for Poe to live south of the Potomac'.[3] Tate in fact is too honest a commentator on the South not to put his finger squarely on the problem involved in the South's literary failure in the ante-bellum period: 'Yet the very merits of the Old South tend to confuse the issue: its comparative stability, its realistic limitation of the acquisitive impulse, its preference for human relations compared to relations economic, tempt the historian to defend the poor literature simply because he feels that the old society was a better place to live in than the new. It is a great temptation – if you do not read the literature.'[4]

As a major poet, novelist, and critic, Tate's standards of literary excellence are high. Not all students of the Old South would agree that such literature as it did produce is quite as bad as Tate implies. Nonetheless, by any standard the literary culture of the Old South is undistinguished. Why this was so exercised the minds of commentators from the early nineteenth century on, and it remains a significant question. As early as 1816 George Tucker was explaining Virginia's backwardness in cultural matters in terms of the structure of its social life: the scattered plantations, and the absence of cities, combined with a preoccupation with practical pursuits and a preference for foreign authors, had produced a situation in which a native literature could not be expected to flourish. Later writers tended mainly to develop Tucker's points. Towards the end of the nineteenth century, for example, Thomas Nelson Page argued in *The Old South* (1892) that the region's failure to produce a major literature resulted from its essentially non-urban, agricultural society, the consequent absence of publishing houses, and the failure to develop a reading-public within the South itself for Southern authors. To these sociological explanations, Page added the equally conventional one that the literary powers of the Old South had been directed towards the worlds of politics and polemical controversy, and that the existence of slavery had led to 'the absorption of the intellectual forces of the people of the South in the solution of the vital problems it engendered'.[5]

It is probably true that the political debate with the North did absorb a large share of the intellectual energies of the South. Hence it was natural that the way ahead for a talented young Southerner should lie in a career in politics or in the related field of law; a career in the arts was scarcely a possibility. In 1842 Charles Dickens received a letter from Thomas Ritchie of the *Richmond Enquirer* which suggests that the cultural life of Virginia had remained much as it was when Tucker was writing in 1816: 'the *forte* of the Old Dominion is to be found in the masculine production of her statesmen, her Washington, her Jefferson, and her Madison, who have never indulged in works of imagination, in the charms of romance, or in the mere beauties of the *belles lettres*.'[6] A still more dismissive view of the imaginative writer is evident in a story told by the minor Southern poet, Philip Pendleton Cooke. Cooke reports how after he had gained some repute as an author, a friendly neighbour said to him: 'I wouldn't waste time on a damned thing like poetry; you might make yourself, with all your sense and judgement, a useful man in settling neighborhood disputes and difficulties. . .'.[7] Equally revealing are the lives and careers of some of the better writers whom the Old South did produce. William Gilmore Simms, for example, now hardly read, but in his own day the most important figure in the literature of the Old South, never felt that his native city – Charleston, South Carolina – adequately recognized and acknowledged his merits as a writer. Certainly until 1860, at least, his many novels were much more widely read in the North than in the South; and, early in his career, it was only by frequent visits to the North, and to New York in particular, that he was able to meet other writers, editors, and publishers and so establish himself as an author. Again, John Pendleton Kennedy, whose novel *Swallow Barn* (1832) played a crucial part in propagating the plantation myth of the Old South, wrote only two further novels before more or less abandoning literature for a career in politics. Then the wayward genius of Edgar Allan Poe could find no permanent home in the Old South. Poe's aim was to be a professional writer and live by his pen; but, in the society of the Old South, there was no way in which he, or any other imaginative writer, could fulfil such an ambition. For a year or two in the 1830s Poe made the *Southern Literary Messenger* in Richmond, Virginia, into a literary periodical of distinction; but his professionalism, and the seriousness of his commitment to art and literature, soon brought him into collision with the amateur, genteel tradition of southern writing. Poe too was compelled to abandon the South.

Indeed, the evidence all suggests that the society of the Old South was not one likely to foster a major literary talent; it is post-bellum Southern writing that we think of when we speak of the powerful Southern literary tradition. No doubt the cultural centres of America were in the North, but this still leaves us with the question of why such literature as the Old South did produce is of only indifferent quality: why is the work of the Simmses, the Kennedys, the Cookes, so unrewarding?[8] Perhaps the answer is that the literature of the Old South is fundamentally dishonest, reflecting the uneasy forms and structures of the society in which it was produced. At one level, its hollowness is a question of the rhetorical forms in which it is couched: an ornate, pompous or weakly sentimental language conceals rather than reveals the reality it purports to describe. This is the high-flown Ciceronian style of the Southern orator – or what Allen Tate describes as 'Confederate Prose', which he and his fellow-writers of the later Southern Literary Renaissance strove above all to avoid. It is also the language of sham sentiment and empty attitudinizing that Mark Twain, a creative psyche in some ways divided between North and South, satirizes so devastatingly in several books, and associates with the unhappy influence of Sir Walter Scott on the South's feudal cultural mentality. In *The Adventures of Huckleberry Finn* (1885), both the successful frauds and deceptions of the King and the Duke and the meaningless massacres of the Grangerfords and Sheperdsons are, in the end, products of Southern society's linguistic corruption: Southerners cannot, in Twain, distinguish between linguistic posturing and genuine expressions of feeling, and are eager to act out the shabby rhetoric they admire. Just how brilliantly Twain's book reveals the underlying flaws of the Old South is suggested by the way it also illuminates a second level of evasion and deception which undermines much Southern writing: for *Huckleberry Finn,* unlike most Southern writing, goes on to probe, at last, the truth about slavery. What Huck has to learn is that Jim, his companion on the raft in the Mississippi, is not an object, somebody else's property, a runaway slave, but a man, an individual with feelings and needs exactly like his own. But the essential humanity of the Negro was precisely what the institution of slavery formally denied. And this was the one simple truth that Southern society and Southern literature could not afford to recognize.

One of the most striking features of the cultural life of the Old South after the early 1830s is its intolerance of criticism. On such crucial subjects as slavery, state's rights, and relations with the North, freedom of debate was denied. Southern society had taken its stand on these issues; the time for argument was over. What was needed was the preservation of the South's ideological purity from the contamination of new or different ideas expressed either without or within. In this show of solidarity, Southern writers were expected to play their part. In such a situation, critical social comment, the probing of accepted orthodoxies and values, the exploration of underlying social or ideological tensions, even the dramatizing of basic conflicts, ceased to be modes or strategies a writer could adopt. Rather than challenge, the Southern writer had to conform to society; so it is hardly surprising that in his work the great issues facing the ante-bellum South remain largely unexplored; the 'cordon sanitaire' the South had drawn around such a crucial issue as slavery was so tight that it could not be penetrated by the literary imagination – at least, not by the imagination of a writer who wished to remain a Southerner and be accepted by the South.

The world-wide success of *Uncle Tom's Cabin* (1852) perhaps suggests that the Old South was right to believe that the subject of slavery was best left alone. To write about the slave, whether well or badly, was inevitably to humanize him. Harriet Beecher Stowe's Northern abolitionist novel may have limitations in its portrayal of Negroes, but its treatment of such themes as the economic basis of slavery, racial prejudice in the North as well as the South, and the predicament of the intelligent Southern slave-owner, is lacking neither in insight nor subtlety. Certainly *Uncle Tom's Cabin* remains a much more interesting book than the plantation romances of the Old South. And if Sir Walter Scott is not to be accused, as Twain did accuse him in *Life on the Mississippi,* of having caused the Civil War by imbuing the Old South with a bogus sense of aristocratic values, medieval notions of chivalry and nobility, and romantic nationalism, he can be seen as responsible for the creation of the characteristic historical romance of the ante-bellum South. Writing within a society reluctant to face squarely the major issues confronting it, Southern novelists such as William Gilmore Simms, John Pendleton Kennedy and William Alexander Caruthers began to turn increasingly toward the past for their subject and, modelling their work, often, on that of Walter Scott or James Fenimore Cooper, began an entire tradition of historical romances on such topics as the Southern frontier, the Indian wars, or the American Revolution. Most emerged during the 1830s, when indeed there appeared a notable promise of a Southern literary movement. Kennedy's *Swallow Barn* (1832) is undoubtedly influenced by Irving, and explores an idealized but recent Virginia plantation life in a series of delicate sketches. Caruthers' *The Cavaliers of Virginia* (1834–35) is a sentimental looking back at the 'cavalier' connection and the South's 'feudal' origins. Simms's *The Yemassee* (1835), perhaps the best Southern book of the period, is about the impact of whites on the Indians of the South Carolina border, and compares favourably with Cooper's Indian novels. The historical novel was indeed a fashionable genre, but in the South it became increasingly sentimental, as well as a way of turning to times when problems were less pressing. The difficulties of the Southern writer were expressed in the uncertainties and difficulties of the careers that followed. Thus Kennedy became by the time of the war an anti-Southerner in Baltimore; Simms became a defender of the

South's 'Greek democracy' and was ruined in the war.

The South after 1865

In the Old South there were thus signs of a nascent literary impulse which finally grew evasive or stunted; and there were those who later came to argue that the South lost the Civil War because of its lack of writers. This was the view of Thomas Nelson Page, one of several writers who emerged after the war to write the enlarging myth of the Old South, and to explore the world of Reconstruction from a Southern standpoint. 'It was', Page wrote in 1892, 'for lack of a literature' that the South 'was left behind in the great race for outside support, and that in the supreme moment of her existence she found herself arraigned at the bar of the world without an advocate and without a defence.' According to Page, the South 'was conquered by the pen rather than by the sword'; but he is honest enough to concede that the fault was the South's own: 'We denied and fought, but we did not argue. Be this, however, our justification, that slavery did not admit of argument. Argument meant destruction'.[9] Page of course oversimplifies and overstates. The South did, as we have seen, argue and attempt to justify – though having allowed the Northern abolitionists to determine the area of debate it could only lose. But it is also true that the South lost the propaganda war for the hearts and minds of the outside world: *Unle Tom's Cabin* dismayed and outraged the South, but the damage it did to the Southern cause was irreparable. In imaginative terms, the Old South could find no answer. On the other hand, even had she enjoyed the support of the finest writers imaginable, it is hard to see how the South could have survived once the North had demonstrated its determination to fight first to restore the Union and later to abolish slavery. Certainly the South believed in itself and the righteousness of its cause. Its soldiers fought well and bravely; its generals were often skilful; and it had the advantage of defensive positions and internal lines of communication. But in most other ways the South was severely handicapped: eleven states against twenty-three, 9 millions against nearly 23 millions, and an equivalent Southern weakness in such crucial areas as iron and steel production, railroad mileage and equipment, shipping and naval power, mechanics and technicians, banking and finance. In government and diplomacy, too, the North's advantage proved overwhelming. Even in terms of political leadership the contest was an unequal one: Jefferson Davis, the head of the Confederacy, could not rival the charisma, the moral authority, or the unyielding determination of the Northern Lincoln. The longer the war continued, the more inevitable total Southern defeat became.

Yet there is a sense in which the weakness of the literature of the Old South is indeed an index of the weakness and ultimate failure of the culture and civilization of the Old South itself. Literature and society were both fatally weakened by their unwillingness to face up to the reality of slavery. Not even the shock of defeat in the Civil War – how could the dare-devil, hard-riding, courageous, Cavalier South be conquered by the money-worshipping Federals, the corrupt employers, downtrodden artisans and meddling abolitionists of the North? – was sufficient to make the South face the truth about itself. The unavailing bravery and self-sacrifice of the Confederate armies served only to heighten Southern pride and sectional self-consciousness. In the period of Reconstruction, which occupied the years subsequent to the ending of the Civil War, a new chapter was added to the mythology of the South: a prostrate South was now the helpless victim of rapacious Northern politicians and businessmen ('carpet-baggers'), compliant white Southerners ('scalawags'), and their Negro allies. The romantic aura surrounding the Old South, and an idealized vision of a lost cause, a lost society, and a lost way of life, increasingly obscured the historical realities. And in the works of a new generation of post-war Southern novelists, such as Thomas Dixon and Thomas Nelson Page himself, the romance of the Old South was written and re-written.

About 1870, John W De Forest, a Northern novelist – his excellent *Miss Ravenel's Conversion from Secession to Loyalty* is one of the few significant novels to emerge directly from the Civil War – identified the sources of the continuing weakness of Southern writing:

Not until Southerners get rid of some of their social vanity, not until they cease talking of themselves in a spirit of self-adulation, not until they drop the idea that they are Romans and must write in the style of Cicero, will they be able to so paint life that the world shall crowd to see the picture.[10]

In the twentieth century it has happened. Responding to the astonishing power of a revitalized South literary imagination, the world has crowded to see the picture painted by the writers of the modern South. From the mid-1920s, American fiction, poetry, drama, and literary criticism have received a massive Southern imprint, and Southern writers have everywhere demanded and received recognition and acclaim. The crowning achievement of the South's literary renaissance is the fiction of William Faulkner, but Faulkner's success has been brilliantly supported by that of other influential figures such as John Crow Ransom, Allen Tate, and Robert Penn Warren, while the continuing vitality of Southern writing is abundantly evident in the work of a whole range of authors from Katherine Anne Porter, Eudora Welty and Carson McCullers, to Flannery O'Connor, Elizabeth Spencer, Shirley Ann Grau, Peter Taylor, William Styron and Reynolds Price. For all these writers the South and its history, the South and its society, the South and its identity or meaning, provide a major source of creative energy and stimulus. But when they turn, as they frequently do, to portray the living face of the South, what the world sees is not the moonlight and magnolia of the old romantic image of the South. Instead, what it sees is in the end an image of itself. In the colourful, controversial, but inevitably tragic history of an Old South doomed by the burden of slavery, the twentieth century has come to recognize a powerful and compelling symbol of our flawed and fallible human condition.

Notes and references

1. Lipscomb and Bergh (eds), *Writings of Thomas Jefferson*, xiv, 247–9. Quoted by Clement Eaton, *A History of the Old South*, New York, 1975, p. 200.
2. Mary Boykin Chesnut, *A Diary from Dixie*, Boston. 1949, p. 20. Quoted by W R Taylor, *Cavalier and Yankee*, New York, 1957, p. 332.
3. Allen Tate, *Essays of Four Decades*, Swallow, Chicago, 1968, p. 520.
4. *Ibid.*, p. 527.
5. Thomas Nelson Page, *The Old South*, New York, 1892, p. 59.
6. Quoted by Louis D Rubin, Jr, in *The Writer in the South*, University of Georgia Press, Athens, Georgia, 1972, pp. 12–13.
7. Quoted by Jay B Hubbell in *The South in American Literature*, Duke U.P., 1954, p. 504.
8. The work of Edgar Allan Poe is frequently far from unrewarding. But Poe's relevance to an account of the characteristics of the literary culture of the Old South is not self-evident. Certainly much of his life was spent in the South; on one occasion at least he described himself as 'A Virginian'; and he must have been familiar with Southern society, its attitudes and habits of mind. Yet his imaginative writing remains entirely detached from any recognizable Southern or even American landscape, and he never writes directly about the South. He studiously avoids comment on any social or political issue, including even that of slavery – indeed there are only two recorded instances in his whole life of even a mention of Negro slaves in the South. It may be that the colour symbolism of *The Narrative of Arthur Gordon Pym* alludes indirectly to the slave society of the Old South, but to lay claim to Poe as a Southern writer is essentially to locate the sources of his peculiarly exotic, sensational or Gothic imagination exclusively in his experience of a tense and fearful Southern society.
9. Page, *op cit*, pp. 50–1.
10. Quoted by Tate, *op cit*, pp. 578–9.

Chapter Five
The Frontier West

R A Burchell and R J Gray

What was the Frontier?

A popular idea exists of the Frontier West of the United States as a vast
and empty area where Nature dwarfs man and the only figures in the
landscape are the cowboy and the Indian, with perhaps an occasional
trapper, prospector or troop of United States cavalry filling a
supportive role. A wagon-train may now and then cross from right to
left, taking pioneers towards the sun, but it does not stop to deposit
settlers, and the wagons disappear over the mountains on their way to
a further land. There may be settlements within this wilderness – small
forts, Indian villages and sickly cow-towns – but they do not appear to
follow normal urban functions, seeming rather to stand and wait in
silence, coming alive only when the cattle arrive from Texas or the
calvary ride out to mount a deserved counter-attack on fractious
Indian tribes. There is, however, very little historical truth in this
single static snapshot, which ignores all variety of time and space, and
also excludes one of the great motifs of the Frontier West – that is, the
continuous arrival and departure of people who connect it with, and
make it part of, a much wider world.

The men and women who came to the Frontier West brought with
them cultural preconceptions which they hastened to impose on their
new homes. Their Frontier West was no limbo sitting outside the
pattern of national development: it was rather an area of rapid change
connected intimately with national expansion. The history of the
Frontier West was ever one of defeat for difference, separation and
individuality. The victory went continuously to the traditions of the
East. One of the earliest and most powerful image-makers of the
frontier, James Fenimore Cooper, portrays this paradox in the five
novels of his 'Leatherstocking' sequence. Natty Bumppo, 'Leather-
stocking', is the romantic borderer of early nineteenth-century
historical fiction; he explores virgin land and space, but his actions are
set firmly in a process of historical time, and 'civilization' comes in
stages that finally overwhelm him.

The Frontier West requires careful definition. It was not equivalent
to the wilderness: it was, rather, the intermediary between it and the

developed East. Moreover, in the history of the United States, the frontier was not always synonymous with the West, nor was the West always the same as the frontier. In 1607, when the Virginia Company initiated the first successful English settlement, all the continent outside Jamestown was the new settlers' Frontier West. The frontier did not always lie *to* the west. In the 1850s parts of Maine, Florida and Georgia being opened to white settlement were certainly frontier areas. At the same time, however, newly settled parts of New York, Pennsylvania and western Virginia were not on the frontier, the essential difference being that the true frontier is not surrounded by civilization. Nonetheless, from the 1840s, the nation had in fact *two* frontiers, one to the east and one to the west, for, with the acquisition of Oregon in 1846, and California in 1848, population – particularly drawn in by the gold discoveries of 1848 – began spreading from both coasts into the unsettled land between. But the most important fact about the frontier is that it was an historical process – the process whereby newcomers incorporated an area into the culture of the East, until the sum total of activity in it came so closely to resemble that of areas earlier settled that the frontier period can be said to have ended. 'Culture' here refers not to the schoolmaster from Boston, nor to the spread of music, art and ideas: it means all those patterns of behaviour that evince a society's values.

The idea of process involves the notion of time. The process did not go forward in uniform ryhthm, decade by decade; it was affected by surrounding circumstances that altered themselves as time passed. Briefly, the history of the Frontier West can be divided into four phases. The first lies in the colonial period; the second in the pre-railway age of the early national period; the third falls in the decades between the spawning of the railways and the statement made by the Superintendent of the Census in 1890 that there was no longer any frontier line (that is, a single line marking off areas with less than two persons per square mile from those with more); and the fourth phase covers the period since the 1890 census, during which areas that could still be classified as frontier-parts of Oklahoma, Montana, Wyoming, New Mexico, Arizona, Nevada, Idaho and Alaska – have proceeded toward 'civilization'. On some frontiers this process was long and slow, particularly in the first two periods; on others, such as in northern California, the frontier could pass in half a decade. Most historians and literary critics too have regarded the second and third periods as having played the most significant and formative roles in the development of the American Nation.

The frontier as re-culturation

There has been much debate over how best to visualize what happened during the phase when an area was part of the Frontier West and underwent the process of cultural re-creation. Frederick Jackson Turner, in his famous paper on *The Significance of the Frontier in American History*, suggested that the 'frontier was the line of most rapid and effective Americanization' and was responsible for creating 'a new product that is American, an American mind marked by restless, nervous energy'. Some have argued that significant change took place in the failure to re-create precisely what had formerly existed in the East, and that successive failures to reproduce identical cultural patterns are at the heart of the development of a separate American culture away from mainly British roots. We can hardly deny that the varieties of context in which the reconstitution took place affected the lives of those who experienced the process – to do so would be to say that man can remain impervious to his social and cultural environment. It was, however, clearly the case that the pioneers brought with them, if they were Anglo-American, or soon adopted, if they were foreign born, a fundamental and formative ideology of republicanism that in broad outline remained an unchanging guide to what they expected in the way of government and politics, in the control and distribution of resources, and in the general right to anticipate a certain level of socio-economic mobility.

The debate over the rate and quality of cultural change has often been concentrated on one point in particular: the question of whether the westward movement of peoples produced an increasing democratization of society. It has been claimed that, particularly in the period 1815–60, ruling groups and their institutions in the United States, previously able to maintain a deferential social order, found it more and more difficult to control affairs with the same success, because the rapid expansion of the settled area taxed and then overwhelmed their resources. Hence new elites emerged in frontier areas; however, these did not succeed in reconstituting the old conservative order, since they had no inherited power bases from which to work, and so they were vunerable to challenges from other groups as eager to rise as they had been. At the same time, the democratic content of the republican ideology that had been adopted by the nation at the time of the Revolution was given ever more stress to legitimize the shifts in power that were taking place.

Inasmuch as these were times of poor communications, of scattered, largely rural communities concentrating on self-sufficient agriculture, of weak national government, and no national army through which a proto-aristocracy might seize or perpetuate power, the nation did indeed undergo cultural transformations that came through the weakening of institutions through expansion. Yet it is important to recognize that the eastern ruling groups received their major challenge at home, in the fast growing areas of the east, which increasingly acquired groups of alien European immigrants who could not be peaceably incorporated into the power-structure, but whose entry into the system governing rewards could not be denied without doing great harm to the sentiments of the Declaration of Independence and the Constitution. The Conservatism of both Hamilton and Jefferson was undermined by every immigrant ship's arrival, as well as being slowly outdated by the creation of new societies to the west of the Appalachians.

How the West was won

The conventional imagery of the westward movement includes ideas of simplicity and intimacy with Nature: the meeting with the 'virgin land'. Yet at all times, technology – especially the technology of communication – stood between Nature and man. Before the coming of the railways, communication was difficult, restricting economic growth and the total sense of social cohesion, and thus enhancing the impact of the wilderness and the frontier. In 1756, for instance, it took three days to go by coach from New York to Philadelphia, travelling eighteen hours a day across some of the most settled parts of the colonies. Before the Revolution there was only one hard-gravelled road: that leading out of Portsmouth, Maine. The first canal, from Middletown to Reading, Pennsylvania, was surveyed in 1762, but was not begun until after the Revolution. Consequently, if settlement had not been concentrated near the coast or along navigable rivers, for reasons of defence and marketing, and if the British government had not provided a centripetal cultural force, then colonists might well have succumbed to isolation and experienced marked cultural change. Some observers of back-country society, especially in the western parts of the colonies running south from Pennsylvania, argued that this was already happening by 1776; but if it was, it was also occurring within a situation where both Colonial and British governments intended to control the pattern of settlement and its rewards.

A change did come with the revolution; government control over expansion weakened. The new federal government tried to institute an ordered policy of land distribution, but largely failed, for want, among other things, of an efficient bureaucracy. Significantly, the Indian threat to white settlements east of the Mississippi was ended in a series of engagements, of which the most important were the battles of Fallen Timbers in north west Ohio, in 1794, Tippecanoe in Indiana in 1811, the Battle of the Thames in 1813 in Michigan, and of Horseshoe Bend in Alabama in 1814. Simultaneously, transportation improved, aiding the spread of population. By 1821, 4,000 miles of new turnpikes had been completed, although by then interest was turning toward canals. Further, the *Clermont* went from New York to Albany and back in August 1807, and inaugurated the age of the steamboat. The United States had secured title to the Mississippi Valley in 1803, but it was the round-trip of the *Washington* in 1817, from Louisville, Kentucky, to New Orleans, that ensured the area's growth and development. In

1818, it still cost between 100 dollars and 125 dollars to travel between the two cities; but by the 1830s the price had fallen to between 25 dollars and 30 dollars. Fares on other routes fell proportionately, further easing the way west. The opening of the Erie Canal in 1825, linking the Hudson River with the Great Lakes, where steamships had also been lately introduced, gave yet another boost to westward expansion.[1] By 1840 the population of the western states of Ohio, Indiana, Illinois and Michigan stood at 2,893,000; that of the southern states of Kentucky, Tennessee, Missouri, Arkansas, Louisiana, Mississippi and Alabama at 3,410,000. In 1800 the two areas had contained 51,000 and 336,000 people respectively.[2]

Yet despite all these improvements, travel, even in long settled areas, remained slow. As late as 1833, it took 33¼ hours to travel from Boston to New York: the maximum speed of the fastest form of transport, the stagecoach, was only around 11½ miles an hour on good roads. The canal boats taking migrants west along the Erie Canal travelled at about 1½ to 2 miles an hour, while no boats anywhere appear to have been capable of exceeding 5 miles an hour.[3] Such slow travel hindered communication, which in turn hampered the development of markets, and importantly, the communication of ideas and the control of government and institutions. Localism was very important in this period, while the level of technology in general made men dependent on climate, topography and local supplies, vulnerable to flood or blizzard, and conscious of their isolation. This was a Frontier West of a relatively low level of agricultural technology and, linked to it, of low agricultural productivity. At first farmers relied on wooden ploughs and then, between 1825 and 1840, on cast-iron ones. They were without Hussey's and McCormick's reapers until the mid-1840s, and without even the cradle (a frame attached to the scythe to lay the grain evenly) until about 1820. There was not much sense of a margin between man and Nature under these conditions. This period of the Frontier West was thus characterized by a sense of loosening social bonds, and a healthy respect for – if not a fear of – the face of Nature and the problems of expansion and development.

There has been debate over what shape the American economy might have taken had it been restricted to a transportation system based on canals, rivers and oceans. Whatever the economic consequences, the social and ecological results would have differed from what did take place, and would have extended the period of weak central control and cultural diffusion. The late 1820s, however, saw the introduction of railways, and thereby made it possible to construct a national transportation system to arrest some of the centrifugal tendencies that were at work. To judge by the American response, the railway met a deeply felt need: by 1840 the country had 3,328 miles, whereas the whole of Europe had only 1,818. There was no systematic plan behind this development: many lines were short and differed in gauge from their neighbours. Chicago was not linked to New York until 1855; and it was not possible to travel from the Great Lakes to the Gulf of Mexico before the Civil War without at some point having to leave the train. Nevertheless, the railway was surpassing all other forms of transport, and grew by 28,000 miles between 1840 and 1860. In twenty years after 1851, the federal government granted over 150 million acres to railway companies to help them build into sparsely settled areas, as well as over 64 million dollars in loans to six companies to build transcontinental routes. Without the railways, and to a lesser extent the telegraph service, which first appeared in 1844 and connected the Pacific coast in 1861, a continental United States would have been far more difficult to integrate and control. Road conditions were very primitive throughout the nineteenth century: as late as 1905, the country had only 161,000 miles of surfaced roads.

It is arguable that it was national expansion before the Civil War that had the most important effects on the national culture, and yet the popularly held idea of the Frontier West would not seem to include the expansion over the humid, forested areas east of the Mississippi. By the Civil War, the tide of developers had reached the increasingly arid and treeless areas of the Great Plains, where low rainfall levels were particularly important in slowing down the pace of agricultural growth and, in the absence of costly schemes of irrigation, in turning men's minds towards cattle and sheep, which took far more room than wheat and corn. The Indian made his last stand in this West in the quarter-century after the ending of the war; but, although the classic period of White-Indian relations did not come to an end until the Battle of Wounded Knee in December 1890, the issue of which group would dominate was never in real doubt. The Frontier West of the late nineteenth century came into being in a society that had already changed the balance between man and Nature through new technologies that were bound to give the whites the advantage. In general, pioneers now had steel ploughs and reapers; after 1874 they had barbed wire; and from 1863 it was possible to enjoy the benefits of a cheap federal postal service. Although it was not possible to telephone from New York to San Francisco until 1915, no pioneer of the late nineteenth century ever experienced the isolation of the backwoodsman of seventy years before. This, of course, is the frontier of the 'Western' film.

Those who take their images from the movies find it difficult to imagine the West as dotted with mine-shafts; yet mining played a very important part in opening the trans-Mississippi West, beginning with the Californian gold discoveries. Scarcely any far-western state went untouched by rumours of gold, while mining excitements brought gold-seekers as far east as the Black Hills of South Dakota in 1875. Although the first wave of prospectors would include a large number of unconnected individuals, each seeking a personal fortune, even early arrivals soon found that the race in which they had engaged went to the forces of organization and of capital, and that the individual prospector too soon became an archaic survival in an age of wage labour. Many refused to accept the conditions imposed by employers, and very recognizable forms of industrial unrest soon characterized the mining industry. Even in the Californian gold rush, the individual found little place within two or three seasons. The employers found it easy to retaliate against recalcitrant white labour by, for instance, bringing in Chinese, so that had it not been for vestigial unionism, and for the sense that the worker could leave the mines to try his fortune elsewhere, many 'argonauts' would have found themselves part of a proletariat, a sad reflection on the dreams with which they had started out for the West.[4]

Land policies

One of the most bloody Western mining strikes, at Coeur d'Alene in Idaho in 1892, is usually mentioned in any survey of the labour history of the United States. Less bloody, but more interesting in the way it highlights misconceptions, was the first big strike of cowboys, in the Texas Panhandle in 1883. Although the frontier was always seen as the home of economic opportunity, it generally obeyed the laws of capitalism very faithfully, apart from, perhaps, its earliest years, which were often so unlike what was to follow that they may be seen as no more than an aberration from the main line of development. Some men came with capital or credit, bought up land or prime urban sites, and remained to build fortunes on these foundations. Others came as wage labourers, and stayed no longer than three or four harvests. The frontier gave more to those that had than to those that had not, for no government intervened to use it as a site for social engineering to create a utopia of greater social and economic equality.

Land policies might have been used in this direction, especially the Homestead Act of 1862, which offered any citizen or intending citizen who was head of a family and over twenty one years of age 160 acres of surveyed public land free, if he or she should reside there continuously for five years and pay a registration fee of from 26 dollars to 34 dollars. But there were at least four main reasons why the act did not lead to an egalitarian society with uniformly rising living standards. These reasons were equally important whether the pioneer bought his land from the government or other agencies.

First, although the land might be 'free', its cultivation required capital. In the 1850s, in areas with fewer problems and costs of irrigation than the arid Far West, it could require 1,000 dollars to bring a farm into cultivation and 2,000 dollars on a 100-acre farm to maximise profits.[5] Second, only a minority of even the farming population had sufficient skill and motivation for pioneering. It has been suggested that the United States shows not a stream of would-be farmers flowing from the cities to the West, but instead a flood of disgruntled farmers seeking their fortunes in the city. Possibly twenty farmers moved to town for every industrial labourer who moved to the land, and ten farmers' sons went to the city for each who became the owner of a farm anywhere in the nation.[6] Consequently, it is quite possible to argue that, as this migration shows, the industrial, not the agricultural, frontiers were the areas of opportunity for the nineteenth-century American.

The effect of the Homestead Act was limited, thirdly, because the United States government disposed of the majority of its land by other means: by auction; by grants to states for educational and other purposes; by grant to states and corporations for transportation improvement; and in return for military service during war. The government did try to control the amount of land going in to any individual's control in 1862 by distinguishing between offered land, available for private purchase in unlimited amounts, and unoffered land which could only be taken up in limited amounts under the Homestead Act and other land laws. Much of the land west of the states of Minnesota, Iowa, Missouri, Arkansas and Texas was defined as unoffered land, but those intent on large acquisitions could always buy from intermediaries like the railways or the states, or simply break a very loosely applied law. Between 1862 and 1904, only one-quarter of the public domain went to settlers under the Homestead Act, though it did have some success between 1863 and 1880 in the area that runs from Oklahoma through the Dakotas to Minnesota.[7]

The fourth reason for the failure of land policies to provide general opportunity has to do with the increasing difficulties all farmers faced in the United States as the century progressed and a world market was produced for agricultural products in which there was a long term decline in prices. Small units of production were inefficient, while it has been calculated that only 28 per cent of the total number of homesteads begun under the act of 1862 were sited in areas suitable for 160-acre farming. There was no successful irrigation policy before the Newlands Act of 1902, and irrigated land was naturally expensive. California tried an Irrigation Law in 1887 and by 1889 unimproved land with water could cost between 100 dollars and 200 dollars an acre.[8] In the Dakotas, a farmer needed to raise 20 bushels of wheat from 1 acre and receive 80 cents to 1 dollar a bushel for it if he was to do no more than stay out of debt. Between 1881 and 1914 he never received more than 1 dollar.[9]

It was by no means totally impossible to overcome this list of difficulties and acquire a farm, bring it into cultivation and make a living, albeit a modest one in most cases. It has been calculated that between 1820 and 1850 it might take a careful saver, who was well-paid and had continuous employment, ten years to acquire 500 dollars; and that after 1850, higher wages meant he might do it in five to seven years. The determined could usually rely on some credit and could begin by renting. A capital of 500 dollars in animals, equipment and cash could give a renter two-thirds of his product in the later nineteenth century.[10] The likelihood was, however, of a long and probably unsuccessful struggle to make ends meet. In 1900 only 22 per cent of all farms were owner-operated, and increasing tenancy seemed inevitably to go hand in hand with the development of the frontier.[11]

The closing of the frontier

In fact, as the nineteenth century progressed, agriculture ceased to be the single dominant employer of labour even on the frontier. In 1890 no more than half the labour force in the states and territories west of the tier from the Dakotas to Texas was employed in agriculture. In most, fewer than one in three was. After the North East, the West was, indeed, the most urbanized area of the nation. Despite the fact that there were only three cities west of St Louis in the list of the nation's fifty largest – namely San Francisco, Omaha and Denver – 30 per cent of the population of this area lived in settlements of more than 8,000 people. Altogether, there were twenty-four urban areas of over 8,000 people in the West in 1890.[12]

The growth of urban areas occurred at the same time as the development of the surrounding countryside, so that in many cases there were, simultaneously, two frontiers: one urban, and one rural. In many ways, the urban West was of great value in the process of westward expansion, for the concentration of population permitted the exercise of some centralized cultural control. The fact that the first Beethoven symphony to be heard in the United States was performed not in Boston but in Lexington, Kentucky, showed how culture in the narrow sense emanated from urban centres as culture in the broader sense did more importantly, too.[13]

The replacement of the Indian by the white man was one of the most important features of the cultural process that defined the Frontier West. This process began long before the final battle or the forced removal of tribes cleared an area of white settlement, for Indian cultures were deeply shaken by the technologies and diseases of the whites long before white men in any number appeared on the scene. There were many separate Indian cultures, so that the popular image of the Indian is no more than a careless agglomeration of characteristics taken from different tribes. Some Indians – the Pueblos are a striking example – were sedentary farmers, living in villages or small towns. One Pueblo tribe, the Hopi, was, as the name translates, pacifist – though more tribes resembled the warlike Apaches who did not, however, begin to take scalps until well into the nineteenth century, when they adopted the practice from whites. Only tribes like the Siouan-speaking Mandan and Hidatsa of the northern plains wore the familiar feathered war-bonnets, but they lived in large dug-out lodges, usually half underground, and only took to teepees on hunting expeditions. The Indians of the north-west coast had the totem pole, for theirs was a culture that worked wood, but their cedar-bark loin cloths and mountain goats' wool blankets, together with their decorated hats of basket-work, gave them an appearance quite unlike that usually associated with the Indian.[14] As so often in the construction of images of the Frontier West, that of the Indian has been reduced to a particular time and place, the post–Civil War High Plains, and then extended to all others.

The settlement of the Frontier West has been seen as a quintessential American experience, providing folk heroes and a central tradition. The winning of the West has necessarily been seen as the work of the spiritual descendants of the Plymouth and Jamestown settlers. Yet to uphold such a view it is necessary to ignore certain facts, since, for instance, about 25 per cent of the cowboys who ranged northward after the Civil War were black and perhaps another 10 per cent were Mexican. At the same time, probably three times as many foreign-born immigrants were being attracted to the trans-Mississippi West as native-born Easterners.[15] Even in the colonial period it was the Germans and the Scotch-Irish who were prominent on the frontier.

But the story of the Frontier West has been seen as a single crucial American experience for important reasons. The United States necessarily suffered great problems in establishing a sense of its own identity after the Revolution, since independence could not mean the resumption of idigenous cultural patterns, while the constant flow of goods, ideas and people, from Europe in particular, made cultural isolation impossible, and hindered the development of distinctiveness. Even before 1776, the Indian and the black posed their cultural problem, for the decision to accord them an inferior status demanded a definition of American society. In the ninetenth-century, the immigration of non-British, non-Protestant stocks posed a further challenge, increasing the possibility of cultural fragmentation. The ideology of republicanism helped prevent this, offering values that all immigrants could share, but equally as important a cohesive force was the experience of the developing Frontier West, where the challenges of distance, isolation, hardship and misfortune helped mould a common response that ignored national origin.

Thus the opening of the Frontier West and its acculturation was the result of a general commitment to a common future – even if the rewards of development were not equally distributed. By the end of the nineteenth century, a sense had grown that the steady incorporation of successive Frontiers West into the nation was of the utmost importance in maintaining a cultural identity. In a sense the new frontier was already there, in the city; still, the view of the Superintendent of the Census in 1890 that the frontier was fast disappearing was bound to introduce a period of anxious introspection, to be seen at one level in the emergence of very strong frontier themes in the national literature. At the same Chicago Columbian Exposition where Turner enunciated his thesis on national identity, the novelist Hamlin Garland, who had grown up in the 'Middle Border' of Wisconsin, Iowa and South Dakota, called in effect for a new literary frontier of realism, of local colour, of western writing – though only to find his audience from the railhead of the plains preferring a romantic gentility. But it was around this tension that the frontier began to stabilize its meaning. In the long run, the disappearance of a frontier line did not turn out to be culturally catastrophic: the nation survived, though one result of its sense of intrinsic connection between frontier and national identity was that the United States began to contemplate ending unrestricted immigration, in order to diminish the potential danger from the centrifugal forces of ethnic cultural diversity. This did not occur until the 1920s, but the frontier question underlay a number of issues in the intervening period; some, for instance, in foreign policy. During the previous 300 years the expansion of settlement and the extension of eastern cultural forms westward had together been of the utmost importance in giving a particular meaning to the European experience in North America – turning Europeans into Americans and producing a central cultural tradition to hold the nation together. Though much of that tradition rested on myth, that very fact was a reason for its success in relieving some of the tensions of a culturally pluralistic society.

The frontier in literature

Given the mythical force that came to be attached to the idea of the frontier in American culture, it is hardly surprising that it deeply affected the American literary imagination, and indeed the very nature and form of American writing. The idea of the new-found land to the West, the iconography of the wilderness, the fundamental encounter between man and Nature, the figure of the Indian: all these came to be, for the earliest American writers and their successors, among the most important motifs and themes in the national literature. Such themes, indeed, have extended beyond the boundaries of American writing to appear in European literature as well – in the pastorals of the Elizabethan and Renaissance period, for instance; in the romanticism of Chateaubriand's short Indian novel *Atala* (1801); in the ironic realism of Charles Dickens's venture to the American frontier's edge in *Martin Chuzzlewit* (1844); and in the 'Shatterhand' Western novels of the German Karl May, who did not even visit the United States until the end of his career. The sheer range of these images and myths is one of the obstacles facing those who try to define what we mean by 'the literature of the frontier'. It is, in effect, one of the reasons why the fictional form, like the historical fact, poses so many difficulties. And another reason for these difficulties is that, while the frontier has always been a central theme *in* American writing, it has also become, increasingly, an important source *of* American writing – as the cultural boundaries of the nation, and perhaps even its centre, have moved ever further westward. As a direct result of all this – the cultural shift to the West, that is, and the sheer complexity of the Western myth – the very term 'frontier literature' can be interpreted in a number of radically different ways. We could, for instance, take frontier literature to mean anything that was actually written or devised by the settlers – that is to say, literature that comes *from* the frontier. Then again, we could take it to embrace books and poems from elsewhere, which use the life of the pioneer or the Indian as their subject and setting – in other words, literature *about* the frontier. Beyond this, we could expand the term even further, to include any writing that bears the imprint of the pioneering experience and the westward movement; it could, to put it another way, also mean literature that has somehow been *inspired by* the frontier. This problem of definition is a serious one, the seriousness of which is indicated, not least, by the radical disagreements to be found among those who have considered the subject. [16]

Quite apart from these problems of form or definition, there is also the question of period. If, as the textbooks usually suggest, we identify the frontier period as being from 1607 to 1890, this might seem to mark the parameters of frontier literature: frontier literature, we could say, was written over the 300 years the frontier was actually there. But again, as in the historical discussion, there is the problem of emphasis. Was it, for example, as Turner insisted,[17] the settlement in the Middle Region in the nineteenth century that provided the definitive frontier experience and, by extension, the true sources of frontier culture? Some critics have assumed this to be so; yet this does less than justice to the Puritans and the early settlers of the Virginia Tidewater region, and it leaves out of the picture the work of modern writers, like Willa Cather and William Faulkner, who were profoundly affected by the frontier past. The specifically literary problems are the greater because literature reaches across time and space: it mythicizes, recreates, and incorporates structures from history. Indeed, if we accept the idea that literature *inspired by* the frontier is relevant, then no terminal date of any kind is possible. Even the heroes of a contemporary novelist like, say, Norman Mailer can be regarded as 'spiritual pioneers', trying to recover the frontier sense of possibility; even contemporary American literature can be seen – to quote one commentator, Van Wyck Brooks – as a 'sublimation of the frontier spirit'.[18]

The last phrase suggests a third problem. In a sweeping and memorable passage in his essay on the significance of the westward movement, Turner suggests that the frontier was 'the line of most rapid and effective Americanization' and, as such, was almost entirely responsible for creating 'a new product that is American'.[19] Literary critics have not been slow to take up Turner's suggestion and argue that what makes American *literature*, in turn, characteristically American is the consciousness of the frontier – or, more simply, that all American novels are really Westerns.[20] The flaw in this argument is, of course, that it ignores the existence of other historical factors. It evades all the problems posed by the fact that what Turner calls, at one point, 'the American mind' was formed out of a dialectical interplay between various, and often quite separate, events and structures of belief. The frontier experience did not occur in a vacuum, historical or ideological; in fact, it was itself profoundly affected, even shaped, by certain distinctively European notions. For as Lewis Mumford puts it, in his classic study of American culture, *The Golden Day* (1921):

in the episode of pioneering a new system of ideas wedded itself to a new set of experiences: the experiences were American, but the ideas themselves had been nurtured in Savoy, in the English lake country, and on the Scots moors.[21]

These are the basic problems then: the ones of definition and period, and those created by the unavoidable recognition that other forces have been at work in American history. And the first step – to adopt a pioneering metaphor – in clearing a pathway to some solutions is to admit that no blanket definition of the term 'the literature of the frontier' is possible. There are, quite simply, different types and different periods of literature associated with the westward move-ment. The second step, perhaps, is to admit that, while this does necessarily complicate matters, the frontier as a fact and a myth *has* been a formative influence in American literature – and, as such, provides a useful framework both for studying that literature and for relating it to American history and culture.

Types of frontier literature

Perhaps one indication of the sheer variety of frontier literature is that, at the most basic level, that of literature *from* the frontier, it is not even *writing* that we are talking about: a good deal of what the early pioneers actually created comes under the heading of folklore. The frontier heritage, some scholars have argued,[22] has provided most of the peculiar experiences and culturally unifying memories which enable us to talk about an American folk culture in the first place. And, even if this is open to dispute, it is still clearly the case that certain things, like cowboy songs, ballads of the '49 Gold Rush, and early songs of pioneering offer us some unique commentaries on the advance across the continent. So do the innumerable comic yarns, legends, and tall tales which helped make heroes out of the likes of Davy Crockett, Mike Fink, Paul Bunyan and Pecos Bill. The oral tradition also reminds us that there is a vast spoken tradition of Indian legends and poetry, much revived by the modern ethno-poets; but we can hardly identify that as frontier writing, however much we must root it in the classical experience of those whom the frontier displaced.

Moving away from the oral to the written, one might include in the category of literature issuing directly from the frontier certain reports and chronicles produced by the early settlers: the writings of the Puritan William Bradford, or of William Byrd the younger, in the colonial period, for instance, or of James Hall in the nineteenth century.[23] But at this point the definitions begin to blur, if only because these reports were often produced for non-frontier audiences – in colonial times across the Atlantic, and later on in the East – which inevitably affected the way in which they were written. Besides that, many of those who provided them could be described, in a way, as agents of Eastern culture – set apart from their pioneering neighbours by their background, tastes, and literary pretensions. In short, literature *from* the frontier tends to merge with the literature *about* the frontier, being written either for those elsewhere, or in retrospect. A good deal of the actual folklore of the pioneer was indeed eventually 'civilized', taken up by writers and editors further east, where it became part of the national literary tradition. The knockabout comic stories and tall tales of the frontier, for example, helped lay the foundations for south western and vernacular humour, which in turn became nationally popular through figures like Mark Twain and Artemus Ward. Davy Crockett was transformed into a national hero, thanks to his autobiography, and other widely circulated narratives; and stories about Daniel Boone, Pecos Bill, and Kit Carson provided the staple diet of the late nineteenth-century 'dime-novel'. The distinction is still there, perhaps, between a cultural document and a literary version, but it is a shifting and occasionally elusive one. Mark Twain is a useful indication of this shift. Writing of the Mississippi Valley and the mining camps of the Sierras, he inherited the comic and vernacular traditions, but amended them and at the same time moved eastward. What further complicates matters is that after the Civil War, when American literature was less clearly identified with the New England establishment, the former pioneer areas became regional literary centres, producing a good deal of writing of their own. Usually, this writing is related in some way to the last stages of the frontier process. It offers a background record of 'local colour', for example; or it concentrates, as Hamlin Garland's *Main-Travelled Roads* (1891) and *Prairie Folks* (1893) do, on the problems of declining homesteads, viewed from the standpoint of economic naturalism. But works about the experience of late-immigrant pioneers, like O E Rolvaag's *Giants in the Earth* (1927), which describes Norwegian homesteaders in the Dakotas, were still appearing in the early years of this century.

It is, however, when one turns from literature *from* the frontier to literature *about* the frontier that the floodgates begin to open, because the real impact of frontier life, as a myth or idea as well as a fact, was felt in the rest of American society, the culture of which the pioneering experience formed only one, separable part. Such literature is not only vast, it is also extraordinarily varied, ranging, as it does, from simple documentary through popular writing to imaginative work of the very first rank. First, and most obviously, there are the reports of exploration or conquest, which offer us fascinating versions of the various stages of the westward movement. From colonial times, there are the many narratives collected by Richard Hakluyt and Samuel Purchas; while the works of James Adair and Jonathan Carver provide two quite unique accounts of the frontier during the period immediately before the Revolution. The advance across the Alleghenies is vividly commemorated in the writings of John Filson *(The Discovery, Settlement and Present State of Kentucky*, 1784, which introduced Daniel Boone to the reading public) and in the work of Gilbert Imlay. Exploration of the Louisiana Purchase territory, in turn, is the subject of the journals of Lewis and Clark, prepared for publication by Nicholas Biddle (1814); while Josiah Gregg's *Commerce of the Prairies* (1844) deals with the journey along the Santa Fe Trail into the Spanish outposts of the Southwest. The migration across the plains and intermountain region to the Pacific Coast is memorably registered in Lieutenant John C Frémont's account of his expedition to the Rockies *(Report of the Exploring Expedition to the Rocky Mountains*, (1845) which among other things, established Kit Carson as a national celebrity); and the settlement of the Great Plains, and absorption of the West into the Nation, is described and interpreted in the narratives of the journalists Bayard Taylor and Horace Greeley. [24] This, however is only the beginning. Quite apart from these narratives (coloured, in most cases, by the imagination and frequently sprinkled with legend), there is a popular literature about the west, particularly in the nineteenth century. Mention has already been made of the south western humorists, whose work grew out of the folk culture of the frontier. From about 1835 until 1861, a number of writers from such old south western states as Georgia, Alabama, and Mississippi produced tall tales, scenes from provincial life, and sketches of backwoods rogues and eccentrics which were characterized by three things: broad humor, the use of dialect, and a tendency to emphasize the earthier aspects of frontier experience. Most of these writers – people like Augustus Baldwin Longstreet and George Washington Harris – liked to think of themselves as gentlemen of education and breeding. This, though, did not inhibit them when it came to recording the cruder side of pioneer life and character.

Nor did it prevent them from reproducing the language of the frontier, bold, racy and idiosyncratic, and so preparing the way for the absorption of the vernacular into American literature as a whole. [25] At the other end of the spectrum from these humorists stand the popular romancers, creators of sentimental legends. These include such writers as Timothy Flint and Robert Montgomery Bird in the earlier half of the nineteenth century, but above all the 'dime novelists' in the latter half. The 'dime novel' was devised by the editors of weekly story papers in the 1840s, and then exploited remorselessly by people like Erasmus Beadle (who manufactured millions of such books between 1860 and 1900). It was invariably written to a formula. Any exotic setting could be exploited, as the background to a series of thoroughly predictable adventures, but, for obvious reasons, the 'Wild West' was particularly favoured. The purveyors of this fiction (they can scarcely be called creators) helped to turn the Western adventurer, sometimes called Buffalo Bill or Deadwood Dick, sometimes given another name, into a popular hero. Strong, self-assured and self-reliant, he became a part of the newly emerging mass culture – and he has remained so, of course, ever since.[26]

Finally, and perhaps most importantly, as far as writing *about* the frontier is concerned, there is the work of the major writers, who incorporate the frontier into a fundamental thematic tradition. James Fenimore Cooper is of crucial significance here, since his five 'Leatherstocking' novels – *The Pioneers* (1823), *The Last of the Mohicans* (1826), *The Prairie* (1827), *The Pathfinder* (1840), *The Deerslayer* (1841) – are among the first American books to realize the epic potential of the westward movement. They are also the first to describe, however implicitly, the paradoxes on which the myth of the frontier depends. For Natty Bumppo, Cooper's hero, is at once uneducated and learned, simple and noble, practical and idealistic, innocent and experienced. He is a romantic hero, as Cooper's is a romantic perspective. And so, above all, he is at once a philosopher of primitivism, fleeing from the settlements, and an empire builder, helping to chart the wilderness and so spread those same settlements wherever he goes. This is suggested by the closing sentences of *The Pioneers*, the first of the Leatherstocking novels:

This was the last that they ever saw of the Leather-Stocking. . . He had gone far towards the setting sun – the foremost in that band of pioneers who are opening the way for the march of the nation across the continent.[27]

Natty leaves Templeton, the setting of the novel, because he feels threatened by the growth of civil society, and yet he prepares the pathway for that society – indeed, he is in some senses a part of it. He exists, at best, in a neutral territory between the forest and the clearing, nature and culture, belonging wholly to neither: which is true not only of him, really, but of all major American heroes associated with some kind of pioneer territory. 'Between savagery and civilization',[28] Turner's famous description of the American frontier area, possesses a special poignancy, not only for Natty Bumppo, but for characters like Hester Prynne, who lives on the edge between the Puritan settlement and the forest in Nathaniel Hawthorne's *The Scarlet Letter* (1850), and Huckleberry Finn, Mark Twain's innocent hero in *The Adventures of Huckleberry Finn* (1885), who gravitates all the time between the freedom of the river and the riverbank communities of the old Southwest. In a way, it has a similar poignancy for a figure like Ike McCaslin in William Faulkner's *The Bear,* who cannot commit himself, finally, either to the beliefs learned in the wilderness or to the ideas instilled in him by Southern society – and for many other heroes in modern American literature, characters who are often, in fact, several generations removed from the actual, historical frontier.

At this point, of course, we are moving towards the third and most intractable of the types of frontier literature; that is, literature *inspired by* the frontier. The danger here is that virtually every American book can be said to reflect the pioneering experience in one way or another, if only because that experience has become an integral part of the national consciousness. A certain amount of tact is required, really, to distinguish between those works which have been affected, profoundly if circuitously, by awareness of the westward movement and those in which other influences are of greater significance. For example, it is surely correct to say that much of Thoreau's writing belongs in this category. For although Thoreau was not very interested in the actual frontier (and, indeed, often said that he felt repelled by the typical pioneer's excessive materialism), he was clearly fascinated by its potential as myth. As he saw it, using a characteristic pun, the real frontier was to be found wherever a person tried 'to front only the essential facts of life'. Thinking that 'it would be some advantage to live a primitive and frontier life' even 'in the midst of outward civilization',[29] he turned himself into a pioneer of the imagination, constructing his own version of the Western experience at Walden Pond and in his books, *A Week on the Concord and Merrimack Rivers* (1849) and *Walden* (1854). Thoreau, we could say then, was writing a *kind* of frontier literature; as was Herman Melville in a work like *Moby-Dick* (1851), which describes the frontier of the sea, and Henry James, when he examined – in such novels as *The Portrait of a Lady* (1881) and *The Ambassadors* (1903) – the American frontier with Europe. But, on the other hand, we would probably be wrong to claim, as at least one critic has,[30] that Poe can be put in this category as well. Certainly, he was interested in the unknown and in dominion over nature, and many of his heroes can be described as explorers. But *his* unknown is totally inward and associated entirely with the past, while the realm his heroes explore has a heart of darkness. The burden of his imagery, if fact, and the thrust of his narratives suggest that the Old South was more important to him, imaginatively, than the West was. Obviously, this is a contentious area, where the evidence has to be weighed very carefully; and it becomes, finally, a matter of deciding at what stage an inheritance that all Americans share, by the mere fact of being Americans, is crucial to the understanding of an individual text.

The periods of frontier literature

If frontier literature needs to be seen in terms of different types, it also deserves to be looked at, just like the frontier process itself, in terms of different periods: periods in which there were not only varying historical forces at work in society but changing aesthetic assumptions at work in art. The first of these periods, the colonial, was notable chiefly for the establishment of certain crucial images of the frontier: images that became deeply attached to the very idea of America itself. Seen from the standpoint of Europe, or from the Atlantic seaboard, the newly discovered wilderness of America was transformed into what one enthusiastic commentator called

a Virgin Countrey, so preserved by Nature out of a desire to show mankinde fallen into the Old Age of the Creation, what a brow of fertility and beauty she was adorned with when the world was vigorous and youthfull. . .[31]

The myth of the virgin land was born, or rather resurrected in a new context, and with it the linked images of the pioneer and the good farmer – the one of them a man who cleared a pathway into the wilderness, and the other a sturdy yeoman who transformed his surroundings into a garden of the world.

The writers of the early national period developed these images and several others associated with the frontier,[32] bathing them in the light of Romanticism and a burgeoning nationalism. In Crèvecoeur's *Letters from an American Farmer,* for example, the small farmer inhabiting the 'intermediate space' between sea and forest is presented as someone who has experienced 'a sort of resurrection' and become, as a consequence, 'a new man'. He is another Adam, and the American wilderness offers him the possibility of recovering Eden. The point is made, without embarrassment, over and over again in the literature of this era – and often in ringing terms, as in these lines by Philip Freneau:

. . . Paradise anew
Shall flourish, by no second Adam lost,
No dangerous tree with deadly fruit shall grow
No tempting serpent to allure the soul
From native innocence.[33]

Utopianism and nostalgia are neatly combined in visions like this, as they are, of course, in the figure of Natty Bumppo. For the American West was by this time a focus for conflicting feelings; the longing for lost innocence, and a return to primal nature, was mixed with the emerging belief in some sort of manifest destiny for the nation, and the realization of a new imperial culture.

It was in the third period, however, that the belief in an imperial destiny was brought into full flower. As the westward movement accelerated with the help of the railways, and the Atlantic and Pacific seaboards were gradually bound together into one nation, so the association of the West with the idea, not merely of innocence, but of power grew steadily as well. This new assertiveness, growing out of the rapid advance of the pioneer across the entire continent, as well as a transcendental expectation of wholeness, is perhaps most noticeable in the work of Walt Whitman – as in 'A Broadway Pageant':

> I chant the world on my Western sea. . .
> I chant the new empire, grander than any before – As in a vision it comes to me;
> I chant America, the Mistress – I chant a greater supremacy. . . .

The assertiveness is there, of course, not merely in what Whitman says but in how he says it. For while celebrating the westward movement, and the experiment in living it implied, Whitman was also conducting what he called his own 'language experiment' – developing new forms, a new line and a new vocabulary, which could adequately express the vitality of this 'new empire'.

In a sense, Whitman's equivalent in prose is Mark Twain, since Twain's best work is as formally innovative as Whitman's is: *The Adventures of Huckleberry Finn* (1885), for example, which grows directly out of the tradition of Southwestern humour, is a masterpiece of the American vernacular. But, in another way, Twain is very different from Whitman because the frontier Eden described in *Huckleberry Finn* is clearly a part of the past. The book was published, after all, only five years before the official closing of the frontier and it is set, significantly enough, in a prelapsarian, ante-bellum world. Utopianism is easily outweighed by nostalgia here; the pastoral, such as it is, has tragic implications. For Twain's audience must have realized, even as they read about Huck Finn lighting out for the Territory to escape being civilized, that America had come of age and the Territories were practically gone. Here, in fact, and in some of his other books – most notably, *Life on the Mississippi* (1883) – Twain is already moving towards that image of a lost pioneer world that would haunt Sherwood Anderson, in *Winesburg, Ohio* (1919), and which permeates the novels of Sinclair Lewis, such as *Main Street* (1920). Behind the main streets of Winesburg and Lewis's Gopher Prairie lie the last remnants of a pioneer past, a past that is now being trampled under by boosterism, commerce – and by young people beating a retreat to the big city.

All of this is by way of saying that Twain does, to some extent, anticipate the literature of the fourth of our periods: an era, including the present, when the frontier as an historical fact has disappeared and when its pastoral associations must be balanced against an awareness of those changes – that process of advance towards a modern – urban society, which the frontier experience itself helped to bring about. To borrow a phrase from Leo Marx, the legend of the West and its accompanying imagery have acquired now the character of 'complex pastoral'.[34] The virgin land and the pioneer, the small farmer and the garden of the world: the possibility of actually realizing these dreams in experience has more or less vanished – and yet, as dreams, they remain alive in American thought and writing. They survive as sources of inspiration, creative myths. Of course, the forms this survival assumes are pretty various and often very subtle. The frontier and its legends may be located purely in memory, as they are in Twain's work and, more recently, in the novels of Willa Cather, like *O Pioneers!* (1913) and *My Antonia* (1918). Alternatively, the legends themselves may assume parodic form, and so act as a measure of the distance between ideal and fact: the Joads in John Steinbeck's *The Grapes of Wrath* (1939), for instance, find themselves enacting a cruel parody of the pioneer experience, journeying westward only to find a closed society and further oppression. A new setting may be sought for the imagery of pioneering – in the anonymity of the city, perhaps, where Fitzgerald's heroes, like the central figure in *The Great Gatsby* (1925), try to recreate themselves, turn themselves into sons of Adam, secreting a tale of the West in a tale of the East. Or, then again, from disorderly modern experience the writer may look back into the space of primitivism, and the apparent coherence of past history; so Hemingway's heroes return to the rituals of hunting and fishing, while some of Faulkner's characters explore the possible implications of the destruction of the wilderness. The writer, and his hero, may favour a purely inner freedom: witness the protagonist in John Barth's *The End of the Road* (1958) or the private detective of modern legend – characters who enjoy independence, and a sense of belonging to some world elsewhere, while nevertheless retaining a function within society. Or he may seek a kind of refuge in perpetual mobility – as Jack Kerouac's heroes do in, say, *On the Road* (1957) – conducting a journey without destination across the American continent, as an outward and visible sign of an inward quest. Finally, and even more subtly, the writer may take upon *himself* the role of pioneer, pursuing, as Hart Crane once put it, 'new thresholds, new anatomies'. He may try, in effect, as Crane tries in his epic poem, *The Bridge* (1930), to cross new frontiers of language and imagination, and so turn the actual text into a kind of neutral territory between the clearing and the wilderness, the familiar and the unknown.

At this point we have returned, by however circuitous a route, to the basic problem: where does 'the literature of the frontier' begin and where, if at all, does it end? What do we mean when we say a writer has been affected by the movement west? As this discussion has tried to show, there are ways of at least approaching answers to such questions, involving, among other things, a recognition of the sheer variety of frontier literature, and an acknowledgment of what is, in any case, part of the problem – the fact that the frontier (both as an experience and an ideology) has been involved in a dialectical relationship with many other forces and influences in American life.

But even if these approaches were carried through in far more detail than is possible here, it is likely that many of the problems would remain. For the legacy of the pioneer is, in some ways, like a ghost, a familiar spirit haunting the national literature. It is there when we least expect it, and are perhaps not even prepared to see it; and very often the simple question of its presence or absence must remain open to debate.

Notes and references

1. Richard B Morris, (ed), *Encyclopedia of American History,* (updated and rev. edn), Harper and Row, New York, 1965, pp. 433, 436, 442, 443, 444.
2. Ben J Wattenberg, *The Statistical History of the United States From Colonial Times to the Present,* Basic Books, New York, 1976, pp. 24–37.
3. George R Taylor, *The Transportation Revolution 1815–1860,* Holt, Rinehart and Winston, New York, 1951, pp. 141–4.
4. Mark Wyman, 'Industrial Revolution in the West: Hard-rock miners and the new technology', *Western Historical Quarterly,* **5** (1974), 45–53.
5. Clarence H Danhof, *Change in Agriculture: The Northern United States, 1820–1870,* Harvard U.P., Cambridge, Mass., 1969, pp. 95–100, 114–16, 120–1, 125.
6. Fred A Shannon, 'A post mortem on the labour-safety-valve-theory', in Ray Allen Billington (ed), *The Frontier Thesis: Valid Interpretation of American History?* Holt, Rinehart and Winston, New York, 1966, pp. 41–50.
7. Paul W Gates, 'The Homestead Act: Free land policy in operation, 1862–1935', in Howard W Ottoson (ed) *Land Use Policy and Problems in the United States,* University of Nebraska Press, Lincoln, 1963, pp. 28–46.
8. Gilbert C Fite, *The Farmer's Frontier: 1865–1900,* Holt, Rinehart and Winston, New York, 1966, p. 170.
9. Robert V Hine, *The American West: An Interpretative History,* Little Brown and Company, Boston, 1973, pp. 169–70.
10. Danhof, *op. cit.,* pp. 78, 81–93.
11. Paul W Gates, *Landlords and Tenants on the Prairie Frontier: Studies in American Land Policy,* Cornell U.P., Ithaca and London, 1973, pp. 166–7.
12. United States Bureau of the Census, *Compendium of the Eleventh Census: 1890* (3 parts), Government Printing Office, Washington D C, 1892–1897, Part I, pp. lxxiv, lxxv; Part III, pp. 400–33.
13. Richard C Wade, *The Urban Frontier: The Rise of Western Cities, 1790–1830,* Harvard U.P., Cambridge, Mass., 1959, p. 239.
14. Oliver La Farge, 'When the white man came', *History Today,* **5** (1955), 287–97.
15. Shannon, *op. cit.* pp. 46–7.
16. Compare, e.g. Lucy L Hazard, *The Frontier in American Literature,* 2nd ed., 1927, reprint. Ungar Publishing, New York, 1961; Percy H Boynton, *The Rediscovery of the Frontier,* University of Chicago Press, Chicago, 1931; Jay B Hubbell, 'The Frontier', in Norman Foerster; (ed), *The Reinterpretation of American Literature,* (3rd edn.), 1929, (reprint.

Harcourt, Brace, New York, 1959): Edwin Fussell, *Frontier: American Literature and the American West*, Princeton U.P., Princeton, 1965. Hazard accepts all three meanings; Hubbell concentrates on the first two; Fussell is interested only in the third; and Boynton suggests that there is, strictly speaking, no literature *from* the frontier (see pp. 34–5).

17. F J Turner, 'The Significance of the Frontier in American History', in F J Turner (ed) *The Frontier in American History*, Holt, Rinehart and Winston, New York, 1963, pp. 27 ff.

18. Van Wyck Brooks, cited in Hubbell, *op. cit.* p. 50. The phrase 'spiritual pioneers' appears in Hazard, *op. cit., passim.*

19. Turner, *op. cit.*, pp. 3–4, 37.

20. See, e.g. Hazard op. cit.

21. Lewis Mumford, *The Golden Day: A Study in American Literature and Culture,* (3rd edn.), 1926, (reprint. Dover Publications, Toronto, 1968), p. 20.

22. See, e.g. 'Folklore', in Robert E Spiller *et al.* (eds), *Literary History of the United States,* (3rd edn), 1946, (reprint. Macmillan, New York, 1963), Vol. 1, 704.

23. See, e.g. William Bradford, *Of Plymouth Plantation* (begun about 1630 and first published in 1856); William Byrd II, *History of the Dividing Line Run in the Year 1728* (first published in 1841); James Hall, *Legends of the West,* 1832.

24. See, e.g. Richard Hakluyt (ed), *The Principall Navigations, Voiages, and Discoveries of the English Nation,* 1589; Samuel Purchas (ed), *Hakluytus Posthumus; or, Purchas His Pilgrimes,* 1625; James Adair, *The History of the American Indians,* 1775; Jonathan Carver, *Three Years Travel through the Interior Parts of North America,* 1778; John Filson, *The Discovery, Settlement, and Present State of Kentucky,* 1784; Gilbert Imlay, *Topographical Description of the Western Territory of North America,* 1792; Meriwether Lewis and William Clark, *History of the Expedition Under the Command of Lewis and Clark,* 1814; Josiah Gregg, *Commerce of the Prairies,* 1844; John Charles Frémont, *Report of the Exploring Expedition to the Rocky Mountains in the Year 1842,* 1845; Bayard Taylor, *El Dorado; or, Adventures in the Path of Empire,* 1850; Horace Greeley, *An Overland Journey, from New York to San Francisco,* 1860.

25. For further details see, e.g. Constance Rourke, *American Humor: A Study of the National Character,* Doubleday, Garden City NY, 1931; Walter Blair, *Native American Humor (1800–1900),* American Book Co., New York, 1937: Hennig Cohen and William B Dillingham (eds), *Humor of the Old Southwest,* Houghton Mifflin Co., Boston, 1964.

26. See, e.g. Timothy Flint, *Francis Berrian; or, The Mexican Patriot,* 1826; Robert M Bird, *Nick of the Woods,* 1837. For further details about the 'dime novelists' and their heroes see, e.g. Henry Nash Smith, *Virgin Land: The American West as Symbol and Myth,* Harvard U.P., Cambridge, Mass., 1950; Edmund Pearson, *Dime Novels; or, Following an Old Trail in Popular Literature,* Little, Brown, Boston, 1929; Richard J Walsh, with Milton S Salsbury, *The Making of Buffalo Bill: A Study in Heroics,* Bobbs-Merrill, Indianapolis, 1928.

27. James Fenimore Cooper, *The Pioneers; or, the Sources of the Susquehanna,* 1823, Ch. 41.

28. Turner, *op. cit.* p. 3.

29. Henry David Thoreau, *Walden*, Ch. 2.
30. Fussell, *op. cit.*, pp. 132 ff.
31. Edward Williams, *Virginia, more Especially the South Part Thereof, Richly and Truly Valued*, 1650, in Peter Force (ed), *Tracts and Other Papers Relating Principally to the Origin Settlement, and Progress of the Colonies in North America, from the Discovery of the Country to the Year 1776*, (2nd edn.), 1836–46 (reprint. P. Smith, New York, 1947), pp. 3, 19,
32. For example, the two opposed images of the Indian created by the white imagination: the Indian as noble savage and the Indian as imp of the devil. See, e.g., Russel B Nye and Norman S Grabo (eds), *American Thought and Writing, Volume I: The Colonial Period*, Houghton Mifflin, Boston, 1965, pp. 119, 121.
33. Philip Freneau, 'The Rising Glory of America', lines 443–7; Hector St John De Crèvecoeur, *Letters from an American Farmer* (1793), Letter 3.
34. Leo Marx, *The Machine in the Garden: Technology and the Pastoral Ideal in America*, Oxford U.P., New York, 1964.

Chapter Six

The immigrant experience

R A Burchell and Eric Homberger

A teeming of nations

From its colonial days the United Sates has been a society of immigrants. 'Whence came all these people?' asked Crèvecoeur in the 1770s. 'They are a mixture of English, Scots, Irish, French, Dutch, German and Swedes. From this promiscuous breed that race now called Americans have arisen.' Or, as the poet Walt Whitman put it some eighty years later, 'Here is not merely a nation but a teeming of nations.' In over 350 years, close to 50 million men, women and children have entered the United States as immigrants. Yet in Crevècoeur and Whitman, as in most other descriptions of this process, there is an ambivalence, suggesting on the one hand the singularity of American society and on the other the variety of those entering it. Not surprisingly, the attempt to accommodate within a single nation these disparate, often mutually hostile, groups of newcomers, with their particular national and ethnic habits and loyalties, has been one of the key themes in American history.[1]

Broadly viewed, immigration is the product of two sets of factors: those pushing migrants from their homelands, and those drawing them towards particular destinations. Both were invariably involved, although often in differing proportions. Mid-nineteenth-century Irish immigration, for example, was largely the result of the expelling force of the famine, just as late nineteenth and twentieth-century Jewish migration was triggered off by pogroms. Sometimes an individual voice speaks out: 'My father had been an upholsterer, doing a very good business, but having always had a great wish to go abroad, thought it, I suppose, a good opportunity, when his place burned down.'[2] Often, too, one can detect in literature, as in the following late nineteenth-century Swedish 'American Ballad', the nature of the forces of attraction:

> Out there in the fields
> There grows English money.
> Ducks and chickens come raining down
> Roasted geese, and others yet
> Fly onto the table,
> With knife and fork stuck in 'em.[3]

In the early twentieth century, farm and factory labourers in East Prussia, workers in the Russian anthracite coal fields, and unskilled labourers in Poland, could not but be impressed that their American counterparts were enjoying, respectively, double, three times, and five times, the income they were earning.

High wages due to labour shortages in the United States drew immigrants across the Atlantic. So too did the 'padroni', or immigrant bosses who propagandized and mediated between the immigrant labourers and their new society. Steamship companies, and the agents of American land speculators, railroads and private employers, combined to present potential immigrants with attractive images of the United States. The supply and demand for information grew together. In January 1867, William Hepworth Dixon finished his *New America* and published it in London. By April 1869, he was writing a note to the eighth English edition and stating that 'in the two years of its young life this book has already passed, in various languages, through more than forty editions'. Among its main attractions was its image of an America, where 'a man will find himself growing free. . .in daily contact with the newest forms of life, with a world in the earlier stages of its growth, with a society everywhere young in genius, enterprise and virtue'.[4]

These images of America derived in large part from its dynamic economy. But immigrants also felt impelled to move by virtue of the massive increases in Europe's population from around 192 million in 1800 to 423 million in 1900.[5] Improvements in communications and transportation further encouraged populations long since used to migrating within the continent of Europe to consider trans-Atlantic movement. In 1825 a passage to America could cost £20, but by 1865 steamships were charging only £5 and by the 1890s it was possible to cross for less than £4. Moreover, once the first members of a particular group had settled, they could help to pay for later comers. Perhaps as much as one-third of all emigrant passages to the United States were paid for in this way.

Generally speaking, the history of American immigration divides into four periods: from Jamestown to the Revolution; from the Revolution to 1896; from 1896 to 1921; and from 1921 to the present day. In the first period, the immigrants came mainly from Great Britain and Ireland, with a sizeable eighteenth-century German contingent. In the second, the composition remained roughly as it had been, but with the addition of Scandinavians and a higher proportion of Irish and Germans. In the third period, the majority of immigrants arrived from southern and eastern Europe. In all three periods immigration went virtually unrestricted, though not unregulated; since 1921 the United States has imposed an annual limit on the numbers permitted to enter.[6]

Table 6.1 sets out immigration by decade for the period for which reliable figures are available. Immigration will be seen to have reached its first peak in the Famine years of the 1850s; to have been comparatively low in the Civil War decade and in the 1870s and 1890s, decades in which the United States experienced economic recessions; and to have reached an all-time high in the decade 1901–10, when southern and eastern Europe in particular poured out millions of emigrants. To be more accurate, immigration peaked in the ten-year period 1905–14, when over 10 million people entered the United States, Throughout the period 1841–1920, the annual rate of immigration never fell below 5.3 per thousand of the United States population, reaching close to 10 per thousand in the decades 1841–50, 1851–60, 1881–90 and peaking at 10.4 per thousand in the decade 1901–10. Since 1931 the rate has not exceeded 2.3. The figures for the preceding decades help to explain why unrestricted immigration produced native hostility.[7]

Table 6.1 Total immigration by decade: 1820–1970 (in thousands)

1820–30	152	1871–80	2,812	1921–30	4,107
1831–40	599	1881–90	5,247	1931–40	528
1841–50	1,713	1890–1900	3,688	1941–50	1,035
1851–60	2,598	1901–10	8,795	1951–60	2,515
1861–70	2,315	1911–20	5,736	1961–70	3,322

Although immigrants have arrived in the United States from all over the world, some societies have provided a disproportionate share. The most significant sources of immigration to date are set out in Table 6.2. together with the year in which immigration from each peaked, and at what total. Briefly, until recently, Europe has been the major source of immigrants, though since 1965 and thanks to new legislation this has changed. Between 1820 and 1975, 76.4 per cent of immigrants came from Europe; 4.8 per cent from Asia; and 17.7 per cent from the Western Hemisphere. But between 1971 and 1975, the figures were 21.1, 31.7, and 44.7 per cent, respectively, the last representing principally immigration from Mexico, the Caribbean and Latin America.[8]

Some parts of the nation have been more affected by immigration than others. Table 6.3 shows the position in the United States in 1890, on the eve of the massive immigration from south-eastern Europe, and in 1920, on the eve of restriction. By 1890 the immigrants of the preceding decades had mostly moved away from the ports of entry, but the immigration of the next decades stopped very largely on the east coast. This table shows how much the development of the northern and western states owed to immigration and how little effect it had on the southern states. Scandinavians and Germans tended to settle in the Mid-West in the earlier period; the English and Irish to prefer New England and the Middle Atlantic states. In the later period, Jews, Italians, and Slavs, finding themselves excluded from American

Table 6.2 Total immigration by major area of last permanent residence, together with year and numbers at the peak of immigration: 1820–1971 (in thousands)

	Total	Peak immigration	
		Year	Number
Germany	6,926	1882	251
Italy	5,199	1907	286
Great Britain excl. Ireland	4,805	1888	109
Ireland	4,715	1851	221
Central Europe excl. Germany	4,528	1907	339
Canada and Newfoundland	3,991	1924	201
USSR and Baltic States	3,379	1913	291
Scandinavia	2,483	1882	105
Mexico	1,643	1924	89
Other North-western Europe	1,628	1882	28
Southern Europe excl. Italy	1,187	1921	76
Poland	488	1921	95
China	451	1882	40
Japan	370	1907	30

agriculture, in part by its high costs, tended to settle in eastern urban and industrial areas. Not surprisingly, therefore, Italian literature set in the rural Mid-West is rare, as is Jewish literature relating to the South. Willa Cather's Bohemians farmed in Nebraska; their story could not easily have been put into a New England setting; likewise Peter Finley Dunne's Irish philosopher, Mr Dooley, dispensed his wisdom from an urban environment; it would not have been the heat alone that would have shrivelled him to representative insignificance had he set up his saloon in Arizona. There is a regionalism to the history and literature of American immigration, and a need to explain the career of each ethnic group in terms of its own history, its character before migration, its period of arrival and its place of settlement. These factors ensured very different experiences for immigrants from each group.

Table 6.3 Percentage total population native-born, by region: 1890, 1920[9]

	1890	1920
New England	52.8	39.0
Middle Atlantic	52.6	46.0
East North Central	55.5	57.4
West North Central	58.7	62.1
South Atlantic	94.1	93.8
East South Central	95.4	96.9
West South Central	88.4	88.7
Mountain	54.4	63.2
Pacific	49.0	53.4

Uprooting and re-rooting

Although it is difficult to generalize about the effects of migration upon the individual, it is plain that some succeeded better than others in pulling up old roots and planting new. Those from societies which were more like the United States had fewer problems of recognition, less trouble in understanding their new home, and consequently experienced less dislocation. British immigrants, familiar with the language, with either the agricultural techniques or the contours of urban and industrial living, aware of common political, religious and cultural roots, generally had fewer problems, particularly as their migration was in the main voluntary. Much the same applied to the Protestant Irish (Scotch-Irish according to American terminology) and English-speaking Canadians. The Catholic Irish, on the other hand, found themselves set apart by their religion. Anti-Catholicism was a prominent feature of American life, then and well into the twentieth century. Not all Catholic Irish were peasants; those who came from Dublin, Limerick or Cork, with legal skills, or who were able to buy property, did not find themselves completely excluded from wealth, power or status, but many others did.

The Catholic Irish, in fact, are an instructive example of what could happen to immigrant groups in the United States. In their case, as in many others, their sense of group solidarity, their 'ethnicity', was in part an American creation – a defensive response to a hostile environment which led to the smoothing over of internal feuds within the Catholic Irish community itself, such as the traditional hostility between Cork men and Limerick men, Dubliners and Far-Downers. Furthermore, the Irish community provided a level of opportunity within itself for its more able, educated and wealthy members. Enterprising Irishmen achieved upward social mobility by providing political, legal, economic and cultural leadership for their fellows. The Irish also took control of the Catholic Church and used it to give them national importance and status, and their familiarity with the language and the forms of politics brought them early rewards which put them into the mainstream of the republic's life. Thus, as time passed, and even when the group had achieved a significant socio-economic position, provided a President of the United States, and overturned earlier stereotypes of the shanty Irish, a sense of ethnicity continued to exist, sustained by marriage, residential and educational patterns. As the Catholic Irish experience clearly shows, ethnic groups did not want, even if indeed they could, to diminish their identity in important respects by giving up what made the world intelligible to them – their culture.

The Jewish flight to America encountered not only native hostility and an unfamiliar culture but a strange language as well. Their great strengths were their sense of group identity and their belief in the values of education. Education opened the professions, though anti-semitism attempted to close them, and acquisition brought wealth and status in a capitalist, plutocratic republic.

Less well adapted to life in the new land were the peasants. These included many Irish and Germans as well as the Italians, Slavs and other southern Europeans who arrived at the end of the nineteenth century. These were not men and women loyal to the land so much as loyal to their immediate kin and locality. They had neither the capital nor the entrepreneurial skills and knowledge for American agriculture at the turn of the century, and so went from being unskilled rural to unskilled urban and industrial labour in general in one move. Scandinavians, however, were the most likely of all groups to transfer from agriculture in the old country to the same in the new.[10] Groups that left agriculture necessarily had to adjust to more than a change of homeland: in some cases they moved from a pre-modern rural to a modern urban situation with the further problems that this entailed.

Religious prejudices affected many of these immigrants, while colour or 'racial' prejudices affected others. Although, geographically, Mexicans did not move far to reach the south-west of the United States, they entered a world in which they were far from welcome once they had provided their labour. They were not, for instance, classed as white by the United States census of 1930. Colour prejudice – that is, the assumption that a different skin colour implied biologically inherited social incapacities – was also evident in the treatment of Oriental immigrants, exacerbated by the fact that a wider cultural gulf separated them from the members of the host culture than was the case with most European immigrants. The Oriental experience also illustrates the fact that much of the bitterest hostility encountered by immigrants came not from the native-born but from other immigrant groups – as the Chinese discovered in their encounters with the Irish on the West Coast in the 1870s. Nativist fears of 'the yellow peril' led to the ending of unrestricted Chinese immigration in 1882 and of unrestricted Japanese immigration in 1907–8. Even this, however, did not fully allay fears, with the result that although the descendants of German immigrants suffered no significant discrimination during the Second World War (one of them was indeed put in charge of the invasion of Germany), almost the entire Japanese–American community spent the war languishing in camps under close armed guard.

It is important to recognize that the immigrant world functioned at two levels: the public and the private. Accordingly, the immigrant's dislocation or uprootedness had two very different dimensions. Most immigrants found it hard to assimilate the public values of the new society, but they managed to do so in the long run – so achieving what has been termed *behavioural assimilation*. By contrast, they were often significantly reluctant to adopt other, more private aspects of American life – attitudes toward marriage or child-rearing, for example – and American native stock was not often eager for close personal ties with the newcomers; this diminished the possibility of what has been called *structural assimilation*.[11] Although the sometimes dogged retention of old-world values made groups conspicuous, and vulnerable to nativist attack, it also strengthened the immigrant in the hour of need. Immigrants embraced the republican ideology of the United States, with its accent on political equality and equality of economic opportunity. But, while they adopted many cultural externals, they found it difficult to be sure about what they should give up in exchange. There was inter-generational disagreement over what values of the new society could be safely adopted, what additions might be psychologically destructive. Parents often suffered as they saw their children acculturating faster than they did. One immigrant later recalled that even in the first weeks after arrival,

We had to visit the stores and be dressed from head to foot in American clothing; we had to learn the mysteries of the iron stove, the washboard, and the speaking-tube; we had to learn to trade with the fruit pedlar through the window, and not to be afraid of the policeman; and above all we had to learn English. . . . With our despised immigrant clothing we shed also our impossible Hebrew names.[12]

Clearly, some of these changes made life easier, but some – like the change of name, a common occurence – had consequences that could be far-reaching. Not only traditionalists would worry about the prospect of being renamed in adult life.

The experience of uprooting, migration and re-rooting was thus a complex rite of passage. Often, however, individuals could rely on more than their private efforts in experiencing it. Once the first few migrants had pioneered a connection between the old world and the new, others could follow, in what has been called a 'chain migration'. For instance, between 1887 and 1947, 8,000 people followed the original emigrant Francesco Barone from Valledolmo in Sicily to Buffalo, New York.[13] Italians, however, tended to be the extreme case: among those who settled in Cleveland around 1900, fully a quarter arrived in chains of 100 migrants or more, while the median number of Romanians in village chains was only around 5, and of Slovaks less than 4.[14] Of families, Italian, Irish and French Canadians seemed to hold up particularly well during migration, so supporting the individual. Another important supportive role was played by locally based associations, particularly in the form of the myriad benevolent societies (the Mafia indeed functioned as one such), often first founded in the new world. Often they were very particular in membership: for instance, in Cleveland, twenty-five of the thirty-five Italian mutual benefit societies incorporated between 1903 and 1910 limited members to persons born in a particular village – though once again, Italians seemed to have more local sense than other groups, and Rumanians, Greeks and Slovaks in Cleveland formed general associations, as did Poles and Lithuanians in Massachusetts, and Irish,

Germans and Scandinavians in San Francisco.[15] Entry to such associations was the easier since many newcomers lodged with fellows from their old village: one immigrant, looking back, recalled that her parents' home 'always contained a "greener" or two from Polotzk, whom we lodged as a matter of course until they found a permanent home.' Such clusterings as these certainly helped to produce what can be called immigrant ghettoes, where like sought out like, especially in the very difficult early years. But it is wise to remember, in using the term, that these ghettoes were temporarily created from a flood of immigrants who overwhelmed housing stocks; that they did not occur automatically, especially when immigrant numbers were small; that they had a voluntary side to them; and that they were not – except in rare cases, as in Chinatown – monolithic blocks of population, excluding all other groups. Thus the American immigrant ghettoes were not synonymous with the Jewish ghettoes of Europe. The present-day Jews of Providence, Rhode Island, may jocularly refer to their largely upper-class suburb as 'a gilded ghetto', but no more than a brief genuflection to a now distant historical memory is implied.[16]

Inevitably, there were failures – men and women who found that migration took more than it gave. Some foundered in America, others returned to their homeland (though groups like the Irish or Jews could not do so, and had to sink or swim where they were). Figures are hard to come by, but between 1908 and 1924 more Croats, Slovenes, Russians, Italians, Slovaks, Magyars and Rumanians actually returned home than stayed in the United States.[17] Of course their transience had something to do with expectation and intention; many came to work for short periods only. But some returned as failures, and it is relevant that these groups were culturally quite removed from the host society. Still, this point should not be taken too far – eight out of ten Ruthenians who arrived between 1908 and 1924 appear to have migrated permanently, just as did eight out of ten Scots, Germans, English and Scandinavians, all of whom had, by this date, fewer cultural barriers to breach than the southern and south-eastern Europeans.

The Melting Pot?

In a famous passage in *The Melting Pot* (1909), Israel Zangwill, an English Jew, described his vision of how immigrants and America would interact. His major character David Quixano proclaims, pointing downward from his garret window:

There she lies, the great melting-pot. Listen! Can't you hear the roaring and the bubbling? There gapes her mouth [points East], the harbour where a thousand mammoth feeders come from the ends of the world to pour in their human freight. Ah, what a stirring and seething! Celt and Latin, Slav and Teuton, Greek and Syrian, black and yellow . . .

VERA [his girl friend] Jews and Gentile–
DAVID Yes, East and West and North and South, the palm and the pine, the pole and the equator, the Crescent and the Cross, how the great Alchemist melts and fuses them with His purging flame. . .[18]

No cultural anthropologist, aware of the inner strength and coherence of cultural patterns, would today treat Zangwill's views as founded on anything more than sentimental optimism. Those Americans, mainly of British Protestant origins, who supported the Know Nothing party of the mid-1850s, the American Protective Association of the late 1880s and early 1890s, or the Ku Klux Klan in the 1920s, all partly reactions to rising immigrant numbers, would also have opposed Zangwill, but for different reasons. Ostensibly they wished the immigrant to give up his cultural differences and accept the necessity of what has been called Anglo-conformity, that is, to take on native-stock values in their entirety. Such a demand was fundamentally hypocritical, as the following two passages suggest. In 1877 the Chinese were attacked by the California State Senate because they insisted on their separate identity:

During their entire settlement in California they have never adapted themselves to our habits, mode of dress, or our educational system, have never learned the sanctity of an oath, never desired to become citizens, or to perform the duties of citizenship, never discovered the difference between right and wrong, never ceased the worship of their idol gods, or advanced a step beyond the traditions of their native hide.

In 1910, however, the Japanese in California were reminded that

Had the Japanese labourer throttled his ambition to progress along the lines of American citizenship and industrial development, he probably would have attracted small attention of the public mind. [But] Japanese ambition is to progress beyond mere servility to the place of the better class of American workman and to own a home with him. The moment that this position is exercised, the Japanese ceases to be an ideal labourer.[19]

Attitudes to the Chinese and Japanese immigrants were likely to be partly the result of racial prejudices, but the underlying irrationality of the nativist's position recurred through all their views on the immigrants. At the end of the nineteenth and beginning of the twentieth centuries, it was argued, drawing on the work of Charles Darwin and particularly on that of Herbert Spencer, that there were essential 'racial' differences between north-western and south-eastern Europeans, which must prevent the latter from ever achieving full parity. These ideas, and fears of the 'dilution' of the American racial stock, helped to justify ending unrestricted immigration.

In the 1920s, when immigration restriction was increasing and the long-term multi-ethnic character of the United States was much more apparent, a third view of the immigrant began to be conceptualized, especially among sociologists. This was 'cultural pluralism', the warmest advocates of which tended to be Jewish social scientists and politicians, who saw their own position in the United States as inextricably related to the broad acceptance of diverse ethnic cultures within the nation. They argued that the survival of ethnic differences would actively enhance and strengthen national life through the richness of diversity. The balance between ethnic variety and national homogeneity was always delicate in the United States, functioning on the margin of the yet more intractable problem of relations between blacks and whites. It is perhaps easier to describe ethnic diversity than it is to define the national cultural norms upon which the demand for Americanization rested. It would certainly not be correct to say that the national culture can be described as the sum of the constituent ethnic cultures. Although ethnicity survives in the United States, and affects many individuals in important ways, correlating with such factors as occupational prestige, family size and income, length of education, the character of political participation and voting, marriage, residential patterns and religion, there are whites who do not consider themselves to belong to any ethnic group. Likewise, there are those whose remote ethnic origins are Protestant British, but whose difficult case cannot be dealt with merely by making out that White Anglo-Saxon Protestants are themselves a single, identifiable and discrete ethnic group. [20] The fact that, in 1972, three-fifths of those surveyed by the Bureau of the Census identified themselves with a single country of origin suggests why ethnic cultural patterns persist, but it tells nothing of the strength of the identification. The fact that two-fifths of those surveyed failed to specify a single nation of origin illuminates the problems for any generalizations about the degree and intensity of present-day ethnic awareness in the United States. [21]

Other societies have experienced mass immigration, but none of such size and diversity as the United States. Whereas other societies have been clear about their national culture, against which immigrants could be measured and usually found wanting, the birth of the United States in a revolution that ended in national independence without the resumption of indigenous cultural patterns left the nation searching for an identity. The national culture was being defined as politically egalitarian and democratic when the first large-scale immigration (including men and women who were not culturally identical to those already settled in the United States) occurred. Immigrants and native stock alike thereafter had to work out a common national destiny, with important disagreements over the proper content of the national culture. Such a process could come to no easy or early resolution, and the resulting tensions were at the heart of much of the social conflict that occurred in the United States in the century after the Great Hunger.

Yet, paradoxically, the virulence of ethnic conflict has led to a relative absence of class conflict in the European sense, for ethnicity in the United States warped the traditional European class structure, making it difficult to analyse class relations in America with the conceptual tools deriving from European experiences. Ethnic diversity meant that the American labour movement would differ in several important respects from the European. The divisions within the workforce along ethnic and racial lines weakened labour, and prevented the emergence of a political party which expressed its ideology. Socialism developed independently of the labour movement, and its failure to become a significant force in American politics may in part be attributed to the historic weakness of the labour movement. Throughout all ethnic groups there are ample indications of class-based behaviour, even of class-consciousness; but the fact of ethnic variety produced a pattern of political and social relationships which is highly idiosyncratic by European standards.

The immigrant experience in literature

Certainly by the later nineteenth century, America was a nation of immigrants, but there was a perceptible gap between the social reality and the way Americans customarily thought about their society. In cultural terms, the immigrants remained largely invisible and irrelevant until well into the present century. In the nineteenth century, 'culture' was white, Anglo-Saxon and Protestant; perhaps most strikingly, Americans looked to German universities, Parisian *salons,* and British writers for cultural models. A provincial society, with a provincial culture, young American artists and writers streamed across the Atlantic towards the great capitals of European culture. The lowly immigrants on board the ship carrying Wellingborough Redburn back from Liverpool (in Herman Melville's *Redburn,* 1849) were 'the most simple people I had ever seen. They seemed to have no adequate idea of distances; and to them, America must have seemed as a place just over a river. Every morning some of them came on deck, to see how much nearer we were: and one old man would stand for hours together, looking straight off from the bows, as if he expected to see New York city every minute, when, perhaps, we were yet two thousand miles distant, and steering, moreover, against a head wind'.[22] Melville was appalled by the conditions faced by the Irish immigrants in steerage: 'In every corner, the females were huddled together, weeping and lamenting; children were asking bread from their mothers, who had none to give; and old men, seated upon the floor, were leaning back against the heads of the water-casks, with closed eyes and fetching their breath with a gasp'.[23] Melville makes a number of suggestions for improving conditions for the immigrants, in the name of Christianity and of sheer humanity, and resolutely opposes any attempt to restrict immigration.[24] It could hardly be expected that such 'simple people' could make a contribution to American life. Even in provincial America the cultural gap between Melville, married to the daughter of the Chief Justice of the

Massachusetts Supreme Court, and the illiterate.Irish immigrants was too great. Generations would be required. During the rest of the century, the immigrants are occasionally brought within the purview of literature, but usually in a passive manner as part of a richly heterogeneous culture (for Whitman), or as a newly complicating factor in American life (for Howells).

Yet in the nineteenth century there were works by those who had been through the fundamental experience of immigration – works by Irish writers, or German emigrants like 'Charles Sealsfield', the pseudonym of a runaway German monk, who wrote *Das Cajutenbuch* (1841). Immigrant communities produced newspapers, magazines and, in larger cities, were able to support theatre and vaudeville in their native tongue. The settled communities of Germans, Scandinavians, Poles, Hungarians and Jews sought to preserve their cultural traditions in various ways. Pioneer settlements on the plains sought to preserve their own cultural tradition (the story of pioneer Scandinavian experience was to be powerfully recorded by writers like O E Rolvaag, who emigrated in 1896, and whose *Giants in the Earth* (1927) would prove the classic novel of immigrant life in the Dakotas). Levels of literacy were high, and educational activities flourished. Ethnic newspapers, like the Jewish *Daily Forward,* played a major role in sustaining the sometimes tenuous cohesion within immigrant communities, and provided a crucial window upon the larger arena of American life. The most highly educated immigrants still lived within the stream of European culture. They read Manzoni or Goethe or Chekhov and Gorky, and knew nothing of Twain and Howells. Ironically, Europe remained the focus for culture in the dominant American society as well as within the immigrant community. Or at least, that part of it which was literate. Many Americans were appalled at the ignorance of the newcomers. In the eyes of European visitors, the immigrants seemd particularly contemptible:

And the emigrants! They are horrible. They're not at all like those who made America. Today's emigrant is simply Europe's rubbish, its waste matter, a lazy, cowardly, impotent little manikin drained of energy without which there's no getting on here. A modern emigrant is incapable of making life, all he can do is look for a ready-made, safe and smug existence.[25]

Ironically, in this withering judgement Gorky was merely voicing the prejudices of those Americans whose materialism and hypocrisy he found so disgusting.

Progressives and muckrakers wrote with great concern over the conditions within immigrant ghettoes. The classic text, written by a former immigrant who had worked for a dozen years as a police reporter, was Jacob Riis's *How the Other Half Lives* (1890). The horrors of the urban slum were revealed. Hoping to arouse public conscience, Riis more specifically tried to show landlords of tenements that improved sanitary conditions would be in their own economic interest. With Riis we are on the edge of a modern approach to the problem, but do not cross the barrier. In the end his appeal is to a change of heart, and not action by the state:

The gap between the classes. . .is widening day by day. No tardy enactment of law, no political expedient, can close it. Against all other dangers our system of government may offer defence and shelter; against this not. I know of but one bridge that will carry us over safe, a bridge founded upon justice and built of human hearts.[26]

Ultimately, the immigrants themselves were the major 'social problem' and a more sympathetic approach to their dilemmas was made through the Social Settlements.[27] The most famous of these was Jane Addams's Hull House in the west side of Chicago. The settlements championed the immigrant poor, encouraged their cultural development, and defended their economic cause. Jane Addams in Chicago soon discovered that it was not enough to suggest ways in which capitalists might make a profit by improving conditions for the immigrants: she saw, unlike Riis, that the political arena was precisely the place where improvement should be sought. She led the fight for labour legislation, improved treatment of juveniles in the legal system, sanitary regulations, and a host of other areas. The immigrants were pawns, in one sense, in a struggle between the high-minded reformers and the corrupt bosses of the urban political machines. But with the appearance of Jane Addam's *Twenty Years at Hull House* in 1910 it is clear that the immigrants are beginning to be perceived as subject as well as object.[28]

It was no mere coincidence that at the time when the Settlements were founded, and when the 'New Immigration' was dramatically increasing, immigrants become a real presence in literature. One of the earliest examples is Stephen Crane's *Maggie: A Girl of the Streets* (1893). Crane, excited by the new possibilities for literature opened up by the naturalism of Zola, portrayed the violence, drunkenness and corruption of slum life in New York. *Maggie*, which asked searching questions of the relations between moral codes and social conditions, gave a powerful portrait of the culture of the new immigrants. When Pete and Maggie go to the 'show', Crane beautifully captures the scene:

As a final effort, the singer rendered some verses which described a vision of Britain annihilated by America, and Ireland bursting her bonds. A carefully prepared climax was reached in the last line of the last verse, when the singer threw out her arms and cried, 'The star-spangled banner.' Instantly a great cheer swelled from the throats of this assemblage of the masses, most of them of foreign birth. There was a heavy rumble of booted feet thumping the floor. Eyes gleamed with sudden fire, and calloused hands waved frantically in the air.[29]

Upton Sinclair's *The Jungle* (1906) contained an explosive account of the conditions in 'Packingtown' (Chicago). The Lithuanian immigrants who have been brought into the stockyards to depress wages are abused on a systematic basis. Sinclair records the weakening of traditional customs under the pressures of capitalism and dog-eat-dog individualism. His main concern was to make a case for socialism. No one could have been more surprised than Sinclair, the most famous socialist propogandist in America, when the public seized upon his portrayal of the unsanitary conditions in the canning industry. Hoping to build the New Jerusalem, he created the Food and Drug Administration: 'I aimed at the public's heart and by accident I hit it in the stomach'.[30]

But all too often the vaudeville caricatures of Wop, Polack, shanty Irish and Jew prevail in literary representation. The same sterotypes in fact appear within the ghetto, but serve rather different purposes: they enabled the partly assimilated to mock the greenhorn. The cultural life of the ghetto was richer than generally credited, as Hutchins Hapgood suggested in *The Spirit of the Ghetto* (1902). There was, however, an undercurrent of sadness: the cultural achievements of the immigrants were self-extinguishing. Social mobility continually creamed off the cleverest and most adaptable. The inexorable pressure toward assimilation into the dominant way of life left a ghetto culture unable to believe in its own permanence. Its memorials are in diaries, letters, native-language newspapers and journals, and, supremely, in auto-biographical memoirs.

The literary forms which lent themselves to immigrant writing were the realistic novel and fictive memoir. An important moment of recognition came when William Dean Howells welcomed Abraham Cahan's *Yekl: A Tale of the New York Ghetto,* when it appeared in 1896.[31] The author was a recent immigrant from Russia who had established himself as a socialist and journalist. A disciple of Howells, Cahan wrote consciously within the modes of realism. Although *Yekl* is not the first book by an immigrant, it is the first to be seriously considered as literature. Howells noted that Cahan, like Stephen Crane in *Maggie,* has done his duty as an artist by having drawn aside the thick veil of ignorance which parts the comfortable few from the uncomfortable many in this city. Such books as *Yekl,* a bitter-sweet tale of love in the ghetto, and autobiographies like Mary Antin's *From Plotzk to Boston* (1899) and *The Promised Land* (1912), Jacob Riis's *The Making of an American* (1901), and Edward Bok's *The Americanization of Edward Bok* (1920), now began to establish the dominant forms of immigrant writing. It was strongly autobiographic-al, and usually took the form of a success story, if often with an ironic twist. The immediate ancestry of this body of writing lay in the self-improving ideas of Samuel Smiles, the Horatio Alger books, and the underlying myth signified by the story of the man who rose 'from log cabin to White House'.[32] In the late nineteenth century such ideas were the staple product of American popular culture, and they repeatedly enforced the message that, by hard work, perseverance, and quick wits, it was indeed possible to achieve an unimaginable success within American capitalism – an idea that had attracted many immigrants to the United States in the first place.[33] The immigrant experience, despite the difficult adjustments which were required, reinforced this aspect of American ideology, and the immigrant autobiographies and memoirs became an addition to the genre.

The immigrant success story, however, had another side which was suggested by the titles of the now neglected novels of Anzia Yezierska: *Hungry Hearts* (1920) and *Children of Loneliness* (1923).[34] Where for Mary Antin the immigrants' arrival in America was the beginning of a new life, for Yezierska, America was at best a mixed blessing. Promising so much, America cruelly frustrated those who came most open-heartedly. For Antin, 'America' was an idea which stood not only for a new society but also for the very possibility of human self-fulfilment. Inevitably, romantic dreams came into contact with the intractable and often harsh reality of life in the urban ghetto. This is the theme of Abraham Cahan's later, better-known novel, *The Rise of David Levinsky* (1917). It is a remarkable book which spoke directly to the romantic dreams of the immigrant, but contained many home truths about America and about immigrants themselves. Cahan was an ironic writer, and irony was a way to comprehend the sometimes harsh distance between dream and social reality that was so often characteristic of the immigrant experience of American life. Levinsky arrives in America from the Pale of Settlement in Russia, and gradually comes to terms with the new reality of American life. A crucial symbolic threshold is crossed when Levinsky, strongly advised that 'one must be presentable in America', has his fore-locks cut off. A scene follows which was enacted hundreds of thousands of times:

I stood before him, necktie and collar in hand, not knowing what to do with them, till he showed me how to put them on.

'Don't worry, David', he consoled me, 'When I came here I, too, had to learn these things'. When he was through with the job he took me in front of a looking-glass. 'Quite an American, isn't he?' he said to the barber, beamingly. 'And a good-looking fellow, too.'

When I took a look at the mirror I was bewildered. I scarcely recognized myself.

I was mentally parading my 'modern' make-up before Matilda. A pang of yearning clutched my heart. It was a momentary feeling. For the rest, I was all in a flutter with embarrassment and a novel relish of existence. It was as though the hair-cut and the American clothes had changed my identity.[35]

Cahan follows Levinsky's schooling in the new land: he learns to deceive and cheat, to exploit workers, and how to make a fortune. Levinsky is a success story, and his narrative, related in the first person, is obviously modelled upon the autobiographies of figures like Riis and Bok. But at the end of the book Levinsky is a hollow, lonely man, more to be pitied than envied. Cahan is not trying to score a narrow or partisan point off the budding Levinskys of the lower East

Side. Certainly his well-known sympathy for the unions and advocacy of democratic socialism provides a way of looking at Levinsky – as a 'fleecer of labor' and a 'cockroach manufacturer'. We are given other perspectives on Levinsky, especially those offered by the women he has met, which make it clear that Cahan's criticism of the dream of success has more than a political meaning; rather, Levinsky's failure is to be judged on an emotional and humane basis. Instead of cut-throat competition, through the portrait of Levinsky's emotional failure Cahan holds up an alternative image of selflessness, sacrifice and solidarity.

Cahan's irony was based on a perceived gap between the intensity of the immigrant's aspiration and the reality of its fulfilment in America. Although there was nothing like a uniform 'immigrant experience', the basic events of passage from the past and the familiar to the present and the new imposed a form on consciousness itself. The dichotomy between old world and new, and the division of identity (which Cahan so vividly captures), expressed a larger economic and social dilemma which all immigrants faced. The space between one world and another, or one generation and another, was often filled with irony. There are kind and affectionate ironies, as when Mike Gold in *Jews Without Money* (1930) describes his father as an 'upright conservative pauper'. There is a deeper irony, however, in the father's disillusionment and bitterness at his own failure in America:

'Look at me,' he said. 'Twenty years in America, and poorer than when I came. A suspender shop I had, and it was stolen from me by a villain. A house painter foreman I became, and fell off a scaffold. Now bananas I sell, and even at that I am a failure. It is all luck.'

He sighed and puffed at his pipe.

'Ach, Gott, what a rich country America is! What an easy place to make one's fortune! Look at all the rich Jews! Why has it been so easy for them, so hard for me? I am just a poor little Jew without money.'

'Poppa, lots of Jews have no money', I said to comfort him.

'I know it, my son,' he said, 'but don't be one of them. It's better to be dead in this country than not to have money. Promise me you'll be rich when you grow up, Mikey!'

'Yes, poppa.'[36]

Mikey, of course, has other ideas, which lead him to Max Eastman's *Masses* and *Liberator,* to the *New Masses,* and to the Communist Party. That we know all this adds yet another layer of irony to his father's words of advice. Gold and Cahan's political irony is not characteristic of immigrant writing as a whole, but is a useful reminder that the seemingly straightforward autobiographies and realistic novels become, through their use and emendation of the structural irony in the immigrant experience, complex texts in their own right.

There were other points of tension which complicated the 'rags to riches' myth. In the nineteenth century, traditional religious cultures came into open conflict with the materialism and secular spirit of the modern world. This was to give yet another ironic tension to the immigrant experience. As Sarah Reznikoff writes in hear 'Early History of a Seamstress', her desire for education (traditionally allowed only to men in orthodox Jewish culture in the *shtetl*) initiated a conflict which could only be resolved by migration to America – but in America there was no time for education, only work.[37] In Nathan Reznikoff's autobiographical narrative, a young boy in America finds the ritual fast more an endurance test than a meaningful religious observance. Religious faith itself becomes an unintended casualty of immigration. The conflicts within families and between sexes altered the way people viewed each other. Expectations long-sanctioned by tradition were undermined, and tradition itself became problematic. Irony became one of the great liberating tools in the struggle against the burden of tradition. But such ironies had an uncomfortable habit of cutting the other way. For the thoroughly Americanized second and third generation, modern America was ashes in the mouth, and tradition suddenly seemed more relevant. When asked to write about the Jewish experience in America, the hero of Joseph Heller's *Good as Gold* (1979) discovers that he knows nothing at all about it. That is the bitterest irony of all.

Growing up in America

By the second and third generation, these ironies were sharpened and made more specific because America itself was more accessible. Literary life became visibly more plural as a German-Jewish generation of writers emerged (Hergesheimer, Hecht, Frank, Lewisohn – to say nothing of Dreiser, not Jewish of course, but close to his immigrant roots). Throughout the 1920s Gertrude Stein was a liberating influence on younger writers, Sherwood Anderson in particular. Stein's experimental use of language taught Anderson, in the words of Irving Howe, that 'at least in the actual process of composition, words could have an independent value: they could be fresh or stale, firm or gruelly, colored or drab.'[38] Stein's *The Making of Americans* (1925) is both a Cubist novel and a classic story about the myth of American success. Along with the emergence of a conspicuous presence in literature, the sons and grandsons of immigrants began to appear in every area of American cultural life: popular entertainment, music, painting, photography, the theatre. So pronounced was their arrival that the conflicts facing second- and third-generation immigrants emerged in the popular culture. The struggle between tradition and the American way of life was exceptionally difficult in real life, but on the stage reconciliation was not too difficult to bring about. In the third act of Anne Nichol's *Abie's Irish Rose* (1924), gentile Rose keeps a kosher kitchen for her husband Abie, but makes ham for her non-Jewish friends. They have two babies: Patrick Joseph and Rebecca. Relations between Christians and Jews may have been uneasy in the real world, but on Broadway the priest and the rabbi shake hands and agree that love conquers all. *Abie's Irish Rose* is a 'melting pot' play, after Zangwill, in which the old heritage of distrust in wished away:

What with all the shells bursting [on the Argonne], and the shrapnel flying, with no one knowing just what moment death would come, Catholics, Hebrews and Protestants alike forgot their prejudice and came to realize that all faiths and creeds have about the same destination after all.'[39]

Sociologists might remind us that intermarriage between Jews and Catholics was fairly uncommon. At the turn of the century the rate of Jewish 'in-marriage' was just under 99 per cent. By 1950 the figure was 96 per cent.[40] How, then, can we explain the immense popularity of *Abie's Irish Rose?* Mainly in terms of the perfectly reasonable wish for some easing of ethnic tensions. The play symbolically enacts not so much the end of Jewish apartness as the beginning of Jewish integration, as Jews, into the community. It evades the reality of racial and religious tension, but not the underlying process, which was to bring Herbert Lehman to the governorship of New York.

The prosperity of 1920s acted as a great solvent in the ghettoes of New York. Business was good, and as immigrants prospered they moved into middle-class neighbourhoods. A decade later there was an explosion of interest in what it had been like to grow up in the ghetto. Mike Gold's *Jews Without Money* set the fashion in 1930, and was followed by a novel of substantially greater merit: Henry Roth's *Call It Sleep* (1934). Roth's recreation of his childhood was heavily influenced by psychoanalytic thought, by then well established in New York,[41] and by the techniques of stream-of-consciousness narrative and the use of symbols pre-eminently shown in the work of Joyce, Gertrude Stein and Virginia Woolf. *Call It Sleep* is, with Faulkner's *The Sound and the Fury,* one of the very few American books which belong to the period of high-European modernism between the wars. What may be Roth's greatest innovation is his treatment of one of the most fundamental of all immigrant dilemmas, the linguistic one. The Schearl family use Yiddish at home, which Roth represents by a clear, lean, standard English devoid of mannerisms. Roth counterpoints this with a close phonetic transcription of a grotesque Brooklyn-Yiddish-American-English as spoken on the streets of New York (Howells, writing of Cahan in 1896, prophetically wondered whether 'we shall have a New York jargon which shall be to English what the native Yiddish of his characters is to Hebrew, and it will be interlarded with Russian, Polish and German words, as their present jargon is with English vocables and with American slang.')[42]:

'Aaa, dawn be a wise-guy! Hooz tuckin' f'om vinninn'! A dollar 'n' sexty-fife gestern! A thuler 'n' sompt 'n – ove hadee cends – Sunday! An' Monday night in back f'om Hymen's taileh-shop, rummy, *tuh* sevendy. Oy, yuh sh'd die. An' I sez if yuh ken give a good dill, Abe, yuh sheoll dill in jail auraddy!'[43]

Which might be translated as:

Oh, don't be a wise-guy! Who's taking [anything] from [the] winnings? A dollar and sixty-five yesterday! A thaler [?a half-dollar] and something-over eighty cents – on Sunday. An [on] Monday night in [the] back of Hymen's tailor shop, [we played] rummy, [and I won] two [dollars and] seventy [cents]. Well, you would have died to have seen it! And I said, if you can't give [me] a good deal, Abe, you'll surely [wind up] dealing in jail!

Roth helps us to see that within the ghetto it was *English* which was the bastard tongue.

Call It Sleep is an 'education' novel, if not a full-blown *bildungsroman*, and throughout the decade memoirists like Joseph Freeman (*An American Testament*, 1936) and novelists from immigrant families were busily at work on multi-volume novel sequences reconstructing the way ethnic children grew up. The most famous of these realistic narratives was James T Farrell's portrait of Irish-American life in Chicago (*Young Lonigan*, 1932; *The Young Manhood of Studs Lonigan*, 1934; *Judgement Day*, 1935). No less striking was Daniel Fuchs's trilogy describing Jewish life in the Williamsburg section of Brooklyn (*Summer in Williamsburg*, 1934; *Homage to Blenholt*, 1936; *Low Company*, 1937).

By this time mass immigration was over, and the tragedy of European Jewry was beginning to unfold in Germany. As the process of acculturation proceeded, many Jews, especially among the younger intellectuals, identified Jewishness itself with the restraints which foreignness imposed on their families. Lionel Trilling's rejection of a Jewish dimension to his criticism, and his lack of interest in Jewish culture, defines the situation with clarity. On the left, the Communist Party offered a different path towards integration, but one which no less comprehensively demanded the abandonment of the traditional religious culture. Many Jewish and ethnic writers drifted into the Party orbit, and some, like Clifford Odets (*Waiting for Lefty*, 1935), actually learned from the experience. But for most the attempt to write proletarian literature was an unhappy and brief adventure before proceeding on their various ways. The Jewish presence in the Party was always strong, and throughout the 1930s influential. But the Stalin – Hitler pact and the war itself accelerated the process of integration by which ethnic intellectuals became simply Americans and joined the national consensus. The writers of Trilling's generation in New York had 'arrived' by the 1940s, and the New York family, as it was later called, emerged as the dominant voice of post-totalitarian humanism. Critics including Trilling, Meyer Schapiro, Harold Rosenberg, and Philip Rahv; the poets Delmore Schwartz and Howard Nemerov; and novelists such as Norman Mailer and Saul Bellow signalled the presence, on a massive scale, of writers from immigrant background. The arrival had taken approximately fifty years from Howell's review of *Yekl*. When Trilling wrote a long piece rescuing Howells from neglect, no one seems to have caught the irony.[44]

The temper of immigrant writing after the Second World War was almost exclusively set by Jewish writers. Few of them wrote from within the religious faith. Judaism, rather, was an embarrassment, to be mainly dealt with in terms of comedy and irony. Ethnic consciousness declined throughout the 1950s, as assimilation proceeded apace. Inevitably a new round of ironies began. Philip Roth portrayed a comic confrontation between unworldly religious orthodoxy and the new, assimilated suburban Jew in 'Eli, The Fanatic' (*Goodbye, Columbus*, 1959). Not wholly free from nostalgia, Roth finds the fanatic more praiseworthy in the end than the surburbanites. The title of the volume is ironic, but it is the knowing irony of Sholom Aleichem and Mendele Mocher Sforim rather than the specific form of structural irony which had been so characteristic of immigrant writing. The preoccupations of immigrant literature lost some of their uniqueness in this period, when the living experience of immigration passed on to other ethnic groups. The urban ghetto now belonged to the blacks, and to their literature. It was mainly through nostalgia and humour that this experience was recalled by Jews (the numerous books by Harry Golden and the H*Y*M*A*N K*A*P*L*A*N novels of Leo Rosten). There were important exceptions, such as Bernard Malamud's *The Assistant* (1957), but for most Jewish writers their roots in the immigrant experience loomed less significantly than their awareness of the travails and complexity of contemporary American life. Characteristic tones of Jewish writing in the 1960s were either grossly self-indulgent (Roth's *Portnoy's Complaint*, 1969), blackly comic (Joseph Heller's *Catch-22*, 1961) or else painfully introspective (Saul Bellow's *Herzog*, 1964): in each case the novels transcended the specific historic experiences of Jews in America and spoke to the common experience.

The return to ethnicity in the late 1960s was a general phenomenon whose causes are complex. The war in Vietnam and the civil rights movement divided America, and shook the complacent assumption that there actually was a consensus within which one could find a place. The great renewal of interest in ethnic foods, peasant dress, music and drugs were cultural signs of a political crisis. Many groups which had previously been content to ignore their roots in the immigration experience began to rediscover their own, and their family's roots. The greatest beneficiaries of this new mood were undoubtedly the blacks, but the consciousness itself was widespread. The trend toward comprehensive assimilation could not be reversed by an epiphenomenon like this (it had an economic basis), but the feeling was widespread in the literature of the 1970s that ethnic attachments mattered. It appears in the work of poets like Louis Simpson (*Adventures of the Letter I*, 1971), Philip Levine (*1933*, 1974), and Jerome Rothenberg (*Poland/1933*, 1974), who take advantage of a new tone of personal immediacy in contemporary American poetry to use their ethnic heritage. The poetry of Charles Reznikoff and Carl

Rakosi was discovered in this period. Reznikoff, in particular, is of interest because he is one of the very few Jewish writers in America to be seriously interested in Jewish and Biblical history. The novels of Chaim Potok and Robert Kotlowitz (*Somewhere Else,* 1972; *The Boardwalk,* 1977) are infused with a new ethnicity, as are the stories of Cynthia Ozick, Grace Paley and Hugh Nissenson. In figures like Kenneth LePeters and Stan Buchta, central characters in novels by Bruce Jay Friedman (*The Dick,* 1971) and Irvin Faust (*The File on Stanley Patton Buchta,* 1970), we see the uncomfortable rebirth of ethnic awareness on the part of Jewish policemen.

The achievement of Isaac Bashevis Singer, whose books have all been written in Yiddish, inevitably stands to one side of the general movement of Jewish and ethnic writing in America. Singer is an undoubted genius, and, since Heine, the greatest of all Jewish writers. But he can never truly be part of an American literature (the same point might hold true for Nabokov) in that the exile and *émigré,* as opposed to the immigrant, only reluctantly if at all consciously accept a new identity for themselves. Those of Singer's stories and novels which have been set in America do not constitute the most important part of his work. Perhaps Singer's reputation was helped by the rebirth of ethnicity, but that is purely fortuitous and accidental; in any culture 'Gimpel the Fool' and *The Slave* would be acknowledged as the masterpieces they undoubtedly are. (Except that is, in his native Poland where Singer's books are wholly unknown.)

It is no small irony that the run-down slums of the lower East Side in New York, and similar ghettoes elsewhere, have come to stand for values which for many people are now under threat. The ghetto was remembered in the 1960s as the place where one's hopes for America survived intact. It was a symbol of an unalienated way of life, at once warm and human. And thus it joined the great procession of popular myths and fantasies feeding American culture. The ghetto and its immigrants have been transformed from the tense and ironic locale of Abraham Cahan to the chic sepia-tinted Little Italy of Mario Puzo's Don Corleone (*The Godfather,* 1969). Nostalgia, like other commodities, is now packaged and promoted. Even in such an implausible guise, the ghetto retains its power to remind us of a world we have now lost.

Notes and references

1. The continuous record of immigration to the United States begins with an Act of 1819. Between 1820 and 1976, 47.5 million immigrants reportedly entered the United States. See US Bureau of the Census, *Statistical Abstract of the United States 1977,* Government Printing Office, Washington D C, 1977, p. 83. The figure of 50 million excludes blacks whose experiences under slavery distinguished them from voluntary

immigrants. The quotation from Whitman is taken from *Leaves of Grass*, (1855).

2.   Percy G Ebbutt, *Emigrant Life in Kansas,* Swan Sonnenschein, London, 1886, p.1.

3.   Quoted in H Arnold Barton,*Letters from the Promised Land: Swedes in America, 1840–1914,* University of Minnesota Press, Minneapolis, 1975, p.34.

4.   William Hepworth Dixon, *New America* (8th edn), Hurst and Blackett, London, 1869, pp. x, 220.

5.   *Chamber's Encyclopaedia,* (New and rev. edn), Pergamon Press, Oxford, 1966, Vol. XI, p. 78.

6.   Brinley Thomas, *Migration and Economic Growth: A Study of Great Britain and the Atlantic economy,* (2nd edn), Cambridge U.P., Cambridge, 1973, p. 96; Philip Taylor, *The Distant Magnet: European Emigration to the U S A,* Harper and Row, New York, 1971, pp. 94–5; M A Jones, *American Immigration,* University of Chicago Press, Chicago, 1960, p. 105.

7.   Figures for Table 6.1 taken from Ben J Wattenberg (ed), *The Statistical History of the United States: From Colonial Times to the Present,* Basic Books, Inc., New York, 1976, p. 105; figures for decadal rates of immigration against population are from *Statistical Abstract 1977,* Government Printing Office, Washington D C, 1977, p. 81.

8.   Figures for Table 6.2 from Wattenburg, op. cit., pp. 105–9; *Statistical Abstract 1972,* Government Printing Office, Washington DC, 1972, p. 92; for the overall composition from *Statistical Abstract 1977,* p. 83.

9.   Native-born here comprise native-born whites of native-born parents; Blacks and Indians. Figures for 1890 and 1920 compiled from *Compendium of the Eleventh Census: Population,* Government Printing Office, Washington DC, 1892, pp. 473–4; *Abstract of the Fourteenth Census,* Government Printing Office, Washington DC, 1923, pp. 98, 100.

10. Rudolph J Veccoli, '*Contadini* in Chicago: a Critique of *The Uprooted*', *Journal of American History,* **51** (1964), 404–17; US Bureau of the Census, *Abstract of the Thirteenth Census of the United States 1910,* Government Printing Office, Washington DC, 1914, p. 197; Constantine M Panunzio, *The Soul of an Immigrant,* Macmillan, New York, 1921, pp. 77–8.

11. See Milton M Gordon, *Assimilation in American Life,* Oxford U.P., New York, 1964.

12. Mary Antin, *The Promised Land,* Houghton Mifflin, Boston, 1912, p. 187.

13. Virginia Yans-McLaughlin, *Family and Community: Italian Immigrants in Buffalo, 1880–1930,* Cornell U.P., Ithaca and London, 1977, p. 17.

14. Josef J Barton, *Peasants and Strangers: Italians, Rumanians, and Slovaks in an American City, 1890–1950,* Harvard U.P., Cambridge, Mass., 1975, pp. 53–4.

15. Barton, op. cit., pp. 60–1; *Report of the Massachusetts Commission on Immigration,* Wright and Potter, Boston, 1914, pp. 202–5; Bradford Luckingham, 'Immigrant life in emergent San Francisco', *Journal of the West,* **12,** (1973), 600–17.

16. Antin, op. cit., p. 273; as Louis Wirth said, 'The ghetto is not only a physical fact; it is also a state of mind.' See Wirth, *The Ghetto,* Chicago U.P., Chicago, 1969, p.8.

17. Imre Ferenczi and Walter F Willcox, *International Migrations* (2 vols), National Bureau of Economic Research,Inc., New York, 1929, 1931, Vol II, p. 477.

18. Israel Zangwill, *The Melting Pot: A Drama in Four Acts,* William Heinemann, London, 1919, pp. 184–5. These are almost the play's closing lines.

19. Quoted in Mary R Coolidge, *Chinese Immigration,* Henry Holt, New York, 1909, p. 87; and in Harry H L Kitano, *Japanese Americans: The Evolution of a Sub-culture,* Prentice-Hall, Englewood Cliffs, NJ, 1969, p. 16.
20. An attempt is made is Charles R Anderson, *White Protestant Americans: From National Origins to Religious Group,* Prentice-Hall, Englewood Cliffs, NJ, 1970.
21. For correlations today with ethnicity, see Andrew M Greeley, *Ethnicity in the United States: A Preliminary Reconnaissance,* John Wiley and Sons, New York, 1974, especially pp. 35–89, 122–55.
22. Herman Melville, *Redburn: His First Voyage,* (ed Harrison Hayford, Hershel Parker and G Thomas Tanselle), North-Western U.P. and the Newberry Library, Evanston and Chicago, 1969, p. 260.
23. Ibid. p. 287.
24. Ibid. p. 292.
25. Maxim Gorky to K P Pyatnitsky, August 1906, *The City of the Yellow Devil: Pamphlets, Articles and Letters About America,* Progress Publishers, Moscow, 1972, p. 133.
26. Jacob A Riis, *How the Other Half Lives,* with an introduction by Donald N Bigelow, Sagamore Press, New York, 1957, p. 226.
27. See Allen F Davis, *Spearheads for Reform: The Social Settlements and the Progressive Movement 1890–1914,* Oxford U.P., New York, 1968.
28. See Jane Addams, *Twenty Years at Hull-House,* with a Foreword by Henry Steele Commager, New American Library, New York, 1961; and Allen F Davis, *American Heroine: The Life and Legend of Jane Addams,* Oxford U.P., New York, 1974.
29. Stephen Crane, *An Omnibus,* (ed Robert Wooster Stallman), Alfred A Knopf, New York, 1968, p. 67.
30. Upton Sinclair, *The Jungle,* with an Afterword by Robert B Downs, New American Library, New York, 1960, p. 349.
31. 'New York low life in fiction', New York *World,* 26 July 1896, reprinted in *Howells às Critic,* (ed Edwin H Cady), Routledge & Kegan Paul, London and Boston, 1973, pp. 256–62.
32. John G Cawelti, *Apostles of the Self-Made Man,* University of Chicago Press, Chicago and London, 1965.
33. See, for example, the obituary of Cornelius Vanderbilt in the New York *Herald* in 1877, reprinted in Henry Nash Smith (ed) *Popular Culture and Industrialism 1865–1890,* Anchor Books, Garden City, NY, 1967, pp. 102–124.
34. Yezierska's *Bread Givers* (1925) has been reprinted with an Introduction by Alice Kessler Harris, Braziller, New York, 1975.
35. Abraham Cahan, *The Rise of David Levinsky,* with an Introduction by John Higham, Harper and Row, New York, 1960, p. 101.
36. Michael Gold, *Jews Without Money,* Horace Liveright, New York, 1930, p. 301.
37. Charles Reznikoff, *Family Chronicle,* Norton Bailey with The Human Constitution, London, 1969.
38. Irving Howe, *Sherwood Anderson,* Methuen, London, 1951, pp. 95–6.
39. Anne Nichols, *Abie's Irish Rose,* (acting edn), Samuel French, New York, 1937, pp. 78–9. Nichols's play was one of the most popular ever produced on Broadway, running for 2,532 performances. It was adapted for the movies in 1928 and again in 1945.
40. Gordon, op. cit., p. 181.
41. See Paul Roazen, *Freud and His Followers,* Alfred A Knopf, New York, 1975.

42. *Howells as Critic*, p. 261. See also Howells's writings on dialect in literature, pp. 231–242.
43. Henry Roth, *Call It Sleep*, Michael Joseph, London, 1963, p. 408.
44. Lionel Trilling, 'W D Howells and the Roots of Modern Taste', *Partisan Review*, **18** (September–October 1951), pp. 516–36.

Chapter Seven

The black experience

C W E Bigsby and Roger Thompson

Blacks and Slavery

Between 1619 and 1860 some 400,000 blacks were transported from Africa to what is now the United States. This was not a large number as compared with the total Atlantic slave trade which carried around 9.5 million Negroes to the New World, most of them to the sugar plantations of Brazil and the Caribbean. Whether slaves were transported direct to North America or by way of the Caribbean made little or no difference to the blacks themselves; torn from their families and villages, marched to the coast, confined in Barracoons to await a passing ship, then crammed below decks for upwards of two months, they were finally brought ashore to be auctioned off. How many enslaved blacks perished in Africa it is impossible to say, but on average (depending on period) between 6 and 16 per cent died during the voyage and perhaps as many again during the subsequent period of seasoning.

In one respect, however, those Africans who found themselves in North America may be deemed to have fared better than those who went elsewhere; they became part of a population which was not only self-sustaining, but which actually grew at more or less the same rate as the surrounding white population. Thus, the abolition of the slave trade of the United States in 1807 did not bring about a decline in slave numbers, as was the case in Britain's West Indian colonies. The great westward cotton boom of the early nineteenth century depended on ever-increasing numbers of American-born slaves. In fact, the original 400,000 black slaves transported to North America had, by the time of the Civil War, increased ten-fold to more than 4 million.

One consequence of the natural increase of slaves in America was that among them little in the way of specific African practices, institutions, customs or beliefs survived. Except in the very earliest years, blacks born in Africa were always outnumbered by the American-born; and probably less than one in a hundred of the slaves emancipated by Lincoln had actually seen Africa. Even in the eighteenth century, when recently arrived African captives, recognizable by their tribal scars and wild appearance, were to be found in sizeable numbers, their ability to communicate with one another, on account of differences in language and culture, was strictly limited. For them, as for the native-born, the only common language and institutions available were those provided by their white masters. And yet it would be hasty to assume that, because it is difficult to trace specific linguistic and institutional links, nothing from the African past survived. It is hard to imagine, for example, that slave songs, slave stories and, closely associated with both, slave religion, were entirely the product of their American experiences – that *any* group, consigned to slavery, whatever its previous history, would have produced the same songs, stories and beliefs. Altogether it makes much more sense to suppose that, as with other immigrants, something survived, even though it is definable only as a style of music or a way of seeing things. Culture, as Lawrence Levine has argued, is 'not a fixed condition but a process: the produce of the interaction between the past and the present'. This was, of course, true of white American culture no less than of black; the difference was that blacks looked back on *two* pasts – their own, dimly remembered, African past; and the Euro-American past from which the dominant culture drew its strength, and to which they themselves owed not only their language but also many of their beliefs.

This mixed and ambiguous note is equally evident in the work of the first black American poets emerging, surprisingly enough, in the eighteenth century. Phyllis Wheatley (1753–84), the young slave of a Bostonian family, celebrated in verse the enforced move from Africa to America as a liberation from paganism, a redemption of the soul consequent upon an enslavement of the body. Yet, despite the patent prejudices of her audience, she was equally capable of observing the ironies of her situation, linking a conventional opposition to tyranny with her own circumstances. In her poem to the Right Honourable William Earl of Dartmouth she observes:

> Should you, my lord, while you peruse my song,
> Wonder from whence my love of *Freedom* sprung,
> Whence flow these wishes for the common good,
> By feeling hearts alone best understood,
> I, young in life, by seeming cruel fate
> Was snatched from *Afric's* fancied happy seat:
> What pangs excruciating must molest,
> What sorrows labor in my parents' breast!
> Steel'd was the soul and by no misery mov'd
> That from a father seiz'd his babe belov'd.
> Such, such my case. And can I then but pray
> Others may never feel tyrannic sway?

The mere fact of her ability to intrude her own racial perspective into the orthodoxies of English poetics stood as a challenge as well as an apparent, if inevitable, act of capitulation. Her ability to learn was itself a social as well as a literary fact at a time when the presumption of incorrigible ignorance in blacks was uneasily bolstered by laws prohibiting their education. And her command of literary form was potentially a subversion of the intricate balance of social and political as well as aesthetic structure.

Much the same could be said of the slave narrative, which was intended to do much more than narrate a history of injustice. It was a declaration of literary and social independence. It was simultaneously an assertion of selfhood and a set of political propositions. By definition, such narratives celebrated an achieved freedom but they were also agents of that freedom in offering paradigms of social action and in constituting evidence of an achieved selfhood. The man who narrates his own experience thereby possesses it, reclaims it from those who had asserted rights over all aspects of his experience. The narrative changes the passive into the active voice. For the most part these narratives were unsentimental, if naïve. Sentimentality was displaced into fiction, into works like William Wells Brown's *Clotel* (1853), the first novel written by an American Negro. But this, in turn, generated a series of stereotypes which, in seeking to liberate the black from enslavement, entrapped him in a myth which proved more enduring than slavery and which, primarily through popular culture, constituted a sustained assault on the black American's identity. Indeed, the patronizing caricatures of plantation literature (Thomas Nelson Page's *Red Rock,* 1898; Margaret Mitchell's *Gone with the Wind*), the vicious distortion of Thomas Dixon's *The Clansman* (1905), and the casual stereotypes of Hollywood films, generated social fictions which were all too easily transmuted into social fact by those seeking a single model of political, economic and metaphysical reality.

But the emergence of black culture was itself not simply a matter of asserting command over the written word. The work songs, hollers, and chants of the field slave were both sustaining a heritage whose roots lay elsewhere than the soil of Alabama and Tennessee, and laying down the material out of which black folk and popular culture would itself grow. Ironically, one consequence of imbibing white culture was to strengthen blacks' awareness of the contradictory nature of their own bondage. How to justify holding some people in slavery while permitting freedom to others had been a perennial problem for pro-slavery apologists, but it created particular problems for Americans on account of their country's proclaimed dedication to the principles of freedom, equality and democracy. How could a nation which valued such ideals hold four million of its inhabitants in bondage? This was a troubling question because the obvious answer – that the two could not be reconciled and that the slaves should be freed – carried with it the implication not only of bloodshed but of the possible destruction of the nation itself. In the event, the Civil War came and the nation survived, although only after half a million soldiers North and South – one for each eight slaves emancipated and more than the original number of blacks imported – died in the struggle. Yet it was only when the war was over and the slaves had been emanciptated that it became clear that this was merely a first step and that, if ever blacks were to achieve equality in the fullest sense, much more would be required.

The black experience and radical reconstruction

It was in 1865, with the South's defeat in the Civil War, that the black American entered history, in the sense of being able to control his own experience and, at least potentially, deflect the course of the social and political system which was now required to take cognizance of his freedom, even to the extent of legislating against its too effective utilization. Slavery may have fed, clothed and sheltered him adequately, organized his work, trained him in artisan and agrarian skills, even treated him less cruelly than Harriet Beecher Stowe, in her abolitionist novel *Uncle Tom's Cabin* (1852), had imagined. But the 'peculiar institution' had systematically denied literacy, freedom of movement, and any sense of racial pride or personal autonomy to blacks; they were pitched unprepared into the world of freedom. As Union armies rampaged across the South, Negroes, automatically emancipated by Northern conquest, stopped work, walked off plantations, to follow Sherman's marauders or to revel in unfettered movement. The task that followed – that of social and personal reconstruction, the reconstruction of a selfhood harrowed by slavery and denied by patronizing and proprietorial whites, who had imposed on them the twin images of 'sambo' or the 'uppity nigger' – was complicated by the fact that the South, where most blacks lived, was ravaged, pauperized and bitter in defeat. Its immense investment in slavery had been liquidated, its manhood decimated, its cotton-based economy dislocated. The underdeveloped section of ante-bellum America had become a post-bellum disaster area. But some Southern institutions survived. One was the belief in white supremacy; the most degraded 'poor white trash' knew himself superior to the most elevated 'nigger'. The immediate Southern answer to emancipation – symptomatic of what the black could expect in the South for a century – was the Black Code, which continued the restrictions of slavery and reduced Negro constitutional rights to a mockery.

Blacks looked to the North, especially to the radical abolitionist wing of the young and still insecure Republican Party, led by Thaddeus Stevens, Charles Sumner, and others. But Republicans were partly distracted by partisan considerations: confrontation with Lincoln's successor Andrew Johnson, the prospect of a revived Democratic Party, based on increased Southern representation arising from emancipation, the fear that politically innocent Negroes could be used by their ex-masters as voting-fodder. It was these conflicts and apprehensions that conditioned the policy of 'Radical Reconstruction', which sought to disfranchise rebel leadership and also to politicize blacks on the Republican side. This policy was effected by the passage of the Fourteenth (1868) and Fifteenth (1870) Amendments to the Constitution, guaranteeing blacks 'equal protection of the laws', and forbidding states from disfranchising any person because of 'race, color, or previous condition of servitude'. The result of 'Radical Reconstruction' was that the South, deemed now to be a territory, was placed under military rule. General O O Howard organized the Freedman's Bureau, initially for welfare assistance to unsupported blacks, later as a facility for their education, legal protection and economic aid. By 1868 adult male Negroes had the vote. This they used, under protection of Northern bayonets and prompted by Republican Union League agents, to return not only scalawags – white Southern Republican sympathizers – and carpetbaggers – Northern migrants into the South – but also significant numbers of their own race to county, state and federal offices. The lower house of the South Carolina legislature had a majority of Negro members: 87 blacks to 69 whites; South Carolina, Mississippi, Louisiana and Florida all had blacks in high executive and judicial posts; 14 Negroes sat in the House of Representatives, 2 in the Senate. They took part in the state constitutional conventions, which guaranteed freedmen full political and civil rights. South Carolina and Lousiana even forbade educational segregation in their public schools. Such blacks were rarely newly freed men. Many had lived in the ante-bellum North; some were ministers or teachers by profession; a few – like Senator Hiram Revels of Mississippi – had college educations, or – like Jonathan J Wright, Supreme Court Justice of South Carolina – had been members of the bar in the North.

Reconstruction has had a bad record, and indeed there was corruption, embezzlement and incompetence, especially from carpetbaggers, in several Southern states. But there was a serious attempt to replace the shattered economic infrastructure, and to spread educational opportunities. Blacks eagerly grasped the educational chances offered by state, religious and philanthropic organizations. 'It was a whole race trying to go to school,' Booker T Washington later recalled, 'Few were too young and none too old to make the attempt to learn. As fast as any kind of teachers could be secured, not only were day-schools filled, but night-schools as well.' In office, some inexperienced and easily-swayed blacks were certainly guilty of excesses, but the record of black leaders in Reconstruction states and counties merits James G Blain's praise of their federal colleagues: 'The colored men who took their seats in both Senate and House did not appear ignorant or helpless. They were as a rule studious, earnest, ambitious men, whose public conduct would be honourable to any race.'

But if every black office-holder had been a paragon, the days of

Radical Reconstruction would still have been numbered. As the Republican party strengthened itself, and its radical spokesman died or retired, the cost of administering the defeated South came more and more in question. By the 1870s most Northerners were convinced of the need to let the South return to home rule. The Reconstruction regimes were weakened by factionalism, and the mass of the white population repudiated them. White intimidation and racial demagoguery had grown as secret organizations – the Ku Klux Klan, the Knights of the White Camelia, the White Brotherhood, the '76 Association – terrorized blacks and their allies, murdering, lynching, raping, beating. What ended Reconstruction was the cliffhanging presidential election of 1876, when the Republican candidate, Rutherford B Hayes, conceded the removal of the last federal troops from the South in return for disputed electoral-college votes that put him in office. The South was returned to the South, and the black abandoned to 'the party of the fathers'.

His position was not strong. Radical Reconstruction had shakily provided the vote, and educational opportunities. But it had not brought economic independence. Wartime plans for confiscating rebel plantations to provide each ex-slave with 40 acres and a mule had foundered. Many abolitionists had seen emancipation as a moral victory, not an economic and social challenge. The business wing of the Republican party emphasized the sanctity of property rights, and was not averse to having a cheap, landless black labour force in the South. But blacks could not eat votes, and book learning did not nourish the body. The Southern economy was in disorder; despite an increase in the area of land under cotton after the Civil War, production did not recover to 1860 figures until the end of the 1870s. In any case, the last three decades of the nineteenth century were no time to try small-scale cotton farming. Thanks to world overproduction and the tight money policy of the American government, the price of cotton fell from 17 cents a pound in 1871 to 4.6 cents per pound in 1894. The freed black was trying to make his way in circumstances of agricultural depression.

Some blacks managed, through homesteading, accumulated savings, or Northern philanthropic contributions, to acquire their own land; most, however, engaged in sharecropping, 'the planter', as Edward King explained, 'taking out the expenses of the crop, and, when it is sold, dividing the net proceeds with the negroes who have produced it.' Other patterns existed, but most of them exposed blacks, and poor whites too, to problems of capitalizing their next crop. Sharecropper farmers fell under the sway of the furnishing merchant. who supplied seed, food, fertilizer, implements and mules against notes pledging the cotton crop as security. Local merchants charged exorbitantly for supplies and conventionally undervalued the crop. If the crop failed, the hard-won land had to be mortgaged. Monopolistic trusts came to control vital supplies – ploughs and fertilizer, for example – and, because the value of the dollar was appreciating, interest rates grew exorbitantly. The Depression reduced the value of Southern land to a level where it was virtually unmortgageable and unsaleable. Blacks shared, and suffered with, the decline of the South.

The rise of black protest, 1890–1918

In 1895, thirty years after the end of the Civil War, the Negro leader Booker T Washington was asked to speak at the Atlanta Cotton States Exposition – designed as a shop-window for 'The New South', now rapidly industrializing with ramshackle cotton mills and factories. The son of a slave and a white man, born in West Virginia shortly before the Civil War, Washington had worked as a miner and house-servant in his youth before walking and riding the 500 miles to the Hampton Institute, a Northern-financed agricultural school, where he gained an education while working as a caretaker. By 1881 he was appointed principal of the Tuskegee Institute in Alabama, which he raised, through a policy of strict discipline, self-help, and successful approaches to Northern philanthropic institutions, into the leading centre of Negro industrial education in the country. The story of his own development he would tell in *Up from Slavery* (1901), an autobiography that was to become the first classic of black writing since Emancipation; his achievement at Tuskegee, where he inculcated in successive generations of bricklayers, carpenters and mechanics the protestant virtues of thrift, providence, politeness and hard work, he would record in *Tuskegee and Its People* (1905). Washington's address at Atlanta expressed his racial pride in black achievements; it called for legal protection for his people, and it asserted his philosophy of gradual Negro self-improvement. Yet there is no mistaking an obsequious tone in his biblically inspired rhetoric, a tone that was soon to be attacked, most notably by W E B Du Bois. He recalled the loyalty of slaves, he accepted social segregation and inequality, and questioned Negro political ambitions. His message was a plea for, in essence, mutual co-operation between unequal partners.

But at this time most blacks accepted Washington's message and his leadership, especially if, like him, they remained loyal to the Republican Party. The period was one of political tension, racial violence and economic depression, exacerbated by the Great Crash of 1893. From 1887 some black farmers had been attempting to solve their economic problems by joining Colored Farmers Alliances, based on white models. But these attempts at co-operative buying and marketing had largely failed under the combined hostility of plantation owners, merchants and financiers; they had, however, raised the political consciousness of white and Negro members, and led to the formation of the People's Party. Populism called for a third party of masses against classes; in some areas of the South, blacks did align with the People's Party, and were even elected to offices in it. But the ruling Democrats reacted with violence: terrorism, electoral fraud and economic threats were used mercilessly. The decade of the 1890s holds the record for the frequency of lynchings of blacks. In such a conflict, where white Bourbons controlled the political and economic system and would stop at nothing to maintain their rule, where white support from blacks was fragile and the chances of success frail, the 'uppity nigger' became an inevitable scapegoat. Humility and accommodationism were at this time perhaps the only policies which could have secured the continuance of Northern philanthropy and safeguarded the southern blacks.

Booker T Washington's personal reputation burgeoned after Atlanta; he became the acknowledged leader and spokesman of American blacks and the recognized voice of their aspirations. He published books, like *Sowing and Reaping* (1900) and *Character Building* (1902), expressing his gradualist philosophy. The 'Tuskegee Machine' became not only the channel for all philanthropy to Negro causes, but also the clearing house for the Republican party and federal patronage. Washington was consulted by President Theodore Roosevelt between 1901 and 1909, and unprecedentedly bidden to breakfast at the White House. Yet politically, Washington had sadly miscalculated. Lynching continued unabated, the frustration of poor whites at the collapse of Populism in 1896 adding to the violence. Worse, quasi-legal disfranchisement and segregation deprived blacks of what little political power they still had in the South. Ever since Redemption, disfranchisement had been a danger to the blacks. When and where it happened depended more on the white political factions in the different states than on such 'trivial' matters as constitutional rights. In the 1880s, for instance, black voters were useful to black-belt Bourbons. However, in South Carolina, where blacks were in the majority, various stratagems like the Registration Law of 1882 gave white electoral officials wide discretion to prevent blacks from voting. The first wholesale exclusion of Negroes from the polls occurred in Mississippi in 1890, after the failure of Henry Cabot Lodge's so-called Force Bill, which would have given them federal protection. Through poll taxes, residence requirements, literacy tests and the 'understanding clause', the new Mississippi constitution effectively removed blacks from political life. After 1896 and the Populist debacle, disfranchisement came everywhere, and often disqualified poor whites as well. The decision rested with the Electoral Registrar, who ensured that the South was a White Man's Land. The 'solid South' was effectively one-party; the Democratic nominating primary was more important than actual elections. To make assurance doubly sure, primaries were limited to white delegates.

Booker T Washington resisted disfranchisement, and used the funds he had to challenge the new constitutional arrangements in legal battles that went to the Supreme Court. But the hostile judgement in

William v. *Mississippi* (1898) doomed such efforts to failure, while in *Plessey* v. *Ferguson* (1896) the Supreme Court (over the famous dissent of Mr Justice Harlan, who described the constitution as 'color-blind') sanctioned the concept of 'separate but equal' facilities for blacks and whites, in this case on transportation in Louisiana. This condemned blacks not only to inferior, money-starved school systems but to wide-ranging segregation, 'Jim Crow Laws'; segregation of buses, railroads, schools, hotels, hospitals, restaurants, lavatories, theatres, trade unions, and many other institutions and facilities. This move to institutionalize the colour-line had also been spurred by the growing urbanization of the South, which brought blacks to Birmingham, Roanoke, Raleigh, Natchez, Atlanta and New Orleans in search of work in new industries; it was estimated that one third of the black population of the South lived in urban areas by 1890, and whites sought new 'rules' to protect themselves.

Thus the two decades from 1890 to 1910 were to prove disastrous for black Americans. Political and civil rights were sacrificed; education, which betweeen 1865 and 1900 had reduced black illiteracy from 90 per cent to 30 per cent, was now at the whim of whites. Economically, the black farmer was reduced to peonage, or else to the lowest-paid jobs in southern industry. Moreover, despite Theodore Roosevelt's tentative overtures, Progressivism offered little to the Negro. In North and South, consciences were salved by popular pseudo-scientific versions of Darwinism and genetics, which proposed fundamental racial differences. A syrupy romanticization of an aristocratic Old South, in fiction and folklore, pulled a veil over its contemporary shortcomings: political stagnation and corruption, cultural and economic backwardness, violence, illiteracy, ignorance.

Yet the 1890s were a decade that both raised and suppressed many hopes in American life, not least those of blacks. It saw the rising promise of a new black writing, for instance in the work of Paul Laurence Dunbar, the first black poet with a national reputation. The son of a slave, he was best known for his dialect poetry, a style which he himself resisted but which was popular with white publishers. Ironically, such experiments were efforts towards establishing that kind of cultural distinctiveness which a century later would be *de rigueur* with many black writers. Dunbar also wrote a fascinating novel about a black Christian who loses his faith in the naturalist wilderness, *The Uncalled* (1898). Charles W Chesnutt published black fiction, notably *The Marrow of Tradition* (1901), in which a black doctor, abused and ill-treated, eventually wins the support of the better element in a white community as a result of his selfless treatment of a white child. But at the same time, Chesnutt draws a sympathetic portrait of a black rebel who is willing to die rather than accept a subservient role. Chesnutt touches here on the ambiguity of the black man, but also of the black writer, forced to mediate his expression through white publishers to a white audience, and so half-compelled to conceal the self he wishes to express. Most early black literature – from Phyllis Wheatley on – tends to be imitative of white modes, and to display some of the servility felt to be the necessary price of success. Yet, often, the subversive spirit survives, and articulateness itself becomes a kind of political assertion.

Two long-term reactions now began to make themselves felt. One was protest, epitomized in the career of W E B Du Bois. A northern Negro from a family of ante-bellum freedmen, he grew up in Massachusetts, experiencing only mild racial prejudice. It was when he visited the South in his vacations from Fisk University that he discovered the force of the colour-line. He gained his doctorate at Harvard for a dissertation on the slave trade, and after studying in Berlin became a professor of sociology first at Wilberforce and then at Atlanta University. His first strategy for helping his race was typical of the prevailing Progressive mentality: disseminating factual information by pioneering sociological studies of the Negro in Philadelphia, Atlanta, and the black-belt of Georgia. But as he witnessed his people's decline, and growing racial violence (there were serious race riots in Atlanta, Boston, Brownsville, New York, and Springfield, Lincoln's home-town, in the first decade of the twentieth century), he grew more outraged and outspoken. In 1903 he published his classical collection of historical, socio-economic, political, mystical and fictional essays, *The Souls of Black Folk*. Its most famous passage expressed the idea that the Negro was blessed and cursed with a double consciousness: he was both black *and* American, even if his Americanness went unrecognized. This conferred a privileged, 'underside' insight into the moral weakness of the culture; it also encumbered him with an ambiguous response which left him alienated, not just from society but, more profoundly, from himself. He noted:

The Negro is a sort of seventh son born with a veil and gifted with second sight in this American world – a world which yields him no true self-consciousness, but only lets him see himself through the revelation of the other world. It is a peculiar sensation, this double consciousness, this sense of always looking at oneself through the eyes of others, of measuring one's soul by the tape of a world that looks on in amused contempt and pity. One ever feels his twoness – an American, a Negro; two warring souls, two thoughts, two unreconcilable strivings, two warring ideals in one dark body, whose dogged strength alone keeps it from being torn asunder.

'The History of the Negro' he concluded, 'is the history of this strife', and it is this strife and sense of doubleness that much Negro expression in the arts and music has gone on to express.

In one essay in the book, Du Bois mutedly attacked Washington; in another, propounding the idea of 'The Talented Tenth', elitist, intellectual spokesmen and leaders of the Negro race, he offered alternative policies. Now the gap began to widen between Du Bois, like-minded black leaders such as Kelly Miller, Dean of Howard

University or Charles Chesnutt, and the 'Washington camp'. In 1905 the 'Niagara Movement' promoted a journal, *Horizon*, to protest against disfranchisement and racial inequality, but it was poorly organized and suffered Washington's hostility. Du Bois attacked Washington with increased bitterness and turned to the Progressive wing of the Democrats, but was soon disillusioned; Woodrow Wilson, elected President in 1912, was a Southerner, one of whose first executive orders segregated the federal civil service. Du Bois, now the leader of the militant wing of blacks, had in 1909 become a founder of the National Association for the Advancement of Colored People (NAACP). He edited the NAACP journal, *Crisis*, and directed research, publicizing the injustices and discrimination suffered by blacks, to arouse the moral outrage of the American people. In his turbulent relations with his white progressive backers, Du Bois oscillated between calls for the complete integration of the races and the idea that black Americans, in alliance with black Africa, must go it alone. As an editor, he encouraged young black writers, assured his position as a leading voice of black protest in America, and led the way into the black intellectual revival that followed the war.

The second response to the triumph of Southern racism was also a form of protest: black migration to Northern cities. From emancipation onward, there had been much migration by Negroes, westward into Texas, townward into the fledgling mills, factories and mines of the New South. But from the 1890s onward, increasing numbers of Negroes, initially often young males, began the movement northward, the Great Migration, which in little more than a generation changed the black from predominantly a Southern farm labourer into predominantly a Northern city-dweller. The factors behind the 'push' from the South have been indicated, though the spread of the boll weevil between 1910 and 1920 added to them. The 'pull' of the Northern cities – Chicago, St Louis, Pittsburgh, Cleveland, Detroit, New York, Philadelphia, Boston – was aided, in classic immigrant fashion, by descriptions in letters and the propaganda of Northern black newspapers (like Robert S Abbott's Chicago *Defender*). Du Bois's *Crisis* also favoured migration. The First Word War turned a steady stream into a flood. Northern factories geared to war production were starved of labour by the drop in European immigration and by conscription. The South was flooded with job advertisements; labour touts offered cheap fares to the North. Southern industrialists used intimidation to stop the flight of labour, though the poor whites were doubtless less sorry to see their competitors pack train after train to 'The Promised Land'. Between 1890 and 1920 some 2 million Negroes had migrated to northern cities; the flow continued thereafter until recently.

Some migrants had already experienced urban life in the South, but the cultural shock of arrival in the North's great cities for field-hands or sharecroppers has rightly been compared to the trauma of enslavement. City life, as for all new immigrants, meant ghetto life. White residential blocks had been 'busted' by realtors intruding black families. After white flight, family homes had been divided, subdivided and sub-subdivided, to pack the black tenants in at exorbitant rents. Surrounding white neighbourhoods adopted restrictive convenants, formed 'improvement associations', or, as in Chicago, resorted to bombings and terrorism, to prevent black ghetto expansion. As more and more migrants arrived, overcrowding reached disastrous levels. It has been estimated that by 1940, had population density in the rest of Manhattan borough equalled that of Harlem, all the population of the USA would be contained in the one borough. Household and civic services could not cope, and neglect by landlords and municipalities made an appalling situation even worse. Inadequate plumbing, bad ventilation, poor hygiene, spasmodic refuse collection and malnourishment all helped to push infant mortality figures to two and three times the white level. Bad schooling, working mothers, lack of social amenities and of parental authority brought high crime rates and generational conflict. The ghetto became a magnet for exploiters and racketeers; the patent medicine man, the pimp, the storefront church and numbers racket became ghetto institutions. Even job prospects, which had drawn hopeful Negroes from the South, began to collapse with the post-war recession and the return of demobilized whites to the labour market. 'Last hired, first fired' was the rule for blacks.

Black arts and black politics between the wars

President Wilson's 'War to Save Democracy' proved a hollow slogan for American blacks. Encouraged by such leaders as Du Bois, and by government propaganda, Negroes flocked to the colours, only to find that Jim Crow ruled the armed services. Negro regiments were customarily assigned demeaning fatigue duties. They were forbidden to fraternize in France, though they could not fail to notice the relaxed racial conditions there. When they returned home, they were attacked by white mobs if they had the effrontery to wear their uniforms in public. Negro veterans who returned to northern ghettoes likewise found claims to racial liberalism exposed as hypocritical cant. In 1917, East St Louis suffered a terrifying outburst of racial violence: 39 blacks were killed by rampaging white mobs, 500 were injured, and 312 buildings were destroyed. 1919 was, in James Weldon Johnson's words, the bloody 'Red Summer', with a major four-day race-riot in Chicago which killed 23 Negroes and injured 342, and outbreaks of racial tension in a dozen other cities. The 1920's were not to be a tolerant decade, but the changed social situation, and black migration, had some advantages. Compared with scattered Negro settlements in the rural South, the ghetto created a black community, homogenized by shared suffering, which quickly established its own institutions and began to recognize its own potential strength. Urbanized, the black was near to national cultural activity. He began to be celebrated in some white literature, in the fiction of Sherwood Anderson, Carl Van Vechten, William Faulkner and Du Bois and Dorothy Heyward's *Porgy* (1925). Black writers, black singers and black music were in vogue. Fashionable whites invaded Harlem nightclubs, catering to exclusively white clientele. White playwrights, like Eugene O'Neill and Paul Green, wrote on Negro themes; artists found inspiration in not-so-primitive African primitive art.

The spirit of the decade was summed up by Alain Locke in his 1925 anthology, *The New Negro*. A collection of essays, verse and prose, this proposed the emergence of a new breed of writers who wrote 'as Negroes' rather than necessarily 'for the Negro'. In other words, cultural identity was no longer problematic; it was an assumed fact. For Locke, indeed, this charged the American Negro with a responsibility to liberate his African brothers. But in fact the 'New Negro' was less interested in black Africa, except as an image of lyric innocence, than he was with examining his own environment, defining his own identity and announcing his own new-found sense of cultural independence. He may have been in vogue with the whites, who tried to promote an image of the black as a spontaneous, unrepressed sexual being – an image which served their own psychic and mythological needs – but his own concern lay elsewhere. It lay in a process of personal and group discovery which could express itself equally in defiant poems like Claude McKay's 'If We Must Die' (quoted by Winston Churchill in the House of Commons during the Second World War), or lyrical celebrations of the black past.

The mood of black writers was one of celebration. Where white literature of the period tended to dwell on images of sterility, unfulfilled hopes, unrealized dreams or disappointed aspirations, black literature tended to assert the sensual vitality and lyric potential of life. With the exception of Langston Hughes's poetry and Jean Toomer's *Cane* (1923), it was a literature to one side of the modernist concerns of Stein, Hemingway, Pound and Eliot. The imagination was not to be a last desperate resource; it was a key to shared experience, part of the process of liberation. No wonder, perhaps, that they shared so little with the whites who fondly imagined that their interest in jazz implied an understanding of the experience from which it derived. At a time when whites were deploring the collapse of community, identifying the alienation and social dislocations of urban life, the black American saw in the city a cultural and political potential which was cause for hope.

The black writer was not blind to the debilitating nature of the physical environment but for the most part he chose to emphasize the complex cultural resources of a black community in the process of creating its own values, images and myths. And if this was expressed in poetry, prose and, to a lesser extent, drama, it was also centrally expressed through jazz. A major influence on twentieth-century American music, more centrally this was an art which expressed a specific cultural experience. For F Scott Fitzgerald, the 1920s were the 'jazz age'. But he was simply appropriating what he took to be its apoliticism, its sensuality, its antinomianism. Its buried history was a cipher he was not inclined or equipped to decode. But it was central to the black experience. For Hughes, its rhythms were those of Negro life. For Ralph Ellison, its subtle combinations of improvisation and fixed form, the dialectical relationship between individual and group, stood as an image of the individual Negro's relationship to his community. Where the blues offered a lyric sublimation of suffering, jazz proposed a more active and complex model. Jazz was folk, rather than popular, culture in that it was embedded in a shared experience. It was never simply social anodyne. The spaces in the music demanded collaboration not only by the soloists but also by those whose experience was the material out of which the music was made.

In the 1920s black writers, especially poets and novelists, found it relatively easy to publish and for a decade the 'First Black Renaissance', more usually known as the 'Harlem Renaissance' or the 'Negro Renaissance', flourished. Yet there was still a radical disagreement as to the objective of black writing. Claude McKay announced that he did not regard himself as a Negro poet, wishing to transcend 'the narrow confined limits of one people and its problems', while Countee Cullen confessed to a race-consciousness which grew stronger and stronger. Partly, of course, it was still a question of audience. James Weldon Johnson suggested, indeed, that in many ways this was the primary problem for the black American writer – for whom does he write, for blacks or for whites? This was a dilemma felt every bit as strongly half a century later.

This emphasis on the nature of black identity, this desire to make a declaration of cultural independence, was reflected on a social level by Marcus Garvey's Universal Negro Improvement Association (1916). A West Indian, one of many 'black jews' who migrated to Harlem in the early twentieth century, Garvey headed a back-to-Africa movement: indeed, though he never set foot on the continent, he declared himself Provisional President of Africa. In many ways, his organization was touched with farce, with its ostentatious uniforms and mass parades. He established a Black Star Shipping Line, but because of incompetence his ships either sank or were impounded; he himself was indicted for fraud in 1924, and eventually died in London. But it would be a mistake to see him simply as a clown or charlatan – though Du Bois moved from cautious support to indicting him as 'the most dangerous enemy of the Negro race in America and in the world'. But he instilled in individual Negroes a sense of pride and dignity, suggested the need for black Americans to control their economic destiny, and demonstrated the possibility of creating a mass movement among blacks, indicating a political potential that could be mobilized to win advancement. He himself despaired of this in America, seeing the black future in a return to Africa. Thus there was an atavistic dimension both in the First Black Renaissance and in Garvey's economic and political plans. Yet, though this was a period in which northern black communities became a demonstrable fact of urban and cultural life, the political lessons were not yet drawn, and Garvey's predominantly working-class movement was hardly reflected in the largely middle-class black writing of the period.

The 1930s brought an abrupt change of mood. The 1929 Stock Market crash and the Great Depression of the 1930s were, in Villard's words, 'an unparalleled disaster' for 'the great masses of colored people'. In the South, a further fall in cotton prices deepened the persistent agrarian depression of the 1920s. In many areas, lien farmers and sharecroppers were evicted wholesale as credit dried up; livestock, implements, foodcrops and household furniture were seized by creditor landlords and merchants. In the cities, North and South, Negro unemployment rose to 50 per cent or higher, far above the level for whites. Established black organizations like the NAACP – which now concentrated on legal actions and legislative lobbying against lynching, segregation, and inequality of pay – and the Urban League, founded in 1910 to foster educational and economic opportunities for ghetto blacks, were overwhelmed by the scope and scale of disaster. In this near-revolutionary situation, the American Communist party, on orders from Moscow, made determined efforts to win black support. Its interracial Southern Tenant Farmers Union enrolled 31,000 members in the South for its labour-union tactics against landlords, who often responded with bullets. In 1931, the party's International Labor Defense grabbed the limelight from the NAACP in the trial of the Scottsboro boys, nine young blacks accused of raping two white girls from Alabama, and Southern 'justice' was exposed in a carefully orchestrated international propaganda campaign in which the pathetic defendants often seemed forgotten. The Communist Party also fostered Negro unionization among miners and textile workers, and Tenants' Leagues among ghetto-dwellers. The difficulty was that the party was itself undecided about the nature of the Negro's dilemma. Hence it tried simultaneously to present blacks as colonial peoples fighting for freedom, seeking independence in their own socialist republic in the Black Belt, and as simple victims of class warfare with common interests with the white working class.

It is this ambiguity that is reflected in such works as *Uncle Tom's Children* (1938) and *Native Son* (1940), by the period's most famous black writer, Richard Wright. Wright was, like many intellectuals of the time, a party member, but became increasingly disillusioned as he came to feel that the party's deterministic theories, hostility to bourgeois individualism, and cynical Comintern-ordained shifts of policy were inimical to his own liberal and existentialist impulse. *Native Son*, the story of Bigger Thomas, a Chicago ghetto black, has a naturalist, theme but his move is towards selfhood, an existential redemption; a theme that would return in Wright's later novel, *The Outsider* (1953), written in Paris. Like Ralph Ellison, whose portrayal of the Harlem 'Brotherhood' in *Invisible Man* (1952) stems from similar depressive experiences, Wright and other perceptive black intellectuals found themselves being used as pawns for the political ambitions of others, amd moved towards a separate path. To Wright, the black artist had a crucial role: to create the values by which the black American was to survive, to 'furnish moral sanctions for action, to give a meaning to blighted lives, and to supply motives for mass movements of millions of people'. Many black writers would tread this anxious path, for the black writer – an example of Du Bois's talented tenth – felt charged with forging the myths, creating the symbols, the heroes and animating fantasies of a people constructing their own self-definition: a task all the more difficult when menaced by public myths and dominant stereotypes which demeaned him, made him invisible, or distorted his nature through cultural and political prejudices.

The 1930s brought new political awareness into American life in general. Even so, the response of the Roosevelt administration to the plight of blacks was ambivalent. On the one hand, the president's reliance on electoral and legislative support from Southern conservatives and demagogues meant that 'FDR' (Roosevelt) could show blacks no overt favour. On the other hand, leading New Dealers like Harold Ickes and Eleanor Roosevelt were outspoken enemies of racism, and helped ensure that blacks benefited from relief and social security measures. Black sharecroppers found New Deal farm policies raised their pitiful incomes; the galaxy of work projects brought some hope to the mass of black unemployed; and the newly formed Congress of Industrial Organizations welcomed Negro support in unionizing traditionally unorganized industries. The first great spokesman for Negro labour emerged in A Philip Randolph, of the Brotherhood of Sleeping Car Porters. The Federal Theatre project encouraged black playwrights and expressed Negro problems. Looking back on the 1930s, Du Bois declared that 'Negro Americans made more progress towards their goal of full citizenship' then than since Emancipation. Blacks responded with massive support for the Democratic party; and their growing importance to its new urban power-base was reflected in federal appointments.

Yet Roosevelt had to be forced into his major concession: the Committee on Fair Employment Practises. As in 1940, the United States took on its role as 'the Arsenal of Democracy'; shaking off its depression malaise, it soon appeared that those Negroes who had been first fired a decade before would be last hired, or not hired at all, by wartime industry. Randolph threatened to march 100,000 blacks on Washington to demand the end of Jim Crowism in the war-machine, the services, and federal government. The threat of direct non-violent action was sufficient: on 25 June 1941, the President signed the Executive Order 8802 'to provide for full and equitable participation of all workers in defense industry, without discrimination'. The limited victory of the March on Washington movement served as a pregnant example for the future. Immediately, though, the gradual intergration of munitions factories produced widespread racial tension. In Detroit the worst of several wartime race riots broke out in June 1943. Blacks were attacked by white mobs in the ghetto and elsewhere; twenty-five Negroes were killed, hundreds injured, and much property destroyed. Moreover, Order 8802 neglected the armed services. Black officers and other ranks met white hostility, insults and violence. Negro troops were forced to eat separately on Southern trains; meanwhile German prisoners of war dined in the white restaurant car. Randolph bitterly described black troops as 'Jim Crow slaves in the army', and a Negro soldier serving in the Pacific suggested the disillusioned epitaph: 'Here lies a black man killed fighting a yellow man for the protection of a white man.'

American blacks since the war

It has been in the three decades since the Second World War that the biggest revolution in Negro status, and in the articulation of black consciousness has occurred. A major engine of change was black leadership, political and cultural, and the heroism, sometimes turning to rage, of many ordinary Negroes reacting against oppression. American liberal and radical opinion was aroused, partly through the impact of television reporting. The independence of Black Africa represented at the UN in New York City and the growth of international anti-racist ideology put American racism in a new embarrassing perspective. Was America to be classed with South Africa as an international pariah? The new Democratic party strategy stressed the importance of the black vote, as changes in the Senate undermined Southern political power in Washington. Liberal Democratic nominations altered the formerly conservative balance of the Supreme Court. Emergence from the Cold War mentality and the growth of radical idealism and activism by a new generation of white Americans brought a new attitude to domestic issues. Massive black achievements in literature, the arts, theatre and scholarship undermined assumptions of racial inferiority. So did dominant theories in social science and psychology. From the early 1960s, the role of the black in America became a fundamental theme of American life.

Moreover, the growing role of the federal government in giving positive protection and assistance to oppressed minorities led to a cumulatively interventionist mentality in Washington. Truman, in 1946, appointed a Presidential Committee on Civil Rights which presented a blueprint for action for the executive, the Congress, and the states. It would, painfully and exhaustingly, have to be forced on to the statute books over the next twenty years against a determined Southern resistance. One positive achievement of the Truman era was the gradual desegregation of the armed forces from 1949, effected by presidential executive order. But other initiatives ran on to the sandbanks of Southern control of congressional committees, and filibustering by Dixieland Senators.

A second crucial breakthrough for black civil rights was judicial. On 17 May 1954 – 'Black Monday', to recalcitrant Southerners – Chief Justice Earl Warren delivered the unanimous opinion of the Supreme Court in the case of *Brown* v. *Topeka Board of Education* that 'in the field of public education the doctrine of "separate but equal" has no place. Separate educational facilities are inherently unequal.' Significantly, the court's decision culminating sixteen years' erosion of *Plessey* v. *Ferguson*, cited findings by psychologists and social scientists. Subsequently the court ordered educational desegregation 'with all deliberate speed'.

But whatever the Supreme Court might order, it relied on the executive branch to enforce. President Eisenhower, who had made considerable Republican inroads into the South, showed no eagerness for the task. He did break a tradition going back to Redemption by sending federal troops to Little Rock, Arkansas in 1957 when Negro parents sought to register their children in an all-white school. Television viewers across the world saw Governor Orville Faubus vainly try to block the school entrance – an oft-repeated sight, for Southern racists now girded themselves to thwart the Court decision. White Citizens' Councils, pioneered in Mississippi, and Klan-like organizations spread race hatred and anti-integrationism across the South. The familiar weapons of intimidation – bombings, burnings, stabbings, mob-violence, murders – were reactivated against 'niggers' and 'nigger-lovers'. Every kind of subterfuge to circumvent school integration was used: private white academies sprang up, sometimes helped by state subsidies; Virginia even closed down its entire public school system. But the struggle was spreading to other areas. Within eighteen months of *Brown* v. *Topeka*, another sacred cow of Southern segregation, transportation, was attacked through the Montgomery Bus Boycott, sparked off by the arrest of Mrs Rosa Parks, in December 1955, for refusing to give up her seat to a white passenger. For over a year the boycotters organized by SCLC endured massive white intimidation before desegregation was conceded. Victory led to national recognition for its black organizer, the Rev. Martin Luther King, Jr. King fitted the traditional mould of Southern black leadership. A minister, and son of a minister, he used the evangelistic rhetoric employed by black preachers for generations. He also brought less familiar qualities to his mission. Travelled and well-educated (he had a doctorate from Boston University), he was in touch with world opinion on race, specifically with the Gandhian doctrine of non-violent resistance, which gave a cutting edge to his Christian commitment to love as an all-conquering power. A man of surpassing charity, courage, dignity, organizational ability and determination, the articulate author of *Stride Toward Freedom* (1958) and *Why We Can't Wait* (1964), he quickly came to symbolize the Negro's new-found purpose and integrationist ambition.

There were other expressions of a new mood. The 1950s saw the emergence of a new generation of black writers of great influence. In 1950 the poet Gwendolyn Brooks became the first black to win a Pulitzer Prize. A conscious innovator, she drew upon folk ballads and experimental modes alike. It was a double tradition which lay at the heart of her literary strategy. Yet the social pressure created by her racial identity constantly informs her work. She is not a polemical writer but she has expressed accurately enough the shifting mood of the black community in the second half of the century, proving remarkably sympathetic to, and supportive of, the poetic rhetoricians of the 1960s, writers whose urgent politics left little room for the ambiguities so precisely located by her own verse.

The 1960s did, indeed, have little room for ambiguity, and the thrust of LeRoi Jones's poetry moved from a Beat-derived 'soft' metaphysics to a conscious mythicization of black experience. Poetry was, for a time, blunted into a weapon of crude but effective force. It became a kind of political and cultural mantra, a chant from the soul, a reiterated invocation of racial spirits. It was a poetry designed for the voice, for public performance – at its best in the work of Sonia Sanchez, at its weakest, perhaps, in the work of Nikki Giovanni, who, however, proposed the collapse of poetic structure as a correlative of the collapse of personal and public illusion.

As far as the novel was concerned, the 1950s began with Ellison's brilliant parable of the Negro's fate, *Invisible Man*, the story of a faceless, identityless black whose anguish is as much social as metaphysical. But it *is* both; that is, it is an account of a racially derived sense of alienation and a metaphor of alienation. The literature of victimization sounds through the 1950s: Ellison suggests that the alienated plight of blacks matches that of all modern sufferers of disorientation and persecution, and urges the need for the individual to accept a private and public responsibility for reality. In *Invisible Man*, imaginatively, at least, the black American was already insinuated into the realm of American moral concern – a fact which later made Ellison a target for some abuse by certain black critics. For the novel takes as its central strategy the need to infuse life into those very liberal principles enshrined in the Constitution but systematically denied in relation to the Negro.

In 1953 another essentially liberal voice was heard, in the person of James Baldwin. His first novel, *Go Tell it on the Mountain* (1953), was a sensitive account of a young boy's initiation into the realities of racial, sexual and religious life. With *Giovanni's Room* (1956) he linked this theme of black identity with that of homosexual love. But it was as an essayist that he made the greatest impact, with *Notes of a Native Son* (1955), *Nobody Knows My Name* (1961) and *The Fire Next Time* (1963), the latter a controlled polemic which expressed the apocalyptic anger that the moral failure of Americans to deal with race had generated in him. But his was an ambiguous voice. When he used the pronoun 'we' it frequently meant 'we Americans' rather than 'we blacks', and his retreat to France seemed to many blacks evidence of a failure of commitment, a failure which bred a guilt which expressed itself in fictions which became less controlled as they became more shrill. By the mid-1960s there were other voices which seemed to speak more clearly for the younger generation which now set the tone of racial revolt. Baldwin now found himself the target for attack, more especially by Eldridge Cleaver. Divided in his own mind between indicting white society for the 'unforgivable sin' of racism and proposing a sentimental synthesis in the form of 'love', he eventually allowed ambiguity to collapse into simple contradiction.

For all Baldwin's denunciation of liberals, his work can scarcely be characterized by any other word. His belief in the integrity and reality of the individual, his model of a society of socially responsive individuals, his stance as moral teacher, his 'devotion to the human being, his freedom and fulfilment' is liberal in origin and intent. And, despite an apocalyptic imagination, much the same could be said of John A Williams (*Journey Out of Anger*, 1963), William Melvin Kelley (*A Different Drummer, 1962)*, Alice Walker (*The Third Life of Grange Copeland*, 1970), and Toni Morrison (*Song of Solomon*, 1977). Indeed, freed of some of the social pressures of the 1960s, black writers have now begun to permit themselves a commitment to experimentation which would earlier have been regarded with intense suspicion (see Ishmael Reed, *The Free-Lance Pall Bearers*, 1967).

In theatre, Lorraine Hansberry's liberal drama about a black family's desire to integrate itself in a white community, *A Raisin in the Sun*, 1959, quickly gave way to more powerful accounts of racial conflict in the form of James Baldwin's *Blues for Mr Charlie*, 1964, and LeRoi Jones's *Dutchman*, 1964, and *The Slave*, 1964. Indeed, the Black Power movement had its cultural wing in the form of the Black Arts Movement, whose focus was LeRoi Jones.

Formerly an avant-garde writer in New York, Jones moved his activities to Harlem, where he founded the Black Arts Repertory Theatre, an organization which served as a model for many other ventures in urban centres across America. Jones's plays, which proved so successful downtown, when transferred to the ghetto were seen as menacing revolutionary tracts. It was a logic which he accepted, writing, now, 'black revolutionary plays' whose declared intention was to create new black myths, to identify heroes and villains, to denounce the white man as the source of evil and to raise the consciousness of the black masses. He divorced his white wife and changed his name to Imamu Amiri Baraka. Throughout the 1960s and early 1970s he was the dominant and defining influence on the black arts movement. Ed Bullins in particular was inspired by his example, though his own plays were sensitive examinations of the black community rather than agit-prop sketches or revolutionary rituals.

The 1960s also witnessed the creation of a number of significant black drama groups, in particular the Free Southern Theatre, designed to take theatre to Southern rural communities, and The Negro Ensemble Company, founded in New York by Douglas Turner Ward and funded by the Ford Foundation. Both have survived into the 1980s, though undergoing certain changes which reflected the shifting orthodoxies of racial opinion.

The 1960s were indeed dominated by discussions of those orthodoxies, more especially by the propounding of the notion that the black writer should celebrate and define an experience distinct from that of the white American. Literature and criticism alike were to conform to an orthodoxy vigorously if imprecisely announced by critics like Addison Gayle Jr (ed. *The Black Aesthetic*), by social historians such as Harold Cruse (*The Crisis of the Negro Intellectual*) and by writers such as Amiri Baraka. White critics were warned off. White writers, such as William Styron, who attempted to 'appropriate' black experience (*The Confessions of Nat Turner*), were denounced. Black writers and historians like Lerone Bennett (*Before the Mayflower*) re-examined, and, in some cases, re-invented their past, deliberately subverting a view of history and black identity which had been defined by whites. Literature was to be part of the process of redefinition; not simply a reflection of reality.

During the 1960s blacks won even more phenomenal advances. Martin Luther King's widely acclaimed achievement sparked off a wide range of attacks on segregation. Young Negroes in 1960 began sit-ins and picketing of segregated lunch-counters in the South. In 1961, the Congress of Racial Equality organized 'freedom rides' through the South to highlight segregation on interstate transportation. After savage reprisals by Southerners, the Interstate Commerce Commission outlawed discrimination on interstate travel. In the same year, the interracial Student Non-violent Coordinating Committee began its assault on the basis of white political power, with its campaign to register blacks as voters. Northern liberals and students were seeing Southern violence at first hand.

The continued shift of Democratic party support for black aspirations was symbolized during the close-run 1960 election campaign by John F Kennedy's widely publicized telephone call to Coretta King, whose husband was in gaol. The new President, and his brother Robert, the Attorney-General, were faced with a rising tide of racial confrontation, reported almost nightly on television. In 1962 tanks and hundreds of federal troops and marshals had to be sent to the University of Mississippi to enforce the admission of James Meredith, a black freshman. In June 1963, the President mobilized the Alabama

National Guard to ensure the enrolment of two black students at the state university when Governor George Wallace physically attempted to prevent it. In the same month, Kennedy's civil rights proposals, hastened by the revulsion of the public at the savage over-reaction of Southern policemen, politicians and thugs to unarmed, unresisting black and white protesters, were put before Congress. They covered both voting and segregation, involved the Attorney-General in the enforcement process, and threatened sanctions by withdrawal of federal financial aid. In the summer, Martin Luther King delivered his 'I have a Dream' speech to an estimated quarter of a million people who had converged on Washington. By the time of the President's assassination that autumn in Dallas, Southern politicians had already organized a dogged and time-consuming resistance. The following year, 1964, President Johnson, a liberal Texan and brilliant congressional strategist, helped by emotional reaction to Kennedy's assassination and to the bombing of a Negro church in Birmingham, Alabama, which killed four young Negro girls, was able to force the Civil Rights Bill through the Senate after 534 hours of filibuster.

Johnson's triumph was short-lived. Southern registration officials continued to use literacy tests and poll-tax requirements in a blatantly discriminatory way. King and other civil rights leaders organized renewed registration drives and marches. In March 1965, Alabama police, under the command of 'Bull' Connor, attacked peaceful demonstrators *en route* for Montgomery on the bridge at Selma, using tear gas, electrified cattle prods, night-sticks and savage dogs. James Meredith was shot while leading another such march. The administration introduced a new Voting Rights Bill to throw the full weight of federal power behind Negro rights. In still resistant areas of the South, the federal government would take over voter registration and would police the polling stations; the literacy test would be abolished, and poll-tax requirements nullified. The Bill became law in record time in August 1965, and thereafter in the South, after a century of struggle, blacks at last had that basic political right 'without which all others are meaningless'.

The revolution of rising expectations had not escaped the attention of Northern ghetto blacks. The disadvantages under which they struggled had been articulated by President Kennedy in 1963:

The Negro baby born in America today, regardless of the section or the state in which he is born, has about one-half as much chance of completing high school as a white baby, born in the same place, on the same day; one-third as much chance of becoming a professional man; twice as much chance of becoming unemployed; about one-seventh as much chance of earning $10,000 a year; a life expectancy which is seven years shorter and the prospects of earning only half as much.

Five days after Johnson signed the Voting Rights Act of 1965, the Los Angeles ghetto of Watts exploded into a week of black rioting, looting, shooting and burning. The pattern was repeated in ghetto after ghetto in the next two 'long hot summers'. Few major Northern cities escaped outbursts of Negro frustration and rage. In 1968, the murder of Martin Luther King in Memphis triggered a new phase of outraged destruction. Parts of Washington D C resembled a blitzed city.

Meanwhile, young blacks in the North had become increasingly disillusioned with King's insistence on integration and Christian charity, which they found inadequate or irrelevant to their needs. The cry of Black Power, the title of one of Richard Wright's books, but first used by Stokely Carmichael (like Garvey, a West Indian) on a voter registration drive in the South in 1965, was enthusiastically taken up. The Black Muslim Movement, dominated since the 1930s by Elijah Mohammed in Chicago, recruited many disillusioned young blacks, among them Malcolm X and the young heavyweight boxing champion Cassius Clay. With its celebration of the non-white world, its programme for forming a separate black nation in America, its contemptuous reversal of Christian myths–a white devil, for instance– and its insistence on Islamic asceticism and self-discipline, its rigour gave a new purpose to many young ghetto blacks lost in a chaos of drug addiction, crime, unemployment, truancy or vice. In 1966, as a protest against pervasive police harrassment and brutality, Huey Newton and Bobby Seale formed the Black Panther party in Oakland, California: a militant organization, visibly armed and rhetorically violent. Else-where, ghetto communities agitated for community control of education and welfare services. Black students demanded lenient admissions procedures to universities and vocational training and the mounting of black studies programmes in schools and colleges.

Increasingly, emphasis was placed on the separate identity of the Negro; indeed the word 'Negro' itself now became a term of abuse, be-tokening racial appeasement. Where Du Bois had once waged a battle to ensure that the word was written with a capital 'N', now Baraka insisted on using the word 'black' and the dominant tone was an aggressive assertion of cultural identity. Ironically, the Johnson anti-poverty programme strengthened this movement by channelling money directly into the ghettoes, thereby bypassing the conventional civil-rights leadership.

Initially the new generation of young black leaders who emerged with heightened polemical styles concentrated on consciousness-raising, on a distinctive life-style, on confronting the black American with the question of his own authenticity. Du Bois's double-consciousness was to be resolved in favour of blackness; 'Black is Beautiful' was their early rallying cry. Yet, as their ideas developed, the essence of their message came to emphasize racial separation less than radical revolt. Indeed, people like Eldridge Cleaver (*Soul on Ice*, 1968), Malcolm X (*The Autobiography of Malcom X*, 1966), Bobby Seale (*Seize the Time*, 1970), Huey Newton (*Revolutionary Suicide*, 1973), George Jackson (*The Prison Letters of George Jackson*, 1969), and Angela Davis (*Angela Davis: An Autobiography*, 1974), moved towards a class-critique of black problems and programmes stressing the need for black and white equally to perceive their deprived state.

Paradoxically, in the 1970s, while these radical and racial ideas were mulling, the black stake in the established American educational and political systems was increasing. The percentage of Southern blacks in all-black schools dropped from 58 per cent in 1968 to 9.2 per cent in 1972. By 1978, 2,200 blacks held political office in the South, compared with less than 100 before 1965. Though significant discrepancies remained between black and white employment (13 per cent black unemployment compared with 7 per cent white in 1977) and though a black could still expect to receive a markedly lower income than a similarly qualified white, equal-rights legislation forced on employers the onus of justifying the non-hiring of minorities. By 1976, black families had a median income of $9,252, an increase of 105 per cent over the decade though still $6,000 below the white median; 30 per cent of all black families earned $15,000 or more, compared with 2 per cent in 1966. The rise of the black middle class, an increasing number in white enterprises, has occurred at a time of economic recession. In the South, more than half the eligible blacks were registered voters by 1978. Not only had northern cities like Los Angeles, Cleveland, Detroit, and Washington black mayors, but so also had the leading southern cities of Atlanta and New Orleans. Black students now constituted a higher proportion of the student body at the University of Alabama than at many northern universities; the police force of McComb, Mississippi, known in the 1960s as 'The Bombing Capital of the World', was now fully integrated; Selma had a Dr Martin Luther King Street. The easing of the burden of racism from the South brought relief to whites as well as blacks. Symbolic of the ending of that section's pariah status was the election to the presidency of Jimmy Carter, the first fully-fledged Southerner since the Civil War.

Curiously enough, these very real Negro gains in the last decade, though founded on the liberal measures of the 1960s, took place at a time when racial conflict had been shifted out of the limelight. Nixon's policy was one of benign neglect. The trauma of Vietnam and then of Watergate distracted liberal consciences from the unfinished business of achieving racial equality. Though the thesis of inherent racial inferiority, gaining new life from Arthur Jensen's experiments with intelligence quotients, was greeted with a chorus of northern liberal criticism, the problem of segregation in the North, where whites had left the inner cities for non-metropolitan suburbs, proved far more resistant to change than did that in the South. The legally enforced solution of bussing to achieve racial balance in public schools led to violent white reactions in Boston in 1974. The recession and the financial crises of northern cities threatened the welfare programmes of poor ghetto blacks at the same time as their more fortunate brethren were joining the American middle classes. The general conservatism of the decade extended equally to the black community. The Black

Panthers had been effectively destroyed by police bullets; the Muslims retreated from the separatist doctrines. Bobby Seale became a Washington lobbyist; Eldridge Cleaver converted to Christianity; Amiri Baraka joined the ranks of radical conservatism as an orthodox Marxist. Alex Haley' *Roots* could hardly be described as revolutionary. There were even signs of a black re-immigration back to the South. While many problems remained, however, notably that of the poorest blacks – 26 per cent of black families still earned less than $5,000 per year – the general prospect at the end of the 1970s was one of hope, compared with the despair felt by many blacks during the first century of 'emancipation'.

Chapter Eight

The loss of innocence: 1880–1914

Brian Lee and Robert Reinders

Forces of change: The machine and the city

Innocence, it could be argued, is a state of mind which prefigures dual feelings of loss and guilt. Thus childhood is a period of innocence; to become adult is to sin and lose innocence. Primitives are often considered innocents dwelling in a pre-lapsarian Eden close to the divinity of Nature, but Western man with his sense of collective guilt can only yearn for and never attain the innocence of the primitive. There is, however, another sense of loss of innocence that arises in many people when the values, *mores,* even physical qualities of the lives they have inherited and take for granted appear to collapse in a world undergoing change with a rapidity that to many signifies chaos and catastrophe. The thirty-seven years after 1880 produced deep changes in the quality of American life which seriously tested older value systems and behavioural patterns. These changes – chiefly associated with industrialization and urbanization – required new disciplines, new goals and a new kind of consciousness from a predominantly rural folk. The value system based on the existential realities of an agrarian society had to be adapted and partly transformed to meet the new realities. As relations between people and their surroundings altered, new methods of description and new forms of observation had to be devised. Of course, old ways of living, thinking and seeing persisted, or at best were reluctantly accepted, and to some the new times were times of crisis and despair. But after 1900 there are indications that some elements in American society saw in the new urban-industrial structures the potential for a society which was logically ordered and humanely satisfying.

If one speaks of a loss of innocence in this period it may be measured – assuming one can quantify a feeling as tenuous as innocence – in selected statistics which, underneath the cold numbers and percentages, reveal a society undergoing a process of industrialization and urbanization unprecedented in American history. If, in Wilbur Cash's words, 'Men who, as children, had heard the war-whoops of the Cherokee in the Carolina backwoods lived to hear the guns at Vicksburg', then the teenage Illinois soldier who faced Confederate artillery at Chancellorsville would live to see the miracle of man's flight, and his Cook County corn fields consumed by the steel furnaces, stockyards and apartment houses of Chicago, and

> A midnight bounded by the bright carnival of the
> boulevards and the dark girders of the El.
> Where once the marshland came to flower.
> Where once the deer came down to water.[1]

Industry had begun in America long before 1880, and technological principles had been governing many areas of American society from well before the Civil War – a war that further accelerated industrialization and commerce, and was followed by a period of massive entrepreneurial activity. Yet the presence of the open frontier still helped sustain an image of a rural, agrarian, unmechanical America. However, once the Depression of the 1870s had ended, the United States entered on a period of unprecedented technological expansion. The indices of growth from the end of the 1870s to the advent of the Great War were unparalleled. Gross national production (in five-year averages) far outstripped population increases, and more than tripled between 1882–86 ($11.3 billion) and 1912–16 ($38.9 billion).[2] Capital in manufacturing industries (in 1929 dollars) rose from 2.7 billion in 1879 to 20.8 billion in 1914. The goods turned out by industry increased at the same level: the index of manufacturing production (1899 = 100) rose from 42 in 1880 to 192 in 1914. America was now competing with the great industrial nations, Britain and Germany, and was outstripping both combined. The result was a change in the landscape, a change in the direction of American energy, and a change in consciousness. Americans, said the historian Henry Adams – contemplating the American industrial marvels on display at the World's Columbian Exposition, held in 1893 in the massively expanding city of Chicago, where skyscrapers rose and new commercial enterprises flourished – needed a new kind of education, a new type of awareness, to confront the world of proliferating energy now surrounding them. As Americans looked forward into the twentieth century, they began to sense a futuristic, industrial world ahead.

At the heart of this industrial transformation, touching almost all aspects of American growth, was steel. With the coming of the Bessemer and Open Hearth processes, raw steel production (in units of 1,000 short tons) grew from 597 in 1876, to 6,785 in 1895, to 35,180 in 1915. By 1900 – the year when, according to Henry Adams, the machine had turned America into a modern pluriverse – the American steel industry was outproducing Great Britain and Germany combined. The signs of industrial growth were everywhere. Although by 1880 the United States already had the longest railroad network in the world, this continued to expand from 115,547 miles of track in that year to 394,944 in 1915, while the number of passengers more than doubled between 1890 and 1912. Oil production, literally and figuratively the lubricant of an industrial society, leaped (in thousands of 42-gallon barrels) from 5,261 in 1870 to 26,286 in 1880, tripled by 1900, and more than quadrupled again by 1915. The output of coal, which remained the basic energy source throughout the period, more than doubled each decade, rising from 50 million tons in 1880 to 443 million tons in 1915. When Henry Adams felt that new laws of history were needed, based on theories of exponential energy, he was expressing the sense of change and acceleration these developments brought.

Steel, railroads, oil and coal were industries that had their inception before 1880; more revealing were industries almost totally created in the period. From Frank Sprague's first commercial electric railway in Richmond, Virginia (1887), the industry mushroomed; in 1890 there were 789 electric street railways with 8,123 miles of track and carrying 2 billion passengers; twenty-two years later, 1,260 companies operated 41,065 miles of track and carried 9½ billion passengers. Electric light and power, unknown in 1880, and with a total value in plant and equipment of only $34 million in 1890, took off in the 1890s as plant and equipment values grew to $234 million in 1900, $964 million in 1910, and $1,500 million in 1914. If the growth of the electric industry aroused the enthusiasm of financiers and manufacturers, it also increasingly provided light and electric services to an expanding population; in 1907, 8 per cent of all dwelling units had electric service: the figure doubled by 1912 and tripled by 1917. Net production of electrical energy (in millions of kilowatts) rose from 2,507 in 1902 to 11,569 in 1912. The telephone, a curiosity at the Philadelphia Exposition of 1876, and still a rarity in 1890, when only 3.6 persons per 1,000 enjoyed the dubious honour of owning these primitive implements, increased so rapidly that by 1915 the ratio of telephones to population was one to ten. All of this growth – and the above figures are only selective – meant an outpouring of goods available to a consuming public. The value of semi-durables (in current producer's prices) more than tripled between 1879 and 1915 ($828.2 million to $2,636 million) and consumer durables increased nearly 600 per cent ($304.3 million to $1,700 million).

Attendant on the growth of industry was the expansion of urban centres. The urban population (measured as communities of 2,500 and over) grew from 14,130,000 in 1880 to 41,999,000 in 1910, and although it was not until 1920 that the census indicated the urban population exceeded the rural population, it is likely that such a figure had been reached by 1914. In 1880, 28 per cent of the population lived in urban areas; by 1910, 44 per cent did so. Established cities grew at an unprecedented pace. The ten largest cities in America in 1910 – New York (including Brooklyn), Chicago, Philadelphia, St Louis, Boston, Cleveland, Baltimore, Pittsburgh (including Alleghany), Detroit and Buffalo – had had an almost three-fold population increase in the preceding thirty years: 4,835,688 to 12,631,602. New York alone increased its population from 1,772,962 to 4,766,883; Chicago, the Topsy of American major cities, doubled its 1880 population in a decade (503,185 to 1,099,850) and had nearly doubled that figure again by 1910 (2,185,283). In the same thirty years, St Louis, Boston, Baltimore, San Francisco, Washington, Jersey City, Pittsburgh and Providence doubled their populations, while Cleveland, Buffalo, Milwaukee, Detroit and Newark more than tripled theirs.

All of these cities had, of course, been urban centres before 1880. More dramatic still, perhaps, was the growth of cities which were almost totally created in the period. It is in these cities that the sense of rural to urban change must have appeared most challenging and, to some most traumatic, as the figures in Table 8.1 indicate.

Table 8.1 Populations of newly created cities, 1880 and 1910

	1880	1910
Los Angeles	11,183	319,198
Minneapolis	46,887	301,408
Kansas City	55,785	248,381
Seattle	3,533	237,194
St Paul	41,473	214,744
Denver	35,629	213,381
Portland, Ore.	17,577	207,214
Atlanta	37,409	154,839
Oakland	34,555	150,174

But perhaps the main agency for diffusing urban life-styles and values were smaller cities. Their numbers grew rapidly between 1880 and 1910, as shown in Table 8.2.

Table 8.2 Numbers of urban centres

Population(,000s)	50–100	25–50	10–25	5–10	2.5–5	1–2.5
1880	15	42	146	249	467	—
1890	30	66	230	340	654	1,603
1900	40	82	280	465	832	2,128
1910	59	119	309	605	1,060	2,717

In the period 1880–1910, thousands of sleepy little townships, with their few services for the surrounding agricultural population, were transformed into 'cities'. Where once had been a few false-fronted stores, a blacksmith's ship and a church or two, now there would be a bank, a weekly or even a daily newspaper, paved streets, a YMCA, a Masonic Hall, an Odd Fellows Hall, perhaps an armoury, speciality stores, a department store, an expanded railroad station, a street railway line, a hospital, uniformed police, and a scattering of small factories and warehouses. Small as some of these communities were, each had its own sense of urban identity, and the citizenry was increasingly conscious of itself in contrast to the rural folk that invaded the town on Saturday nights, 'whiskered adults self-conscious in their Sunday "best", young swains beauing bashful sweethearts, thin-chested mothers herding restless broods.'[3]

Improvements in medical care helped urban areas to grow by natural increase, but this alone could never have accounted for the dramatic rate of development experienced by cities after 1880. The largest immigration to urban areas came from farms and villages. Thanks to mechanization, agriculture required fewer workers: in 1880, one farm worker could supply 5.6 persons and by 1920 he could feed 8.3; the number of man-hours required to cultivate an acre of wheat or corn dropped by one-third between 1880 and 1914. Agricultural areas, with their high birth rates, provided a surplus labour supply which could not be absorbed by the opening of new agricultural lands in the Great Plains. The 'Buckwheats' drifted into cities, often by way of a few years spent in a village or township. New England, where rural depopulation had begun before the Civil War, saw a continuous farm-to-city migration. In the decade 1880–1890, 932 of 1,502 townships in New England lost population. In 1880 the urban and rural populations of the north-eastern states almost balanced, but while the rural population thereafter remained constant at 7 million, the urban population had risen to 18½ million by 1910. By the 1880s, rural depopulation had spread to the Mid-West; over half of the townships in Ohio and Illinois declined in population during the decade. Blake McKelvey estimated that 11 million urbanities in 1910 had moved from rural homes after 1880, and that one-third of all urban residents in 1910 were of rural American origin.[4]

Urban centres were also swollen by large numbers of foreign-born citizens, chiefly from southern and eastern Europe. (In 1910 over half of all foreign-born originated in southern and eastern Europe). Between 1880 and 1914, over 13 million immigrants entered America's portals. Some were temporary residents and eventually returned to their native countries; others took up agricultural occupations, often after a sojourn in a major city, but the majority of the foreign-born settled in cities. In 1910 there were 9,635,900 foreign-born in America's cities, and an additional 12,346,900 native-born of foreign or mixed parentage. The European immigrants were concentrated particularly in large urban centres. According to he 1910 census, of the ten largest cities in America, 3,183,116 residents were of white native American parentage, 4,605,860 were of foreign or mixed parentage, 4,106,117 were foreign-born, and 336,493 were Afro-Americans. In only four cities – Philadelphia, St Louis, Baltimore and Buffalo – did those of native American parentage outnumber the foreign-born; and only in Baltimore did the native population exceed the foreign-born and American-born population of foreign or mixed parentage. Thus 75 per cent of the population of America's ten largest cities were either foreign-born or only a generation removed from a foreign parent or parents. The memory of Europe hung heavily over the American city.

Looking backward

Yet these new experiences and those immigrant forces found little direct reflection in the expressive culture, little presence in literature. Life in the new American city, whether for the immigrant or the in-migrant, did not, it seemed, transmute easily into art. Indeed, in the face of change American writing seemed generally slow to react. Since the Civil War, the dominant movement had been realism, a realism that explored some of the new communities and settings of American life, that looked in the manner of 'local colour' at the life of the Plains or the Mississippi Valley. The three major novelists were Mark Twain, writing his vernacular, deflationary realism from roots in South-West humour; William Dean Howells, arguing the case for realism as the discourse of democratic ordinariness and 'smiling' American values; and Henry James, refining realism to an aesthetic precision in Europe. Howells's best novel, *The Rise of Silas Lapham* (1885), brings a self-made paint manufacturer forward from the 'day of small things' before the Civil War into the new world of trusts and mergers. The corruptions of the system defeat him financially, but his morality remains: Howells imposes on the new landscape of commerce and industry the old, domestic, moral image of the family. Enthusiasts now began to proclaim in the last decades of the century that new literary movements and centres were emerging; but their proclamations remained no more than brave acts of faith as long as they were issued – like Hamlin Garland's statements on behalf of the movement of 'veritism', in *Crumbling Idols* (1890) – from the traditional literary capital, Boston. There were perceptible signs of shift; in 1889 Howells moved from Boston to New York, celebrating the new venture in a book in a fresh manner, *A Hazard of New Fortunes* (1890), which nonetheless indicates within itself that a new language of fiction must be found. Garland would attend the Chicago Columbian Exposition to proclaim the need for a new middle-western literature, but it is not really until after 1900, with Theodore Dreiser's *Sister Carrie*, that we see the signs of this, and the real outcome had to wait for the 'Chicago Renaissance' of twenty years later, when writers like Carl Sandburg, Sherwood Anderson and Vachel Lindsay distilled the experience of the 'Second City' and the 'Hogbutcher of the World' into poetry and prose.

In 1887, Eleanor and Edward Marx Aveling, in their book *The Working Class Movement in America*, complained that American literature had so far produced no studies of factory hands or dwellers in tenement houses: no *Uncle Tom's Cabin* of capitalism. By 1906 Jack

London would be proclaiming that Upton Sinclair's *The Jungle* had done this, but in the 1880s the promise seemed slim. That American culture at that time was backward looking, more aware of lost innocence than future power, is nicely demonstrated by Larzer Ziff in his *The American 1890s,* where he describes a benefit reading given in 1887 for the American Copyright League by the day's major writers, including John Greenleaf Whittier, Oliver Wendell Holmes, James Russell Lowell, Mark Twain, Edward Eggleston, George Washington Cable and James Whitcomb Riley. Some of these were realists, but all were writers whose talents had been nourished in a different America and whose best literary efforts were employed to chronicle its passing. Others like Henry James and Henry Adams also felt themselves to be lone survivors from a golden past, but they elected to recapture it in Europe rather than America. And when they did turn their attention to contemporary America – in James's *The American Scene* (1907), Adams's *Education of Henry Adams* (1907) – it was to express a sense of void and despair at the chaos and ugliness or the mental disorder created out of the 'large and noble sanities' of the past. Thus the excitement generated by a society transforming itself within a generation did little to affect their gloomy conviction that there 'cannot really be any substitute for roundabout experience, for troublesome history, for the long, unmitigable process of time'. All, perhaps, sensed the need for a new language but it was slow to come, though gradually the 1890s made the great formal transition, from moral realism to a deterministic, process-centred naturalism, a writing that increasingly found its centre in the new urban and industrial America.

But perhaps this slowness is understandable. Certainly now many native-born Americans could claim two or more generations of urban dwelling; moreover, many foreign-born, especially Jews, now came to America from European urban centres. Yet though exact statistics are not available, indirect evidence indicates that the bulk of the native- and foreign-born who moved into the American cities after 1880 came from rural and village backgrounds. They were, as Herbert G Gutman contends, a pre-industrial folk 'who brought into industrial society ways of work and other habits and values not associated with industrial necessities and the industrial ethos.'[5] Under the conditions of urbanization and industrialization, their folk behaviour and values were seriously challenged and transformed. Rural traditions and localism, lynchpins of identity, broke down in urban anonymity. The Polish peasant came from a society where 'Every tree, every large stone, every pit, meadow, field, has an individuality of its own and often a name. The same tendency shows itself in the individulization, often even anthropomorphization, of time. . .time becames part of nature, and individualized periods of time become natural objects.' Whereas in America time takes on a different character: 'I long terribly for my country,' Aleksander Wolski wrote home to Poland, 'nothing gives me pleasure in America. We must be very attentive in our work, every hour, because if anything is bad we are without work.'[6] In Europe the peasant's social environment was bounded and determined by primary groups. 'The Sicilian peasant's interests are literally limited by the skyline. His only interests are the local interests of his village. . . The spirit of *campanilismo*, of dwelling under one's church tower, of jealous loyalty to *Paesani*, to his fellow villagers, circumscribes the Sicilian's social, religious, and business life.'[7]

Industrialization imposed on the immigrant and native American of rural backgrounds a novel discipline which required conformity and routinized behaviour rare in rural society. The wage system separated the individual from ritual duties and obligations. Factories and mills required regularized, clock-based attendance, and a repetitious and constant work pattern. What was expected of the immigrant worker is found in a booklet to teach English to Polish labourers of the International Harvester Corporation.

Lesson One. I hear the whistle. I must hurry. I hear the five minute whistle. It is time to go into the shop. I take my check from the gate board and hand it on the department board. I change my clothes and get ready to work. The starting whistle blows. I eat my lunch. It is forbidden to eat until then. The whistle blows at five minutes of starting time. I get ready to go to work. I work until the whistle blows to quit. I leave my place nice and clean. I put all my clothes in the locker. I must go home.[8]

Discipline was imposed on workers by men who themselves were part of a hierarchical system. In industry, unlike rural society, there existed a separation of ownership, direction and labour.

In the rural mind, accommodation was interwoven with land, and, without land, the family 'cannot act as a unit with regard to the rest of the community; it ceases to count as a social power'.[9] Even where rural dwellers were tenants, they had certain 'rights' to property by law or custom, and they were normally closely associated with property owners. In the city, dwellings were separated from land. The individualized, if often substandard, character of the rural home became in the city the tenement, and with the tenement block came an enforced and unnatural community. The relationship between the individual and his dwelling-place was casual and contractual – the contract often being made with an owner several agents removed from the tenant. Throughout the period, two-thirds of all housing was tenant-occupied: in 1900 in New York 87.9 per cent and in Chicago 74.9 per cent of all housing units were rented. Chicago was notorious for its railroad flats and New York for its tenements. In 1893, the year in which Stephen Crane published *Maggie,* over half of New York's population lived in tenement houses. The conditions of such lives have never been better described than by the twenty-one-year old protégé of Garland and Howells:

Eventually they entered a dark region where, from a careening building, a dozen gruesome doorways gave up loads of babies to the street and the gutter. A wind of early autumn raised yellow dust from cobbles and swirled it against a hundred windows. Long streamers of garments fluttered from fire-escapes. In all unhandy places there were buckets, brooms, rags, and bottles. In the street infants played or fought with other infants or sat stupidly in the way of vehicles. Formidable women, with uncombed hair and disordered dress, gossiped while leaning on railings, or screamed in frantic quarrels. Withered persons, in curious postures of submission to something, sat smoking pipes in obscure corners. A thousand odours of cooking food came forth to the street. The building quivered and creaked from the weight of humanity stamping about in its bowels.

Indeed, Crane's *Maggie* would begin to fulfil the Avelings' appeal for a literature of the American tenement, just as in 1899 Frank Norris's *McTeague* and in 1900 Dreiser's *Sister Carrie* would help fulfil Garland's prophecy of a Western literary movement based on the new realism: not, as H L Mencken said, 'the old, flabby, kittenish realism of Howells's imitators', but a new vision that got under the surface of things. Where James, Adams and Howells himself emphasized the chaos amid the crumbling eighteenth-century and nineteenth-century principles, their successors now began to chart the powerful forces that were to shape twentieth-century America. *Maggie* works by an observant indifference, noting inexorable processes at work, refusing moralistic conclusions. *McTeague* applies a naturalistic system to the story of a brutish San Francisco dentist and his thrifty Swiss immigrant wife. *Sister Carrie* explores the almost biological ascent of Carrie Member through the world of goods and cities from poverty to dominance. The older realism, morally concerned, was now giving way to new languages and codes for charting the new order of things. It explored the detail of city life, the workings of heredity and environment, the sense of social struggle. Even fiction about rural America – Frank Norris's *The Octopus* (1901), for example, set in California's San Fernando valley – is about the impact on farmers of the pressures of the monopolistic railroad; in the world of pastoral, machine and the system prevail.

The same shift was evident in other areas. Before the Civil War, opportunity had been defined in largely agrarian terms, in the spirit of Horace Greeley's advice: 'Go west, young man'. But now it was increasingly described in an urban context. Thus, in the novels of Horatio Alger – the most popular novelist in American history – the hero, with a few variations, comes from a farm or village, and with luck and pluck succeeds in the city. Or to use another example: in a famous lithograph of the period, a young man resting on a rural hillside, plough beside him, looks upon an idealized industrial city, aglow and challenging, which in its complexity contrasts with the simplicity of the rural setting. The picture is called 'The Lure of the City'. Dreiser, who first saw Chicago in 1884, never forgot the 'urge and sting' of his first days there, and used the experience to write the opening chapters of

Sister Carrie. He also recalled his feelings directly in *Dawn:*

I washed my face and brushed my clothes, then knelt down by the window – because I could hang farther out by doing so – and looked out. East and west, for miles, as it seemed to me, was a double row of gas lamps already flaring in the dusk, and behind them the lighted faces of shops and, as they seemed to me, very brightly lighted, glowing in fact. And again, there were those Madison Street horsecars, yellow in color, jingling to and fro, their horses' feet plop-plopping as they came and went, and just as they had when I sold papers here four years before. And the scores and scores of pedestrians walking in the rain, some with umbrellas, some not, some hurrying, some not. New land, new life, was what my heart was singing! Inside the street cars, like toy men and women, were the acclimated Chicagoans, those who had been here long before I came, no doubt. Beautiful! Like a scene in a play: an Aladdin view in the Arabian nights. Cars, people, lights, shops! The odor and flavor of the city, the vastness of its reaches, seemed to speak or sing or tinkle like a living, breathing thing. It came to me again with inexpressible variety and richness, as if to say: 'I am the soul of a million people! I am their joys, their prides, their loves, their appetites, their hungers, their sorrows! I am their good clothes and their poor ones, their light, their food, their lusts, their industries, their enthusiasms, their dreams! In me are all the pulses and wonders and tastes and loves of life itself! I am life! This is Paradise! This is the mirage of the heart and brain and blood of which people dream. I am the pulsing urge of the universe! You are a part of me, I of you! All that life or hope is or can be or do, this I am, and it is here before you! Take of it! Live, live, satisfy your heart! Strive to be what you wish to be now while you are young and of it! Reflect its fire, its tang, its color, its greatness! Be, be, wonderful or strong or great, if you will but be!'

The cultural dominance of the city led to a changing image of the farmer. Before the Civil War the farmer was deemed an ideal type: the noble yeoman, the horny-handed son of toil, a man of nature, a Cincinnatus. But after the war the farmer became, in urban parlance, a 'hayseed', 'rube' or 'hick'. Where once his nobility was extolled, the farmer became a comic figure on the stage, dressed in overalls and sporting a goatee. One of the earliest Edison records was entitled 'Moving Day in Pumpkin Center' and reinforced the stereotype of the bumbling, backward farmer already common on the stage. By the 1880s a literature about rural degeneracy appeared which would have been inexplicable before the Civil War. 'My people are degenerates; the people all through my district are degenerates,' a New England rural pastor wrote to a Boston newspaper. Robert Dugdale's 'Jukes' of New York, Frank Blackmuir's 'Smoky Pilgrims' of Kansas and Henry Goddard's 'Kallikaks' of New Jersey, all came to symbolize a drama of rural decay.

Farm protest in the nineteenth century had its roots in real, economic grievances. The farmer was exploited by industrialists and businessmen who respresented an urban-based elite. Adding fuel to farm bitterness was the knowledge that the urban exploiter also attracted their children. The city was the symbolic Babylon which lured the rural children of Israel. And as the city ways dominated, so rural inferiority increased. In Will Carlton's *Farm Ballads* the mother – soon to be sent 'Over the hill to the poor house' – rails at her daughter-in-law who had come from town: 'She was quite conciety, and carried a heap o' style.' The rural hostility is poignantly captured in Hamlin Garland's story, 'Up the Coulé', in *Main Travelled Roads* (1891), where the city and farm brothers face each other:

> They stood and looked at each other. Howard's cuffs, collar and shirt, alien in their elegance, showed through the dusk, and a glint of light shot out from the jewel of his necktie. . . As they gazed in silence at each other, Howard divined something of the hard, bitter feeling which came into Grant's heart as he stood there, ragged, ankle-deep in muck, his sleeves rolled up, a shapeless old straw hat on his head.

This sense of bitterness, combined with inferiority feelings, was a persistent strain running through farm protest movements before 1900. Richard Hofstadter, in his *The Age of Reform*, contends that 'The agrarian myth encouraged farmers to believe that they were not themselves an organic part of the whole order of business enterprise and speculation that flourished in the city, partaking of its character and sharing in its risks, but rather the innocent pastoral victims of a conspiracy hatched in the distance. The notion of an innocent and victimized population colors the whole history of agrarian controversy . . .'

The farmers mourned for their children in the cities; equally important was the fact that the children bemoaned the lost innocence of a rural past. In 1910 over half of the city population had an American or European past rooted in the land or in a local rural community. It was almost inevitable, therefore, that a literature of rural nostalgia would appeal to their collective memory. Indeed the school of local-color writing, an important phenomenon of this period, must be considered in the context of an urban nostalgia for a rural past. Unlike much of the literature of the 1920s, with its acerbic views of village and country life, pre-First World War writing is almost elegiac in recreating rural joys. This is true of Mark Twain's Hannibal, Zona Gale's Friendship Village, Sara Orne Jewett's Maine Villages, Edward Eggleston's Flat Creek, and Hamlin Garland's Wisconsin and Iowa farmers. Nowhere is this sense of rural nostalgia more vividly portrayed than by the popular and commercially successful poet James Whitcomb Riley. Born in the small Indiana town of Greenfield, he moved to Indianapolis, and lived there until his death in 1916. His poems are a paean to rural Indiana with Doc Sifers, Little Orphan Annie, Old Aunt Mary, Squire Hawkins, Tradin' Joe, and Uncle Sifers offering sage rural advice from the front porches of Griggsby Junction. In the country Riley saw man close to Nature; there was a different time scale, different sounds, colours, and smells:

> The husky, rusty, russel of the tassels of the corn,
> And the raspin' of the tangled leaves, as golden as the morn.

The city, by contrast, was artificial:

> My son-in-law said, when he lived in town,
> He jest natchurly pined, night and day
> For a sight of the woods, er a acre of ground
> Where the trees wasent all cleared away!

The contrast between the country (natural) and city (artificial) is a common theme in Riley's poems. Rural nostalgia is probably a less common theme in ethnic literature because much of it was written by relatively assimilated second and third-generation Americans. That it existed on an intimate and personal level is indicated in the letters of Polish peasants collected by W I Thomas and Florian Znaniencki. Letters from Poland are filled with references to rural concerns, and from urban America came letters enquiring about crops, livestock, and the village community.

For other writers, rural values and country scenes were beyond recapture, and nostalgia, however comforting, was an unsatisfactory emotion. Yet the rural memories remained, as they would through into twentieth-century literature, in Anderson, Hemingway and Faulkner, and the lure of the city never quite obliterated the sense of loss which the move from the country entailed. One simple escape from this dilemma was into an untroubled and unconditioned future; and it is significant that, with the decline of Utopian communities during the third quarter of the nineteenth century, Utopian literature simultaneously increased in volume – in works like Edward Bellamy's *Looking Backward* (1888), or Ignatius Donnelly's *Caesar's Column* (1891). Often reformist and populist in spirit, these works often expressed, in the form of romantic pastoral, a fear and hatred of modern technological and industrial society. Essentially it derived from the same impulses that lay behind another popular form, the historical novel, and it mattered little whether the authors looked backwards or forwards; it was always away from immediately contemporary America. One of the exceptions was Mark Twain's *A Connecticut Yankee in King Arthur's Court* (1889), a parody of this type of yearning romance, which squarely confronts the complex issues of primitivism and progress. Out of ambivalent feelings toward past and present, he creates a complex ironic pastoral which ends with his Yankee mechanic in sixth-century Camelot trapped behind an electric fence, surrounded by corpses. When one of his characters laments in the postscript 'We had conquered; in turn we were conquered,' this sums up not only Twain's ambiguity about industrial innovation, but what many sensitive Americans felt about the progress or otherwise of the Gilded Age.

The image of the new America, industrial and urban, proved in fact hard to grasp. One way of measuring it was in its changing relationship with Europe: a theme, of course, in the novels of Henry James. America had once stood, to itself and others, for innocence (one need only recall the vogue for James Fenimore Cooper in Britain and Germany) and a predominantly agricultural America had been seen by many as, in Jefferson's words, 'the last best hope of mankind'. By contrast, Europe was old, class-ridden, wise (or at least sly): mobs roamed its cities, and its poor filled its prisons, workhouses, mines and mills. In President Monroe's words, the European political system was 'essentially different. . .from that of America'. Europe was beyond redemption. But what of an America which filled its sky with acrid smoke, sent its children down mine-shafts or into textile mills, and created its own chaotic and formless cities? Old ideals seemed lost; perhaps the simplest answer was to follow Marx and state that the United States was no exception to the contradictions of capitalism and to class struggle, nor immune to a proletarian revolution. Or one might ignore differences, and fall back on belief in a community of interests, as in the cult of Anglo-Saxonia popular among upper-class Americans and North Europeans, but also present in the writings of Frank Norris and the socialist Jack London. Others argued that America had now become corrupt: that the world of Henry Adams's Arcadian boyhood in Quincy had, in a short time, become the world of banks and trusts, dominated by J P Morgan, John D Rockefeller, and other business predators. To such people, Europe often beckoned, much as it does in the fiction of Henry James and Edith Wharton, with the promise of cultural values that could transcend the vulgarity of American materialism. One might thus conceive of a culture irrevocably split between culture and process, dream and reality. Or one might argue, like Henry Adams in his *Education,* that the New World called for a new account of history, a new type of consciousness, or perhaps a new pragmatism that could order the increasing sense of chaos.

Looking forward

And there were indeed those who found justifications for and challenges in the new society. These individuals did not idealize a bucolic past, nor apparently did they feel any sense of innocence betrayed. Rather, they saw factories and cities as the inevitable products of Progress. In terms of the American past it was relatively easy to justify industrialization and laissez-faire capitalism. The factory was merely the large-scale manifestation of industrial processes that had been going on in New England homes since the seventeenth century. It was said of Henry Ford that when he looked out of his office window he never saw the massive River Rouge plant, but only his machine shop in Greenfield village. Certainly machines to save time and cut costs were essential in a nation with a chronic shortage of labour. On the level of ideology there were few problems. The Puritan ethic with its stress on thrift, industry and frugality, its admonition to 'work for the night is coming', was as applicable to the industrialist Amos Lawrence in the nineteenth century as it had been to his agricultural forebears in the Massachusetts Bay Colony. The Jacksonian division between productive and non-productive classes may have cast aspersions on bankers and stockholders, but not on the honest industrialist. Alexander Hamilton, Matthew Carey and Henry Clay had an image of an industrialized America long before the Civil War. Even in the South, where rural and patriarchal values lingered the longest, ante-bellum proposals for industrial expansion were greeted with enthusiasm, albeit with little money. In the Gilded Age the movement to extend railroads and open cotton mills and iron foundries was carried forth on a wave of Southern nationalism and crusading rhetoric. The general American delight in statistics – agricultural, commercial, industrial – reflected the faith of a nation which identified its validity not in a hoary past but a bright future. Americans were by nature teleological in their thinking.

Social Darwinism reinforced the older American business and industrial ethos. Charles Darwin and Herbert Spencer offered a scientific rationale for a laissez-faire system based on competition, and flattery for those who survived the struggle for competitive existence. Most importantly, Spencer argued that social evolution was inevitable, and that its apogee was in Western industrial society. The Americans, Spencer stated, could 'reasonably look forward to a time when they will have produced a civilization grander than any the world has known'.[10] Furthermore, Spencerians could invoke the 'Master' – as Andrew Carnegie called Spencer – to oppose any criticisms of the industrial system. Scientific 'laws' supported laissez-faire capitalism; to interfere with them would be harmful in the short term and absurd over the long perspective. Nor was Spencer's scheme at odds with the rise of big business. John D Rockefeller, half Spencerian, half Puritan divine, expressed this view in a Sunday School address:

The growth of big business is merely the survival of the fittest. . . The American beauty rose can be produced in the splendor and fragrance which bring cheer to its beholder only by sacrificing the early buds which grow up around it. This is not an evil tendency in business. It is merely the working-out of a law of nature and a law of god.[11]

'Not evil, but good', Carnegie declared, 'has come to the race from the accumulation of wealth by those who have the ability and energy to produce it.'[12]

The critics of laissez-faire capitalism did not, with the exception of Henry George, decry industrialism. In part this was because they were soaked in Spencerian thought, and their criticisms of Spencer's conclusions were usually argued in terms of evolutionary premises. John R Commons stated that 'I was brought up on Hoosierism, Republicanism, Presbyterianism, and Spencerianism.' And Commons was not alone in American intellectual circles. The economists and sociologists who studied in Germany or at Johns Hopkins accepted evolution and with it the concomitant view that the growth of industry was inevitable and desirable. Lester Ward contended that human evolution proved the validity of co-operation rather than competition, and nowhere was this more true than in advanced industrial states.

What the critics of laissez-faire capitalism wished to do was to measure the effects of industrialism by moral considerations. And they were willing to advocate the use of the State not to destroy industry – few were interested in William Morris's neo-Medievalism – but to use its powers to ensure competition and soften the impact on those least able to survive in the industrial jungle. Thus Edward Bellamy's *Looking Backward,* the most popular Gilded Age criticism of contemporary society, depicts a good and humane future world which is both pastoral and intensely industrial. Bellamy's readers could easily extrapolate his Boston of 2001 from potential tendencies of 1887. Perfection no longer was dependent on a close harmony and communion with Nature. Right reason, a touch of 'true' Christianity, and the rational organization of industry could provide the good society and a higher form of mankind.

Evolutionary thought, in particular its concepts of inevitability, and the realities of industrialization and urbanism, forced literary figures to observe and analyse the world in a new way, and to discover new literary forms in which the new dimensions of society could be expressed. Writers were freed from the incubus of the past which was, in Spencerian terms at least, meaningless. The contemporary scene was found in the spatial dimensions of the city, the binding discipline of commerical or industrial work, and all determined by forces over which the individual had little control. Stephen Crane's *Maggie* in New York could no more prevent her tragic fate than could Upton Sinclair's back-of-the-yards Lithuanians in *The Jungle* of Chicago. Frank Norris' Grain Exchange and the working of the Southern Pacific Railroad in *The Octopus* (1901) and *The Pit* (1903) were locations in which the universal rules of competition and the struggle for existence were carried out. Its actors were puppets in some dimly perceived evolutionary plan. The Naturalists seldom seriously question a society based on competition and one that produced mill hands and millionaires. They might consider it vulgar, as Dreiser and Samuel Fuller did, but it existed, and existence transcended moral judgements. Paul Dressler might have sung about the memories of 'new mown hay' along the banks of the Wabash, but his brother Theodore Dreiser had no such romantic notions. In Theodore's world there were no innocents, least of all in Indiana.

In many ways, industry was easier to justify and adjust to than was the city. The discipline imposed by the factory may have been alien to immigrants and Americans of rural origins, but the factory as such was not incompatible with America's past value system. And in Social Darwinism the large factory and monopoly capitalism had the sanction of Science and the aura of Progress. The literature of naturalism and realism found its roots in and its defences in an industrial society. Although the city was a logical result of industrialization, it seemed a more alienating force – somehow less 'American' than the Carnegie Steel Works. Josiah Strong, writing in 1885, saw the city as a 'serious menace to our civilization'. It was filled with unassimilated foreigners and Roman Catholics, along with 'gamblers, thieves, saloon keepers and all the worse elements of society'. 'Here the sway of Mammon is widest and his worship the most constant eager.'[13] In the city where riches contrasted with dire poverty, governments were apt to be corrupt and thus the heresy of socialism was likely to find advocates.

The city impinged on people's consciousness more than the work place, and the city contrasted vividly with real or imagined memories of a rural past. Where the factory and office were efficient and work was routinized, and to that extent acceptable, the city was filthy, ugly, chaotic and alienating. A girl from Emporia, Kansas, desperately lonely in Chicago, caught this sense of alienation:

The city is like that. In all my work there had been the same lack of any personal touch. In all this city of three million souls I knew no one, cared for no one, was cared for by no one. . .I had read how the universe is composed of millions of stars whirling about. I looked up at the sky. I was just like that – an atom whirled about with three million other atoms, day after day, month after month, year after year.[14]

There was no focus, no sense of community except what the individual might create out of his organizational ties: the lodge, ethnic saloon, trade union, fire company, political club, literary society, church.

By the turn of the century the bleak view of the city began to change. Progressive reformers became increasingly convinced that the city was politically redeemable, that corrupt bosses could be overthrown, and that the city could be operated efficiently and humanely. The structure of city government, hitherto modelled on two-house legislatures, typical of state and national governments, could be transformed by the strong mayor system, or by introducing city manager or commision forms of government. Urban reformers declared that the city need not look like a treeless jungle, that parks, boulevards and recreation centres would provide breathing space and beauty to an urban population. While many reformers had an ambivalent view of the foreign-born, others, chiefly from the settlement houses, saw in the immigrant community values which were lacking in American natives. Then, too, there were millions who by 1910 were born in cities, and for whom there was no alternative living place; nor was there a rural past except as a folk memory passed down from an older generation.

The concept of the city as a distinct urban form, and as a positive and beneficial force, was reflected by the turn of the century in a new physical appearance and in new ways of interpreting life in the metropolis. A remarkable group of engineer-architects – William LeBaron Jenny, Dankmar Adler, Daniel Burnham, John Wellborn

Root, Louis Sullivan – created in the steel-girdered skyscraper a *city* architecture. The skyscraper evolved from technological advances and urban commercial motivations. Structural steel and the hydraulic and, later, electric elevator, allowed for an upward extension of buildings, and high land prices in central business districts made the skyscraper economically viable. The skyscrapter presented a unique cityscape. Tall buildings – offices, factories and apartment houses – came to distinguish the town from the country. The city was now not merely the town overgrown, but physically a new creation. The skyscraper became the symbol of a triumphant urbanism.

Men who could change the skyline of American cities could also determine other aspects of its physical appearance. Throughout America, planners were stimulated by the World's Columbian Exhibition of 1893 with its overall contribution of architecture, landscaping and lake-shore setting. Parks, parkways, recreational centres, were expanded or created in all major American cities. It seemed possible, as Daniel Burnham and Edward A Bennett remarked in their general plan for Chicago, for a city to 'be made an efficient instrument for providing all its people with the best possible conditions of living'.[15] The concepts and plans which Burnham and others in America drew and put into practice was popularly called the 'City Beautiful' movement. The title itself indicates a new and positive conception of the city.

Settlement houses, starting with Chicago's Hull House in 1891, and numbering over 400 by 1915, became the locus for a new evaluation of the city. Settlement-house residents accepted the city as the basic context in which they lived. Their efforts to create a sense of community in the slums did not grow out of any desire to re-establish a rural or village society, but rather because community was a means of breaking down urban alienation. They argued that their experience showed that the city was capable of regeneration by reforms, example and community spirit.

Settlement-house workers usually stressed the 'scientific' character of their work, by which they meant that they developed a methodology for observing and studying the social and economic conditions of the city. Sociologists, in particular Robert E Park of the University of Chicago, developed a theory of urban ecology which assumed that cities lent themselves to scientific observation, that change – the life blood of sociology – could be charted, and that in the city human behaviour was as 'natural' as in a rural society. Although the Chicago school of urban sociology operated from environmental premises which stretched back to Jefferson, it denied that there were associations between evironmental conditions and moral results. Park and other American urban sociologists rejected such categories as rural innocence and urban depravity.

In his autobiography, the progressive urban reformer, Frederick C Howe, writes of his conversion to a new conception of the city:

The possibility of a free, orderly, and beautiful city became to me an absorbing passion. I had an architectonic vision of what a city might be. I saw it as a picture. It was not economy, efficiency, and business methods that interested me so much as a city planned, built, and conducted as a community enterprise. The city was the enthusiasm of my life. And I saw cities as social agencies that would make life easier for people, full of pleasure, beauty and opportunity.[16]

Except in Whitman, or city booster literature, it would be rare to find such a fulsome view of urban life in the nineteenth century. By the time Howe was writing, the city need no longer represent sinful menace, but promise. In *Sister Carrie,* it lures like a magnet or a lover: in *The Jungle* it contains the political seeds of its own amelioration. And for the writers of the developing new arts movement that stirred the United States around 1912, when Progressivism seemed dominant, Woodrow Wilson was elected, radical and *avantgarde* causes abounded, and the impact of European modernism began to reach American shores, the city was experimental bohemia, dislodging the Puritanism of an old and confined America. When Sherwood Anderson in 1912 walked out of his paint factory in Ohio and moved to Chicago and the modern arts, he felt he was experiencing the transition of an entire generation, advancing, certainly, into the complexities of modern industrialism, but away from the confinements of the small town and the past. In any case, as the tentacles of railroad lines and, later, highways spread to the farthest reaches of the country, the old rural–urban distinctions began to collapse. By the early 1920s, America was sure of its modern condition. Around this time, too, Professor Charles J Galpin of the University of Wisconsin was discovering 'rurban' areas where farm and town had developed a symbiotic relationship, so that the distinction of behaviour and value systems between them diminished. Certainly rural nostalgia, and appeals to the virtues of agrarian life, as well as to images of the city as Waste Land or Slough of Despond, persisted in American thought and art after the First World War. But increasingly these struggles were focused in recognition of the complex power and pull of the modern city, or else they became defensive and cranky. Innocence, in so far it was based on images of pioneers, noble yeoman and villagers, itself became either complex – as in Hemingway – or suburbanly sentimental. Factories and cities, and an acceptance of their life-styles and discipline, had created a new reality.

Notes and references

1. Nelson Algren, *Chicago: City on the Make* (3rd edn), Angel Island Publications, Oakland, 1961, p. 59.

2. Unless otherwise stated, all statistical information is from the US Bureau of the Census, *Historical Statistics of the United States: Colonial Times to 1970,*

Bicentennial Edition (Two parts), Government Printing Office, Washington DC, 1975.

3. A M Schlesinger, *The Rise of the City 1878–1898*, Macmillan, New York, 1933, p.63.
4. Blake McKelvey, *The Urbanization of America 1860–1915*, Rutgers U.P., New Brunswick, 1963, p. 63.
5. Herbert G Gutman, *Work, Culture and Society in Industrializing America: Essays in American Working-Class and Social History*, Alfred A Knopf, New York, 1976, p. 15
6. William I Thomas and Florian Znaniecki, *The Polish Peasant in Europe and America*, (2 vols), Alfred A Knopf, New York, 1927, Vol. I, pp. 207,760.
7. Harvey Zorbaugh, *The Gold Coast and the Slum: A Sociological Study Chicago's Near North Side*, University of Chicago Press, Chicago, 1950, p.162.
8. Gutman, op. cit., p. 6.
9. Thomas and Znaniecki, op. cit., Vol. I, p. 162.
10. Quoted in Richard Hofstadter, *Social Darwinism in American Thought*, Beacon Press, Boston, 1955, p. 48.
11. Quoted in *ibid.*, p. 45.
12. Quoted in Richard Hofstadter (ed), *Great Issues in American History: From Reconstruction to the Present Day*, Vintage Books, New York, 1969, p. 88.
13. Quoted in Charles N Glaab (ed), *The American City: A Documentary History*, Dorsey Press, Homewood Ill., 1963, pp.330–6.
14. Zorbaugh, op. cit., p. 80.
15. Quoted in Christopher Tunnard, *The Modern American City*, D Van Nostrand, Princeton, 1968, p. 48.
16. Quoted in Allen M Wakstein (ed), *The Urbanization of America: An Historical Anthology*, Houghton Mifflin, Boston, 1970, p.213.

Chapter Nine

The Twenties

Jacqueline Fear and Helen McNeil

What were the Twenties?

When the United States economy teetered and then crashed in the last months of 1929, 'The Twenties' became an entity for the first time, defined in retrospect. Initially the significance of the stock-market crash was not grasped; financiers looked confidently toward recovery. But, as the nation slid into depression and despair, with banks and factories closing, bread-lines lengthening, and one-quarter of the labour force seeking work, the year 1929 assumed a mythic quality. In 1931, F Scott Fitzgerald called the past decade of economic boom and high personality 'the Jazz Age', and Frederick Lewis Allen's sparkling book *Only Yesterday* characterized the eleven years from the end of the First World War to the stock-market crash as 'a distinct era in American history'.[1] Detailing the changing state of the public mind, and recording the facts, fashions and follies which touched the daily lives of millions of Americans, Allen synthesized a now-familiar picture of the Twenties, as an era of bootlegging and Babe Ruth, Fords and Flappers, Babbits and Bohemians – an era which, in 1931, had already receded into the past, leaving Allen wondering 'What was to come in the nineteen-thirties?' In fact, of course, the idea of 'the decade' as a principle of historical interpretation can be both misleading and ahistorical: it necessarily ignores the slow and uneven development of social and economic organisms, and exaggerates superficial qualities and differences. Yet some of the most vital changes during the Twenties did occur in exactly the sphere that Allen documents – in the nation's mood and style of life.

Certainly, after the First World War, it seemed to many that the pace of life in America greatly quickened, and that the war drew a barrier between generations and across many areas of experience. In *Middletown* (1929) their sociological study of Muncie, Indiana (a book that interestingly compares with Sinclair Lewis's fictional treatments of middle America, *Main Street* (1920) and *Babbitt* (1922)), Robert and Helen Lynd set out to chronicle the changes that had occurred in a representative mid-western city between 1890 and 1925. Acknowledging that 'any people are in a process of change', they asserted, however, that 'we today are probably living in one of the eras of greatest rapidity of change in the history of human institutions.'[2] The Lynds's conviction of uniqueness may well have been incorrect, but many echoed their opinion,. and generational oppositions and distinctions mattered greatly to the politics and discourse of the Twenties. Considering the problem of cultural change, the anthropologist Ralph Linton has observed:

Even in the most progressive and forward-looking community, changes in culture produce some individual discomforts. At least some of the members of the group will develop nostalgic attitudes toward a past which appears rosy in the light of present difficulties. The more intense and widespread the discomfort due to change, the more widespread the attitudes are likely to be.[3]

And indeed, as Lawrence Levine has noted,[4] a struggle between progress and nostalgia seems strikingly central to the Twenties, a decade in which many Americans looked back with yearning to a past age which seemed simpler, morally surer, more pastoral, and less troubled. Yet they were simultaneously forced to grapple with the problems and demands of the present. There was no war to be fought, no depression to be beaten. The singularity of the Twenties lies in the fact that it was a post-war, economically hopeful decade when Americans confronted the onrush of the modern world with no distractions.

War and post-war

In April 1917 the United States had entered the First World War in support of the Allied cause. Woodrow Wilson defined the war aims in moral terms: 'The world must be made safe for democracy. Its peace must be planted upon the tested foundations of political liberty.' In 1918, while the war still raged, Wilson formulated his famous Fourteen Points, which outlined the need for a peaceful world and provided a 'guarantee' of continued peace through a 'general assembly of nations'. It was this League of Nations which became the focus of hostility for the Republican party and other Americans opposed to the war or to Wilson. While on a speaking tour to win support for the League, the President suffered a debilitating stroke; the Senate rejected both the Treaty of Versailles and the League of Nations; and, in the election of 1920, when a small-time politician, Warren Gamaliel Harding from Marion, Ohio, was thrust forward as the Republican candidate by the party powers, H L Mencken, who scourged the 'Booboisie' of the decade of 'normalcy', predicted that:

the overwhelming majority of Americans are going to vote for him. They tire, after twenty years, of a steady diet of white protestations and black acts; they are weary of hearing high fallutin' and meaningless words. . .Today no sane American believes in any official statement of national policy, whether foreign or domestic. . . .He wants a renaissance of honesty – even ordinary, celluloid, politician's honesty. Tired to death of intellectual charlatanry, he turns despairingly to honest imbecility.[5]

The progressive coalition, founded on a shared belief in reason and man's ability to build a better world, had been shattered. The reform impulse did not die, but it was fragmented. Americans suffered economic troubles: 4 million men from the armed services were suddenly demobilized; inflation spiralled, rising by a shocking 28 per cent in 1919–20 in New York City; farm prices fell, and continued to fall. Progressive or naturalist writers like Theodore Dreiser or Edgar Lee Masters were dealing with dead issues. There was also an alarmist psychological mood, described by William McAdoo as 'a strange poison in the air', which fostered hostility towards labour and radicals and resulted in riots and lynchings. After 1919, the ugly fervour of the Red Scare died, but the unity of political vision which had characterized the Progressive period had gone.

The Twenties may be said to begin with the end of the Great War, as they finished with the Great Crash. Yet in social developments, politics and art alike there was an inevitable element of continuity with what went before, though the war symbolized the stark distinction between past and present. The Twenties continued a process of modernizing and standardizing technology that had been evident in the United States since the Civil War; and the famous experiments of Twenties' arts had pre-war roots. Eliot and Pound had already moved American poetry into Modernism by 1914; and Imagism had been founded in 1912; the Armory Show (1913) had brought the innovations of French cubism into American art; James in his later novels and Gertrude Stein had begun a stylistic revolution which deeply affected American writing after 1913.

The enormous achievements of the American novel in the Twenties were, of course, partly triggered by the war, which became a symbol for the cut-off of the past. For Fitzgerald, Hemingway, Dos Passos, Faulkner, and for O'Neill, Williams, Stevens and Crane the literary modernism of the Twenties was the beginning of a new age. Yet for American writers the war as political, social and personal experience hardly seemed to have occurred at all.[6] American post-war fiction was not marked, as in Europe, by a struggle to understand the relations between the war, state power, and capitalism. In American writing, the public arena of history was approached, if at all, through myth, sometimes overlaid with a naturalist determinism. American writers were struggling to understand the self and validate the role of the artist in language; these 'aesthetic' themes and problems of their relation to modern American society became fundamental artistic issues.

None of the important writers of the Twenties had actually served at the front except Hemingway, who was wounded while an ambulance driver in Italy, 'the picturesque front' of *Farewell to Arms* (1929).

Fitzgerald was at training camp in Alabama when the Armistice was signed; William Faulkner was learning to fly with the RCAF in Canada, not in France, as he liked to say later. For British authors the war meant the death of friends, even one's own death (Rupert Brooke, Wilfred Owen, Issac Rosenberg); the hideous reality of trench warfare exposed official cant and either broke the survivors or marked them for life. But for Americans the war was more often a symbolic event: a chance to explore freedom, courage, and personal maturation. The impossibility of personal heroism turned the literary war into an incomplete, unreal experience, but one which released energies instead of crushing them.

The Great War thus gave a sense of impetus, power and discontent, even a feeling of generational separation. But by mid-decade it had become one of the many events in American life in which something promised, some important event, had its fulfilment in meaning mysteriously withheld. In 'Echoes of the Jazz Age', Fitzgerald felt that he had succeeded with *This Side of Paradise* (1920) 'simply for telling people that he felt as they did, that something had to be done with all the nervous energy stored up and unexpended in the war.' In E E Cummings's *The Enormous Room* (1922), ambulance driver Cummings paradoxically first feels free when he is imprisoned by the French military, who become the enemy in his private war: Cummings's language bursts into surreal vigour the moment the prison gates shut and he is let loose into 'the Delectable Mountain' of bizarre personalities. John Dos Passos's *Three Soldiers* (1921) shows the dehumanization of war with bitterness camparable to Robert Graves's *Good-bye to All That* (1929); but he went on to write the energetic urban collage of *Manhattan Transfer* (1925), a characteristic work of Twenties experiment. Almost inevitably, other war novels, such as Don Passos's earlier *One Man's Initiation* (1920, complete version 1969), and William Faulkner's *Soldiers' Pay* (1926), assimilate the war to the fictional model of the young man growing to manhood that was set for American literature by Stephen Crane's *The Red Badge of Courage* (1895), another convincingly realistic war novel written from imagination.

The most famous American war novel, Hemingway's *A Farewell to Arms* (1929), appeared when the war was a decade in the past. Here the collapse of the Italian front confirms Frederic Henry's belief that effort is futile since 'they get you in the end'. However, the destructive symbolic rain that washes away Frederic's 'separate peace' falls mainly on the non-combatant Catherine Barkley, the English nurse who dies giving birth to Frederic's dead child, conquered not by war but by her body's biological fate. For Hemingway, all is vanity. To this day *A Farewell to Arms* remains a compelling mixture of compressed realism and ritualized dialogue, despite its misogynist tone and its rather less-noticed ambivalence about war itself. Somewhat like Byron in *Childe Harold*, Hemingway hates war for its stupidity, its sloppy arbitrariness, its slaughter of the good, but is attracted to it for its ability to make heroes who can display what Hemingway calls 'grace under pressure'. Vivid as it is, Hemingway's Great War exists to validate a nihilism already fixed by *The Sun Also Rises* (1926; published in Britain as *Fiesta*), in many ways his true war novel. Hemingway's terse tale is set in an expatriate's Paris where the wounds of war have created what Gertrude Stein, Hemingway's stylistic mentor, called 'a lost generation' of men and women adrift in a chaotic hell of their own solipsism.[7] Lady Brett Ashley, the heroine, destroys everything she touches by her sexual greed; even her pseudo-Christian renunciation of a vulnerable young matador doesn't heal her. In such a sterile age Jake Barnes, the cynically idealist hero who narrates the story, must by definition be impotent, like T S Eliot's Fisher King, in *The Waste Land* (1922), who sits 'the dull canal' of post war 'Unreal City' musing 'on the king my brother's wreck/and on the king my father's death before him.'

Such images of impotence and alienation coloured much modernist American writing, darkening the more familiar picture of energy and excitement. Jake Barnes's friend Bill parodies the supposed case against the American expatriate: 'You've lost touch with the soil....Fake European standards have ruined you. You have become obsessed by sex. You spend all your time talking, not working.' Yet the fact that Hemingway, Fitzgerald, Hart Crane and hundreds of other writers and would-be writers invaded Europe in the 1920s, in a literary migration unequalled before or since, suggests not so much a developed nihilism as a disillusion with American limitations, a belief that art separated from one's society could redeem what politics could not.

Above all, while nineteenth-century American expatriatism expressed a Jamesian thirst for an older, richer culture, Twenties expatriatism displayed a flight away from provincial and puritan constraint, one that overshot New York and turned to a Parisian artistic bohemia large enough, *avant-garde* enough and sexually liberated enough to accommodate the most rebellious American. These American writers did not generally absorb French language or culture, as earlier writers and contemporary artists had; they went, as Gertrude Stein put it in *The Autobiography of Alice B. Toklas* (1933), to be 'all alone with English and myself'; or they went, like Hart Crane, to join a restless crowd of other English-speaking expatriates, possibly reading Joyce's *Ulysses* at Sylvia Beach's bookshop,[8] certainly drinking and living a bohemian life at the favourable exchange rates brought about by the post-war superiority of the American economy, at a time when the United States, having now become an economic creditor, was on its way to becoming a cultural one.

A hunger for new styles of life and art went hand in hand with an anxious need to have these new sensations explained. If one sign of major literature is its ability to give meaning to the great social events of its age, then Sinclair Lewis's *Main Street* (1920) and Fitzgerald's *This Side of Paradise* (1920) are the major works through which the nation perceived its new sensations at the beginning of the Twenties. Both novels exposed American social patterns which their readers desperately needed to understand; a grateful public made them both best-sellers. *This Side of Paradise* was read as a chronicle of the young in revolt against convention, even though the very young Fitzgerald had clearly already read James Joyce's *Portrait of the Artist as a Young Man* (1917) with profit. Lewis's *Main Street* crystallized the shift of national values from rural to urban. For the heroine, Carol Kennicott, the city is 'good': complex, free and modern, but the petty, constrained middle-American society of Gopher Prairie finally grinds her down. As in Sherwood Anderson's poetic, psychological short stories, *Winesburg, Ohio* (1919), the only way to mature and escape Puritan repression is to flee for the city, preferably into the life of art.

Many Americans in the Twenties clung to their lost Age of Innocence; others, recognizing the force of change, sought explanations. Politicians and pulpits had lost credibility: literature, newspapers, and the burgeoning mass culture of popular magazines, radio, and the movies had to bear the weight of a new quest for social and personal models. Fitzgerald, Lewis, Dreiser and Mencken genuinely influenced their avid readers, but when the questions raised seemed too complex or the answers too shocking, the work was rejected. This pressure for the easy answer deepened the split between high culture and mass society, as writers forged a self-reflecting literary society through modernist *avant-garde*s and a bohemian life-style.

A fragmented culture

Some literature thrives on its own resources: it can appear perversely peripheral to contemporaries, yet in retrospect seem close to the heart of an era. In a changing society, some separation between literature and life is essential; literary attention to form can give an age a shape by which we can perceive what is happening to it. Symbolic illusion and fragmentation were two such formal modes of the Twenties. American theatre, dominated by Eugene O'Neill, tried to shape social and psychological issues by what O'Neill called 'the touch of the poet': heightened language, expressionist staging, psychological plots, mythic allusions. In *The Emperor Jones* (1920), the black, vitalist hero reverts to a Freudian savagery under pressure; in *The Hairy Ape* (1922) class conflict is acted out through sexual conflict with Darwinian overtones; *Desire Under the Elms* (1924) sets a mythologized Oedipal struggle in New England. Many of O'Neill's plays have great theatrical impact; others, like the Expressionist *Dynamo* (1929), look like crude cobblings together of European influences. But it was above all Modernist poetry that played, for the Twenties, the form-giving and form-shattering role. By the Twenties, American poetry was already ahead of phase, and its complex forms were absorbing historical changes rather than simply recording or being influenced by them. The Imagist and Modernist strand of American poetry had become cosmopolitanized, threatening the culturally less urbane native vein. As the aspiring poet Hart Crane wrote from Cleveland, Ohio, in 1920; 'there are still Rabelais, Villon, Apuleius and Eliot to snatch at occasionally ... a small Gauguin I have on the wall, Japanese prints, and Russian records.' Anything to blot out Cleveland.

Eliot's *The Waste Land* (1922), probably the most important and influential American poem of the decade, thus has almost no American references. Its themes of impotence and loss are structured through accumulated shards of 'impersonal' myth and history, fragments 'shored against my ruins' and it draws on the European sense of cultural collapse. Widely read during the Twenties as a summary of post-war disillusion, it now looks more like an intense, even personal outcry, its famous fragmentation a means of psychological and stylistic investigation as well as an indictment of modern decay. *The Waste Land* made fragmentation seem the appropriate structure for the modern age; this pattern recurs in Ezra Pound's *Hugh Selwyn Mauberley* (1920), Pound's disgusted farewell to London and his younger Imagist self as he moved on to Paris and later Italy. *Mauberley* portrays American cultural immaturity (E P is 'born in a half-savage country, out of date'), and a philistine, anti-artistic Western society, 'an old bitch gone in the teeth', which either kills its young artists in useless war, or disposes of them by making them drifting hedonists like M Verog or Mauberley. With his brilliant, uneven *Cantos* (1925, 1928, 1934, etc.) Pound undertook his life work, a modernist epic that makes a positive Odyssean quest to balance *Mauberley's* satiric negative. But where Eliot's 'difficult' fragmentary references make a conservative ideological point about the fragmentation of Western tradition, Pound's eclecticism here seems designed to give what he considered to be the most vivid modern form of expression: his collage of classical, oriental, Renaissance and contemporary imagery is meant to build toward what Pound called a 'paideuma' or culturally unified society, to be led by an enlightened ruler-patron, a line that unhappily led him toward Mussolini, 'the Boss' of Canto XLI (1934).

William Carlos Williams commented sourly in the Preface to his surreal prose poem, *Kora in Hell* (1920), that a meeting on contemporary American poetry in Paris would find half the poems submitted in French or ancient Provençal. Like the 'Chicago Renaissance' poets, Masters, Lindsay and Sandburg, Williams wanted a specifically *American* modernist poetry. He attempted to make his 'Objectivist' short poems into tools of social change *and* literary experiments. 'The Red Wheelbarrow' insists that 'so much depends on' the way a particular red wheelbarrow looks; it is through small compositions of the real that we know ourselves. But there is need for an 'American measure'; and Williams's short, strongly enjambed poetic line together with his social commitment have made him a powerful influence on subsequent poetry. What Pound and Williams did share was a hope for a mature *and* an American literature: and in the critical perspectives of Edmund Wilson or the poetry of Wallace Stevens, one finds this to hand.

To be an American writer in the Twenties meant that one was free to be European or not as one chose. Wilson showed in *Axel's Castle* (1931) that French symbolism had become the English-speaking modernism of a Joyce or Eliot. Stevens took care never to set foot in Europe; but his *Harmonium* (1923) expresses an almost Emersonian optimism about perception through the radiating ambiguous imagery of French symbolism: 'Poetry is the supreme fiction', replacing religion. For Stevens's Poundian *persona* Crispin, the hero of 'The Comedian as the Letter C', the American soil inspires first a 'green brag', then through 'disguised pronunciamento' yields a relation between the real and the imaginary which is always imperfect but always evolving. By the end of the decade, the diverse modernist experiments of Eliot, Pound, Williams and Stevens had irrevocably become the American poetic – a poetic in which the resources of language and culture were seen as fully available even if the audience stayed small.

In American painting, however, the struggle between Europeanized moderns and nativists was not resolved. The separation took dramatic form in the Armory Show of 1913, where both Cubists and the realist Ash-Can School were represented. Walter and Louise Arensberg's New York salon (1914–21) introduced European Dadaists like Marcel Duchamp and Francis Picabia to the American photographer Man Ray, the painters Charles Sheeler and Charles Demuth, the poets Amy Lowell and William Carlos Williams, and the socialist Max Eastman. But the American painters influenced by Cubism and Dada lacked both talent to go beyond a decorative Cubism and the nihilist rage of Dada: instead they celebrated the machine and the city, much as did Hart Crane in his modernist epic *The Bridge* (1930). Realist and regionalist painters like George W. Bellows and Thomas Hart Benton went on working; Benton's mural cycle, 'American Historical Epic' (1919–26), suggests he is almost waiting for the Depression to bring realism back. It was, ironically, Benton's pupil Jackson Pollock who was finally to create a profoundly American abstract art owing nothing to this realist and national imagery.

Perhaps the most impressive American visual art of the Twenties was photography. It had behind it a secure *avant-garde* tradition, coming from Alfred Stieglitz's and Edward Steichen's '291' gallery and its successors; and the experimental photo-journalism and advertising photography in mass-circulation magazines profoundly influenced popular taste. Margaret Bourke-White, Paul Strand, and Charles Sheeler, photographer as well as painter, abstracted machinery and skyscapers into powerful angular forms whose stark presence and often ambiguous scale gave a critical edge to the photographer's awe, a perspective that the European futurists never achieved. Other photographers – Ansel Adams, Edward Weston – and artist Georgia O'Keefe, made sharply focused dramatic studies of wilderness, nudes, or individual objects that share the spirit of poetic 'objectivism' ('No ideas but in things', said William Carlos Williams).

A divided society

Although the tensions and fragmentation of the Twenties were keenly felt, there was, superficially, a basic political and economic consensus. A journalist wrote in *Harper's Magazine*, in 1929:

When ten thousand widely scattered hearts are beating high with hopes of a rise in some favourite discovered overnight ... When the whole country follows the same tips ... finds comfort in the same reassuring signs that normalcy is here to stay, we know without doubt that this is a united people.[9]

But that earlier conflicts had continued to fester through the decade, despite the prosperity, was well demonstrated when Sacco and Vanzetti were executed in 1927. Convicted in 1921 after a payroll robbery in Massachusetts, Sacco and Vanzetti were both Italian immigrants and self-confessed anarchists. The evidence against them was regarded by many as inconclusive, and their cause attracted world attention. They were condemned to death after a group of Boston 'Wasps' (white Anglo-Saxon Protestants) refused a retrial. 'All right, we are two nations', John Dos Passos declared in *USA* (1938), writing about this divisive episode.

There was, of course, a Twenties radicalism, but it was mainly preoccupied with such matters as the Red Scare and the IWW (Industrial Workers of the World), with Sacco and Vanzetti's trial and with the implications of the Soviet Revolution, popularized by John Reed in *Ten Days That Shook the World* (1919). Magazines like *The Masses* (1911–18) and *The Liberator*, both edited by Max Eastman, and Michael Gold and Joseph Freeman's *The New Masses* moved on from a permissive experimental radicalism to a call for communist world revolution, even though, as the bourgeois expatriate Matthew Josephson said in 1928, 'the people vote for General Motors'. Scores of American political tourists visited Soviet Russia in the Twenties: Eastman, Freeman, Gold, Isadora Duncan, Lincoln Steffens, Senator Robert La Follette, John Dos Passos, Theodore Dreiser, E E Cummings, Claude McKay. But their experiences had no effect on the American worker; nor did these radicals agree with one another. Eastman explored the post-Lenin struggles in *After Lenin Died* (1925) from a Trotskyite viewpoint; Freeman wrote off the Stalin–Trotsky clash in *An American Testament* (1938), and, like some leftists in the Twenties and many in the Thirties, saw the party as 'selfless, incorruptible'.[10]

The Twenties are often represented as an era of materialist conservative retrenchment when politics were in abeyance. Throughout the decade, Republicans succeeded in winning a high proportion of the popular vote: 60.4 per cent in 1920, 54 per cent in 1924, 58.2 per cent in 1928. Yet, there was underlying strife, occasionally evident in social strife, and perceivable in the struggles between the two major political parties. Within the Democratic Party, the heterogeneous remnants of the Wilson coalition, without direction or leadership, struggled against one another. Issues like prohibition highlighted the conflicts between the diverse dividing elements of American society.[11] The Volstead Act of 1919, making the production and consumption of alcohol illegal, can be read as a progressive measure, based on a belief that social problems could be curbed by legislation; but it also reflected and deepened social divisions, as an older protestant America sought to control a less tractable immigrant minority. Rifts within the Democratic party became clear at the convention of 1924. Big City Democrats supported the Irish Catholic Al Smith, a 'wet' and a product of a big-city machine, who demanded that the party condemn the Ku Klux Klan – a secret organization which terrorized blacks, Catholics and Jews, claiming it was fighting for 'Americanism', and working to 'win a return of power into the hands of the everyday, not highly cultured, not overly intellectualized, but entirely unspoilt and not de-Americanized, average citizen of the old stock.'[12] Smith, when asked what he would do for the states west of the Mississippi, reportedly answered: 'Which are the states west of the Mississippi?' Rural Democrats thus backed William G McAdoo of Tennessee; in the end a compromise candidate, John W Davis, a Wall Street lawyer, was nominated on the 103rd ballot.

Four years later this conflict was re-enacted on the larger national stage. In the 1928 election Al Smith won the Democratic nomination, but lost the Presidency to the Republican Herbert Hoover. Analysing the impression of unity given by the election results, *Harper's Magazine* asked, 'What is the bond of union between a Pennsylvania manufacturer and an Iowa farmer?' and answered, 'Not interest certainly, nor political theory, but a common faith that God loves the typical American as he has been, and that what he has been he should continue to be.'[13] This faith was to be painfully shattered by the Depression. The strife which immobilized the Democratic party during the 1920s in fact concealed a shift in political power which was to guarantee the party's success in the 1930s. In 1922 and after, the big cities, Republican for nearly three decades, went unwaveringly to the Democrats, and western states, already experiencing an agricultural depression, consistently sent radical Democrats to Congress. Even though during the Twenties it appeared that there was an unchallenged political consensus, the Republican majority was being progressively undermined throughout the decade.

If old stock and rural Americans were suspicious of Smith's New York Eastside accent and big-city style, it was partly because they feared the political power of the first- and second-generation Americans who supported him. Demands for immigration restriction were by no means new to America; but in the 1920s, for the first time, the federal government began imposing rigid laws. Congressmen expressed their fears of changes occurring in society by passing the National Origins Act in 1924 (which based immigration to the United States on the proportion of residents of each nationality already resident in the United States); more lowly Americans joined the reorganized Ku Klux Klan. However, the Klan was in decline by 1925 after the disgrace of its leaders, and superficially many of the schisms within society seemed to heal.

To describe political struggles as Dos Passos did in terms of 'them' against 'us' simplifies what was occurring in Twenties America. Mencken blamed the problems of the nation on rural Americans, who, 'abandoned for years to the tutelage of their pastors, have now gone so far into darkness that every light terrifies them and runs them amok.' He insisted: 'In the long run the cities of the United States will have to throw off the hegemony of these morons. They have run the country long enough and made it sufficiently ridiculous.'[14] But the developing mass society of the 1920s was rooted in an industrial economy which reached deep into the countryside. A clear urban – rural division could no longer be made. The year 1920 marked the symbolic moment when over 50 per cent of Americans were found by the census to be urban rather than rural (living in towns of over 2,500); by 1930 this figure had grown to 69 per cent. However, other less quantifiable developments were of greater significance. The automobile gave mobility to both town and city people, and the radio brought the same programmes into rural and urban homes alike. In 1926, the National Broadcasting Company, and the following year the Columbia Broadcasting Service, hooked together hundreds of local stations in national networks. If urbanites like Mencken felt threatened by rural America, farmers reciprocated these feelings. The Scopes Trial, held in Dayton, Tennessee, in 1925, was a staged event which dramatized the cultural dimensions of the Twenties. A young schoolteacher was brought to trial for teaching Darwin's laws of evolution; William Jennings Bryan, three times Democratic presidential candidate and champion of rural protestantism, confronted the agnostic Chicago lawyer, Clarence Darrow. Although it appeared that Bryan and his cause were the losers, and Bryan died a few days after the trial, there were many non-fundamentalist Americans who nevertheless felt ambivalent about the direction their new, technological and scientific society was taking. 'Science', wrote Joseph Wood Krutch in 1929, 'has always promised two things, not necessarily related – an increase first in our powers, second in our happiness or wisdom, and we have come to realize that it is the first and less important of the two promises which it has kept most abundantly.'[15]

An increase in wisdom without a corresponding increase in power was the fate of black Americans in the 1920s. During and after the Great War, millions of blacks emigrated from the rural South to Northern urban centres. Detroit and Chicago offered industrial employment, and New York had a variety of trades, and the magnet of Harlem, even if black employment everywhere was subject to humiliating 'Jim Crow' practices. These urban blacks had a crucial impact on the nation's economy and cultural life. Jazz – primitive, syncopated, improvised, complex – came to seem the necessary music of the Twenties; white writers praised black vitalism: Sherwood Anderson, *Dark Laughter* (1925); Carl Van Vechten, *Nigger Heaven* (1926); the 'Harlem Renaissance' linked black themes with white modernism. These black writers, many well-educated products of W E B Du Bois's 'talented tenth', felt their contradictory position; as Countee Cullen wrote in *Color* (1925), 'Yet do I marvel at this curious thing/To make a poet black, and bid him sing!' Discovered by poet Vachel Lindsay when he put some poems on Lindsay's table in the restaurant where he was busboy, Langston Hughes combined, in *The Weary Blues* (1926), a Whitmanesque free verse with jazz and blues rhythms; Jean Toomer published *Cane*, a finely styled short-story collection, in 1923; West Indian-born Claude McKay wrote militant sonnets trapped within traditional English forms. The problems were focused in Alain Locke's *The New Negro* (1925), an influential integrationist book that pleaded both for racial pride and white acceptance, and saw the Twenties as a 'coming of age' for black Americans. But if Locke was right about the new breadth of black writing and music, he was wrong about white American society (in the Twenties not even American radicals joined the black struggle for equality).

The economy in the Twenties

In 1919, when Congress rejected Wilson's League of Nations, American foreign policy seemed to move decisively toward 'isolationism'. American issues preoccupied the decade, and the world outside seemed a threat. Yet, paradoxically, 1919 was the moment when the United States emerged as the world's leading creditor nation. Now one of the largest producers and exporters of agricultural goods and one of the largest import markets, America's economic health and politics would have more direct effect on the world economic conditions than those of any other nation. If the decade ended with a loud economic crash which left no one unaffected, it opened with a silent transferral of economic power from which many benefited, although, in general, the rich remained rich and many of the poor remained poor. The 'mood' of the Twenties, at once elusive and tangible, followed the same rhythms as the burgeoning production economy. In 1922, after the brief post-war recession, the boom began. Three years later, an overwhelming majority of Americans were to agree with Calvin Coolidge that 'the business of America is business'. The city, not the railroad, was now the main stimulus to the economy; the construction industry accounted for much of the Twenties boom. But industry now manufactured new goods, some of them previously unknown and unimagined – radios, vacuum cleaners, electric irons, toasters, record players and, most important of all, the automobile – to transform the life-style of Americans. Consumer goods became foundation stones of the economy; with manufacturing output growing three times faster than population, the American economy had entered a new phase. Madison Avenue suddenly featured on the map of New York City; a generation of Americans like Zelda Fitzgerald grew up founding their dreams on the infinite promise of American advertising. Articles people could not afford were bought with the help of new instalment credit schemes. The logic of the economy had shifted from saving to spending. 'We've spent close to $100 on our radio,' said a worker's wife in Muncie, Indiana, 'Where'd we get the money? Oh, out of our savings, like everybody else.' (*Middletown*, p. 270)

Americans now enjoyed a higher standard of living than any other people. Yet technological developments transformed more than the economy; they also created new dreams and provided, for some at least, the means of fulfilling them vicariously. In 'Echoes of the Jazz Age', Fitzgerald recalled how:

In the spring of '27, something bright and alien flashed across the sky. A young Minnesotan who seemed to have had nothing to do with his generation did a heroic thing, and for a moment people set down their glasses in country clubs and speak-easies and thought of their best dreams.

Charles Lindbergh's solo flight across the Atlantic stirred the nation. John William Ward has pointed out the dual nature of the popular celebration. Lindbergh was the living symbol of the young, independent American, unbound by organizations and public pressures. Yet, ironically, his achievement was made possible through the refinements of technology, organization and industrial finesse. Lindbergh himself gave equal credit to the plane, 'that wonderful motor', and President Coolidge expressed his pride 'that in every particular this silent partner represented American genius and industry'. As Ward points out: 'The response to Lindbergh reveals that the American people were deeply torn between conflicting interpretations of their own experience.'[16] Committed to the ease, affluence and thrill of their technological age, they nevertheless mourned a simpler, purer, less frenetic past.

Abroad, American business organization was admired and envied. 'The future of America is the future of the world,' wrote Aldous Huxley in 1927, 'material circumstances are driving all nations along the path in which America is going ... speculating on the American future, we are speculating on the future of civilized man.'[17] In the factory the increased rate of technological development meant that costs fell as productivity rose. But as tasks were divided into their component parts, work became repetitious and meaningless.'Ye get the wages, but ye sell your soul at Fords,' complained one worker in the Detroit factory. 'You've worked like a slave all day, and when ye get out yo're too tired to do anything.' In *The Big Money*, Dos Passos saw Ford spreading 'the Taylorized speedup everywhere, reachunder, adjustwasher, screwdown bolt, shove in cotterpin, reachunder, adjustwasher, screwdown bolt,reachunderadjustscrewdownreachunderadjust, until every ounce of life was sucked off into production and at night the workmen went home grey shaking husks.'[18] As enterprises became larger, 'scientific' methods were increasingly employed to control production and labour.

In the Twenties the Ivy League universities founded schools of business studies, training professionals to rationalize the work process and to secure the consent and contentment of workers. This 'welfare capitalism', a confused combination of paternalistic reasoning and hard-headed economic sense, was partially responsible for the staggering decline in union membership: from 5 million in 1920 to 3.5 million in 1929. Many workers were content, as the Lynds showed in *Middletown*, to enjoy the material benefits of the age and let power be concentrated in the hands of the employers. But the Crash of 1929 destroyed the belief in the possibility of welfare capitalism: employers had made a commitment to look after their workers which they had proved unable to fulfil.

The decline in the labour movement cannot be attributed entirely to the new prosperity. The changing structure of American industry undercut union membership. Several unionized industries – coal and New England textiles – were 'sick' and the numerous new industries had no union tradition. Also, the labour force was changing fast. Blacks had never been welcomed in unions, nor women, who made up one-quarter of the workforce, nor immigrants, still more concerned with adapting to life in America. Unions kept their anachronistic craft orientation, even when an increasing proportion of the workforce was unskilled. And despite the reassurances that the interests of labour and capital were identical, no previous era in the Supreme Court's history compared with the Twenties in the number of statutes invalidated, and most of these were labour laws. Whatever the diverse reasons for the weakening of the labour movement, Lincoln Steffens pointed to the main one: 'big business was producing what the Socialists held up as their goal: food, shelter, and clothing for all'.

The family, women, and sex

Some of the most visible changes in American life during the Twenties came not in politics and institutions, but in the unprecedented acceleration of economic development and its influence on life-style, modes of consumption, sexual codes, personal relationships, individual expectations. Life became more 'modern' and familial and sexual change were observed with concern. As divorce increased, some Americans looked back to the stability of the previous age. As one 'Middletowner' explained:

The main reason there are more divorces is that people are demanding more of life than they used to .... In former times ... they settled down to a life of hard work ... and putting up with each other. (*Middletown*, p.128)

Others, though, demanded that the institution of marriage should adapt to changing times. More emphasis was put on emotional fulfilment, less on financial bonds; increasing numbers of people lived in large cities far from their parents; the private as well as the public dynamic of marriage changed. In 1927, Judge Ben Lindsey shocked respectable public opinion by advocating 'compassionate marriage', urging that with divorce and contraception made readily available, only the most suited need or should contemplate parenthood. If individual marriages that broke with traditional forms hit the headlines (like that of the novelist Fanny Hurst, who lived separately from her husband), Americans in general were marrying younger and having fewer children – bringing changes in roles and relationships within the household. One result of the declining birth-rate was that, in relation to the very young, the proportion of people in the 15–24 age group was growing larger; while the shift of the economy towards the service sector meant that more and more young people stayed in educational institutions. In 1920 only 32 per cent of the 10 to 17-year olds were in high school; the figure was 51 per cent by the end of the decade. (There is an interesting parallel between the 1920s and 1960s in educational expansion coupled with a dominant 'youth culture'.) These changes ricocheted back into the heart of the family, altering relations between parents and children. With school classes growing, children were increasingly divided by age; the authority of the family weakened, that of the peer-group increased. Nor was school time necessarily spent on the traditional learning activities. The Lynds found that, for parents and children alike, school education was 'more valued as a symbol of things hoped for than for its specific content' (*Middletown*, p.294) and, as the school's function widened, children engaged in a wide round of extra-curricular activities. Sports teams and social clubs ranked high in priority. When asked what made a girl eligible for a high-school club, a Middletown girl replied: 'the chief thing is if the boys like you and you can get them for the dances' (*Middletown*, p.216). If the older generation decried the precosity and sexual *mores* of the young, changing family patterns, the automobile and the movies meant that over half the junior and senior boys and girls in Middletown marked 'true' in a questionaire stating: 'Nine out of every ten boys and girls of high school age have "petting parties". (In Fitzgerald's *This Side of Paradise*, Amory Blaine is behindhand when, already a sophomore at Princeton, he goes to 'that great current American phenomenon, the petting party'.)

But even more striking, because more celebrated, was the changing image of women: the flapper was, and still is, one of the most compelling symbols of Twenties culture and society. Audaciously flaunting her bobbed hair, hiked skirt, cigarettes and bootleg, she personified the 'new woman', different in spirit and shape from her Victorian mother. 'By sheer force of violence she established the feminine right to equal representation in such hitherto masculine fields of endeavour as smoking and drinking, swearing, petting and disturbing the community peace.' The flapper, with her garish daring, redefined the boundaries between private and public morality. Yet how significant was her victory? According to Henry Steele Commager, the Twenties saw the emancipation of women, begun in the 1890s, 'dramatised by the vote and guaranteed by birth control'. Yet in important areas the situation of women in the 1920s was unchanged. An ex-flapper, writing in 1922, praised the flapper's potential:

Watch her five years from now and then be thankful that she will be the mother of the next generation, with the hypocrisy, fluff and other 'hookum' worn entirely off. Her sharp points wear down remarkably well and leave a smooth polished surface. You'll be suprised at what a comfort that surface will be in the days to come![19]

So the 'fluff' and naughtiness are merely preparation for a woman's traditional role. H L Mencken likewise identified the flapper as a staunch Main Streeter: 'What she dreams of is not an infinitely brilliant husband, but an infinitely *solid* one, which is to say, one bound irretrievably to the claims of normalcy.'[20] Statistics endorse this cynical view. Though more single women now worked and became an important reserve force in the economy, most married women gave their energy to home-making. Those in professions were blocked by prejudice and discriminatory pay practices. Yet more important, home-making itself became professionalized in the Twenties, especially for the middle classes. Women's colleges like Radcliffe, Mount Holyoke and Smith, founded to provide female equivalents of Harvard and Yale, began to turn motherhood into a profession: Vassar created a School of Eugenics in 1924 to re-route 'education for women along the lines of their chief interests and responsibilities, motherhood and the home'. The flapper may have dispelled certain nineteenth-century taboos; but she did not represent a large change of role for women, marriage or the family, as one ex-feminist emphasized in 1926:

In six years of married life I have gradually but surely descended from that blithe, enthusiastic, cocksure young person I was eight or ten years ago to the colorless, housewifely, dependent sort of female I used to picture so pathetically and graphically to my audiences – the kind of woman we must all have a chance not to be.[21]

The American Twenties were the 'sex era', a time when the existence of an instinctive 'sex drive' in young people, especially women, gained wide social acceptance – an emphasis made reputable by Sigmund Freud, whose Clark University lectures in 1909 fostered a popular, optimistic, version of psychoanalysis, which America absorbed with amazing speed.[22] By 1915, psychoanalysis had displaced all other therapies and reached the women's journals; Mabel Dodge serialized her analysis in the Hearst Press. Popularized psychoanalysis meshed with the American belief in self-improvement; Freudian theories seemed a way to get rid of neurotic symptoms without analysing what they meant. 'Do you suffer from headaches, nausea, "neuralgia," paralysis, or any other mysterious disorder?' asked Max Eastman only semi-satirically in *Everybody's Magazine* (June 1915); if so, Freud could 'sink a shaft into the subconscious region and tap it of its mischievous elements'. Sexual problems and analysis became acceptable and then fashionable; sex, in other words, became another American con game. The sexually hungry 'liberated' woman (Zelda Fitzgerald, Mabel Dodge [who, failing to win D H Lawrence from Frieda, married a 'primitive' Navajo Indian], Mae West, Elinor Glyn, Caresse Crosby) became a familiar type; while sexually sophisticated women like Dorothy Parker, the Algonquin table wit, or bohemian poet Edna St Vincent Millay behaved more like the Hemingwayesque 'chap': defiantly tough outside, sentimental and frightened underneath. Others, like poet and editor Marianne Moore, Imagist poet H D (Hilda Doolittle) or, more notoriously, Gertrude Stein, chose a life without men.

The sexual revolution of the Twenties was supposed to belong to the women, but the first great literary erotic revolution was certainly male, and in America at least, it took the form of narcissism or the embattled male trying to protect himself from the sexually aggressive female. In Fitzgerald's *This Side of Paradise* (1920), the trading of sexual favours for social status is still evident, but the rules have changed to allow the narcissistic young to fall in love with the image of their own beautiful, daring selves. And in *The Great Gatsby* (1925), Gatsby's 'Platonic' self-image seeks a reflection in Daisy. So blinding is 'the colossal vitality of his illusion' that Gatsby never sees how Daisy lives only in response to men's images of her – and the stronger and more brutal the imprint, the more she likes it. Daisy is figuratively (and literally) a killer, like Nicole Diver in Fitzgerald's *Tender is the Night* (1934), whose victim is a very American psychoanalyst who thinks neurotics are nice weak creatures who *want* to be saved. In Hemingway the battle lines are even more firmly drawn. Jake Barnes's mysterious groin wound is a necessary defence against Lady Brett Ashley, whose life is determined by her sex drive. Jake and Brett love each other, but when he can't satisfy her sexually, she rejects him: 'It's my fault, Jake. It's the way I'm made.' Meanwhile the housewife learned from popular magazines and movies that unless she had 'It' (sex appeal), she could expect her husband to stray, and her husband saw himself depicted as a machine for making money; after courtship the picture is grim in American popular and high culture alike.

Culture, mass and elite

The exploding mass culture of Twenties radio, film, and popular magazines marketed standardized behaviour models to populations with different backgrounds and needs, generating a new kind of conformity based on lower-middle-class consumer values. In one of the more striking American partnerships of social perception and the profit-making impulse, Hollywood wholeheartedly exploited the flapper type in films such as *Flaming Youth* (1923), *It* (1927), and *Our Dancing Daughters* (1928). The flapper film was a product, packaged by a star, marketed by the studio in the controlled outlets of its nationwide theatre chains, and consumed by millions. Against the undoubted democratizing force of such mass imagery must be set the demoralizing inadequacy that these commercial visions induced in the many who would never be able to buy the pleasures that Hollywood made them think they ought to have.

Ambivalence about the function of mass myth, and a conflict between production and art, were built into the Hollywood studio system. Ever since 'The Biograph Girl' was revealed around 1912 to be someone called Mary Pickford, America worshipped her as its sweetheart or 'silly little saint'.[23] Hollywood had exploited its 'star system', whereby mythic types are created by the star and his or her imitators. Because photography always records a version of reality, every cinematic act is validated by the audience's knowledge that in some way this visual fantasy is also 'real', involving a real person like themselves. From the impossibly innocent Pickford to the impossibly sexy Latin lover Rudolph Valentino, the star image is always based in the body of a human actor: Hollywood myths of youth, success and glamour thus seem 'true' in a way that the manifestly imaginary characterizations of novels can never be. In the Twenties, Hollywood studios wisely promoted audience interest in the stars' lives through publicity and fan magazines. When the human star contradicted the mythic image, a high price was paid: baby-faced comedian Fatty Arbuckle's trial for a sex-orgy murder wrecked his career, even though he was acquitted.

The Hollywood star system still dominates world cinema – so completely that its cultural origin in the American 1920s is not always obvious. Yet the Hollywood-star type is a characteristic product of a society which is deeply mythical while pretending to be pragmatic, passive in its acceptance of mass consumption while considering itself active, and dedicated to the belief that the individual's life is entirely his own responsibility, whatever social conditions might be. The star, like 1920s society, is about illusion, about believing yourself to be what you are not, and enjoying the belief while it lasts. The star images of the 1920s do not, however, provide a simple index of popular taste. Some 'star cycles' competed with others, or expressed urges only dimly articulated elsewhere. In the early 1920s, for instance, the All-American boy Douglas Fairbanks shared popularity with Valentino, and the virginal Pickford competed successfully with the 'vamp cycle' of Theda Bara, who was finished by 1920.

Techniques of classic Hollywood cinema such as cross-cutting between two narratives, flashbacks and close-ups had already been developed by D W Griffith and his cameraman Billy Bitzer in *Birth of a Nation* (1915), as well as by Charles Chaplin and Thomas Ince; the Twenties set these conventions into a language of cinema that we still use today, and which deeply influenced other art forms. The introduction of sound in *The Jazz Singer* (1927) ended the Twenties' expressive style of acting, and temporarily constrained camera movement and editing (montage). But Twenties film succeeded, on the whole, in making star-based melodramas more socially and artistically believable. King Vidor's highly praised, successful *The Big Parade* (1925) had a strong anti-war theme, not surprising since it was scripted by Lawrence Stallings, who also wrote the anti-war play, *What Price Glory?* (1924) with Maxwell Anderson; and William Wellman's brilliant *Wings* (1927), whose aerial photography is still unsurpassed, has a treatment of male comradeship under wartime stress which compares favourably with Hemingway. There were also, of course, melodramatic plots, type casting, and leaden epics (*The Ten Commandments*, 1923, *Ben-Hur*, 1926), and brilliant artistic indulgences like Erich von Stroheim's ten-hour film *Greed*, an adaptation of Frank Norris's naturalist novel *McTeague* (1899).

In the mid-nineteenth century, social change was seen in evolutionary terms. But the generation of the Twenties could no longer equate change with progress. The American version of Oswald Spengler's 'decline of the West' theory was a mild pessimism mingled with quasi-religious awe of the machine. In Henry Adams's meditative memoir *The Education of Henry Adams* (1907, 1918), the dynamo has abolished history and replaced it by a continuous modernity. For Joseph Wood Krutch, and Van Wyck Brooks, as for Lewis Mumford, who praised the cold modern beauty of skyscrapers, mass production's insult to craftmanship and intelligence made a not-entirely coincidental parallel to the insult to the intelligence of their own older, cultured eastern group whose social and political dominance had passed on to the 'booboisie' – a shift from caste power to capital power already analysed in Thorstein Veblen's *Theory of the Leisure Class* (1899). To the extent that critics and creative artists (Hart Crane's *The Bridge*, O'Neill's *Dynamo*, many artists and photographers) were absorbed by *things*, by machine mysticism and the glamourous modern city, they were deflected from any analysis of the people and the investment capital that fuelled those machines and built those skyscrapers. This displacement from causes to results limited critical understanding, despite concerned descriptions of mass production's dehumanizing effects in Sherwood Anderson's *Poor White* (1920), John Dos Passos's *Forty-Second Parallel* (1930) and Charles Chaplin's savagely funny film *Modern Times* (1936), with its scenes of conveyor-belt madness and a Taylorized 'feeding machine' that goes berserk.

Cultural commentators in the Twenties usually took for granted a gap between immaterial culture and a materialist society, an assumption given weight by sociologist William Ogburn's influential theory of 'cultural lag'. According to Ogburn's *Social Change* (1922), material culture (houses, factories, raw materials, manufactures) *always* surged ahead of non-material culture (customs, beliefs, institutions, governments):

When the material conditions change, changes are occasioned in the adaptive culture. But these changes in the adaptive culture do not synchronize exactly with the change in the material culture. There is a lag which may last for varying lengths of time. . .[24]

Not change itself was at fault, but a disharmony of change. Ogburn's theory located all change in technology, but in fact the changes were in the values which determined the use of existing techniques. In the Twenties, few Americans grasped the fact that ideology – as Max Weber has shown – influences change as much as technology. No new technology was needed to bring in the Ford conveyor belt or to 'Taylorize' the workforce.

Understanding of the ways in which the Twenties were indeed an age out of kilter was thus impeded by a belief in the inevitability of 'cultural lag'. Harold Stearn's *Civilization in America* (1921) glibly assumed that Americans should look to other countries for civilization, as the expatriates did. The well-publicized 'victory' of agnostic Clarence Darrow over fundamentalist William Jennings Bryan in the 1925 Scopes Trial masked the fact that evolution no longer made sense as a model for society. Freud's sombre humanism became in America a technique for cleaning up the inner life to fit the outer world.

Yet the 'cultural lag' disappears both as concept and as social reality when the cast of mind of an age is expressed by the form, as well as by the content, of art or literature. The Twenties saw three major works – Hart Crane's *The Bridge* (1930), William Faulkner's *The Sound and The Fury* (1929) and F Scott Fitzgerald's *The Great Gatsby* (1925) – which not only grasped the peculiar American mixture of pragmatism and illusion, but did so through an uncompromising literary modernism. All three works examine symbolism's dual role as carrier of multiple truths and as agent of delusion, so that symbolism becomes a means into social analysis as well as an example of artistic self-sufficiency. It is a critical cliché that American literature has no Dickens or Tolstoi, no great realist to sum up an age – but a symbolic or illusion-ridden society may well best be served by a mainly symbolic literature that uses technique and structure as well as subject matter to occupy the ideological ground between material things and the secret self. American writers who withdrew into the formalism of modernist writing could acquire sufficient space and confidence to bring society back in.

Doubly alienated from his middle-class, mid-west background by literary vocation and homosexuality, Hart Crane had a cautionary modernist career. He fled to New York bohemia; later to Paris and Mexico; a heavy drinker, in 1932 he committed suicide. His epic poem *The Bridge* was intended to be an American, optimistic, 'ecstatic' work opposing *The Waste Land's* European 'pessimism'. It is structured by its central symbol, Brooklyn Bridge, whose 'inviolate curve' is meant to make technology transcendent, and raise the poet-visionary until all America can be comprehended by his myth ('and of thy curveship lend a myth to God'). Crane's balance between a fragmented lyric subjectivity and a public voice lasts as long as the bridge remains a generative symbol, loosening other symbols: rings, curves, flights, returns, the 'arc synoptic' and the 'hellish tunnels that rewind themselves'. The aim is ever-increasing, 'symphonic' resonance. The bridge is both the object of Crane's desire and his image for forging links of past and present, inner and outer. Where *The Bridge* falters is when Crane takes too literally his attempt at synthesis. As in Williams's *In the American Grain* (1925), Crane sees an American heroism – Columbus, Poe, Emily Dickinson, Isadora Duncan – rejected by a venial society; yet he aims for epic confidence. The results are contradictory: the alienated, personal perceptions remain authentic, the effort at an all-embracing positive answer fails.

Beginning with *The Sound and The Fury*, William Faulkner gave his native South an authentic voice which was also at the forefront of modernist experiment. In Faulkner's mythical Yoknapatawpha County, Mississippi, developed over more than a dozen novels, the tragedy – and tragicomedy – of the South was acted out in microcosm. Faulkner's command of the South's social and psychological past is all the more impressive since, in the twenties. Southern historiography consisted of biography and legislative history, and Southern literature (with the exception of Kate Chopin and Ellen Glasgow) culpably ignored the realities of racial oppression and economic inertia which had made the South a separate, almost tribal, nation buried inside the Twenties' consumer society. Faulkner recast Southern history to bring out its murderous heritage (as in *Absalom, Absalom,* 1936), but he was even more concerned to erase the myths which had blighted the South and to form powerful new mythic images which could lead to knowledge. *The Sound and The Fury* is written around its heroine, Caddy Compson – the familiar mythic Southern belle revised by Faulkner into images of defilement, loss, and Christian sacrifice. Caddy is known only in fragments, through the minds of the novel's four consecutive narrators. *The Sound and The Fury* begins daringly with the disjointed Joycean stream of consciousness of Caddy's idiot brother Benjy, for whom past and present are fused into an eternally repeating experience of love and loss: 'Caddy smelled like trees.' Then follow the absurdist, time-obsessed suicide Quentin Compson and the vicious 'modern' brother Jason, who thinks time is money and so loses both. The novel ends with the third-person 'objective' narrative of Dilsey, a saintly black mother-figure to the doomed white Compson family. Paradoxically, Dilsey is the novel's most highly mythicized figure, symbolizing the blacks, who understand and suffer beyond mere history: 'They endured.'

F Scott Fitgerald's *The Great Gatsby* gave the Twenties what now seems its inevitable tragic hero in James Gatz, the mid-western boy who reads Ben Franklin and improves himself into Jay Gatsby, the brilliant hedonist whose tragic flaw is an outdated idealism. Had he loved money for its own sake, and not as a means to win Daisy Buchanan, Gatsby would have been a success, like Daisy's husband Tom, a racist, moneyed brute. But Gatsby must pay for his surreal glitter by a dark contract with the underworld of bootlegging and crooked stock deals. The rich world of suburban West Egg, with its fluttering women in white dresses like sails and the 'green light' of Daisy's dock, is linked with the money and excitement of New York by a waste land of cinders and cars, where the god-like face of Dr Eckleburg gazes balefully down from an advertising poster upon Tom's sexy, vulgar mistress Myrtle, who lives below. At this symbolic crossing-point between getting and spending, image and fact, Daisy crushes Myrtle while driving Gatsby's car, and he takes the blame, believing to the end in his inner image of an absolute love. Yet Daisy, like Twenties America, is simultaneously infinitely innocent and utterly, carelessly corrupt; the object of hopeless desire also for sale to the strongest bidder. In the novel's remarkable closing image, Gatsby's style of illusion is made the basis for all of America, from the moment that Dutch sailors gazed raptly at the 'green breast' of a new land awaiting despoilation.

The pathos of Gatsby's failure to recognize the high inner price of 'old money' prosperity is heightened by Fitzgerald's stress on the destructive illusions generated by new money. The new wealth fostered a complicity to pretend it was real, a confidence which, as John K Galbraith has pointed out, fostered the wild speculation which contributed to the crash of 1929:

Speculation on a large scale requires a pervasive sense of confidence and optimism, and a conviction that ordinary people were meant to be rich.[25]

The prosperity of the 1920s itself was rooted in unanalysed illusion about the availability of wealth. According to *Harper's Magazine*, there would be prizes for everyone:

> One thing that is quite new and definite is the proof that our modern industrial civilization is not going to the bow-wows. . .but is steadily growing more strongly and highly integrated, more stable, and more efficient, meaning thereby that the average livelihood is becoming surer. . .and that we may confidently look forward to a day when what we call poverty will be practically extinct.[26]

Of course the day that came was the day of the stock-market crash, 29 October 1929, the beginning of the end of an era. From the economically obsessed perspective of Depression-era America, the excess and vividness of the Twenties seemed a phantasmagoric illusion. In the Thirties, the cultural expressions of the social trauma of boom and bust were divided between a hectic surrealism and social realism. The Thirties couldn't use the Twenties fusion of regional and personal, outer and inner, through highly styled mythologies.

The contradictions of the Twenties took form in two of its heroes, Charles Lindbergh and Jay Gatsby. Lindbergh, an historic man, was the Twenties' favourite success story. The nation and Lindbergh agreed that he had wedded individualism to the machine in his solo transatlantic flights. His fame served a social need to hide how speculation dominated investment, how investment capital controlled the machine, and how the machine had made individual initiative an anachronism. Gatsby is the Twenties' beautiful loser, whose fictional tragedy forms a passionate analysis of how the supposedly essential American mercantile ideals lead to a fatal romanticism in an age of moneyed duplicity. Lindbergh the man became such a glamourous image of success that two madmen kidnapped and then murdered his young son. *The Great Gatsby,* a fiction that unmasked false images, was a commercial failure for F Scott Fitzgerald, who then exhausted most of his literary energies writing mass-market entertainment stories for handsome fees, which were never enough to pay for his wild, self-destructive life. In retrospect, the Twenties was indeed an age rich in ironies.

Notes and references

1.   F Scott Fitzgerald, 'Echoes of the Jazz Age', *The Crack-Up With Other Pieces and Stories,* Penguin, Harmondsworth, 1965, (orig. pub. 1931) – subsequent references in the text are to the Penguin edition; Frederick Lewis Allen, *Only Yesterday: An Informal History of the 1920s,* Harper and Row, New York, 1959 (orig. pub. 1931).

2. Robert S Lynd and Helen M Lynd, *Middletown: A Study of American Culture,* Harcourt, Brace and World Inc., New York, 1929. Subsequent references in the text are to this edition.

3. Ralph Linton, 'The distinctive aspects of acculturation', in Linton (ed), *Acculturation in Seven American Tribes,* Appleton Century, New York, 1940, p. 517.

4. Lawrence W Levine, 'Progress and nostalgia: The self-image of the nineteen-twenties', in Malcolm Bradbury and David Palmer (eds), *The American Novel and the Nineteen-Twenties,* Stratford-on Avon Studies 13, Arnold, London, 1971.

5. H L Mencken, 'In praise of Gamaliel', in Malcolm Moos (ed), *A Carnival of Buncombe,* John Hopkins Press, Baltimore, 1960, p. 30.

6. Paul Fussell's *The Great War and Modern Memory,* Oxford U.P., New York, 1975, shows the impact of the war on English writers and soldiers (and on some Americans).

7. Hemingway used Gertrude Stein's expression 'We are all a lost generation' as the epigraph for *The Sun Also Rises;* the epigraph is missing from some English editions. Stein heard it from a French petrol station attendant.

8. Gertrude Stein liked to minimize Sylvia Beach's cultural role; see Stein's *The Autobiography of Alice B Toklas,* Bodley Head, London, 1933, and *Paris, France,* Scribner, New York, 1940; for Beach's view see her *Shakespeare and Co.,* Faber, London, 1960.

9. *Harper's Magazine,* Vol. 158 (April 1929)

10. This discussion is indebted to Daniel Aaron's *Writers on the Left,* Oxford U.P., New York, 1961.

11. Joseph Gusfield, *Symbolic Crusade: Status Politics and the American Temperance Movement,* University of Illinois Press, Urbana, 1963.

12. Hiram Wesley Evans, 'The Klan's fight for Americanism', *The North American Review,* March 1926, reprinted in George Mowry, *The Twenties: Fords, Flappers and Fanatics,* Prentice-Hall, NJ, 1963, p. 137.

13. *Harper's Magazine,* Vol. 158 (February 1929)

14. H L Mencken, 'The eve of Armageddon', in Moos, *op. cit.,* p. 208.

15. Joseph Wood Krutch, *The Modern Temper: A Study and a Confession,* Harcourt Brace and Co., New York, 1929, p. 61.

16. John William Ward, 'The meaning of Lindbergh's flight', *American Quarterly,* X, (1958), pp. 3–16; also in R Abrams and L Levine, *The Shaping of Twentieth Century America,* Little, Brown, Boston (rev. 2nd ed), 1971.

17. *Harper's Magazine,* Vol. 155 (August 1927).

18. John Dos Passos, *USA,* Penguin, Harmondsworth, 1975, p. 774.

19. 'Flapping not repented of', *New York Times,* 16 July 1922, in Mowry, op. cit.

20. H L Mencken, *Prejudices, Fourth Series,* Knopf, New York, 1924, p. 114.

21. *The New Republic,46,* 14 April 1926, quoted in Paul A Carter, *Another Part of the Twenties,* Columbia U.P., New York, 1977, p.113.

22. See Nathan G Hale, Jr, *Freud and the Americans,* Vol 1, Oxford U.P., New York, 1971; and F H Matthews, 'The Americanization of Sigmund Freud: Adaptations of psychoanalysis before 1917', *Journal of American Studies,* 1, (1967), 39–62.

23. 'Queen of my people', *The New Republic,* XI, 140 (7 July 1917), reprinted in George C Pratt, *Spellbound in Darkness,* New York Graphic Society, Greenwich, Conn., (rev. ed,) 1973, p. 234. Lindsay, who was one of

America's first serious film critics, was an admirer of Pickford's specifically cinematic style of acting.

24. William Ogburn, *Social Change,* New York, 1922, p. 203.
25. John Kenneth Galbraith, *The Great Crash 1929,* Houghton Mifflin, Cambridge, Mass., 1954, p. 174.
26. *Harper's Magazine,* Vol. 150 (May 1925), 684.

Chapter Ten
The Thirties

Ralph Willett and John White

The crisis of capitalism

It was the Great Crash of 1929 that ended the Twenties. Throughout that decade stock prices had been rising so rapidly that they bore little relation to the earning power of corporations. Yet the Panic of 1929, when it came, was as much a crisis in American confidence as an economic phenomenon. Many factors were involved. President Hoover blamed worsening European conditions, but the federal government had encouraged tax policies that led to over-saving, and monetary policies which were expensive when prices rose and deflationary when they began to fall. There were also dangerous imbalances between agricultural and business incomes, irresponsible practices in the security markets, and structural weaknesses in the banking system. When trouble came, what J K Galbraith calls the 'generally poor state of economic intelligence' made many, including bankers and financiers, oblivious to the worsening situation: in November 1929 Henry Ford was declaring 'Things are better today than they were yesterday,' and the President of the National Association of manufacturers saw 'little on the horizon today to give us undue or great concern'. Until the eleventh hour, and beyond, Americans continued to express their faith in prosperity by stock-market investments. In September 1929 stock prices were 400 per cent over their 1924 level. But, on 24 October 1929, the market finally broke – to usher in a Depression that would deeply test the traditional American faith in economic progress, and redirect many American impulses.

The Wall Street crash now became a continuing and worsening catastrophe. From 1929 to 1933, *per capita* income dropped 100 per cent, and unemployment, notably low in the Twenties, rose from 500,000 to 12 million. Most of the unemployed were without any kind of assistance, and were rapidly reduced to the primitive conditions of a pre-industrial society struck by natural disaster. Millions wandered the country in an abortive search for work; they fabricated, on the outskirts of cities and towns, shanty slums, ironically called 'Hoover-villes'; they rode freight trains across country, risking death or injury by climbing into refrigerated cars. Farmers, unable to meet mortgage payments or to afford coal, burned corn to keep warm, while millions were near starvation. The Commisioner of Charity in Salt Lake City reported adults and children without food or adequate clothing. A member of the Hoover administration seriously proposed that restaurants give the unemployed left-over food in return for work – a superfluous suggestion, for many were already reduced to eating garbage. Apple-sellers, soap-box orators, beggars, bread-lines and soup kitchens appeared in every city. In many instances, the employed were little better off. In December 1932, wages in a wide range of industries averaged from 20 to 30 cents an hour, and a quarter of the women working in Chicago earned less than 10 cents an hour. The economic indicators of unemployment are readily available; the human costs defy quantification.

To many, though, it appeared that the collapse would be short-term. Hoover announced in 1930 that the worst of the Depression was over: billboards appeared asking 'Wasn't the Depression Terrible?' Conservative newspapers ignored or played down economic conditions; *Fortune's* famous attack, 'No One Has Starved (. . .which is not true)', did not appear until September 1932. Between 1929 and 1932, business and industry were united in their view that they wanted unemployment prevented, not treated with welfare programmes. They sought massive government loans to activate industry and regulate the economy, but in vain; Hoover's refusal to adopt proposals for planning and stabilization was at first firm, but it lost him valuable support. Meanwhile the arts and popular culture were equally slow in reacting to the Depression. The glossy middle-class magazine *Vanity Fair* was more interested in prohibition than unemployment; radio copied the ostrich-like behaviour of the press. Yet the hard facts now began to penetrate. Kaufman and Ryskind's prize-winning musical *Of Thee I Sing* (1931) began to show growing public disillusionment with politicians. And Edward Dahlberg's *Bottom Dogs* (1930), a fictionalized autobiography, was among the first of a growing row of books that would now start to explore the 'lower depths' of working-class culture and deprivation. But perhaps the most potent images of the time were the dynamic yet elegant gangsters of the movies, their attraction being their temporary mastery over the urban environment which now seemed, to so many, oppressive, bewildering and defeating.

Vulnerability was not confined to the cities – or the North. In 1931, nine black youths were charged with the rape of two white girls on a freight train in Alabama. The 'Scottsboro case' had national repercussions: both the NAACP (National Association for the Advancement of Coloured People) and the Communist party became involved. But the event which most clearly showed the increasing gap between the authorities and the ordinary people was the savage dispersal of the Bonus Army in 1932. Over 21,000 First World War veterans marched on Washington to demand their war-service bonus:

the majority, many with families, stayed in a huge Hooverville across the Potomac. Hoover complained, 'Their continued presence here will have a depressive effect on Wall Street,' and, after a bonus man died in a skirmish, Hoover panicked. Tanks appeared in Pennsylvania Avenue: but the squatters on Anacostia Flats refused to move, and troops, led by General MacArthur on a white horse, attacked the ex-soldiers' camp with bayonets and tear gas. The shanties were set on fire by the troops; Leo Seltzer, who filmed the event, later described the scene as 'a premature Hiroshima'. MacArthur denounced the marchers as revolutionary Reds; in fact, they were largely conservative men, with a tendency to beat up communists. Many returned home, but hundreds simply joined the jobless drifters who roamed aimlessly across America.

Hoover was not naturally inclined to panic. In *American Individualism* (1922), he had expounded his confident faith in the equality of opportunity and voluntarism: Americans could succeed by their own efforts, developing, in answer to a 'rising vision of service', a sense of community responsibility. In the event, Hoover's response to the Depression was a confused mixture of individualism and 'corporatism' (an economy comprising self-governing, collaborating, monopoly groups). He sponsored a series of White House meetings for large corporations to establish common industrial policies, and, in an effort to ameliorate hardship, used his executive powers to co-ordinate measures of *private* relief. It has been suggested that some of Hoover's policies during the early Depression anticipated the New Deal. Certainly, he approved the creation of the Reconstruction Finance Corporation (RFC) in 1932, a new government credit agency authorized to assist banks, railroads and insurance companies. But its investments were loans and the $1.5 billion it dispersed went mainly to a few large corporations. Hoover's conservatism, his rigid belief in his own wisdom, and his Jeffersonian distrust of strong government severely limited his ability to meet an unprecedented social and economic emergency.

Roosevelt and the New Deal

The Wall Street crash and the ensuing Depression had of course made a bitter mockery of Republican claims to be the 'party of prosperity'. Renominated by his party in 1932, Hoover faced a Democratic challenger with an illustrious name in American politics: Franklin Delano Roosevelt, a distant cousin of Theodore Roosevelt, and a former governor of New York. A landslide followed: Roosevelt received 427 electoral votes to Hoover's 59, and he promised the beleaguered country a 'New Deal'. A master politician, a shrewd manipulator, and a man of extraordinary physical energy (despite being crippled by poliomyelitis), Roosevelt took office with no clearly defined programme, pledged only to get the country moving again. In his first inaugural, Roosevelt warned Congress (and the country) of his intention to act quickly and decisively: 'I shall ask for broad Executive power to wage war against the emergency as great as the power that would be given to me if we were in fact invaded by a foreign foe.' The New Deal measures of recovery and reform indeed operated in and drew on an atmosphere of continuing crisis analogous to war. Between 1933 and 1938 more significant reform legislation was passed than during any other five-year period of American history. The disparate policies of the New Deal – devised and implemented by a carefully chosen group of advisers, often in violent disagreement with each other – were unified only by Roosevelt's commanding personality and strong leadership. For, as President, Roosevelt greatly expanded the powers of his office, and came to assume an executive role not unlike that of a British prime minister. A superb communicator, Roosevelt also dominated the mass media with his informal 'fire-side chats' to a national radio audience and spontaneous answers to reporters at press conferences. For the first time, the presidency became an institution directly in touch with all Americans, with Roosevelt as a hero to his admirers or simply 'that man' to his detractors.

After closing all banks for four days, and placing an embargo on the export of gold, silver and currency to protect US reserves, Roosevelt called the 73rd Congress into special session on 9 March 1933. From then until 16 June – the first Hundred Days of the New Deal – it enacted a mass of complex and sometimes inconsistent legislation at high speed. An Emergency Banking Act authorized the regulated re-opening of banks (2,000 were to remain permanently closed); the Federal Reserve Board was given stronger control over credit. An Economy Act cut the salaries of all federal employees by 15 per cent, reduced veterans' pensions, reorganized government agencies. The Civilian Conservation Corps – a kind of domestic Peace Corps – was founded with a grant of $300 million to enrol 25,000 young men on relief. Direct relief ($500 million) for states and municipalities was to be administered by the Federal Emergency Relief Administration; farming interests were served by the Farm Credit Administration. Bank deposits were secured by the Glass-Stegall Banking Act, which created the Federal Deposit Insurance Corporation. The National Industrial Recovery Act, the Agricultural Adjustment Act and the Tennessee Valley Act represented the early New Deal approach to the problems of industry, agriculture, conservation and community planning. Later, in 1935, the Social Security Act was a notable welfare-state measure, providing for a system of old-age retirement payments and fixed-period unemployment compensation. Much of this programme appeared to have been designed to maintain rather than to dismantle the capitalist system. But the proliferating relief agencies alarmed conservatives as much as they heartened their beneficiaries.

Activity was the hallmark of the New Deal, and H L Mencken observed of Roosevelt in 1934 that 'We have had so many presidents who were obvious numbskulls that it pleases everyone to contemplate one with an active cortex.' Not only did Roosevelt possess a very active cortex, but he attracted to Washington thousands of highly-skilled people who staffed the new agencies and formulated policies and programmes. Roosevelt's 'Brainstrust' – a group of advisers who served him initially when he was Governor of New York – included specialists in economics, law and social welfare: among the more prominent were Raymond Moley, Rexford Tugwell, Adolph A Berle, Frances Perkins, Samuel Rosenman, Harold Ickes, Harry Hopkins, and the conservationists George Norris and David Lilienthal. Collectively and individually, they represented a return to progressivism, a new assertion of the belief that organized social intelligence and its proper application could effectively remould society. To its critics, the Brainstrust was composed of impractical academics, grown arrogant and publicity-conscious because of their sudden elevation to national prominence. They were, in fact, not only the architects and administrators of the New Deal, but Roosevelt's first line of defence against his opponents, often serving to deflect criticism from himself. The Brainstrust devised an 'alphabet soup' of agencies designed to reinvigorate the economy – the NRA, the AAA, the PWA, the CCC, the FSA, the TVA and many more – and constituted the central thrust of the 'first' New Deal.

The National Industrial Recovery Act of 1933, designed to revive industrial and business activity, created the National Recovery Administration (NRA), and was said by Roosevelt to represent 'a supreme effort to stabilize for all time the many factors which make for the prosperity of the nation'. With the Blue Eagle as its symbol, and General Hugh Johnson as its colourful administrator, the NRA was empowered to prescribe codes and standards of fair practice for industries and to punish violaters. Johnson declared grandly that: 'When every American housewife understands that the Blue Eagle on everything she permits to come into her house is a symbol of its restoration to security, may God have mercy on any man or group of men who attempt to trifle with this bird.'[1] The NRA was also designed to stabilize prices, spread employment, raise wages and provide emergency relief through the Public Works Administration (PWA). So industry was to be stimulated and labour protected – Section 7a of the National Industrial Recovery Act authorized workers to organize and bargain on their own behalf. But businessmen dominated the NRA, and wrote its codes, often including unenforceable provisions. Many corporations, in fact, evaded the codes, and doubts about the constitutionality of the NRA Act encouraged evasion. In the event, the NRA was destroyed by a Supreme Court decision in 1935.

The three Agricultural Adjustment Acts (AAA) of 1933, 1936 and 1938 were attempts to maintain farm prices by artificially induced scarcity, thereby laying down the basic lines of the present American approach to the problem of agricultural overproduction. In compensation for a restriction of output, farmers were offered benefit payments through a processing tax on certain farm products – cotton, wheat, corn, pigs, tobacco and rice. Because the 1933 farm season was well under way when the first AAA began operations, large-scale destruction was necessary to cut crop and livestock surpluses. The Secretary of Agriculture, Henry Wallace, reluctantly agreed to a proposal by farm leaders to forestall a glut in the hog market by slaughtering over 6 million piglets and 200,000 sows due to farrow. While 1 million pounds of salt pork were salvaged for families on relief, nine-tenths of the yield was inedible, and was thrown away. Again, faced with the prospect of a huge cotton crop in 1933, AAA agents went to the South to urge planters to uproot their cotton. For ploughing up 10 million acres, farmers received over $100 million in benefit payments. Cotton destruction and the slaughter of pigs fixed the image of the AAA vividly in the public mind, and it was widely believed that these were annual operations. In fact, almost all the actual destruction ended in 1933, and afterwards the AAA restricted yields in a more orderly fashion. The AAA received the active support of large farm organizations and brought benefits to most commercial farmers. But, in limiting acreage and encouraging technological innovation, the AAA forced sharecroppers off the land and did little to improve the conditions of farm labourers. Yet, as W R Brock notes, the AAA 'was successful in its immediate objective, it tied the farmers politically to the New Deal, it turned Jefferson's chosen people into foster children of the federal government, and it raised questions of the ethics of restricting production in a time of scarcity.'[2] The Supreme Court took another view of the ethics of the AAA processing tax, and in 1936 declared the first Agricultural Adjustment Act invalid.

Among other New Deal agencies, the Resettlement Administration (RA), under Rexford Tugwell, attempted to remove farmers to better land and to provide low-paid workers with 'Greenbelt Towns' outside cities, where they could supplement their salaries by part-time farming. The three towns – near Washington D C, Cincinnati and Milwaukee – were to attract more European comment than any other project of the New Deal except the Tennessee Valley Authority (TVA). The RA was also the least discriminating of New Deal agencies in its treatment of blacks, and was the only agency to set up group medical plans. In 1937 it became the Farm Security Administration (FSA), and, against the opposition of Southern conservatives, attempted to regulate the supply, hours and wages of migrant workers. But, lacking a strong political base, the FSA was starved of funds by its Congressional opponents, and its material achievements were limited.

The most imaginative, successful and dramatic of the early New Deal measures was the Tennessee Valley Act. Created in 1933, the ⹁VA was designed to prevent floods in the area of the Tennessee

River, and to provide cheap and plentiful electrical power. A great experiment in regional planning, the TVA was attacked by private power companies as 'creeping socialism', although its farm programme tended to benefit the more prosperous farmers. The TVA was to become the greatest producer of electric power in America, and a manufacturer of low-cost fertilizers. During the Second World War, the TVA provided power for aluminium and arms manufacture. Its successful operation proved that efficiency and social concern were possible in government-owned, non-profit-making organizations. With its emphasis on conservation and reclamation, the TVA implemented proposals urged by progressives since the 1920s.

Of all the New Deal agencies, the Works Progress Administration (WPA) under the direction of Harry Hopkins, did most to implement relief work on a massive scale. By 1939 it had provided employment for 8,500,000 people in activities ranging from highway building and construction work to slum clearance, rural rehabilitation and reforestation, at a total cost of $11 billion. Although accused of inefficiency, waste, and political favouritism, the WPA stimulated private business during the Depression years and completed projects that individual states had been unable to subsidize. Yet the WPA, like other New Deal agencies, could only scratch the surface of unemployment and poverty. With falls in industrial production and agricultural prices, the New Deal appeared to flounder in 1935–36, and new leaders and movements emerged to confront Roosevelt and diagnose the unhealthy economic situation.

In an era of demagogues, America produced a few home-grown and unique examples. Senator Huey Long, the virtual dictator of Louisiana, promised to make 'every man a king' by the gospel of 'Share-Our-Wealth', a simple, sweeping programme to expropriate the wealth of the very rich and provide all families with a $5,000 homestead and an annual income around $2,500. Long's assassination removed the threat, but Roosevelt confided to Tugwell that Long was one of the two most dangerous men in America, the other being General MacArthur. Other popular demogogues emerged, like Father Charles Coughlin, the radio-priest of WJR Detroit, and founder of the National Union for Social Justice, who delivered over the CBS network venomous, anti-semitic broadcasts against the 'Drain Trust' and the 'Pagan Deal'. Panaceas were much in demand: from Long Beach, California, Dr Francis E Townsend started 'Townsend Clubs', demanding monthly payments of $200 for each unemployed person over sixty, appealing to millions who, he said, 'believe in the Bible, believe in God, cheer when the flag passes by, the Bible Belt solid Americans'. Such demagogues, like the hostility of the Supreme Court, the emerging power of labour, and the growing alignment in some intellectual quarters between Marxism and American progressive impulse, helped push Roosevelt left when he appealed to the American electorate in 1936.

Moving Left

There is no doubt that events from 1929 deeply damaged the Twenties'
faith that America was stabilizing itself as a commercial nation secure
in all its institutions, capable of reconstituting old faiths, able to leave
the economy to business, and politics to its supporters. The times
called for a renewal of the progressive impulse and the radical view,
and intellectuals who had felt alienated and displaced in the Twenties
involved themselves in the political urgencies of the Thirties. Many
writers who had previously devoted themselves to a religion of art,
bohemianism and expatriation now became politically active, moving
leftward, reporting on national agonies. Fifty-three writers and artists
explicitly supported the Communist party in 1932, and for much of the
decade authors identified themselves with the Left and the 'toiling
masses'. The modernist impulse certainly did not disappear; indeed its
awareness of fragmentation now seemed the more relevant. Some of
Faulkner's best, most experimental work belongs to the decade: in
1930 came *As I Lay Dying*, and two years later *Light in August*, a
deeply symbolist evocation of the racially divided and historically
disordered South, potentially reintegrated by the pregnant folk-
heroine Lena Groves; in 1936 came *Absalom, Absalom!*, perhaps
Faulkner's masterpiece – an exploration, through several perspectives, of the history of Thomas Sutpen's doomed project to found a
plantation dynasty in northern Mississippi. In most of Faulkner's
writing the grim circumstances of the contemporary South appear only
obliquely, though *Sanctuary* (1931) evokes in the character of Popeye
a modern mechanized dementia, *The Wild Palms* (1939), remarkable
for its counterpointed double plot, explores a disorderly age, and the
story 'Tall Men' (1941) can be read as a conservative rejection of the
New Deal and welfare legislation. But Faulkner's continuing saga of
Yoknapatawpha County offers a longer and more complex historiography of a ceaselessly disoriented South.

Hemingway tried more directly to treat the challenge of the times,
most notably in his journalism ('Who Murdered the Vets?', (1935); the
reports from Spain collected in *By-line: Ernest Hemingway* (ed. W W
White, 1967). His fictional attempt at social criticism in *To Have and
Have Not* (1937) is notably unsuccessful; his novel of the Spanish Civil
War, *For Whom the Bell Tolls* (1940), has remarkable moments, but
also the uneasy lyricism of its central love story, beyond which lies
Hemingway's familiar Twenties universe of waste and death. Perhaps
the writer from the Twenties who most succeeds in the transition is
Scott Fitzgerald, who in his 1936 essay 'The Crack-Up' linked the
economic breakdown with his own psychic collapse, and saw both
pointing to a new kind of art. It was Hemingway who pointed out that
Fitzgerald's *Tender Is the Night* (1934) gets better and better in
retrospect. A novel of moral wisdom informed by a strong Marxist
insight into the economic determination of his moneyed characters, it

traces Dick Diver's finally unsuccessful attempt to hold together a demoralized leisure class from collapsing into psychic decay and sexual disorder. In *The Last Tycoon* (1941), left unfinished on Fitzgerald's death in 1940, there is again a charismatic hero undernourished by an exhausting and exhausted society. Monroe Stahr, the Hollywood director, a tycoon in the original Japanese sense of a great prince, represents responsible authority, humane and imaginative. But he is trapped between Wall Street and communists, and Fitzgerald's notes for the book indicate he was to succumb to illness and corruption: a last dark image of the American dream. However, possibly the most notable experimental enterprise that distinctively belongs to the Thirties – if one sets aside Thomas Wolfe's expansive self-recording through four novels, culminating in *You Can't Go Home Again* (1940) – is John Dos Passos's massive three-volume novel, *USA* (1930–36). An expressionist and experimental work, it uses montage and collage techniques to record America from the turn of the century to the Sacco – Vanzetti case, when the nation becomes two nations. There are fictionalized narratives about the lives of individuals; stream-of-consciousness sections emanating from the author himself ('Camera Eye'); a documentary collage of newspaper headlines, popular song fragments, etc. ('Newsreel'); and 'Biographies' of various strategic real-life villains and heroes – from J P Morgan to Thorstein Veblen, who diagnosed 'the sabotage of production by business'. The book uses modernism's ends to radical purposes (like Eisenstein), showing how capitalism destroys entrepreneurs and radicals alike. But Dos Passos's attempt to bring back Whitman's spirit of 'storybook democracy' tends to work from surfaces; his characters in the end possess only mobility and appetites.

It was those appetites that Henry Miller turned into a Whitmanesque hunger for experience, nonconformity, vitalism, and an anti-puritan celebration of sex. His books were not, he said, novels; in fact they are surrealist acts claiming the rights of the artist while refusing to produce Art. Written from expatriate Paris, *Tropic of Cancer* (1934, Paris: banned in the US until 1961) is fictionalized autobiography evoking a cancerous world which sexuality both exposes and redeems; *Tropic of Capricorn* (1939, Paris) goes back into the 'air-conditioned nightmare' of American experience to evoke working-class Brooklyn life. Nathanael West, too, was briefly an expatriate, and certainly a surrealist. His *A Cool Million* (1934) is another key book of the Thirties, using the clichés of success literature to explore and mock the entire American dream of rags-to-riches. In addition, West warns of latent native fascism, and his novels constitute a savage and satirical attack on an America where, he says, 'violence is idiomatic' and apocalypse is the nightmarish conclusion for a society based on deception and characterized by a tawdry mass culture. His books are a sombre commentary on that culture; his characters are cartoons: *Miss Lonelyhearts* (1933) is told in the form of a comic strip, and *The Day of the Locust* (1939), set in the 'Dream Dump of Hollywood', and ending in the burning of Los Angeles, is modelled on a movie.

But if modernism and surrealism lasted during the 1930s, one of the literary effects of the decade was the emergence of a 'proletarian' literature, though mostly written by and for the middle classes. At best, as in Robert Cantwell's *The Land of Plenty* (1934), or in some of the journalism of Sherwood Anderson, James T Farrell, Malcolm Cowley and others, it took the form of a humane documentary realism. This is a central note in Thirties prose, but other parts of this writing were sentimental, melodramatic and, as the naturalist theme of the beast in man reappeared, excessively brutal. It reached grotesque proportions in the black comedy of Erskine Caldwell, whose *Tobacco Road* (1932) records the exhaustion of the land and the betrayal of Jefferson's agrarian dream as peasants are dispossessed by the banks. The technique is, however, sensationalist and the characters are demoralized, physically repulsive, and degenerate; their emotional inertia presages destruction and death. The book was a popular success, and Jack Kirkland's vulgarized play version (1933) ran on Broadway for over seven years. Caldwell's *God's Little Acre* (1933) is a richer novel; still a tragi-comic dramatization of promiscuous farm-types, it pays homage to the 'strike' novel, and creates a martyr-hero. John Steinbeck deals with a related theme in *In Dubious Battle* (1936), where he identifies 'group-man' (the mob) as a savage, monolithic beast. Steinbeck's subject is not revolution, but transcendence as a biological way through crisis. This is clear in *The Grapes of Wrath* (1939), probably the decade's best-known novel, bringing together many of its central cultural assumptions: a nostalgia for the agrarian past, a documentary desire to record contemporary fact (soil-erosion, foreclosures, industrialized farming, Hoovervilles), a populist faith in 'the people', and an indignation against man-made suffering. The migrating Joads, moving westward from dustbowl Oklahoma, represent 'humanity' rather than 'the workers', and Steinbeck's naturalist analogies with resilient animals emphasize his commitment to stoicism and survival. The appalling conditions of rural life also provided the material for James Agee's *Let Us Now Praise Famous Men*, commissioned in 1936, though not published until 1941. About the lives of three poor Southern tenant-farming families, it is an experimental documentary. Agee's collage form integrates Walker Evans's photographs, quotations from Blake, and other items into a discontinuous text, thus challenging his own professed artlessness, designed to convey the simple dignity and beauty of his subjects.

Not surprisingly, the Thirties also saw a revival of the naturalist urban novel. Henry Roth, in *Call It Sleep* (1934), Mike Gold, in *Jews Without Money* (1935), and William Carlos Williams, in *White Mule* (1937), all explored the immigrant experience, and James T Farrell examined Chicago's Irish lower-middle class in the trilogy *Studs Lonigan* (1932–35). His aim was to reveal the effects of 'spiritual poverty'; so he shows the Catholic Church reinforcing prejudice, while the alternative mass-culture provides only escapist fantasies. In the third novel of the trilogy, *Judgment Day*, the Depression completes the process of human decline; his health shattered by smoking and liquor, the jobless Studs drifts towards death, melancholic, still dreaming. But perhaps the culminating book in this line is Richard Wright's *Native Son* (1940), a major novel about the Afro-American experience, the story of Bigger Thomas, a black raised in the Chicago slums, which combines naturalism and expressionist nightmare; its materials explore loss of identity, ghetto poverty, double murder and liberal explanations from a communist lawyer.

The pressure of events in the Thirties brought about a mood of change in all the art-forms, and a demand for literary relevance. So James T Farrell's sceptical reviews of proletarian books earned him the antagonism of Mike Gold who, on becoming editor of *New Masses* in 1928, had turned it into a revolutionary magazine dedicated to 'the workers' art'. From 1934 to 1949, the weekly *New Masses* printed such writers as Rukeyser, Lorca, Brecht, Caldwell and Dos Passos, and cartoons, drawings and political humour. Though inferior material was published, *New Masses* 'had a bead on the time, which went to its heart'. It was in the New York office of *New Masses* that the John Reed Club – named after the American radical intellectual and journalist who died in Russia just after the Revolution – was founded in October 1929, to disseminate and enact 'the principles and purposes of revolutionary art and literature'. Similar clubs sprang up throughout America: in 1934, the New York branch of the club sponsored a 'little magazine', *Partisan Review: A Bi-Monthly of Revolutionary Literature*, edited by Philip Rahv and William Phillips, an important guide to the intellectual evolution of the Thirties and the schismatic nature of radicalism. The first issue proclaimed its revolutionary stance and offered to combat 'the debilitating liberalism which at times seeps into our writers through the pressure of class-alien forces'. But it also made clear its refusal to countenance attempts to impose 'sectarian theories and practices' on literature: a 'centrist' position opposed to *New Masses* 'leftism'. Several splits followed: the John Reed Club was dismantled by the first American Writers' Congress in 1935; *Partisan Review*, despite absorbing the 'crude vigour' of Jack Conroy's *Anvil* in 1936, began to divide internally. In 1937 it was restructured with additional editors and took on an anti-Stalinist, pro-Trotskyist line (voiced at the second American Writers' Congress that year) while simultaneously making the innovations of modernist European literature, rather than social realism, its focus. As Christopher Lasch has noted, this was a valuable reaction against the proletarian-literature campaign, but it 'melted almost indistinguishably into the retreat from ideology and the emerging postwar "realism"'.[3]

The social responsibility of writers was a much-argued theme of the Thirties, later deeply to affect attitudes in the 1950s. In poetry, two major events occurred in 1930: the publication of Hart Crane's lyrical celebration of mythic America, *The Bridge*, and Ezra Pound's *A Draft of XXX Cantos*, part of his epic enterprise in combining image, vortex, ideogram and rhythmic line in a total spatial action. Pound went on to move toward Social Credit and support for Mussolini, his contribution to the politicization of poetry; in 1930, likewise, the Southern cultural aristocrats who had produced in the Twenties the poetry magazine *The Fugitive* issued a significant statement of Eliotic and Southern agrarian values in *I'll Take My Stand*. But the most important poetic movement of the Thirties was the Objectivists, the group including Charles Reznikoff, George Oppen, Carl Rakosi, Louis Zukofsky and William Carlos Williams. Their sympathies were to the Left, but they avoided the banalities of propaganda poetry, drawing attention to form and shape, to the poem as object or 'an organism with distinct characteristics' (Rakosi). In Williams's intense non-symbolic recreations of direct experience can be found the group's most memorable and influential poetry. Other poets more directly criticized Depression America: Kenneth Patchen, also an important love poet, who would link up with the Beats in the 1950s; Muriel Rukeyser, whose *US 1* (1938) used items from the daily press to show what a social revolution should rectify; and Kenneth Fearing, who attacked bourgeois society with sharp irony through its noisy advertising and specious cinema dreams (see his *New and Selected Poems*, 1956).

In theatre, too, the radical note grew. Clifford Odets, a principal dramatist of the Group Theatre, founded to produce plays of 'social significance' in 1931, likewise exposed Hollywood's escapist images, though the hard-boiled vernacular of *Awake and Sing!* (1935) and *Golden Boy* (1937) owes a debt to the movie language of Cagney and Bogart. No formal experimenter, Odets remains the theatre's leading analyst of the emotions and tensions of the lower-middle-class Thirties family. Other associated playwrights were Maxwell Anderson (*Winterset*, 1935, draws on Sacco and Vanzetti), John Howard Lawson (whose *Marching Song*, 1937, is about the Auto Workers Union), and William Saroyan (*The Time of Your Life*, 1939). Eugene O'Neill, winner of the Nobel Prize in 1936, mitigated his expressionist methods in his drama of the Thirties: *Ah, Wilderness!* (1933) is a 'hazy daguerrotype of Irish family life' (Robert Brustein), calling up small-town life in 1906, but *The Iceman Cometh* (written 1939) looks to social derelicts whose home is the saloon. One consequence of the Depression was the Federal Theatre Project, sponsored by the WPA (Works Progress Administration) to re-employ thousands of theatre workers. It was a national organization of theatre groups, organized by Hallie Flanagan, which by 1937 was playing to weekly audiences of over 350,000. Among its most successful ventures were the Negro theatre and the 'Living Newspaper' project, deriving from revolutionary workers' theatre in Europe. It used projections, statistics, announcements and short dramatic scenes: *One-Third of a Nation* (on housing) was the most popular production, But Joseph Losey's *Injunction Granted* (on labour history) was sharper and more inventive. Other projects included Marc Blitzstein's *The Cradle Will Rock*, a sharp political musical, and Sinclair Lewis's and John C Moffit's exposure of the risks of American fascism, *It Can't Happen Here* (1936). It was the radicalism of the project that provided the excuse for its closure by the Dies Congressional Committee in 1939.

Federal support for the arts was an important stimulus at many levels in the Thirties. The plight of the rural working class permeates the photographs taken for the Resettlement Administration (1935–37) and the Farm Security Administration (1937–42): these pictures of Dust Bowl landscapes, timber-shacks and dispossessed families, taken by Evans, Lange, Delano, Lee and Rothstein, constitute the best-known and most admired collection of its kind. A varied body of work (after 1937 a more heroic mood appeared), it records popular America and its folkloric expression (e.g., Walker Evans's 'Butcher Sign', 1936) and shows even disintegrating America as 'a place of fabrication and assemblage, of house walls patched up ingeniously. . . and trucks elaborately stowed for the journey'.[4] Paul Strand, another great photographer who also worked for the Resettlement Adminis-tration, assisted Paul Lorentz in making the film *The Plow that Broke the Plains* (1936). This and *The River* (1937) use music, dynamic editing and language to extraordinary effect to trace a history of land exploitation and ecological disaster. But since, as New Deal propaganda, the films offered government policies as sufficient solutions, Strand and Leo Hurwitz broke away to form the radical group Frontier Films, whose most notable achievement was *Native Land* (1942), a condemnation of civil-rights violations and the oppression of unionists.

Painting too was restimulated. A key part of the programme of the 'American Scene Painters' – Thomas Hart Benton, John Steuart Curry and Grant Wood – was the expression of vanishing qualities of good neighbourliness, social order, hard work, in a populist mood. (Thus the heroic Washington of Leutze's famous painting is contrasted with the complacent modern 'aristocrats' of Wood's 'Daughters of the Revolution', 1932.) The 'scene' they concerned themselves with mainly was the frontier or small town, often with irony, so that their political attitude defies easy definition. Early sympathetic to the '291' movement and communism, Benton became a populist anti-modernist and anti-Marxist. There was also an urban regionalist tendency working close to poster art and political cartoon, though few of their social paintings had the overt message or force of Ben Shahn's 'The Passion of Sacco and Vanzetti' (1931–32). 'Magic realists' like Peter Blume and Phillip Evergood broke the confinements of realism with fantasy and expressionism. But it was in the work of the mural painters, stimulated by the Mexicans, Rivera and Orozco, who worked in the USA at this time, that politics became especially important, marrying native arts and modernism, protest and public style. Painters employed by the Federal Art Project to decorate banks, schools and post offices drew on the themes of labour, agriculture and history. America's greatest painter at this time, Stuart Davis, achieved four major murals, but, as secretary of the American Artists' Congress, he managed little else. Indeed, his career raises the problematic issue of the times: the appropriate relationship between government and creation, and politics and art.

Popular culture

Like any other American industry, the cinema was seriously affected by the Depression. In 1932, box-office demand slumped to almost half the 1930 level; Paramount and Fox went bankrupt, and by the mid-summer of 1933, 5,000 out of 16,000 movie theatres had closed down. Yet even in the early thirties the cinema was the cheapest and most appealing form of entertainment: for 10 cents, the unemployed bought escape, rest, warmth and even a night's sleep. By 1936 cinema was recovering again, and by 1939 there were an estimated 40 million regular movie-goers, many attending several times a week. Major writers like Faulkner and Hemingway were drawn to Hollywood; the Hollywood novel became a genre (West's *The Day of the Locust*, 1939; Fitzgerald's *The Last Tycoon*, 1941). Genre also preoccupied Hollywood itself, from the early Westerns of William S Hart to the 'disaster movies' of the 1970s; and in the Thirties it produced many memorable films (*Public Enemy, Stagecoach, Forty-Second Street*). But it also contributed to an evasive conservatism. Movie-goers were sustained by the myth of opportunity, and few films actually dealt with the life-styles or problems of working-class Americans or with national politics and economics. Yet this is hardly surprising. The movies had and used their escape function, and most of the 'movie moguls' – though not always their writers – were conservatives (for example, Louis B Mayer, head of MGM, kept portraits of Herbert Hoover, General MacArthur and Cardinal Spellman on his desk). Another powerful conservative force was the Hays Code, established in 1934, which heavily censored sexuality and profanity, and required that sin and crime be shown only if ultimately punished. Many films thus engaged in nostalgia: Walt Disney's cartoons looked back to a sanitized small-town way of life; Shirley Temple offered an escape into the world of childhood; Empire films like Ford's *Wee Willie Winkie* (1937) evoked old hierarchical societies, and so too did films set in the European past (*Marie Antoinette* or *A Tale of Two Cities*, 1935).

But other films, often musicals and screwball comedies, provided sardonic commentary on the Depression years, if without providing any real challenge to the *status quo*. (In *Gold Diggers of 1933*, the 'My Forgotten Man' number dramatically acknowledges the breadlines, but the 'We're In the Money' sequence offers potent alternative images of sex and money, with its Busby Berkeley costumes of shiny silver dollars). Films like *Fury* and *I'm a Fugitive from a Chain Gang* exposed social oppression, but these were gradually replaced by pro-democratic works which boosted public morale and at the same time challenged the rising threat of fascism in Europe. Frank Capra is often considered to offer the purest expression of Thirties' liberalism in cinema. A Sicilian immigrant, he came to believe in the American Dream of which his own success story seemed undeniable proof: his comedies sentimentally evoke both the democratic myths and realities of the American past. In *Mr Deeds Goes to Town* (1936). Longfellow Deeds visits Grant's tomb and praises the United States as the only country where a poor farm-boy could eventually be elected President; in *Mr Smith Goes to Washington* (1939), Jefferson Smith – played by James Stewart, who, like Gary Cooper, provided Capra with a lean, rangy, decent and dependable outdoors type – visits Lincoln's statue when he arrives in the capital. In these films, the simple and naïve triumph over the wicked and powerful; their emotional structure combines sentimental feeling for small-town life with populist resentment of the city, especially the city of intellectuals, politicians, big-businessmen and the press, whom Capra portrays as cynical and corrupt.

Like the populists, Capra was not anti-capitalist, but he distrusted the large-scale trust, and sided with the small businessman against banks, corporations, monopolies. Despite his happy endings, however, he acknowledges the vulnerability of his heroes, and his belief in the 'little man' is complicated by a fear of mob-action – hence his characteristic opposition of independent individual and faceless herd-like crowd. By contrast, John Ford's films are more concerned with the creation of a natural community, strong and resilient – the community of *Stagecoach* (1939), the extended family of *The Grapes of Wrath* (1940). His sympathies, too, are Populist (so, in *Stagecoach*, civilised Easterners confront disreputable Westerners, the whore with the heart of gold, the drunken but humane doctor, the outlaw). His taste for the West is partly nostalgic, but also draws on the wish to show an embryonic society forming rituals and customs which give it value and stability. But the Thirties' major cinematic achievement fittingly appeared at the end of the decade. If *Gone With the Wind* (1939) represents the apotheosis of production values, *Citizen Kane* (1941) was the height of Thirties cinematic invention. An eclectic work, it fused elements of contemporary popular culture (radio, newsreel, theatre) with modernist techniques of montage. Kane's life is revealed gradually from different points of view; old RKO sets and clips from earlier films form an equivalent to theatrical and painterly techniques of collage. The film displays the advances in cinema technique made in the decade, as well as Welles's youthful brashness and enthusiasm.

Network radio was already established by 1928, but in the Thirties it was to function as a unifying force and an antidote to the fragmentation of the times and, as public confidence in the press waned, it increased in popularity. Yet, with half its revenue coming from ten advertising agencies, it was effectively controlled by its 'sponsors'. Controversy was rigorously avoided, most radio drama took place in a social vacuum; current events were kept in the background until the end of the decade. The networks filled the air with comedy and music, but it was the human voice that made the most powerful impression – the apparently casual but carefully planned fireside talks of Roosevelt, the harangues of Coughlin and Long, and, as war approached, the magnificent coverage of European events by Kaltenborn and Murrow for CBS. The success of talking pictures, the rapid increase of radio ownership and, after the end of Prohibition in 1933, the spread of the jukebox, all led to a massive spread in the dissemination and promotion of popular music and records. The Thirties heard some of the best American songs ever written: 'Night and Day', 'In the Still of the Night', 'Smoke Gets in Your Eyes', for example. Jerome Kern, Cole Porter and George Gershwin introduced remarkable harmonic and melodic innovations, though only Gershwin caught the conditions of the age – above all in his opera *Porgy and Bess* (1935), set in the poor black community of Charleston. In the early Depression, songs like 'Life is Just a Bowl of Cherries' (1931) were cheerful and optimistic, giving temporary relief from breadlines and unemployment. But in 1932 one song, 'Brother, Can You Spare a Dime?', caught the bitterness and bewilderment of the times, and sounds more like Kurt Weill than Tin Pan Alley.

However, the detective novels of Dashiell Hammett and Raymond Chandler plunged the reader into a brutal and disordered world closer to the shabby urban environment of the dominant newspaper headlines, and provided a writing close to the form of contemporary anxiety. Hammett was no simple realist, as the eccentric villains and symbolic black bird of *The Maltese Falcon* (1930) demonstrate. His hard-edged pared-down style is the work of a craftsman, and, as Julian Symons claims, *The Glass Key* (1931) bears comparison with any contemporaneous American novel. Hammett's and Chandler's private-eye detectives fill out a vague region somewhere between the criminal underworld on the one hand and the society of money, power and dishonest cops on the other. Chandler's Philip Marlowe indeed represents a vanishing ethical code, like the knight in the Sternwood window panel (*The Big Sleep*, 1939), redeeming the drab, tacky world he encounters with an inventive wisecracking. Yet his wry style and his sleaziness neutralizes his aestheticism. And, though Hammett writes of labour–boss conflict in a company town in *Red Harvest*, 1929, it now seems Chandler's Marlowe, lonely, vulnerable, edgy, who best evokes the mood of the decade.

There were other levels of realism in Thirties writing. John O'Hara, writing of the underlying disturbances of middle-class life, is in fact one of the sharpest social historians of the decade. His *BUtterfield 8* (1935), set in the speakeasy life of New York, a decadent democracy that includes aspiring journalists and dope-pushing debutantes, generates a sense of instability through an ever-present consciousness of unemployment, gangsters and possibilities of revolution. And the instability of social arrangements also pervades his most assured novel, *Appointment in Samarra* (1934), set in a Gibbsville, Pennsylvania, where the surface of public behaviour veils alienation, neurosis, resentment and fear. Julian English's doom is set in motion by a heartless, competitive bourgeoisie; it is completed by his own inner uncertainty and self-destructiveness. O'Hara is a sophisticated writer, whose work appeared in the *New Yorker*, a magazine perhaps never quite as sophisticated as Ross, the first editor, and James Thurber, its distinguished humorist and cartoonist, liked to claim. Its pieces often worked on the tension between the naïve small town and the demanding big city, and Thurber himself created the characteristic *New Yorker* piece about the bewildered, anxious little man confused by the menacing and mechanized society. The mood of many stories – 'The Secret Life of Walter Mitty', 'The Remarkable Case of Mr Bruhl' – reflects the insecurity and tension of the age, the tug between old values and new threats, the struggles of the sex war, the uneasy principles of change, and the powerful images of the popular culture. Mitty's dreams belong in comic books; Mr Bruhl turns into a movie gangster. Thurber has a streak of populist puritanism; the conservative Ross regarded anything serious as 'grim stuff'. In fact, the Depression is only hinted at in the *New Yorker*; the 'realism' of its stories is disinfected, and the trivial often assiduously cultivated, while its advertising (vintage wines, movie cameras, jewelry from Tiffany's) surrounds the text with middle-class fantasies and asserts the permanence of consumer capitalism.

The second New Deal

Renominated by the Democrats in 1936, Roosevelt faced the Republican contender, Alfred M Landon, former Governor of Kansas. Roosevelt stood firmly on the achievements of the New Deal, stressed his basic conservatism, and appealed directly to the electorate as the adversary of 'the old enemies of the peace – business and financial monopoly, speculation, class antagonism, sectionalism, war profiteering'. The result of what was virtually a plebiscite was an astounding victory for Roosevelt, who carried every state except Maine and Vermont, received 523 electoral votes to a mere 8 for Landon, and carried into power a Democratic majority in both houses of Congress. The victory owed much to a highly efficient Democratic party organization masterminded by James A Farley; the support of farmers, small businessmen and organized labour (the Congress of Industrial Organizations (CIO) under Lewis raised $1 million for the Democrats); and to the fact that 1936 was the high-point of recovery under the New Deal. But it was, above all, a personal triumph for Roosevelt, and an endorsement of the principles and policies of the 'first' New Deal. Roosevelt's campaign addresses, one reporter noted, resembled the 'friendly sermons of a bishop come to make his quadrennial diocesan call. Bishop Roosevelt reported on the excellent state of health enjoyed throughout his vast diocese, particularly as compared with the miserable state that had prevailed before he took high office.' His congregation agreed, and entrusted their material, if not spiritual, welfare to him for another four years.

With his landslide victory in 1936, Roosevelt seemed to have sufficient support to enact a 'second New Deal' – with an emphasis on reform and 'security' rather than simply on recovery. But in a 1935 decision, the Supreme Court had declared the NRA codes unconstitutional in delegating legislative power to the president to draft the codes; they were also an illegal intervention in interstate affairs. Six months later the Court declared the AAA processing tax invalid. Those justices opposed to New Deal legislation enjoyed excellent health, and showed no signs of wishing to retire. In a constitutionally sound but crudely handled manoeuvre, Roosevelt proposed to enlarge the Supreme Court from nine members to a maximum of fifteen, in the pretended interests of judicial efficiency. Congress resisted this 'court packing' bill, FDR lost Democratic and popular support, and the Republican opposition, enjoying his embarrassment, was rejuvenated. Yet during the Congressional fight, the Court suprisingly upheld the constitutionality of the Wagner Act by a margin of one vote – eliciting the quip 'a switch in time saved nine'. And by 1941, the Court had authorized sweeping regulatory power over interstate commerce and upheld the principal legislation of the New Deal. But Roosevelt's court-packing bid alarmed conservatives, destroyed the unity of the Democratic party, and tarnished his reputation as an invincible leader; the episode also strengthened the bipartisan anti-New Deal coalition within Congress.

Before 1935, Roosevelt, although pro-labour, was decidedly anti-union, regarding labour as a dependent part of industry. But with the Supreme Court's decision on the NRA codes, the administration needed a new labour policy and with the National Labor Relations Act (Wagner Act), it committed itself belatedly to supporting unions that were independent of management. Company unions were now banned, as was any form of employer discrimination against members of a union. But, as in much New Deal legislation, there were shortcomings: the Wagner Act did not protect the bargaining rights of public employees, workers in intrastate commerce, or service and agricultural workers.

The passing of the Wagner Act, however, did have a decisive and divisive effect on the labour movement. Led by John L Lewis, president of the United Mine Workers, a group of dissident unions left the craft-oriented American Federaton of Labor (AFL) to reach skilled and semi-skilled workers in the mass-production industries. A new organization for labour – the CIO – was formed in 1935, but faced opposition both from the AFL and from employers in the unorganized industries. The CIO began its unionizing campaign when workers at a number of General Motors affiliates staged 'sit-down' strikes to gain recognition for their new union, the United Auto Workers (UAW). Ignoring court orders to leave the buildings, and repulsing police attacks, the auto workers achieved victory in February 1937, when General Motors capitulated to their demands. In March, US Steel signed a contract granting the Steel Workers' Organizing Committee recognition for its members, a wage rise, and a forty-hour week. By the end of 1937, the UAW had gained recognition from every car manufacturer but Ford, and other industrial giants had also recognized the right of their workers to form independent unions. The 'blue collar' revolution was not achieved without violence, most notably in the 'Memorial Day Massacre' (1937) outside Republic Steel's plant in Chicago, when police fired on steel strikers and their families, killing 7 and wounding over 100. At one stage in the steel dispute, an exasperated Roosevelt blamed labour and management alike for industrial unrest, and Democrats in Congress took opposing sides on the unionization issue. But Roosevelt's refusal to use force against the sit-downers, together with his attack on the Supreme Court, alienated many of the New Deal's middle-class supporters. With unemployment remaining high and a sharp business recession in 1937, the New Deal appeared to be running out of steam and ideas. But events in Europe were soon to provide another remedy for American unemployment, and also help to secure Roosevelt's re-election for a third term.

Even before the 1940 election, American attention was being increasingly drawn to European affairs. There is evidence to support the view that Roosevelt perceived the dangers of the German alliance with Italy and with Japan more acutely than did the British, French or Russians. On 5 October 1937, he warned a Chicago audience that Americans could no longer hope to escape from involvement in world events through illusory policies of 'isolation and neutrality'. Yet Roosevelt had never made firm commitments to Britain and France in the event of war, largely because of the strength of American isolationist sentiment, and he expressed relief at the news of the Munich settlement. However Hitler's continuing territorial aggression, Nazi persecution of German Jews, and the new German arms programme brought a swift response from Roosevelt. He announced an expenditure of $300 million on American armaments, and in July 1939 informed Congress of measures 'short of war, but stronger and more effective than mere words'.

With the establishment of the Popular Front in 1935, fascism replaced capitalism as the principal enemy of the American Communist party, and the fight for 'unity, democracy and peace' took precedence over the class struggle. Talk of revolution was discouraged, and by 1939 even 'progressive capitalists' (but not Trotskyists) were considered comrades in the struggle. Thus the communist party was able to attract thousands and to make inroads upon the middle-classes and the unions. But although anti-fascism seemed to bind the Popular Front together, it remained relevant only until the Russian–German pact was signed. And while liberal support for the Loyalists in the Spanish Civil War was not, as Ezra Pound claimed, 'an emotional luxury to a gang of sap-headed dilettantes', those who joined the International Brigade were soon disillusioned by Communist party intransigence and violence towards other groups of the Left.

In the late Thirties, the United States sought to rediscover its cultural heritage; the Popular Front played a significant part in this process, encouraging the fusion of populism and nationalism, and rejecting elitist 'intellectual' forms in favour of folk arts that represented 'the people'. The Communist party sponsored a 'Why I Like America' contest and 'The Star-Spangled Banner' was sung along with 'The Internationale'. The deeply felt urge to rediscover America as an idea and to confront the nation and its cultural history was also fostered by the New Deal, especially the WPA, and by the documentary impulse. Russian and German examples of interest in the land, the worker, and 'the folk' were also influential. America was everywhere, especially in titles. Typical works of reportage were called *Puzzled America* and *America Faces the Barricades*; Elmer Rice's liberal allegory, *American Landscape* (1938), and Kaufman and Hart's anti-fascist play, *The American Way* (1939), were produced on Broadway. Mythic heroes within the democratic heritage (such as Mike Fink, Paul Bunyan and John Henry) were often evoked, notably in Vincent McHugh's vernacular fantasy, *Caleb Catlum's America* (1936). The 'America' revealed in the Thirties was very much a 'New Found Land' (Archibald MacLeish), not only white and middle-class, but also black, Mexican, Indian, immigrant, and agricultural. Historically, this was not a nation devoted to the Protestant ethic but 'a child-like, fanciful, compulsive, absent-minded people' (Robert Cantwell). Thus the historical novels which enjoyed a boom during the Depression were not simply a form of escapism. The past was plundered in the quest for needed values and for those memorable episodes which, as in *Gone with the Wind*, demonstrated the nation's ability to endure and survive. Colonial Williamsburg, its reconstruction completed in 1936, also implied particular social values – individualism, freedom of opportunity – as well as moral and spiritual ones, for despite the surface accuracy, the recreated community of craftsmen represented a fiction which ignored slavery and class gradations.

Generally artists and intellectuals responded to political events in

Europe, and many responded passionately to the Spanish Civil War. Yet a Gallup Poll in 1937 revealed that 94 per cent of Americans favoured a policy aimed at keeping the country out of foreign wars. Reflecting such views, the Neutrality Acts of 1935–37 prohibited American loans to belligerents, embargoed shiploads of arms or munitions, forbade American citizens to travel on the ships of belligerents, and prohibited the arming of American merchant vessels. Implicit in this legislation was the isolationist principle that the United States should refuse to distinguish between the respective moral claims of warring nations. With the German invasion of Czechoslovakia in 1939, Roosevelt (who had increasingly begun to criticize Nazi Germany in his messages to Congress and his fire-side chats) asked for repeal of the 1936 Act. Congress refused but, following Hitler's invasion of Poland, restrictions were relaxed. In 1941, Congress approved the President's request for $7 billion for 'lend-lease', empowering him to lend or lease materials to any nation whose defence he regarded as necessary for the security of the United States, now the 'arsenal of democracy'. With the Japanese attack on the US naval base at Pearl Harbor, in December 1941, the United States declared war on Japan; three days later Germany and Italy declared war on the United States. American isolationism and American neutrality were destroyed at Pearl Harbor and, as Roosevelt later observed, 'Dr New Deal' had to make way for 'Dr Win-the-War'.

What happened in the 1930s?

The historical record is informative – to a degree. The New Deal operated to relieve suffering, and in most of America the spectre of starvation was removed. In addition, social security and unemployment insurance were introduced, and the provisions of the Wagner Act significantly extended the rights of workers. But the rise of industrial unionism meant that Big Labour – bureaucratic and corporate – joined Big Government and Big Business in a national triumvirate. So, under the state capitalism of the New Deal, unions contented themselves with the conservative goal of acquiring a share in the *expansion* of capitalism. There was at that time, however, no significant redistribution of wealth. Roosevelt, in 1936, praised his administration because it had 'saved the system of private profit and free enterprise'. It is hardly suprising that the most popular board game of the Thirties was 'Monopoly'.

New Deal reforms were of greatest benefit to the middle classes; migrant workers, tenant farmers and unskilled labourers were relatively neglected. Also, the New Deal failed to address itself to the problem of the caste system in the South. And the inability of the New Deal to end the Depression – the credit is given to the Second World War – has now become a truism. Nevertheless, capitalism, under pressure, did demonstrate its resilience and even inventiveness.

That the impact of the Thirties was deep and lasting is evident from a work such as Arthur Miller's *The Price* (1968). Set in the present, the play traces the survival mentality of the cop, Victor, to family experiences during the Depression. Yet the mood of the period remains elusive and contradictory. Some 'survivors' report a pervasive camaraderie; others recall the emergence of a predatory mentality. A sense of powerlessness and fatalism is often apparent, but Roosevelt clearly re-kindled hope, and radical politics was at times a source of euphoria.

One of the dominant emotions was fear – fear of others and fear of losing things, the latter instilling a desire for acquisition and for security. Both fears lay behind the affirmation of home and private life. There was also a fear of imminent catastrophe, imaginatively fulfilled by Nathanael West at the end of *The Day of the Locust* (1939). Also prevalent was a feeling of personal guilt and shame, usually brought about by the humiliation of unemployment. Most Americans blamed themselves rather than Wall Street or the government; the ideology of self-reliance persisted as a shaper of consciousness. Nevertheless, bewilderment and shock were widespread responses, and American nervousness was unequivocally demonstrated by the reaction to Orson Welles's radio adaptation of H G Wells's *The War of the Worlds* on 31 October 1938. For the previous month, the American radio audience had been bombarded with news of the European crisis that had been temporarily halted by the Munich agreement. So conditioned to disaster was the public that the broadcast triggered a national panic. Traffic was blocked by fleeing citizens, and scientists rushed into the open to look for meteors.

Assisted by technological innovation, radio and cinema together constituted a powerful ideological apparatus, sustaining the myth of a mobile, classless society containing endless possibilities for success. Increasingly, passive consumerism was to become characteristic of American leisure. But in the Thirties, people bravely continued to believe that the actions of individuals and groups could influence history. Those years, when a considerable quantity of liberal idealism was manifested, were, in Harold Clurman's phrase, 'fervent years'. Saul Alinsky, interviewed at the end of the 1960s, lamented, 'It's a cold world now. It was a hot world then.'[5]

Notes and references

1. Quoted in Bernard Bailyn et al., *The Great Republic. A History of the American People*, D.C. Heath, Lexington, Mass., 1977, p. 1080.
2. William R Brock, *The Character of American History*, Macmillan, London, 1965, p. 217.
3. Christopher Lasch, *The Agony of the American Left*, André Deutsch, London, 1970, p. 56.

4. Ian Jeffrey, 'New World Pictures', in *From Shore to Shining Shore*: *Photographs of the USA – FSA – 1935–43*, Impressions Gallery, York, 1978, p. 5.
5. Quoted in Studs Terkel, *Hard Times*, Avon Books, New York, 1973, p. 361.

Chapter Eleven

War and cold war

Howard Temperley and Malcolm Bradbury

The age of anxiety

In 1947, W H Auden, the British poet now settled in the United States, published his 'baroque eclogue' *The Age of Anxiety*. This long poem, set in a New York bar in wartime, clearly transfers to the United States that sense of historical dislocation, of post-Christian absurdism, amid bleak consciousness that had already darkened the arts of Europe in the pre-war period. Auden himself was one of many intellectual *émigrés* (Bertold Brecht, Thomas Mann, Igor Stravinsky) who were pushed westward by the European turmoils of the Thirties, and whose passage seemed to many a sign of a changing balance of cultural power; it was the modern arts themselves that seemed to be moving westward. But so did the anguishes that went with them, and the way in which Auden transfers his cosmopolitanism and his sense of bleak modernity across the Atlantic is apt; America was indeed now touched by the uneasy thought-movements that derived from world historical disorder. Equally apt was his title: 'the age of anxiety' is as good a name we can find for the two decades of the 1940s and 1950s, a period during which the United States went through some of the most profound and disturbing changes of its modern history – changes that altered national direction, shifted the ideological mood, shifted and enlarged the nation's world-role, and redirected American consciousness.

It was a fundamental and abrupt transition, foreseen by very few. The United States began the 1940s an inward-looking nation, preoccupied with economic fears, unemployment, the need to heal internal ideological division and assert the values of American identity. A decade later, nearly all the issues were changed, and the voices that spoke for the nation and its issues spoke an altered language. Now the United States was a global superpower, the one outright victor from the Second World War, functioning with international responsibilities in an international arena, her fortunes affected by world developments, her problem to define her intentions to the world. The anxieties that preoccupied her were no longer economic but atomic: a new age of power politics had begun. America was now experiencing an unprecedented affluence, making the Depression seem an historical aberration, creating the belief that ideological division in the nation was over, and that a future of limitless, self-sustaining growth lay ahead – if, however, world peace could now be preserved, and with it the future of the 'free' world. But the world in which she now acted was itself changed: it was a modernizing, post-colonial world of changed political alignments, altered spheres of influence, intensifying expectations. In that world, the United States represented one of the two essential modernizing principles – the successful, 'American' way of capitalism, individualism, free institutions, free market, facing, in a posture of growing confrontation, the 'Communist' way of socialist collectivism and the managed economy. American issues were world issues now, and American influence ran wide. Its attitudes and achievements, its position in politics, science and arts, attracted many from elsewhere; at the same time its politics, science and arts, as well as its economics and mass culture, spread through other countries. Yet the new world order was based on tension and contained conflict, and over it all was the shadow of the 'bomb', the atomic weapon that had ended the Pacific war. The post-war period was, indeed, for most Americans an 'age of abundance', and even an 'age of equilibrium'.[1] But it was indeed also an 'age of anxiety', and atomic anxiety at that.

Thus, whatever else it did, the Japanese attack on Pearl Harbor on 7 December 1941 precipitated the United States into areas of experience for which the years before had hardly prepared it. Nor, when the United States dropped its atomic bombs on Hiroshima and Nagasaki in 1945, were many prepared for the way in which a 'hot' war against the Axis powers would lead forward into that long era of 'war by other means' against a former ally, Russia, in the uneasy aftermath of which we still live, though there were times when it seemed that such a future of survival was unlikely. It is no doubt because we still live with the consequences that the 1940s and 1950s remain strongly in our minds, that its issues and arts still seem close to us, that we constantly revisit the period in fiction and films, memoirs and historiography, and with such a mixture of nostalgia and doubt. If the Fifties – taking that term broadly to mean the founding period of cold war and cosmopolitanism in the United States – seemed in endless quarrel with the Thirties (that quarrel reaching, with McCarthyism, the dimensions of a purge), then the Sixties quarrelled likewise with the Fifties. Radicals now interpreted the Fifties as a period of social and indeed sexual repression; 'revisionist' historians and political scientists questioned the 'traditionalist'justifications of the political choices and intensions of the years from VJ day onward – the decisions to support the United Nations, resist communism, support European economic recovery through the Marshall Plan, organize a Western military alliance through NATO, develop nuclear strategies, give aid to Russia's enemies round the world, and intervene, as in Korea in 1950–53, in foreign conflicts. To many in the Sixties, the Truman and Eisenhower eras after Roosevelt's death were a period when the progressive intent of the nation was sacrificed, when American capitalism embarked on a course of world domination and of confrontation, and when intellectuals and scientists betrayed their functions and became weapons of government. Today, in the longer light of the 1980s, all these issues look rather more complicated. As one observer, Donald Watt, has noted: 'American historiography of the Cold War tells us very little of the Cold War, much of American intellectual history in the 1960s and 1970s.'[2] Was it indeed American interest and misjudgement which brought about the Cold War, or was there indeed a communist threat to world stability, or an unavoidable process of entry into the post-war political vacuum? Did the 'liberalism' of the Fifties indeed betray American progressivism, or was it not a characteristic development of the American way of mediating between conservatism and reform? Was that liberalism simply a mask for what David Caute has characterized as an outrageous machinery of repression in American life,[3] or was the main enterprise one of preserving a pluralist system against a widely feared totalitarian threat to it?

What certainly is clear is that the period of war and post-war deserved a more complex interpretation than the Sixties, in its reactive swerve, could give: and above all an interpretation that is capable of recognizing that political choices are made in the midst of events that often seem frighteningly incomprehensible. This was clearly the case in post-war years, marked as they were by fears of totalitarianism which could provoke neo-totalitarian responses; by a new awareness of man's wickedness and potential for cruelty consequent on the hideous revelations of Auschwitz and Buchenwald; by guilt about the political *naïvetés* of the past, which seemed to have permitted the rise of Nazism; by, above all, apocalyptic fears of nuclear threat and annihilation (displaced into black comedy, often, as in the film *Dr Strangelove*: *Or How to Stop Worrying and Love the Bomb*). The main political choices were forged uncertainly, and were undoubtedly shaped by fears of a reversion to the economic and political conditions of the Thirties. Was the world best served by a reversion to sphere-of-influence politics, or could a new age of universalism emerge? Were the interests of those who wanted peace achieved best by appealing to men's reason or their fears? Should the United States seek support from any power prepared to ally with her, or only those who genuinely shared her values? Internal choices were equally difficult. Was a society of materialist conformity better than one of economic instability? Should intellectuals and artists ally themselves with a political order that seemed to defend, globally. the values of liberalism, even if sometimes by illiberal means? Darkened and internationalized by war, fearful about the liberal capacity to handle the illiberal humanity, Americans found themselves having to make decisions which as a nation and as individuals they had hitherto avoided. It was a period of discovered internationalism, fed by global responsibilities in a world where the United States now faced as much west as east, and of reasserted nationalism, as Americans found themselves custodians of 'basic' values. It was a time of uncertain compromises and stoical acceptances, when the works of modern existential thinkers like Heidegger, Buber, Niebuhr and Sartre became authoritative, when myth, faith and the tragic sense seemed truer world-views than the innocent radical faith in history that had served in the pre-war years. In art there was a revived liberalism that also distrusted its own premises and capacities. These were the times of absurdism, of writing and painting left pained and sometimes almost silent in the face of recent history, haunted by fears both of the inner self and the outer life of a society where totalitarianism was an ever-present danger, yet often hungering for reconciliation of the two.

Thus to look on the larger record of the 1940s and 1950s – not only on historical events, but on the records of consciousness and conscience given us by intellectuals, writers and artists – is to look on a time of uneasy reappraisals. The intellectual urgencies of the Thirties often yielded to what Lionel Trilling, one of the larger spokesmen of the mind in the Fifties, called 'moral realism': a sense not of clear good and evil but of good-and-evil.[4] Some of the time's best writing came from authors who saw themselves as survivors of wartime agonies – especially from Jewish writers, who identified with the 6 million who had *not* survived, and spoke the message of a new tragic humanism. At the same time the radical impulse was far from stilled, and the questioning of the new affluence and the contemporary spirit of American society laid a clear path, among political critics, youthful rebels, the Beat generation, to the reaction of the Sixties. The Fifties were a time of new stabilities and new instabilities, of a dark cosmopolitanism and also of a new self-protectionism, of dangerous choices, some foolishly and others anxiously taken. Its inheritance is with us still.

The impact of war

The event that plunged the United States into its greatest structural change since the Great Crash was, of course, the Japanese attack on Pearl Habor in 1941. But, though national problems had concealed this from most Americans, the event had been long in the making. In Europe the political settlements made after the First World War had been coming apart for many years. In 1933 the Nazis had risen to power in Germany, in 1936 they occupied the Rhineland; then followed the annexation of Austria (1938), the invasion of Czechoslovakia (March 1939), and the assault on Poland (1 September 1939) that marked the outbreak of general hostilities. In the Far East, conflict between China and Japan had begun long before with the Japanese occupation of Manchuria, later broadening out into a full-scale struggle for control of China itself. But it was not until December 1941 – by which time France had fallen, German tanks were rolling towards Moscow, and most of China and Indo-China were in Japanese hands – that America found herself, with a mixture of surprise and indignation, an involuntary belligerent. What made Americans so surprised and angry was not just that Pearl Harbour came totally without warning or, as far as they could see, provocation: it was that nothing remotely like it had happened before. Since the founding of the Republic, they had believed that their geography provided a barrier against potential aggressors. They had been involved in previous conflicts, but at least thay had had some choice in the matter. However, the Japanese assault on the US naval base at Pearl Harbour – and simultaneously on American forces in the Philippines, Guam and Midway Island – forced them into the international arena. The US Congress's declaration of 8 December was a recognition of a state of war that already existed.

But, though Congress's declaration, followed by Germany's and Italy's declarations of war on the United States, marked official American entry into the conflict, her actual involvement had started much earlier. As was noted in the previous chapter, American neutrality legislation in the 1930s had attempted to avoid American involvement in future conflict by preventing Americans from giving assistance to belligerent powers. Many were opposed to these 'isolationist' measures, including Roosevelt, who correctly saw that they provided encouragement to potential aggressors while preventing their victims from looking abroad for assistance. But there was little he could do without the support of public opinion, divided between those who wanted America to attend to her own affairs, and those who saw the need for an anti-fascist front. With the outbreak of European war, Roosevelt hastened to remove Congressional restrictions with as much speed as public sentiment would allow. In November 1939 he repealed the arms embargo, by authorizing 'cash and carry' exports to belligerents, and in March 1941 Congress approved his Lend-Lease Bill, which allowed the President to supply arms to countries whose defence was deemed vital to American interests. An initial appropriation of $7 billion was set aside for this purpose, and eventually over $50 billion would be expended. Meanwhile, secret staff talks were being held between Britain and America to agree on a common strategy in the event of an American involvement. More immediately, arrangements were made to create a defence zone east of Iceland, and to use US naval vessels to convoy American shipping. At home, Americans were pushing ahead with military preparations. During 1941 munitions production trebled: car factories were already being adapted for aircraft and armoured-vehicle production. For the first time in America there was peacetime conscription, and more than 16 million men were registered. Already, then, the switch from peacetime to wartime arrangements, from isolationist to internationalist policies, was underway. If the assault on Pearl Harbor took Americans by surprise, it did not find them unprepared.

The war shocked Americans but it also changed their perspectives and above all their economy. The Japanese attack undercut the position of the 'American Firsters', strengthened those who called for an anti-fascist front, and meant that Roosevelt took the nation into war with a larger consensus of the nation behind him. And an immediate effect of entry was to shift the economy into high gear – something the New Deal, for all its deficit spending, had failed to do. Between January and June 1942, the War Production Board, entrusted with the task of co-ordinating the national economic war efforts, placed orders for goods valued at more than $100 billion – more than the entire Gross National Product of 1940, and more than the military spending of all the other combatants combined. Among the targets the President set were 8 million tons of shipping, 60,000 planes, 45,000 tanks, and 20,000 anti-aircraft guns. In all, federal spending during the war amounted to $320 billion. What was most remarkable was that this production was achieved without any drastic cutback in civilian consumer spending. There was some rationing, but so enormous was America's productive capacity that her response to war consisted largely of superimposing her new military requirements on top of existing peacetime production. Indeed, the output of some luxury goods grew, because of the increases in earning power created by the war economy. Job opportunities boomed: those who – like the 'Okies' in John Steinbeck's *The Grapes of Wrath* (1939) – were still jobless when war started, were quickly recruited into the services or taken into expanding war industries. So were women, many of whom had never thought of working, but now found it gave them a new measure of prosperity and independence. And, though in the armed services as well as in some civilian occupations segregation continued, blacks now prospered too.

The war, of course, produced much real suffering for Americans: 322,000 of them lost their lives in battle; more than double that number were wounded, and many more suffered in other ways. Yet, even when all the casualties were added together, the fact remains that, in a war that claimed upwards of 50 million dead, Americans fared better than most. This could be no consolation to those who took part in the death march from Bataan to Corregidor, or in the murderous jungle fighting at Guadalcanal, or in the Ardennes retreat. Yet it did mean overall that the experiences of American soldiers tended to be different from those of their Russian – and very different indeed from those of their German and Japanese – counterparts. Even in the first stages of the conflict, Americans had little reason to fear that they would *lose* the war, let alone that they would see their cities occupied, or their Jews herded into gas chambers. For most Americans at home, and a good many serving abroad, the war brought compensations as well as hardships, and sometimes the former overweighed the latter. If contact with the military machine was shocking to some, others found the experience liberating, opening new opportunities that would be claimed in post-war life. Unlike the Great Depression, which brought misery to almost everyone, the Second World War was an event in which, J K Galbraith later claimed 'a large number of people found pleasure in jobs they never expected to have, in responsibility they never expected to assume, in travel previously reserved for the rich, and in escape from worthy but routine wives'.[5] Above all, the war dispelled the Depression, and America emerged from it the one outright victor, forced into an experience of world contacts which shaped its subsequent policies in directions far away from those of the Thirties.

The shift of mood is evident in intellectual and cultural life. During the thirties, many intellectuals had been on the Left and aligned themselves with a radical future, usually mediating between American progressive radicalism and revolutionary internationalism. But the effectiveness of the New Deal, the revelations about Stalin's purges, and finally the signing of the Nazi-Soviet Pact in 1939 weakened communist sympathies. In a spectacular defection from the Party after the Pact was signed, the writer Granville Hicks noted: 'However much strength and influence the Communist Party has lost remains to be seen, but it is my belief that the events of the last few weeks have largely destroyed its effectiveness [in America].'[6] With the coming of war, writers who had been leftward in the Thirties now became loyal war-correspondents attached to the cause of American democracy: John Steinbeck in Africa and Europe, John Dos Passos in the Pacific, Ernest Hemingway in France (where he had to be restrained from combat, and took pride in having liberated the Paris Ritz). Around this time, too, a number of major writers from the experimental Twenties and political Thirties died: Thomas Wolfe in 1938, Scott Fitzgerald and Nathanael West in 1940, Sherwood Anderson in 1941, Gertrude Stein just after the end of the hostilities. As in the First World War, a new generation seemed to emerge from the war experience itself. Inevitably, with books like John Hersey's *A Bell for Adano* (1944), John Horne Burns's *The Gallery* (1947), Irwin Shaw's *The Young Lions* (1948), Norman Mailer's *The Naked and the Dead* (1948), James Gould Cozzens's *Guard of Honour* (1948), Herman Wouk's *The Caine Mutiny* (1951), and James Jones's *From Here to Eternity* (1951), the war novel again flourished. But, as in the war novels following the First World War, they also marked the changing mood of the times. Malcolm Cowley has noted that the post-First World War writers went not for disillusion so much as rebellion, and tried elaborate technical experiments: the post-Second World War writers wrote of despair and disillusion, and often used conservative technical forms.[7] Their themes were the dark discovery of European ruination of historical waste, political anxiety, and the threat of totalitarianism which they found not only in the enemy but within the military system itself. Norman Mailer's *The Naked and the Dead*, the best of these works, explores the impotence of liberalism and foresees a new fascist potential released in the psychic and social world by war: 'You can consider the army as a preview of the future', says his General Cummings.

But perhaps the best book from the wartime period is by a writer who did not see the battlefields. In 1944 Saul Bellow, a Jewish writer from *Partisan Review* circles, published *Dangling Man*, a novel about Joseph, who had been a communist in the Thirties, but now lives in a dead, modern, wartime New York City, awaiting his induction into the army. Politics and human and romantic relations having failed him, he moves into solitude, an irritable enclosure. He is a marginal man, who nevertheless notes that 'we have history to answer to', and sets himself the task of defining a humanist world view: 'He asked himself a question I still would like answered, namely "How should a good man live; what ought he to do?"' he says, inspecting his past self. Joseph's is a modern existential dilemma – he exists without an essence in a non-reflecting, hostile world – but what resolves it is the arrival of his induction papers. His final cry – 'Hurray for regular hours! And for supervision of the spirit! Long live regimentation!' – is an ambiguous resolution, a testament to loss and gain: the deprivation of the solitary realm of the free spirit, driving toward solipsism, the acquisition of enforced community and historical attachment. In its very ambiguity, *Dangling Man* is a notably modern novel. Its roots lie in the dark literature of European modernism, especially that concerned with romantic deprivation and historical disorder: the work of Dostoevsky, Kafka, Sartre. It is a breakaway from the pastoral nostalgia or the epical American ambition that shaped many novels in the generation before, a recognition of the contingent modern city, the struggle of individual and community, the wasting of self. It is also – in a period when the Jewish voice both cosmopolitanized and darkened American thought – a Jewish novel, seeking a ceremonial of life in a bleak world. Joseph's stoical acceptance of the system in its inadequacy is a bleak parable or paradox that would resound through much post-war American writing, as writers divided between agonizing fears and liberal desires, struggling with Reinhold Niebuhr's warning that liberal moralism could not cope with 'the ultimately religious problem of the evil in man',[8] an evil that gothicized any innocent expectation.

The Truman years 1945–52

It was thus an uneasy, changing, morally bloodied nation that, after Roosevelt's death in April 1945, President Harry S Truman led through the last months of war and into the uncomfortable peace after

14 August, after the dropping of two atomic bombs on Japan. Americans had no wish to return to the economic disasters of the Thirties nor to the unpreparedness and the chaotic international politics of the inter-war years. But the bomb, the revelations about Nazi genocide, and the tactics of the Russians in Eastern Europe all raised dark shadows over the future. The central fear haunting Americans at home was that the end of hostilities would mean a return to Depression. The great boom of the war years, which had raised the nation's Gross National Product by over 60 per cent in real terms between 1939 and 1945, was so plainly the product of the war economy that it was hard to see how it could continue when military spending was cut. Yet Americans wanted the rewards of peace; there were 12 million returning veterans to be absorbed into the labour force. Severe strikes hit the nation in 1946, and inflation took off again. Distrustful of Truman's capacity to manage these issues, the nation elected a Republican Congress, the first since 1931, against Truman's Democratic administration. Yet the fears were groundless. Although federal spending was slashed by almost 60 per cent, from $98 billion in 1945 to $39 billion in 1947, the actual fall in GNP was less than 10 per cent, and within the next three years this shortfall was made up by growth in the domestic sector. Unemployment rose briefly from its all-time low of 1.2 per cent in 1944 to 3.9 per cent in 1946, but dropped to 3.4 per cent in 1948. By the turn into the 1950s, the promises were that American society was evolving into a new kind of mass society based on more or less general abundance.

How was this managed? Partly it was through government planning of the economy, in part based on continued defence needs. For, though by European standards America was far from being a 'welfare state', Truman saw that there was no going back on the New Deal. Returning veterans were treated with generosity through the GI Bill, with grants on leaving the service, low interest loans for acquiring farms, businesses or new homes, and educational subsidies on such a scale that they fuelled a rapid expansion of higher education, in turn bringing an increasing sophistication, a higher level of scientific, technological and cultural activity, and an enlarged academic elite, into the culture. More important, economically, was the demand for new consumer goods that had built up over the preceding five years, when, despite general prosperity, production for civilian consumption had not kept up with spending power. So now articles that had been scarce or unavailable – cars, refrigerators, radios – needed replacing, while a whole new range of consumer goods – electric clothes dryers, television sets, air conditioners, synthetic fabrics – came on to the market, thanks to new mass-production techniques and new, often war-derived, technologies. Construction boomed: by the late 1940s, commercial and industrial building was more than double the level of the 1930s. Firms ploughed back high proportions of profits into research and development, reflecting growing confidence; American business, freed of the demands of the war economy, turned its enormous energies and resources into creating a consumer society that would soon inspire fascination and envy around the world. The stark contrast between American affluence and European poverty became clear; America was the only nation to emerge from the war with her plant intact and her economy strengthened. In 1949, American *per capita* income was double that of Britain, three times that of France, five times that of Germany, seven times that of Russia. With only 6 per cent of the world's population, America consumed 40 per cent of the world's energy, had 60 per cent of the motor vehicles, 70 per cent of the telephones, 80 per cent of the refrigerators, and nearly 100 per cent of the television sets. Americans, who had dreamt throughout the Depression of recapturing the prosperity of the Twenties, found themselves by 1950 with a *per capita* income 44 per cent above that of 1929. It was the American economic miracle: no other nation had ever been so rich.

But American consciousness of good fortune was tempered by a newly awakened sense of international vulnerability. Pearl Harbor had shown that the Pacific and Atlantic Oceans no longer provided effective barriers against aggressors. It also demonstrated the dangers of hiding away from world responsibilities while major crises developed. During the war, the lesson had already been drawn that the United States must henceforth play an active part in world affairs if issues were to be settled before they reached crisis proportions. It seemed clear that the origins of the Second World War lay in the economic collapse of the Thirties and the consequent rise of the dictators. If prosperity were assured, and international disagreements thrashed out in public, the chance of world peace would be greatly increased. One spectacular convert from isolationism was Senator Arthur Vanderberg, who announced in 1945: 'I want a new dignity and a new authority for international law. I think American self-interest requires it.'[9] The instrument that many Americans looked to was the newly established United Nations, which held its inaugural meeting in San Francisco in April 1945. It was in many ways an American product, reflecting American assumptions about the efficacy of free discussion as the mode of resolving differences, and depended on the willingness of members to abide by majority decisions. American foreign policy was now based in principle on a new universalist approach, a rejection of the old sphere of influence politics of the inter-war years. In retrospect, it now appears that much of the idealism the Americans invested in the UN was a product of their inexperience in world affairs, but it appeared a signal model for the future.

But what immediately alarmed Americans was the behaviour of the Soviet Union. During the war, disagreements between the two powers had been largely concealed from the public, and there was something of a honeymoon period as post-war politics evolved. However, over the next years conflict quickly became open and bitter, especially over the question of the 'satellite' countries of Eastern Europe. What the Soviet Union hoped to achieve in these years will remain mysterious until Russian archives are opened; but it is plain that the Russians had drawn quite different lessons from the Second World War from those Americans had drawn. Their losses had been incomparably greater: for every American killed, some 50 Russians had died, and vast areas of the country had been devastated. For the second time in a generation, German armies had swept east; there was little to suggest that such invasions were the product of economic dislocation, nor that an international debating chamber could prevent their recurrence. Moreover as Marxists, Russians were committed to an inexorable interpretation of history that saw socialism and capitalism locked in life-and-death struggle. The establishment of socialism was justified in the satellite countries by historical world-purpose as well as by security. The Americans were at first prepared to recognize considerable Russian rights in Eastern Europe, in exchange for advantages elsewhere. But, as the Red Army remained in Eastern European countries, as democratic regimes began to fail, and the satellite-state system evolved, American policy, committed to pursuing the principles of political and economic liberalism, found itself increasingly at odds with Russia. To those liberals who regretted their earlier failure to see the fascist threat, what was happening now in Poland, Czechoslovakia and Hungary was all too like the Hitlerite adventures of a decade earlier. Did Russia, too, intend to move west and establish throughout Europe satellite states and occupied powers? If so, there was little except American power to stop her: all the Russians needed to reach the Channel ports, went a saying of the day, was boots. In retrospect, it is clear that much that was menacing and conspiratorial in Russian behaviour could as readily be seen as signs of weakness. But it was hard for Americans not to feel that history was repeating itself, and there were reasons – even good liberal reasons – why a Truman administration might use such fears. With a Republican Congress attacking Democratic programmes for financing aid and development overseas, Truman could justify such activity best on the grounds that it was necessary to fight encroaching communism.

By 1947, the philosophies of containment and confrontation were well evolved. In 1946, Churchill had seen an 'iron curtain' coming down on Europe. In 1947, the term 'Cold War' was coined. In 1949 came the Hiss case, involving Thirties espionage, the news that China had gone communist, and the acquisition, probably through espionage, of the atomic bomb by the Russians. By 1950, American troops were again in action, in Korea. This period was as Eric Goldman says, the 'crucial decade' that transformed the nation.[10] In intellectual circles, events had brought many intellectuals to the position of rejecting their Thirties political attachments to the Left, and taking up positions of 'liberalism' or 'neo-conservatism'. It was partly based on the feeling of the failure of radical-revolutionary principles, as evidenced by events in Eastern Europe, so hard to distinguish from the fate of those nations under Nazism. It was also based on a rejection of American progressive innocence, as intellectuals, bloodied in war and doubtful that history was working in humanity's favour, sought to assess the possibilities of an adequate modern humanism. Time and again the issues of the Thirties, the era of communism, which, as the title of one central book of the period had it, was 'The God That Failed', demanded replay. Older intellectuals looked to their pasts, as did Lionel Trilling in his interesting novel *The Middle of the Journey* (1947), which portrays radical hopes turning to conspiracy and intransigence, an 'imperious and bitter refusal to consent to the conditioned nature of human existence', in that era of politics and history. In this book and elsewhere, Trilling defined a new kind of liberalism that recognized the dangers of Utopianism and of high attachment to History, that recognized too the variousness and complexity of reality, and that sought the realization of that complexity not in politics but in literature. Other intellectuals attempted to reconstitute the 'conservative' principles they saw underlying American life – what Peter Viereck in *Conservatism Revisited* (1947) called 'the permanent beneath the flux' – and there was a turn toward myth, religion and classicism, evident in a good many of the writings of the time.

These intellectual developments might partly explain one of the stranger phenomena of the times: the fear of communist subversion at home. It is easy to see why intellectuals might now feel more fully reconciled with their society, and why Russian behaviour inspired American apprehension. It is hard to understand why, when capitalism was apparently successful and few spoke on behalf of the adversary position, people should feel their society was being internally threatened, though a crucial factor, of course, was the fear of betrayal of atomic secrets, which generated an era of suspicion. Even stranger, however, was the cast of characters constituting the threat: Hollywood scriptwriters, New York intellectuals, Ivy League and other professors and academics not usually thought of as having the power to do much harm outside their own families. According to Joseph McCarthy, the Republican Senator from Wisconsin who gave his name to the 'witch-hunting' phenomenon that now arose, it was 'the enemies from within', 'the bright young men who are born with silver spoons in their mouths', who were responsible for sapping America's strength in a new war that could not end 'except by victory or death for this civilisation'.[11] Like most influential political movements, McCarthyism was made up of many strands. It partly arose from party politics: some Republicans found in the subtle link that was drawn between the New Deal and subversion an admirable weapon for attacking Truman's administration. It partly reflected the resentment and frustration of those – lower-class Catholics, rural mid-westerners, the new middle classes advanced by affluence but uncertain of their status – who feared intellectual change, and who had grounds for envying the groups identified by McCarthy, who had simply chosen to exploit a prevailing mood. It arose from anti-intellectual suspicions fed by an age of expanding education, science and technology, which displaced old values, and by the paradoxes of liberals who could change sides, and therefore formed a climate in which some of those who helped to develop atomic capability also felt the Russians should possess it. McCarthyism, in fact, reflected the ambiguity felt by many Americans about their international role; it revealed their doubts, their traditionalism, their desire for simplicity. It also indicated that to do much that was admirable – finance the Marshall Plan, which set European industry on its feet again, aid the United Nations, make generous gifts to developing countries – Americans needed to persuade themselves that they were indeed 'at war'. They had to draw on reserves of moralism, persuading themselves that the struggle was not just between America and Russia, but between good and evil, right-thinking and wrong-thinking. Insofar as American leaders did encourage this atmosphere of suspicion and the apocalyptic fears that ran through the times, they were, as events would prove, fostering dangerous illusions.

Yet in general Americans could look about them with a sense of achievement and success as they surveyed their society and their role in the world. Intellectuals might have strong doubts about the kind of materialist, conformist society that was emerging, and the increased stratification of political thought in the world, but they too seemed generally strikingly content with an America that had apparently overcome economic disaster, brought new welfare opportunities, expanded education, and entered a new era of intellectual achievement recognized in much of the world. If American freedom was imperfect, it was still freedom. In a famous symposium in *Partisan Review* – that radical focus of the Thirties – in 1952, a group of generally radical intellectuals contributed an article, 'Our Country and Our Culture', and were reasonably positive in their view of the society. They stressed that much of the progressive intent of the New Deal had been fulfilled, and suggested that intellectual and artistic life was closer to power and influence than ever before. Some disagreed. Norman Mailer sensed a new totalitarianism in the culture, stifling dissent, and Irving Howe, in an essay called 'This Age of Conformity', complained:

Far from creating and subsidizing unrest, capitalism in its most recent stage has found an honored place for the intellectuals; and the intellectuals, far from thinking of themselves as a desperate 'opposition,' have been enjoying a return to the bosom of the nation. . . . We have all, even the handful who still try to retain a glower of criticism, become responsible and moderate. And tame.[12]

As many critics in the 1960s would, Howe portrayed an intellectual sector won over by weariness and increased grant-aided opportunities, living in an age of defeat and seeking to withdraw from 'the bloodied arena of historical action and choice'. He noticed the absence of counter-politics, and saw a process of social and intellectual bureaucratization at work, granting the intellectual a secure social place in exchange for his critical function. Howe was implicitly assaulting the model of the liberal intelligentsia that had returned in the Fifties, as against the *avant-garde* or revolutionary model that had grown in the years before the First and Second World Wars. And he noticed the infection in literature too: *avant-garde* experimentalism was fading, 'moral musings' were the order of the day, and the professional writer was replaced by the professional critic, now obsessed with orthodoxy, tradition, and abstract formalism.

Howe's challenge had its weight. A new, post-war literary generation was slow in emerging, and in some ways it lacked the aesthetic radicalism of its antecedents, like Pound, Eliot, Stein or Faulkner. In poetry there was a taste for academic formalism, though in fact major poets were emerging – Robert Lowell with *Lord Weary's Castle* (1946) and *Poems 1938-1949* (1950), Randall Jarrell with *Little Friend, Little Friend* (1945), Delmore Schwartz with *Vaudeville for a Princess* (1950), John Berryman with *The Dispossessed* (1948), and Theodore Roethke with *The Lost Son* (1948) – who were mediating between formal concerns and deep historical tension and psychic anxiety. In the 'Southern Gothic' fiction of Eudora Welty (*Delta Wedding*, 1946), Carson McCullers (*The Member of the Wedding*, 1946), Truman Capote (*Other Voices, Other Rooms*, 1948), Flannery O'Connor (*Wise Blood*, 1952) there is again a mixture of formalism and of the tragic sense brought by historical unease and displacement. The theatre of Tennessee Williams contains much the same mood. Yet if the note of modernist experimentalism was muted, it left its clear traces in the new writing. It was true that, as one critic has since put it, 'the issues of ambiguity and paradox had suddenly taken on a new moral prestige, and politics thus became a gesture in the direction of "the tragic sense of life"';[13] it was also true that literature rather than politics direct became the voice of this tragic sense. But what gave post-war American writing its notable force – there were those who would argue that it had now taken on dominance in the development of post-war literature internationally – was its attempt to relate the search for a form to a comprehension of a deeply disturbing history, and so to bridge the space between the world of the imagination and the world of reality, which itself seemed to grow improbable. In this sense it is a liberal fiction, avoiding either systematic ideology or *avant-garde* extremities of formalism; in it the classic attempt to reconcile the individual to a social and historical world is pursued in all its difficulty. In the theatre Arthur Miller, in fiction the new Jewish writers, in poetry Robert Lowell best exemplify these interests. Miller's plays – like *Death of a Salesman* (1949) – examine social victimization and the power of the historical order: 'How', asks Miller, 'may a man make of the outside world a home?' It is the question Bellow too continued to ask as he followed *Dangling Man* with *The Victim* (1947), a book set in the hot, impersonal, naturalist jungle of modern New York City, where the issue of one man's responsibility for another is debated, and the problem of finding a measure for man in conditions of historical impersonality is central. J D Salinger's *The Catcher in the Rye* (1951), soon to become a student 'bible', portrays Holden Caulfield's attempt to take responsibility for the lives and agonies of others in the hypocritical adult world, and shows his psychic defeat. Norman Mailer's *Barbary Shore* (1951), still his most directly political novel, explores the confusions of modern ideology while insisting on the pressure of history on consciousness. The fragile existential centre of selfhood threatened from every angle is the theme of Ralph Ellison's *Invisible Man* (1952), an extraordinary novel of lost social identity that modernizes black fiction. Yet the sense of historical exposure could lead to an art away from liberalism, an art of exposed surreal consciousness to which moral interpretation is no longer relevant. John Hawkes published with *The Cannibal* (1949) and *The Beetle Leg* (1951), the first set in wartime Germany, the second set in wartime Britain, two novels of extraordinary experimental power whose dream-images and gothic imaginings were equally a part of the new mood. They relate to the intensities of Southern Gothic writing; they also lead the way to the *avant-garde* developments of the 1960s and 1970s. But in fact Howe's gloom about contemporary writing was, as he would later acknowledge, premature. By the early 1950s, there were many signs available that post-war American writing was entering into a remarkable and vigorous new phase.

The Eisenhower years 1953-60

Yet it did seem that when, in 1952, Americans dismissed Adlai Stevenson and chose General Dwight D Eisenhower as the first Republican president since Hoover, the conservative vein in American culture had dominated the nation. Certainly there was nothing in the platform on which he was elected to suggest that his administration would take a more relaxed view of communism, abroad or at home. His running mate Richard M Nixon, who had first made his name on the House Un-American Activities Committee, indicated that there would be no let-up in the drive to root suspected subversives out of government service; Eisenhower himself promised an audience at Billings, Montana, a month before the election: 'We will find the pinks, we will find the Communists, we will find the disloyal.' Nor was his choice of John Foster Dulles as Secretary of State reassuring to those who hoped for a reduction in Cold War tensions. Dulles was committed to a manichean view of the world; he had been highly critical of Democratic 'no win' policies, and referred repeatedly during the campaign, as adviser on foreign policy, to 'the liberation of captive peoples' and the possibility of 'roll back'. The voters had no doubt that an Eisenhower administration would be against any 'softness' on communism. Yet, from the beginning, Republican rhetoric and policies were at odds. 'I will go to Korea', Eisenhower promised in the campaign; what, though, he intended to do there was not to practice 'roll back' but to find a mutually agreeable way of ending a struggle that had gone on too long. In any case, the aggressiveness in foreign-policy statements conflicted with other promises, to cut taxes and balance the budget. If the government was going to do more, it would have to do it with less.

Much the same was true in domestic policy. Eisenhower believed that the Democrats had encroached too much on the legislative powers of Congress; it was not part of the presidential role to engage in unseemly legislative tussles, still less to assume an active role in the management of the economy. Business was best left in private hands; the Democrats had been altogether too interventionist, driving inflation up to unacceptable levels (70 per cent on the Consumer Price Index under Truman) by deficit financing and welfarism. Eisenhower saw his responsibility as being to preserve the value of the dollar and give private enterprise freedom to develop. Thus, for the first time since the 1920s, the United States had a president who believed in masterly inactivity. On the occasions when he did take the initiative, it was as often as not to *prevent* things happening: he vetoed public-works bills, community housing legislation, anti-pollution measures. Yet there is no doubt that in Eisenhower the American people found a president admirably suited to the mood of the times. It was, some critics argued, a case of the bland leading the bland. But most felt that, after thirty years of crisis, Americans deserved a little time to enjoy their material comforts and take stock of their position: a period of 'equilibrium'.[14]

Eisenhower's equilibrium worked. The American economy continued to expand. Some years were better than others: GNP actually dropped during 1953–54 and again during 1957–58, but what was lost then was more than made up in other years: expansion during the decade averaged some 3 per cent a year. It was less than the growth rate of some other nations, notably Germany, Japan and – a fact that caused unease, especially after the firing of *Sputnik* in 1957 – the USSR; but, as Americans reminded themselves, these countries started from much lower base lines. In average income per head, as in roads, factories and accumulated capital assets, no other country could compare with the USA. It was America that set the style in everything from building construction to hoola-hoops. The modern consumer society was, in a sense, her invention; and where she led, others eagerly followed. The new high-rise buildings springing up from the rubble in London, Paris and Tokyo looked, and sometimes were,

American. So was the music and entertainment young people in those cities danced to, listened to, or watched. Every summer, hordes of Americans poured through the airports of Europe, much as their ancestors had poured through the Cumberland Gap, often carrying such novel pieces of latter-day equipment as air-travel bags, king-size cigarettes, disposable paper handkerchieves, and expensive-looking cameras, signs of the richer life across the Atlantic. Most astonishing of all, there was no indication that it would end. Now well into their second decade of growth, it seemed clear that Keynesian economics worked and that, barring some incredible act of government folly, another great depression was inconceivable. Public-opinion surveys indicated that fewer Americans now expected a major depression ahead than expected a major war – though, following the death of Stalin in 1953, and the more liberal policies of Krushchev, even that fear receded somewhat. The idea that gasoline might cease to flow or other resources run out occurred to virtually no one. Looking forward to the 1960s, the editors of *Fortune* magazine noted that there were 'cogent reasons for expecting that output per man-hour will advance at least as fast during the next decade as it has over the last one'. Some of this increase would be absorbed by defence and there would be need for additional investment. But, they concluded, 'for the US as a whole the price of growth will be magnificently easy to bear; the economic pie will expand so enormously that almost everybody can get a substantially bigger cut'.[15]

The society of abundance was so novel that it called for analysis, and the Fifties was an era of sociological revival; 'value-free' sociology seemed the best instrument for recording and analysing the new order. Indeed, some thought that sociology was taking over alike from politics and the novel, offering large-scale explanations that became – as with the Kinsey report on American male sexuality in 1948 – part of the folklore. After all, never had a people possessed so much in worldly goods, or, apparently, been so troubled in spirit on that account. In a succession of best-sellers, Vance Pankard recounted the consumer society's problems. *The Hidden Persuaders* (1957) showed how Americans were manipulated by advertising men; *The Status Seekers* (1959) how they struggled to establish themselves in their own and others' estimations; *The Pyramid Climbers* (1962) how anguish reached even the executive suite. The managerial elite, no doubt because they epitomized the Fifties' idea of success, received more than their share of attention: like the Brookes Brothers suits they were credited with wearing, they represented a distinctive blend of glamour and sobriety. Yet, as film-makers, novelists and sociologists pointed out, their lot was not entirely a happy one. If it was true, said William H Whyte in *The Organization Man* (1956), that they enjoyed many privileges through running the big private and public organizations that increasingly dominated a more and more corporational America, it was also true that to a large degree these organizations also ran them

– putting them through batteries of psychological tests, monitoring their family lives, fostering an attitude of conforming mediocrity. The giant modern corporations were quite unlike the monster trusts of the past, and the robber barons had gone. But control over those who served had not lessened, thanks to modern management techniques and psychological screening processes. Indeed, said C Wright Mills in a study of the rising service class, *White Collar* (1951), becoming part of the non-manual labour force meant not only selling one's work but also one's personality. The employee subscribing to the organization ethic was more a slave than the old factory worker, who at least knew when he was being exploited.

The blandness and artificial coherence of the consumer society disturbed many. J K Galbraith saw, in a book that named the whole phenomenon, *The Affluent Society* (1958), a price for private affluence in public squalor: the prices paid in the shops did not represent the full cost of articles to the consumer, who paid an added premium in the form of unsafe cities, congested highways, polluted rivers, devastated countryside. But Galbraith also suggested the difficulties in arriving at a critique: in a new world of expanding production, old assumptions born in a world of scarcity did not apply. Others extended that point: indeed, in *The Lonely Crowd* (1950), the sociologist David Riesman suggested that affluence and consumer culture were generating a new character type. Riesman divided mankind into three categories: the tradition-directed, found in those parts of the world untouched by industrialization; the inner-directed, found most commonly in those cultures which had begun to experience more rapid change; and the other-directed, living in cultures where change was so rapid that members looked for guidance and values not to ancestors or even parents but to their peers. The inner-directed tended to be job-minded and concerned with resource exploitation; the other-directed were 'people minded', moving freely from role to role, sensitive to the needs of others, reflecting the fact that in a consumer society the major problem was no longer production but handling other people. And in *People of Plenty: Economic Abundance and the American Character* (1954), David M Potter pointed out that material abundance of one kind or another marked American experience from the earliest days of settlement, and played an important part in the formation of American character and expectations. In general, there emerged from these studies a portrait of a new America, rescued from Depression anxieties, changed in life-style and opportunity. It was egalitarian, other-directed, consumerized, sub-urbanized, a compound of traditional individualism and welfarism, with an embourgeoisified working class, a large expansion in service functions, a managerial elite, a corporate order, and large opportunities for personal mobility and opportunity. It was, in short, a prototypical affluent modern mass-society by consent.

Yet the problem of consent, conformity and conservation preoccupied many; the problem was to define the discourse of dissent. Not all intellectuals were content with their culture. In 1955 Herbert Marcuse (a European *émigré* from the Frankfurt School, which moved to Columbia in the 1930s) began, with *Eros and Civilization*, a lineage of latter-day studies from a Freudian-cum-Marxist viewpoint which portrayed affluent capitalist society as socially and psychically repressive. The same romantic-therapeutic case, found in Wilhelm Reich and others of reformist Freudian persuasion, became popular during a decade in which the questions of conformity versus alienation, rationality versus irrationality, conservatism versus romanticism, were widely debated. In 1958 William Barrett published *Irrational Man*, a stoically existentialist study of modern absurdity, which appropriately noted the temptations of indulgent romanticism. In 1959 Norman O Brown published, in *Life Against Death*, a psycho-historical account of the coerciveness of modern industrialism, romantically offering the alternative of a permissive non-capitalist 'polymorphous perversity' which might redeem civilization's discontent. What Philip Rieff called the 'triumph of the therapeutic' was becoming a dominant factor of American life; even Marx had to be taken with a twist of Freud.[16] Beyond the therapeutic critique there were, however, more structural accusations. C Wright Mills, in *The Power Elite* (1956) saw the United States as a militarized society run by a 'military-industrial complex'. Later, in *The Sociological Imagination* (1959), clearly influenced by the British New Left, he attacked the neutral, value-free approach of American sociology, demanding a radicalized version of the sociological imagination which gave men a sense of 'social relativity and the transforming power of history'. Despite the Eisenhower equilibrium, the romanticization of anarchic unreason, and the insistence that a conflict rather than a consensus model of society was necessary, were central themes of the Fifties. Hence, among certain intellectuals and writers, as well as among many of the affluent young, the issues of the Sixties – social and sexual repression, minorities, race, poverty, the military-industrial complex, and the politics of global interference – were already alive.

Writing the Fifties

The sociological imagination, ironically neutral, politically aware, was one important way the Fifties found of writing itself. But another way was through the literary imagination, which Lionel Trilling claimed was also the 'liberal imagination' (in his book *The Liberal Imagination*, 1950), – the imagination that could, he said, in the world of modern complexity, express its social, ideological and historical awareness most fully through the dense medium of literature. Trilling especially looked to the novel – a form that mediated between romantic individualization and social reality, commanding ideas and detailed facts, the working of men's souls and the 'hum and buzz' of the cultural density in which they lived–to perform this task, and the 1950s was a remarkably vigorous period in American fiction: a time when writers like Bellow, Mailer, Salinger, Bernard Malamud, Richard Wright, Ralph Ellison, James Baldwin, Truman Capote, Harvey Swados, John Updike, Gore Vidal, Philip Roth, Mary McCarthy and Vladimir Nabokov came to the centre of the scene. It is sometimes seen as a period of relative realism, by contrast with the 'post-modern' experimentalism that was to follow, but this is to simplify its significance. Evidently, humanism and realism were alike under great strain; and if the novel indeed depends, as Trilling suggested, on the attempt to reconcile the history of individual selves with the larger pressures of society, then we can see that the uneasy, uncertain portrait of modern consciousness that was evolving in philosophy, sociology, psychology and political theory, of an uncertainty about the self-governing independence of the individual, was present in this fiction. Irving Howe (now granting that there was a significant contemporary American fiction) noticed this disturbance in an essay on the novel and mass-society written at the decade's end: writers, no longer able to identify a secure individual or a substantial and convincing social reality in the 'relatively comfortable, half welfare and half garrison society in which the population grows passive, indifferent, and atomized', found themselves dealing speculatively with the metaphysical distance between individual and community, and their forms grew oblique, post-realist, post-modern.[17]

And indeed the Fifties' novel does seem increasingly to move away from realism towards metaphysics, from fact to formalism, from social density to therapeutic myth. Its characteristics have been variously defined, but critics have noted the inclination to portray society as either naturalistic process or inert mass; to delineate heroes who were anxious, alienated, experiencing self-discovery, mixtures of rebel and victim; to write from the standpoint of ethnic or other minorities whose values displace the prevailing blandness; and to develop a remarkable fluidity of forms and genres, a mixture of realism and fantasy, naturalism and grotesquerie. Something of the changing flavour is apparent in Bellow's two novels of the Fifties, *The Adventures of Augie March* (1953), and *Henderson the Rain King* (1959). They break the tight form of Bellow's earlier books, and are expansive, comic, picaresque works about heroes who seek to 'burst their spirit's sleep' and become civil human beings; this, however, they do by moving out from the social world into a world of mythic, therapeutic and metaphysical self-discovery. A like mythic intent appears in Bernard Malamud's first novel, *The Natural* (1952), which applies the Grail legend to a baseball story; his second book, *The Assistant* (1957), is more naturalist, about a small-time Italian hoodlum who, affected by the saintliness of an indigent Jewish shopkeeper, becomes himself an 'imaginary Jew', and enters a metaphysically enriched world. Philip Roth's *Goodbye, Columbus* (1959) questions the metaphysical largeness of Jewish culture, portraying a bland, suburban Jewishness, but other stories appeal to larger moral needs. In the black novels of Ralph Ellison (*Invisible Man*, 1952), Richard Wright (*The Outsider*, 1953) and James Baldwin (*Go Tell It On the Mountain*, 1953), the life of black suffering had acquired a similar generalized, ethical dignity. On the one hand we may read in these novels, and those of Salinger, John Cheever, J P Donleavy and Vladimir Nabokov (*Lolita*, 1955), a feeling of the dissolution of a rewarding and ethically valid social world, so forcing the self into retreat, and generating nihilism, absurdism, and formalism. Yet on the other hand political force remains. History is real, and while it is inhabited by those processes and the disinheritance we associate with mass society and modern urban-technological life, it is also the place in which we seek our normal rotundity. Art hungers for a substance in reality; absurdism must balance with realism, formalism with morality. Bellow, Salinger, Malamud, Nabokov, and, at the end of the decade, Updike and Roth represent the best fiction of the Fifties, and in their work the struggle between the purified wholeness of art and the claim of ordinary reality continues to be seriously enacted, generating a humanist force.

But more romantic gestures of alienation were also on offer. It was some time before 1952 that Jack Kerouac invented the term 'beat', alluding both to a sense of defeat and exposure and the renewing rhythm of jazz, to define a newly emerging cultural tone. In 1955 Allen Ginsberg went to Lawrence Ferlinghetti's City Lights Bookstore in San Francisco and there read his poem *Howl*, the most famous single statement of what came to be called the 'Beat generation':

> I saw the best minds of my generation destroyed by madness,
>   starving hysterical naked,
> dragging themselves through the negro streets at dawn looking for an angry
>   fix
> angelheaded hipsters burning for the ancient heavenly connection to the
>   starry dynamo in the machinery of night,
> who poverty and tatters and hollow-eyed and high sat up smoking
>   in the supernatural darkness of cold-water flats floating
>   across the tops of cities contemplating jazz. . .

Howl was an hysterical, anarchic cry against the void of the Eisenhower years, seen as a destructive nightmare in which the best minds wandered in every sense unfixed. It was not just a poem but the rhythmic statement of a cultural attitude and a clarion call to an entire disaffiliate sector, invoking an art-style but also a life-style, based on jazz, drugs, alienation, sexual permissiveness, psychedelic experimentation. Its significance passed far beyond the poets (Ginsberg, Ferlinghetti, Gregory Corso, Kenneth Rexroth, Michael McClure) or novelists (Jack Kerouac, Chandler Brossard, William Burroughs) who were associated with it, and the arts became a radical centre for bohemian action in writing, painting and theatre, but also in politics, culture and behaviour. It reacted against formalism, and invoked spontaneity and confession – the intersection of all the art forms, chance connections, loose structures, breath-rhythms, happenings. Norman Mailer, who now urged that the novelist must risk his consciousness in the run of the times, explained, in his essay 'The White Negro' (1957), that the age called for the hipster, the modern vitalist hero in reaction against the totalitarian order:

One is Hip or one is Square (the alternative which each new generation is beginning to feel), one is a rebel or one conforms, one is a frontiersman in the Wild West of American night life, or else a Square cell, trapped in the totalitarian tissues of American society, doomed willy nilly to conform if one is to succeed.[18]

'Beat' fed the Sixties; but it was firmly a movement of the Fifties. Its fictional expression came in Jack Kerouac's *On the Road* (1957), which moved beyond Salinger's fragile mysticism into outright disaffiliation, celebrating, in spontaneous 'bop prosody', the mobility, moral and physical freedom and disaffiliation of the young. In *The Subterraneans* (1958), Kerouac explored the collective individualism of San Francisco bohemians; in *The Dharma Bums* (1958) he attempted a philosophical justification from oriental mysticism. But more significant was the work of William S Burroughs, who had written a realistic novel about drugs in *Junkie* (1958), but in *The Naked Lunch* (1959) used the 'cut up, fold in method of Bryon Gysin' to explore in aleatory, chance-oriented text the science-fiction horrors of technological society, and the ambiguous surrealism of drug-induced alternatives. Burroughs claimed that the book was a Swiftian satire on technological and repressive forces assaulting mind and sexuality. In fact the novel has a clear ambiguity, an imaginative engagement with the repressions it claims to reject. It is an ambiguity that would pass into other portraits of the age, and move much writing away from humanistic preoccupations into surreal fantasy rooted in the late technological world. Nonetheless, the novel is a powerful act of invention and a voice of the new art of surreal spontaneity and provisionalism that was entering American culture in a period of buoyant, free invention. The new mood was the product of many events, tendencies and gradually accumulating resentments that had been building up during the Fifties: some of these were political reactions against conservatism, and others predominantly investments in free formal experiment, but both tendencies reached out toward a transformation of consciousness and a repudiation of fixed forms.

By 1959 the signs were that the Fifties were in revolt against themselves, at least if the register of the arts and the way in which they were focusing groups concerned with new consciousness is a fair guide. In 1959, Robert Lowell's most powerful and most confessional book,

Life Studies, came out, meshing personal with social disorders and estrangements. Gary Snyder published *Riprap*, moving beyond 'Beat' principles into a subjective exploration of legend and reconstituted history; two 'Black Mountain' poets, Robert Creeley, with *A Form of Women*, and Robert Duncan, with *Selected Poems*, produced important volumes. Out of a similar context was emerging the 'New York School' of Frank O'Hara and John Ashbery, who had been linked throughout the Fifties with Abstract Expressionist painters – like Jackson Pollock, William de Kooning and Robert Motherwell – whose insistence on provisionality and performance linked them in turn with the development of 'happening', and hence with the Living Theatre and the Arts Theatre. 'Happenings' were a kind of multi-media evolution from the successful poetry readings of the 1950s, which suggested that the arts might become collective and communitarian, that an era of universal bohemianism might be on hand. And it was in 1959 that the painter Allan Kaprow staged his living painting *18 Happenings in 6 parts*, which drew on the ideas and influence of the 'Black Mountain' musician John Cage; around the principles of provisionality, instantaneousness and chance invention many arts were drawing together, including also popular music and film (Andy Warhol). The signs began to show in theatre, for in 1959 the Living Theatre, also using aleatory or chance-based principles, staged Jack Gelber's improvised play about drug addiction, *The Connection*, a step toward the Off-Broadway boom of the Sixties. And, on Broadway, Lorraine Hansberry's *A Raisin in the Sun* promised a new era in black theatre. It was a considerable amassing of the forces of change: much that we associate with the Sixties was already alive. Thus, when, in 1960, the political scientist Daniel Bell published his book *The End of Ideology: On the Exhaustion of Political Ideas in the Fifties* – which argued that the new mass society had reconciled the utopian and the real so successfully that 'the ideological age has ended', a situation which nonetheless generated in many a restless yearning for the ideology they felt should somehow be there – he was both wrong and right.[19] The Fifties was a time in which the whole structure of radicalism and conservatism, romanticism and stoicism, the id and the ego, seemed to be realigned. In some ways the Sixties was a revolt against the Fifties, but in other ways it was a preoccupied revisiting of its options and its tensions, which in many forms survive with us still.

Notes and references

1.   On 'abundance' as a characteristic of the age, see David Riesman, 'Abundance for what?', in *Individualism Reconsidered*, Free Press, Glencoe, Ill., 1954; and David M Potter, *People of Plenty: Economic Abundance and the American Character*, University of Chicago Press, Chicago, 1954.

2. D C Watt, 'Rethinking the Cold War', *Political Quarterly*, (October–December 1978), 446–56. For further useful comments see Arthur M Schlesinger, 'The Cold War revisited', *New York Review of Books*, XXVI, 16 (25 October 1979), 46–52.
3. David Caute, *The Great Fear: The Anticommunist Purge Under Truman and Eisenhower*, Secker and Warburg, London, 1978.
4. Lionel Trilling, 'Manners, morals and the novel', in *The Liberal Imagination: Essays on Literature and Society*, Viking, New York, 1950.
5. John Kenneth Galbraith, 'The moving finger sticks', reprinted in *The Liberal Hour*, Pelican Books, Harmondsworth, 1963, p. 80.
6. Granville Hicks, 'On leaving the Communist Party', *New Republic* (4 October 1939), 244–5. Reprinted in C E Eisinger (ed), *The 1940s: Profile of a Nation in Crisis*, Anchor, New York, 1969, pp. 338–42.
7. Malcolm Cowley, 'War novels: After two wars', in *The Literary Situation*, Viking, New York, 1955, pp. 23–42.
8. Reinhold Niebuhr, 'Ten years that shook my world', *The Christian Century* (26 April 1939). Reprinted in D Aaron and R Bendiner (eds), *The Strenuous Decade: A Social and Intellectual Record of the 1930s*, Anchor, New York, 1970, pp. 493–8.
9. Arthur Vandenberg, speech to the Senate, 10 January 1945. Reprinted in Eisinger, *op. cit.*
10. Eric F Goldman, *The Crucial Decade–And After: America, 1945–1960*, Vintage, New York, 1960.
11. Allen J Matusow (ed), *Joseph R McCarthy*, Prentice-Hall, Englewood Cliffs, 1970, pp. 23, 47.
12. Irving Howe, 'The age of conformity', *Partisan Review*, 1952. This symposium of intellectual's opinions, printed over three issues of the magazine, was reprinted as *America and the Intellectuals*, Partisan Review, New York n.d.
13. Nathan A Scott, *Three American Moralists: Mailer, Bellow, Trilling*, University of Notre Dame Press, Notre Dame, Ind., 1973, p.4.
14. William E Leuchtenburg, *A Troubled Feast: American Society since 1945*, Little Brown, Boston, 1973, pp. 85–91.
15. The Editors of *Fortune*, *America in the Sixties: The Economy and the Society*, Harper Torchbook, New York, 1960, p.71.
16. Philip Rieff, *The Triumph of the Therapeutic*, Harper and Row, New York, 1966.
17. Irving Howe, 'Mass society and post-modern fiction', *Partisan Review* (Summer 1959), 420–36. The essay is reprinted in J J Waldmeir (ed), *Recent American Fiction: Some Critical Views*, Houghton Mifflin, Boston, 1963, pp. 27–35; and in Marcus Klein (ed), *The American Novel Since World War II*, Fawcett, Greenwich Conn., 1969, pp. 124–41.
18. Norman Mailer, 'The White Negro', City Lights Books, San Francisco, 1957, reprinted in Mailer, *Advertisements for Myself*, André Deutsch, London, 1961.
19. Daniel Bell, 'The end of ideology in the West', in Bell, *The End of Ideology: On the Exhaustion of Political Ideas in the Fifties*, Collier, New York, 1961.

Chapter Twelve

The Sixties and Seventies

Daniel Snowman and Malcolm Bradbury

'We stand today on the edge of a new frontier. . .a frontier of unknown opportunities and perils. . .I am asking each of you to be pioneers on that New Frontier.'
John F Kennedy, 1960

'We have come through a long period of turmoil and doubt, but we have once again found our moral course, and with a new spirit we are striving to express our best instincts to the rest of the world. . .For the first time in a generation, we are not haunted by a major international crisis or by domestic turmoil.'
Jimmy Carter, 1978

Which were the real Sixties?

Historians like to divide the past into conveniently labelled eras. People at the time were unaware that they lived in 'The Dark Ages' or 'The Renaissance', but scholars assure us they did. The division of the past into centuries is not quite so arbitrary, but even here the historian's tidy packaging can impose too rigid a shape on what is essentially fluid and inchoate. Scholarly subdivisions notwithstanding, the *real* history of each century often seems to begin some fifteen or sixteen years after the official inaugural date: Luther set the Reformation in motion in 1517; the Thirty Years' War began in 1618; the rule of the Stuarts ended in 1718 and the age of Louis XIV a year later; the Napoleonic Wars finished in 1815; and the fundamental turning-point of our own century occured not in 1900 but in 1914–18.

Even more seductive is history by decade. It is convenient to think of the 1930s in America as an era of Depression, or the 1950s as one of middle-class affluence. But here, too, the reality is rarely as tidy as the label. For instance, those who like to regard the 1960s as a period of conflict and protest in America neatly sandwiched between two 'quiet' decades have some difficulty in accommodating the fact that the heyday of the 'Beat' movement occurred in the 1950s – the era of Marlon Brando's leather-jacket image and the birth of rock music – while the national mood after the assassination of President Kennedy in 1963 produced a nationwide emotional consensus rare in the annals of American history. Even in the dramatic year of 1968 – the year of the assassinations of Martin Luther King and Robert F Kennedy, massive student protests, and violent confrontations accompanying the rowdy Democratic National Convention in Chicago – much of America carried on its business in an orderly way. Most planes took off and landed on schedule, most schoolrooms managed to hold normal classes most of the time, and most politicians and most soldiers in Vietnam did what they were officially expected to do – while the biggest protest against the Vietnam War occurred not in the 1960s at all but in May 1971.

The American Sixties were not *uniformly* rebellious, any more than the Fifties were *uniformly* conservative or the Seventies *uniformly* quiescent. Even if decades, like centuries, might be thought to start a little late, so that we date the 'real' Sixties from, say, 1964 to 1974, the conventional contrasts still do not quite work. Perhaps the most radical grass-roots protest against the way in which the nation's power-brokers ran their various fiefdoms was the reduction in property taxes initiated in California as a result of popular referendum in 1978. Thus, 'The Sixties' is less a term for the state of the nation than a catchword for a state of mind – radical, youth-oriented, counter-cultural, easy-riding, committed to New Left attitudes, minority rights, black consciousness, drugs, psychedelic experience, protest and dissent. Undoubtedly many who lived in the United States during the 1960s and 1970s experienced a shift in tone and expectation between the two eras, and felt that the earlier years were a period of eroding optimism, shattered by the hammer blows of the Kennedy and King assasinations, the great campus and urban riots, and the catastrophe of Vietnam, while the later years certainly saw the gradual, muted return to a more stable, honourable if low-key national life, in which personal problems came to predominate over public ones, and concern about the quality of the physical environment took precedence over the more spectacular political issues of yesteryear. Many sensed a similar change in the arts – a radical phase, starting really in the Fifties, when an energetic *avant-garde* emerged in a great era of festivals, happenings, performances, and multi-media events, then to be gradually followed by more delicate, subjective, confession-al forms of expression, as the bookshops replaced texts about Woodstock or the Black Experience with publications on life-passages, ageing, and the role of women. But these are telescoped, foreshortened images. How accurately do they suggest the actual experience of a great nation over the course of twenty explosive and difficult years of its history? And why did America's history take the forms and directions that it did?

The Kennedy era

On 20 January 1961, John F Kennedy became President, and with him came an expectation of great change. Not that a majority of American citizens had voted for Kennedy, or were convinced that he was the best person to chart the course the nation should follow. In the presidential election the previous November, one-third of all eligible voters had not used their franchise. Ot those who had, 49.6 per cent had cast their vote for the rival candidate, Eisenhower's Vice President, Richard M Nixon, and a further 0.7 per cent for other candidates. Having thus received only 49.7 per cent of votes cast, Kennedy became the fourteenth president to be elected on a minority vote. Many who might traditionally have been expected to support a Democratic presidential candidate hated Kennedy so much that they voted for his Republican opponent – especially in the South, where millions of traditional Democrats distrusted him for his 'airs and graces', his intellectual arrogance, his unearned personal wealth, his apparently casual liberalism (especially on the race issue), his predilection for big government, above all his Catholicism. Nonetheless, the authority of the office worked its traditional magic, and even many of the sceptics found themselves impressed as they heard Kennedy set the tone of his administration in his Inaugural:

Let the word go forth from this time and place, to friend and foe alike, that the torch has been passed to a new generation of Americans, born in this century, tempered by war, disciplined by a hard and bitter peace, proud of our ancient heritage, and unwilling to witness or permit the slow undoing of those human rights to which this nation has always been committed, and to which we are committed today at home and around the world.

Let every nation know, whether it wish us well or ill, that we will pay any price, bear any burden, meet any hardship, support any friend, oppose any foe in order to assure the survival and success of liberty. . .

These were stirring words for stirring times, though few roused by them knew where they might lead: to the moon, to the elimination of poverty and disease, or to the Third World War?

Still, Kennedy's appeal to the modern generation and the younger style of his presidency not only attracted new groups but reflected new attitudes and forces in American life. His America was a nation of 180 million, a large and growing number of whom were white suburbanites living comfortably on the outskirts of great metropolitan areas and engaged in an increasingly white-collar and service-orientated economy. By 1960, nine out of every ten American families owned a television set and nearly three-fifths a car. Average family income was well over $6,000 per annum, which meant close to $2,000 for every man, woman and child in the country – an increase of nearly 50 per cent since 1950, a decade during which inflation had raised most prices by only about 15 per cent. Not only were Americans better off than ever before; there were also far more of them than previously. Indeed, the most significant fact about American society in 1960, alongside its unprecedented wealth, was the startling population increase that had begun to make itself felt. During the 1950s, the US population had risen by a massive 18.5 per cent, a figure unmatched since the great waves of immigration prior to the First World War. Even more significant was the age-profile of the US population by 1960. Much of the increase in the previous decade had been due to a high birth-rate (25 per 1,000 population compared with 18 per 1,000 in the mid-1930s), while medical advances had prolonged average life-expectancy from 60 years in 1930 to 70 years in 1960 – so that by the time of Kennedy's inauguration, as much as 45 per cent of the population was either under 18 or over 65, too young or too old to pull its full economic weight. These general economic and demographic tendencies were to have a major influence upon the history of modern America, and their effects will be evident in much that is contained in the following pages.

There were other important factors: for instance, the ways in which America's wealth and its population were distributed. There is no doubt that the nation as a whole was enjoying a period of substantial prosperity as the legacy of the Eisenhower era. America's gross national product had gone up from $285 billion in 1950 to over $500 billion in 1960 at an annual growth rate of some 3 per cent, and all indicators seemed on their inexorable way upward. However, families in the bottom 20 per cent of the income bracket were still, in 1960, earning only 4.9 per cent of all income, while those in the top 20 per cent were earning 42 per cent. There were other similarly uneven patterns. While it is true that the American population as a whole was rising rapidly, certain areas of the country (the big, new sprawling cities of the south and west like Houston, Phoenix and San Diego) were growing fast, while older East Coast cities like Washington, New York and Philadelphia – and particularly their downtown areas – were experiencing a net *loss* of population as people moved south, west, or to the suburbs. Everywhere in the nation, indeed, surburbia was growing fast and was largely white. Meanwhile, the decaying inner-city areas of the north tended to attract blacks moving up from the rural south, or Puerto Ricans and others from the Caribbean. These new arrivals often found themselves trapped in appallingly squalid ghettoes, in a climate of urban neglect and social deprivation, cut off from the general affluence of the period. Millions of other Americans, white as well as black, were caught in pockets of apparently ineradicable poverty in America's rural hinterland: fruitpickers in California and Florida, strip miners in the hills of eastern Kentucky, black sharecroppers in Mississippi, white smallholders in Iowa. And as the ranks of those too young or too old to work continued inexorably to swell, so did the discrepancy between those who stood to gain from the nation's wealth and those who felt themselves excluded.[1]

But, if the basis for some of the tensions of the later 1960s was already established, hope and expectancy still tended to take precedence over the rumblings of discontent. In foreign affairs, too, most Americans seemed for the moment to take a cautiously sanguine attitude. The later 1950s had been a period of relatively unproductive diplomacy, as the anti-communist alliance-building of John Foster Dulles gave way to the gentler diplomacy of Secretary of State Christian A Herter and to the genial globe-trotting of a well-intentioned but largely ineffective President Eisenhower. Eisenhower's last years in office had been marked by several setbacks – notably the breakdown of the East–West summit in Paris as Khrushchev made Eisenhower look foolish over the issue of US spy planes, and the cancellation of a presidential trip to Japan on the grounds that Eisenhower's safety there could not be guaranteed. As Kennedy ran for the presidency, he made much of the apparent weaknesses of the Eisenhower administration's foreign policy, and some of his most telling points in the televised debates with his opponent, Vice President Nixon, were in this area. Kennedy's 'New Frontier' thus included the promise of a fresh approach to foreign as well as to domestic policy (though he was singularly vague as to details), and it was to America's approach to world affairs that his Inaugural address was largely devoted. With the Cold War still at its height, Kennedy's sparkling but sometimes abrasive rhetoric suggested a new and tough activism towards the Russians ('We will pay any price, bear any burden, meet any hardship, support any friend, oppose any foe'). In the early days of his administration, he was at pains to suggest that he had a carefully considered global strategy, and he talked of his hopes for Western European unity, for a new alliance for progress between the USA and its hemispheric neighbours, and for various other American-backed policies that would regain for his country the initiative that he saw as having fallen into the hands of the Communist bloc.

In talking this way, Kennedy was expressing a widely prevalent American mood. Americans were worried about their country's 'loss of purpose' and the supposed subordination of genuine national goals to the gods of plenty and materialism. Books appeared with titles like *What Ivan Knows and Johnny Doesn't*, accurately reflecting the fear that the Russians were catching up with America in scientific research and military skills and hardware. The *Sputnik* launch in 1957 had dismayed the scientific and educational establishments, and Khrushchev's mixture of sabre-rattling and comedy left most Americans uneasy, remembering his ambiguous phrase: 'We shall bury you!' Though the McCarthyite witchhunts against domestic 'subversives' had largely disappeared, many still felt that domestic communists were conspiring to erode all that America stood for, while there was a widespread conviction that the Russians, and their supposed puppets the Chinese, were being allowed to get away with too much – that it was time America cleared its head, got off its backside, and stood up to them.

Thus, both at home and abroad, the United States at the time of

John F Kennedy's inauguration as president was a country of enormous capacities, anxious to take further its great achievements and yet apprehensive lest the chinks in its confidence show through. This was a time of brave new rhetoric accompanied by an undercurrent of self-doubt, of certainties expressed uncertainly, of promises rather than fulfilments, of transition rather than direction. America in the early 1960s showed unmistakeable signs of being on the move, but whether for good or ill no one could say with confidence.

The ambiguities of public policy and rhetoric were reflected in the realm of intellectual life and the arts. To many, Kennedy seemed the first cultured president America had had since the war – a young, vigorous, intellectually alert figure who surrounded himself with an enlightened 'Camelot' court. The Sixties began, not with signs of schism between the world of art and the world of power, but with evidence of reconciliation. Poets and musicians were made welcome at the White House; Robert Frost celebrated Kennedy's inauguration; to younger writers, the path between culture and government, scarcely trodden during the previous decade or so, seemed to be reopening. Time was to suggest that this new rapport was more apparent than real, and that the cult of intellectual withdrawal from the political world that began to stir in the 1950s – the decade of Allen Ginsberg's *Howl* and Norman Mailer's 'hipster' – represented the deeper current of the times. But for a while not only Stravinsky, Casals and Frost but also Lowell, Bernstein and Mailer himself were drawn by Kennedy's style, power and energy. Mailer went on to publish a collection of essays, *The Presidential Papers* (1963), in which he explored his own identification with Kennedy; in 1965, in *An American Dream*, he fictionalized this link, making his violent, purgative hero a friend of Kennedy, and plunging into fantasies of power, violence and radical vitalism by means of which Mailer – and his hero – hoped the nation's consciousness might be revivified. For Mailer, Kennedy had become by the time of his assassination an ambiguous symbol of political possibility in an age caught between creative and cancerous growth; still, for a moment, the 'hipster' or 'white negro' saw himself in office – and was later to enter the world of real politics by running for Mayor of New York. Indeed, this fable of the possible reconciliation of art and power has run as a fanciful possibility through much modern American writing: it appears in many novels, by, for instance, Gore Vidal, Philip Roth, Saul Bellow and Joseph Heller, all of whom paint heroes who seek to minimize the characteristic alienation of the modern artist and allow him some place in the national counsels. The Camelot era seemed to permit the imagination, and perhaps even the artist himself or herself, to take this chance. And so, as Morris Dickstein rightly notes, a good deal of the writing of the early Sixties shares the Kennedy spirit in a tentative fascination with a newly imperial, globally engrossed, internationalized and historically mobile America: 'Grandiose and experimental in form, these books partook of some of the imperial buoyancy of the Kennedy years. But their vision sometimes had a bleak, dead-end character that belied any official optimism.'[2]

Certainly the problem of the relationship between self and society, individual and politics that had so much preoccupied the Fifties did not go away in the early Sixties. 'The American writer in the middle of the twentieth century has his hands full in trying to understand, describe, and then make *credible* much of the American reality. . .,' wrote Philip Roth in 1961, listing some recent horrors. 'The actuality is continually outdoing our talents, and the culture tosses up figures almost daily that are the envy of any novelist.'[3] 'The power of public life has become so threatening that private life cannot maintain the pretence of its importance,' wrote Saul Bellow in a 1963 essay in which he looked at some recent novels – among them John Updike's *Rabbit, Run* (1960), J F Powers' *Morte d'Urban* (1962), Bruce J Friedman's *Stern* (1962) and Philip Roth's *Letting Go* (1962) – and observed that they tended to divide the world up between a chaotic, fleeing self and a disordered society in which historical process was plot and conspiracy, so forcing modern man to 'hoard his spiritual valuables.'[4] Bellow criticized the tendency, but his own notable novel of the early Sixties, *Herzog* (1964), shows his hero retreating into madness in the face of the mass of modern urban America, even though he manages an ambiguous reconciliation at the end. Other books showed a similar drift. Joseph Heller's absurdist war-novel *Catch-22* (1961) displays a world in which no cause or purpose is rational. John Barth's *The End of the Road* (1961) displays a character who is 'weatherless' and inert before reality ('In a sense, I am Jacob Horner,' is the book's first line). Kurt Vonnegut's *Mother Night* (1961) returns again to war and shows the spy Howard Campbell committing 'the crime of the times' by serving evil too openly and good too secretly; Vonnegut's bittersweet despair shifts into science-fiction in *Cat's Cradle* (1963), which concerns 'Bokonism', a religion of 'harmless untruths', and so examines our need for fictions. J D Salinger's two volumes of fragile stories, *Franny and Zooey* (1961) and *Raise High the Roofbeam, Carpenters and Seymour* (1963) display his Glass family and their psychic stresses and hunger for mystical salvation. In Ken Kesey's *One Flew Over the Cuckoo's Nest* (1962) the social order is seen from the standpoint of the madhouse. And in the most remarkable novel of this striking period in fiction, Thomas Pynchon's *V* (1963), we move through an apocalyptic present towards an historical past, American and European, from which no significant order can be drawn, so that the mind is held teetering in a condition of mental and historical entropy.

The flavour of the times thus generated an ambitious spirit of experiment and a new concern with fictions, sharpened by the influence of Nabokov and the translation of the work of the South American writer Jorge Luis Borges. In poetry, too, the creative energy of the late 1950s continued. The year 1960 was remarkably rich for poetry: 'radical', experimental. The 'Beats' extended their influence and their range, with important books by Ginsberg (*Kaddish*), Corso (*Minutes to Go*, written with William Burroughs and Bryon Gysin), and Gary Snyder (*Myths and Texts*). The following year saw Ferlinghetti's *Starting from San Francisco* and Denise Levertov's *Jacob's Ladder*. The appearance of Charles Olson's earlier *Maximus Poems* in 1960 suggested that a new poetic language and a new epical intent were in process of formulation. Following on from Robert Lowell's *Life Studies* in 1959, a frank new school of 'confessional poets' seemed to be emerging after the 'tranquillized' Fifties: Sylvia Plath published *Colossus* in 1960, and Anne Sexton *To Bedlam and Part Way Back* (1960), also, like the novel of the times, much preoccupied with madness and extremity. From the New York School came Frank O'Hara's *Second Avenue*, followed in 1962 with John Ashbery's striking collection *The Tennis Court Oath*. Important books by Galway Kinnell and James Dickey also appeared in 1960; thus the sense of a new poetic mood was strong. There were also significant new developments in theatre. A new playwright, Edward Albee, began to challenge the hegemony of Arthur Miller and Tennessee Williams, with his drama of absurdist social conflict *The Zoo Story* (1959), his hallucinatory portrait of a modern America where all was not, as he said, 'peachy keen', in *The American Dream* (1961), and, most notably, with what would prove probably the best play of the decade, *Who's Afraid of Virginia Woolf?* (1962), about the power of illusion in a modern marriage and its purgation toward reality. Meanwhile off-Broadway was spreading to 'off-off-Broadway', and new experimental theatre groups were coming to dominate the scene, especially after the Living Theatre's production of Kenneth Brown's provisionalist, absurdist, theatre-of-cruelty play *The Brig* in 1962.

Thus the Sixties began in the arts as an era of rich promises and new experiments, drawing, certainly, on underground or minority tendencies from the Fifties. But the signs were that the moral and realist aspects of much Fifties writing were being rejected, in a flight from the realist centre. So, if the Fifties had emphasized the created object, and stressed craft, completion, and the text as icon, the bolder and more imaginative artists of the Sixties encouraged more open acts of creation and performance, and emphasized chance, spontaneity, confession, or the unfixed or impermanent object. If the Fifties sought to fix the sign, the Sixties sought to make it mysterious and multivalent; if the Fifties had emphasised the liberal synthesis of self and society, the Sixties heightened the sense of lonely subjectivity, in a harsh and threatening history. History had its claims, but functioned as enormity or threat, the commanding but conspiratorial force of novels like Pynchon's *V.* Its absurdities were so great that they called for escape into fantasy, as in the novels of Kurt Vonnegut. Or else, as Vladimir Nabokov put it, reality was a word that meant nothing except in quotes, and novelists and poets looked toward a literature where the word was severed from the world, where writing became introverted or 'fictive'. Some writers and artists seemed to take an opposite path into a deeper realism, but in fact they simply reversed the coin by insisting on realism's artifice; so came the hyper-realism of the 'non-fiction novel', a term used by Truman Capote to describe his *In Cold Blood* (1966), a 'faction' about a real murder in Kansas where a rural America was violated by paranoia and psychosis; the 'New Journalism' of Tom Wolfe, Seymour Krim, Hunter Thompson and others, who sought to jostle the novel off the scene altogether and have 'the whole crazed obscene uproarious Mammon-faced drug-soaked mau-mau lust-oozing Sixties in America all to themselves'[5]; and the painterly movements of Pop Art or the Action Art School of Jasper Johns, Robert Rauschenberg, William de Kooning, Andy Warhol and Richard Estes. Thus confessionalism, spontaneity and free form grew as the Sixties got under way; so did the 'absurd', which, in theatre, merged with the poor theatre of Grotowski, the performance theatre of Stanislavsky, Artaud's theatre of ritual and cruelty, to make drama one of the central artistic excitements of the early years of the decade.

New Frontiers were emerging, then, in the arts as well as in politics. The speculative note could, however, go in various possible directions: toward a mood of *avant-garde* experimentation, for instance, or toward a radical political activism. The arts and politics could come together in a major creative impulse, or the cultural and political worlds could split apart with an impact that could impoverish both. For the time being, nobody could be sure how things would develop – only that the country was, as President Kennedy had urged, undoubtedly 'moving again'.

The Johnson years

There are no effects entirely without causes, and the events of history, however haphazard and unexpected some may seem at the time, generally take their place when seen in retrospect as part of a continuing pattern of development. Even the most jarring discontinuity – like the totally unanticipated murder of the vigorous young President Kennedy in Dallas in November 1963 – can come to seem part of the warp and woof of the times in which it occurred. In perspective, Kennedy's assassination can be regarded as a watershed in American history. It may seem fanciful to suggest that the shot that killed the President also inflicted grave wounds upon the country's traditional optimism. The optimism of America goes back far earlier than the presidency of Kennedy, of course, and was indeed deeply rooted in the whole history of white American civilization with its notion that nothing was impossible if you tried hard enough. Nevertheless, there can be little doubt that America before Dallas tended to display greater confidence than it would thereafter, and that the 'New Frontier' belief that all problems were susceptible to rational solutions grew harder to sustain once the Prince had gone. Under Kennedy, it was widely assumed that domestic conflict could be minimized by the provision of more money and better education and that international conflict could be contained by the firm assertion of America's military commitments. Soon after his death, such assumptions began to go sour as the appalling destructiveness of the urban riots of the mid-1960s and of the Vietnam War etched their way into the national consciousness. When Kennedy had assumed the presidency, Robert Frost spoke of a 'golden age/Of which this noonday's the beginning hour'. Ten years later, a leading historian and political scientist, Andrew Hacker, could write that 'America's history as a nation has reached its end.'[6]

The Kennedy presidency and the way it was brought to an end provided a kind of psychic watershed for the nation. Nevertheless, the seeds of the disaffection and discord that so notoriously characterized the later 1960s had been sown long before the tragedy of Dallas. While the assassination provided an opportunity for people to bewail their nation's failures, it was neither the prime cause nor the first occasion for their doing so. Many signs of what was to come were already there just under the surface of the aggressively conformist, largely acquiescent, wealthy, middle-class America of the 1950s. The unease had already displayed itself in, for example, the growth of the Beat movement, the racial struggles that had occurred in places like Montgomery and Little Rock, the popularity among young people of such symbols of revolt as James Dean or Elvis Presley, and the radical theorizing of social observers like C Wright Mills. Thus, as the excitement and promise of the early 1960s moved toward the tragedy of Dallas, American life was already infused with a spirit of protest – the protest of poets who abhorred the culture of materialism, of blacks whose patient opposition to institutionalized racism was close to boiling point, of students and other young people who, initially through satire or rock or black humour and then through politics, came to realize the depth of their opposition to the standards and values in which they had been raised. The young, the black and the 'unwashed' – all had been largely impotent in 1960. All were to some extent revitalized by the rhetoric of the 'New Frontier', and all felt the end of the Kennedy era left them with important unfinished business to complete.

For a season after the death of John F Kennedy, harmony seemed to reign. The nation grieved for its fallen leader and instinctively closed ranks. Political squabbles were held in abeyance, social conflict seemed of secondary importance, and the new president, Lyndon B Johnson, building upon the foundations Kennedy had begun and appealing to the memory of his departed predecessor, skilfully exploited the new consensus to erect the scaffolding of what he hoped would become a major edifice of social reform. Within months of becoming President, LBJ managed to get a major new Civil Rights Bill and a tax reform through Congress. In November 1964, he was triumphantly returned in his own right to the presidency by the electorate and he plunged himself and his administration into a whirlwind of reformist activity. Proposals emanating from the White House dealt with medical care for the aged, education, housing, immigration, urban and rural development, crime, black voting rights and much else. Nothing like it had been seen since the first hundred days of the New Deal back in 1933 and, although Johnson did not have a Depression to use as a political spur with which to goad the Congress as Franklin D Roosevelt had done, much of what he called his 'Great Society' programme was successfully passed into law.

Alongside this burst of activity, though, were other developments that proved more representative of the directions American history would take. The Civil Rights movement had grown more militant and assertive since the days of Montgomery and Little Rock. Still predominantly southern-based, largely Christian-inspired, strictly law-abiding, and optimistically integrationist in its aims, it had nonetheless shifted tactics. Now, instead of merely boycotting segregated facilities, black and white activists had begun to use them – sitting side by side together on buses and at lunch counters. By 1963, massive confrontations occurred in several southern cities between civil-rights workers and local white officialdom, and in August a rally of a quarter of a million people in Washington D C heard Martin Luther King, the movement's greatest leader, talk of his dream of a multi-racial society. The optimism of the Civil Rights movement did not last long beyond 1963. The next year, 1,000 Northern students, most of them white, went South to help Negro voter-registration campaigns. Many of the civil rights workers were harassed by local whites and three were killed, while, back North, Harlem erupted in a spasm of destructive violence in a pattern that was to prove the wave of things to come. Later in 1964, as Lyndon Johnson was building up his coalition of electoral support, students at the Berkeley campus of the University of California formed a Free Speech Movement (FSM) to protest against the refusal of the university administration to let them use land adjacent to the campus for recruitment drives for various political clubs and groups. The FSM, greatly aided by the inept and insensitive overreaction of the administration, burgeoned into a major campus revolt and, in time, helped to fuel the world-wide student protest movement of the later 1960s.

But in 1964 the greatest issue of all, the Vietnam War, was still scarcely perceptible. That summer, LBJ persuaded Congress, in response to what is now known to have been a largely stage-managed incident in the Gulf of Tonkin off North Vietnam, to give him almost unlimited powers of war. At first he appeared to use them with discretion and in his election campaign that autumn talked plausibly about what he saw as the communist threat from North Vietnam against the non-communist South, while pouring scorn on the hawkish policies of his Republican opponent, Barry M Goldwater. Returned to office, however, Johnson began to outstrip anything that Goldwater had proposed, pouring American troops into Vietnam, bombing the North (just when its capital, Hanoi, was hosting the new Soviet premier Alexei Kosygin), and committing America's global prestige and armed might to a massive land war 12,000 miles from Washington on the basis of an entirely inaccurate reading of the forces involved. To Johnson and his advisers, North Vietnam was a communist puppet-state entirely beholden to the Russians. In fact its leaders had for twenty years been united in nothing so much as their determination to rid their whole country, South as well as North, of foreign influences, whether Japanese, French, Russian or American.

At first, Johnson's Vietnam venture seemed too remote and not sufficiently brutal or unsuccessful to arouse passionate domestic criticism. But as the war absorbed more and more of the administration's time and the nation's money, as LBJ's 'Great Society' and 'War on Poverty' began to take a back seat, as stories began to filter back of the fruitless death and devastation being caused in Vietnam, people in America – particularly young blacks and students already politicized by their own protest movements – came to oppose what was being done in their country's name. As the war continued and the voracious requirements of the American military effort required the draft to creep gradually up the social scale so that the sons of the wealthy, white upper-middle-class began to find their lives at risk, opposition to the war became not only more vociferous but also more respectable, better organized, better financed, and better argued. By 1967, millions of ordinary Americans felt personally bruised by what their nation was doing, and took to the streets in protest. Civil-rights leaders like Martin Luther King, writers like Robert Lowell and Norman Mailer, academics like Noam Chomsky and Robert Jay Lifton, the pediatrician Benjamin Spock – all joined together to denounce the war. America, said some of their more radical followers, was a racist society that would never rain napalm on white populations. Others claimed it was run by a ruthless 'military-industrial complex', to whom profits were more important than lives. America's political leaders, many of the protesters agreed, rode roughshod over all the individualistic and libertarian principles in whose name the republic had been founded.

By the end of 1967, in fact, the optimistic visions of the early 1960s had almost entirely eroded. The conflicts and insecurities of America in the early years of the decade, submerged under the uplifting rhetoric of the Kennedy era, were now bubbling through to the surface as it seemed clear that all attempts to deal with them – the 'New Frontier', the 'Great Society', the Civil Rights movement – had invariably promised more than they could deliver. The black ghettoes were aflame every summer, the campuses every autumn, and Vietnam every day of the week. As 1967 gave way to 1968, sane men predicted apocalypse.

Culture and counter-culture

'If You're Lost You've Come To The Right Place!' said the slogan on the besieged campus of Columbia University in the spring of 1968. It might have served as a text for the nation that year. In February, the North Vietnamese, supposedly wilting under a constant barrage of American might, launched a new offensive so devastating as to undermine the entire US position. Prior to this 'Tet offensive', American opinion had stood behind the War, but from now a majority opposed American involvement. A month after Tet, Johnson announced that he would not run for a second term as president. He had had enough. In April Martin Luther King was murdered in Tennessee and blacks in many parts of the country – including the vicinity of the White House – went on a furious spree of arson and looting. In early June, Robert F Kennedy, the most exciting political figure in the country and the one man who might have had the chance of achieving the White House *and* a vision of what to do once there, was shot dead in Los Angeles. When the Democrats met in Chicago in August for their nominating convention, the proceedings were largely upstaged by the tremendous wave of protest that swept through the streets, as demonstrators of every hue found themselves in pitched battle with the city's armed police. By the end of 1968, it seemed to many that there were two distinct American societies existing side by side – an 'official' America that had just elected as president that throwback to yesteryear, Richard M Nixon; and a 'counter-culture' of hippies, yippies, political activists, angry blacks, alienated youngsters, disenchanted parents. And though 'official' America tried to function just as it always had, it seemed that much of the time it was primarily having to *re*-act to the initiatives of the counter-culture.

The counter-culture, a loose amalgam of forces united by their sense of opposition to officialdom, represented many varied and often mutually contradictory strains. Some of its members emphasized the importance of 'life-style' and tried to shock by ostentatiously making love or consuming illegal drugs in public, or by wearing their hair unconventionally long if men or their skirts unconventionally short if women. Others were more concerned with political issues and would (for instance) urge young men to burn their draft cards and would help draft-resisters to escape to Canada or Sweden. To the 'life-style' people, reality seemed so intractable and unmanageable that they were tempted to let fantasy and play take its place – hence the vogue for hallucinogenic drugs or huge posters in 'day-glo' colours that 'breathed', and for massively amplified rock concerts at which new heights of love or destructiveness seemed equally possible. To the politically active, reality was an oppressive system of ideologies and institutions built up by the misguided liberalism of the early 1960s; armed with the cultural critique of C Wright Mills, Norman O Brown and, above all, Herbert Marcuse, the 'New Left' argued that nothing less than a fundamental overhaul of Western capitalist society could save America from itself.

The counter-culture thus included both a 'soft' and a 'hard' element, people who looked to Zen Buddhism for solutions and others who looked in the direction of the gun, hippies who talked of love and revolutionaries who spoke of the overthrow of society, some who were 'turned on' by the gentleness of the Beatles and others who preferred the progressive snarl of the Rolling Stones. But through all these and other contradictions ran a single line. For the counter-culture in all its manifestations was imaginative rather than intellectual, expressive rather than analytical, interested in trying new types of experience rather than improving old ones. Its language was scatological and apocalyptic and its politics radical. It cared even more about feeling than doing, more about the authenticity of personal experience than about its communicability to others. It was a culture that encouraged styles and images to be constantly remodelled and that offered in every boutique new versions of self and society. Within this atmosphere, a much more mobile, kinetic, politically activist sensibility came to infuse the arts of the later 1960s. The liberal model of the artist as a figure integrated into and expressing his culture was replaced by that of the artist as a provisional consciousness transforming that culture or perhaps refining his own aesthetic resources. No longer did America's principal writers dream of reconciliation with political power. On the contrary, many thinkers in the later Sixties saw an end of Kennedy-style liberal humanism and the coming of a new phase of radical sensibility. Saul Bellow records this confrontation directly in *Mr Sammler's Planet* (1970), a bleak novel that sees in modern history two systems of force, one humane, the other barbaric, moving forward in competition for modern consciousness. There is no doubt that the instinct in the late Sixties leaned toward the barbaric, and it was common at the time to talk as if the entire structure of past art and civilization had been overthrown by a new, non-reverential, chance art of immediacy and spontaneity, unaffected by concern with form or standards, there to serve protest and revolution. In fact the record, seen from the present time, looks rather different: one of the striking features of the late Sixties is its eclecticism, its willingness to generate plural styles without necessary synthesis. And the styles, in painting and elsewhere, are enormously varied, moving between political activism and high experimentalism and formalism.

Certainly, as the Sixties developed, the sense of historical pressure on style increased, and the writers changed in manner. J D Salinger followed the Glass family of his later stories into a mystical silence. Mailer displaced American neuroses from the battlefield to the homeland in *Why Are We in Vietnam?* (1967). John Updike opened the delicate world of his middle-class couples to historical disturbance, following on Kennedy's assassination, and the search for salvation by sexuality in *Couples* (1968). Philip Roth left his early controlled formalism behind and took up the confessional mode in *Portnoy's Complaint* (1969), an address from the psychiatrist's couch. John Barth, in *Lost in the Funhouse: Fiction for Print, Tape, Live Voice* (1968), committed himself to a set of experimental texts for a McLuhanite world; the pieces dwell on their own fictionality in the manner of Borges and Nabokov. History may have seemed in acceleration in 1966–68, but fiction was growing increasingly if desperately concerned with its own business. In *Snow White* (1967), Donald Barthelme offered to replace the traditional novel or fable with the materials for a random collage into which meaning could not be structured. Among other confusions, the book included a questionnaire for the reader; 'Do you feel', it asks, 'that the creation of new modes of hysteria is a viable undertaking for the artist today? Yes ( ) No ( ).' Richard Gilman, reviewing the book, saw it as the art of a new reality:

open-ended, provisional, characterized by suspended judgments, by disbelief in hierarchies, by mistrust of solutions, denouements and completions, by self-consciousness issuing in tremendous earnestness but also in far-ranging mockery. . .[7]

The fluid, unstructured reality that Gilman describes came to be dubbed 'post-modernism', a label that embraces not only Barth and Barthelme but also some of the work of John Hawkes, William Gass, Thomas Pynchon (who followed *V* with *The Crying of Lot 49* in 1966), Richard Brautigan (whose *Trout Fishing in America*, 1967, gently and radically evokes a world of mechanism and its magical alternatives), and Ronald Sukenick, who produced in 1969 the aptly titled *The Death of the Novel and Other Stories*, in which he notes: 'The contemporary writer – the writer who is acutely in touch with the life of which he is a part – is forced to start from scratch: Reality doesn't exist. God was the omniscient author, but he died: now no one knows the plot. . .' Politically committed fiction did exist in the later Sixties, most notably, and understandably, in the work of black writers; but here too the experimental note showed itself, most memorably in the surreal world of Ishmael Reed (*The Free-Lance Pallbearers*, 1967) which shows the new uses, so important to the era, of 'fictiveness' and fantasy.

Poetry and drama, being performance arts for the times, revealed more inclination to commitment. Even so, the same processes are evident: we can see a move toward a theatre of revolt and confrontation, but also a move toward experimentation, fantasy and abstraction. Sometimes both came together: for the Sixties was an era of unexpected aesthetic mixtures, high art and popular art, one medium and another, collectivization and privatization, synchronicity and structure, social protest and surrealism. Marshall McLuhan was the Sixties' guru, and his image of a global village of multiply-intersecting forms predominates: the media were a massage. Poetry may have howled protests from poets like Allen Ginsberg, Allen de Loach and Ed Saunders; it also explored deeply into form, myth and legend, with the work of Gary Snyder, Ed Dorn and Galway Kinnell. In the theatre there was a mingling of socially radical and experimentally surreal forms – in, for example, the Living Theatre's four-hour *Paradise Now* (1968), called by one critic 'a wet dream in a cold universe',[8] with audience participation, collective nudity, and anarchic appeal to universal innocence or, in the work of Joseph Chaikin's Open Theatre, or of the La Mamma Troupe. A playwright like LeRoi Jones (Amiri Baraka) might move from a formal poetry to his play *Dutchman* (1964), a fable of the violent relationship of black and white, and then into the Harlem Black Arts theatre, with its Marxist roots and rejection of white audiences. Others might reverse this momentum, as did Edward Albee, who moved from the psycho-social conflicts of *The Zoo Story* to the minimalism and abstraction of *Box-Mao-Box* (1968), a post-modern commentary on a world in which politics becomes one of the available discourses or fictions. The strength of the Sixties was its artistic eclecticism. When Marshall McLuhan celebrated the extensions of self afforded by the modern global village, he touched on the ambiguity of revolt in the Sixties: it took in much that it revolted against and so came to question its own aims and directions; it displaced reality but incorporated it again into the imagination as a form of fantasy. Its art forms often seemed to expend themselves, but they in fact set up a lineage, and there is a direct continuity between them and many of the developments of the Seventies.

The Nixon years

The year 1968 saw the apogee of the counter-culture. But it also saw the election to the Presidency of Richard M Nixon, a man whose appeal lay primarily with what came to be known as 'Middle America'. Despite all the power and publicity that had attended the manifestations of the 'counter-culture', traditional American values remained strong. To many Americans, a vote for Nixon was a vote for a return to the Puritan ethic of hard and honest work, of thrift, of a laissez-faire economy and of respect for parents and elders. In practical terms, this was widely construed to mean that a Nixon administration would know how to end political protest, street and campus violence, anti-war demonstrations. Certainly the next few years saw a weakening of the more aggressive expressions of protest, and the Nixon administration – which early showed its expertise in cracking heads and arresting protesters, and later graduated to more sensational methods of undercutting legitimate political opposition – claimed much of the credit. Even many observers unsympathetic to the Nixon administration felt that the advent of a genuinely right-wing government had helped steer left-wing protest off the streets and back into its traditional institutional home, the Democratic party. However, this kind of analysis misreads the influence political leadership can normally exert on a society. Great social movements do not rise and fall as the result of a change of party at the top; both, rather, are visible expressions of deeper historical forces. The counter-culture of the late Sixties and the administration of Richard Nixon had one thing at least in common: an arc-like history stretching over a five- or six-year period. The constituent elements in the counter-culture came together in the mid-1960s, reached their peak of visibility and audibility in 1967 or 1968, and largely dispersed, regrouped or declined by the early 1970s. Nixon was elected to the presidency in November 1968, re-elected four years later, and left office in disgrace in August 1974. The two arcs thus intersect in the late 1960s and early 1970s, But to understand the relation between them, it is necessary to consider the underlying social trends against which they occurred.

An important clue to the relationship lies in the nation's vital statistics. The American birth-rate, for instance, so high after the war and reaching 25 per 1000 of population in 1955, had been declining ever since, while the death-rate remained largely constant. One consequence was that, as each year passed, the overall population increase in the United States was occurring at a decelerating pace. Between 1960 and 1965 the annual rate of population increase averaged 1.5 per cent; over the next five years it had gone down to 1.1 per cent. A further consequence was that a slightly healthier ratio was developing between the number of those in the earning bracket and those too old or too young to earn. In 1960, out of every 1000 Americans, 357 were seventeen years old or less; by 1970 the figure had gone down to 342. The orange was sliding down the neck of the ostrich and, by the 1970s, the post-war 'baby boom' had begun to enter the work force and, in general, take on the responsibilities of young adulthood. Some of the pressure was thus lifted off the schools, colleges and youth clubs that had often been the reluctant locus of tension in the 1960s. So one reason why the size and frequency of youthful protests and demonstrations tended to lessen in the 1970s was that the prominence of young people in the population as a whole had somewhat diminished.

Also important were changes in the economic climate. In many ways the US economy was strong and healthy and continued to be so. It was certainly, in the literal sense, delivering the goods. The American gross national product continued to rise (from $503 billion in 1960 to $974 billion in 1970) and so did individual and annual earnings. Personal savings rose over the 1960s from a total of $17 billion to over $56 billion, an average annual increase of a colossal 12.7 per cent. But there is another side to the story. If GNP rose during the 1960s by 4.6 per cent per annum, most of the economies with which the USA might reasonably be compared – Belgium, France, West Germany, Norway, Italy – were doing as well or better, while Japan was streets ahead (though Britain was bringing up the rear!). Inflation in the USA was worse during the later 1960s than in most countries in Western Europe (and Canada) while throughout the decade the US dollar lost its consumer purchasing power to the tune of some 2.7 per cent per annum. Above all, America's annual balance of payments was fluctuating dangerously and showed signs – soon to be all too accurately verified – of tumbling into by far the largest deficit in US history. The reasons for the huge balance-of-payments deficits of the 1970s were complex: the last stages of the Vietnam war provided part of the story and so – particularly after 1973 – did America's vast bill for oil imports. In addition, the once high productivity of American industry slumped badly in the late 1960s, so that domestic output was not able to keep up with demand. Thus, though Americans continued to enjoy the world's highest standard of living, there were tell-tale signs by the late 1960s of some of the economic problems that would face them in the next decade. These removed the economic safety net which in the affluent Sixties had helped to give the young, the black, the transient, and the angry the confidence to challenge the system and run the risk of losing. The harsh fact was that, as the economic situation became tighter, many American students, blacks and political and cultural outsiders came to attach greater importance to obtaining their meal ticket (a college certificate, a good reference, a job, a bank loan) than to fighting for great causes or against intractable establishments. As one radical leader of the 1960s put it a few years later 'You can't make a revolution if you have to make a living!'

Demographic and economic statistics help to suggest some of the underlying influences on social and political behaviour as the 1960s came to an end. But the new social quiescence had other correlates as well. For instance, as middle- and upper-middle-class Americans continued to move out of city centres – a process which the urban riots of the later 1960s both stimulated and reflected – the increase in the rate of big property crimes in cities went down somewhat (though any comfort derived from this had to be balanced against the acceleration of crime in suburbia). Moreover, in the matter of black rights, figures from the South showed massive gains in Negro voter registration and in job and educational opportunities (while Jimmy Carter, the first president elected from the Deep South for over a century, could not have won without a sizeable black vote from the South). Health care, too, was greatly improved over the 1960s and, for those at the bottom of the social heap, expenditure on the federal government's food-stamps programme rose by over 400 per cent. Thus, the young, the black and the physically deprived had had part of the foundations of their discontent cut from under them, partly by the sheer passage of time and the broad currents of change that it had effected, and partly as a result of deliberate social or political action.

However, while it is important to consider trends such as these when seeking reasons for the change in atmosphere in America in the late 1960s and early 1970s, it would be foolish to ignore the more obvious surface explanations. One reason why there was less political protest in the 1970s was that there actually seemed to be less to protest about. Though many important problems remained unsolved, it is arguable that the most blatant evils – extreme institutionalized racial discrimination, for instance – had been alleviated by the point-counter-point of protest and legislation of the 1960s. Similarly, while the mindless death and destruction in Vietnam, and domestic protest against it, continued throughout Nixon's first term as president, it was nevertheless clear that his administration was, however deviously, trying to disengage from that part of the world. When it finally did so, in early 1973, the most contentious single issue dividing the American people was removed from public controversy.

Not only was there less to protest about in the 1970s. Somehow it also seemed more of an effort. The rise and fall of the counter-culture, like that of Ancient Rome, seems almost to have been subject to a natural life-cycle: full of brave feats of daring at the beginning, brilliantly innovative in mid-course, merely going through the motions towards the end. Eventually, as one former leader of the Black Panthers donned a shirt and tie and ran for Mayor of Oakland and another found Christ, as the founder of the radical student group SDS ran for a seat in the US senate and another took up a post in an insurance company, their younger brothers and sisters all over the country no longer had the heart to set up the barricades against 'official' America. It had been done; it had achieved some objectives and failed in others; who had the energy to try and do it all over again? Many still talked of radical revolution and the need to overhaul the fundamental infrastructure of society, made clenched fists and wore jeans and long hair. But gradually these things became vestigial symbols of a revolt that had lost its head of steam, gestures of defiance that the new society of the 1970s found it could accommodate without much trouble. The new radicalisms of the new decade – women's rights, gay rights, gray rights, the ecology movement – adopted their own characteristic styles and tactics. By the mid-1970s, it had become clear that neither the confrontation politics of the counter-culture nor its gentler 'life-style' wing any longer constituted a serious threat to those who upheld more traditional values, and that a *modus vivendi* had been worked out between them.

Watergate

The new *modus vivendi* was not simply a return to the life that the upheavals of the Sixties had subverted, though the rhetoric of the Nixon administration sometimes suggested as much. On the contrary, the Seventies developed a new unique, characteristic tone – a tone for which the Nixon administration and the scandals associated with it were partly responsible. Politically, the decade was dominated to a degree unmatched since the 1920s by the issue of integrity in government, and one must go back to the 1860s to find a period when the relationship between President and Congress was as acrimonious – and Congress as assertive – as in the last year of Nixon's presidency. The presidency had in fact been growing in power *vis-à-vis* Congress for many years, and there was no issue associated with Nixon's tenure of office – the impounding of Congressionally approved funds, the using of federal agencies as a means of putting pressure on political opponents, the prosecuting and widening of an undeclared war, attempts to 'manage' the news, the undermining of political opposition by 'dirty tricks' – which had not fuelled fires of criticism against previous presidents. But in the scale and consistency with which it resorted to these and similar operations, and in the absence of any national crisis by which they might possibly have been justified, the Nixon administration brought to a head American fears of the 'imperial presidency'.[9] The boil was finally lanced by Watergate. It was Watergate – merely the name of a building complex in Washington which housed the headquarters of the Democratic National Committee whose offices were burgled one night in June 1972 – that became the symbol of the political chicanery and illegality for which the Nixon White House came to stand; Watergate that gave the mid-1970s its political colouring; Watergate that, in 1974, brought about the first presidential abdication in American history: and Watergate that was to give the Seventies a political colouring all its own.

It is possible to argue – as Nixon himself has – that the Watergate issue has obscured the significance of his administration's achievement. 'I have done some stupid things,' Nixon was prepared to acknowledge to David Frost in a television interview two and a half years after leaving office, 'particularly the pip-squeak Watergate thing; but I did the big things rather well.' By the 'big things' Nixon had principally in mind his government's achievements in international affairs. Not only was America's involvement in Vietnam at last brought to an end under Nixon; but, through his visit to China in February 1972 and his signature of the first Strategic Arms Limitation Treaty (SALT) in Moscow a few months later, Nixon could with some legitimacy claim to be, with Henry A Kissinger, the architect of a new order in world affairs. Given such an achievement, Nixon and his defenders might argue in the court of history, the sheer pettiness of the Watergate incident – in which, after all, nobody died, nobody's livelihood or reputation was unjustly or irrevocably destroyed, and at the end of which the normal constitutional processes of America were seen to be functioning with renewed authority. It could also be argued that the Watergate improprieties were the activities of underlings whose zeal outweighed their judgement and whom Nixon sought to protect out of a misplaced sense of loyalty. Against such a view the prosecution might go as follows: that if Nixon knew about the Watergate events and similar 'dirty tricks' activities he was a criminal, and if not he was dangerously ill-informed; that however 'pip-squeak' Watergate was when measured against the great crimes of history, it so transfixed the American people and the wider world as revelation after revelation tumbled out in 1973 and 1974 that for more than a year US government business virtually stood still and no serious domestic or foreign policies could be pursued; that Nixon, by his appointments and by the tone he set, brought the US government into disrepute and seriously alienated the American people from their elected leaders and from the political process itself.

Will Nixon go down in history as the Watergate President? The long-term answer must depend in part upon how bad Watergate looks and how good his foreign policy looks in the light of later American history. The short-term answer is certainly 'yes'. The repercussions of the Nixon administration were certainly felt more profoundly on the domestic front, where he failed, than in foreign policy. Abroad, the *rapprochement* with China took seven more years to reach the point of mutual recognition, and it seems probable that China's new acceptability in the world arose more out of modifications in its own policies than out of US initiatives. As for American relations with the Soviet Union, the signing of SALT I in 1972 did not substantially improve the atmosphere between the two superpowers over the years that followed. Indeed, Soviet provocation over human rights and in central and southern Africa increased in the mid-1970s partly as a direct response to the impediments upon presidential action imposed by Congress in the post-Watergate atmosphere. Thus, while many of the international initiatives of the Nixon era were bold and imaginative, they can not now be said to have revolutionized world affairs in quite the way that Nixon apologists might wish to claim. As for the domestic front, the Watergate legacy was everywhere to be seen. Congress reasserted its power *vis-à-vis* that of the president to the point that even a Democratic president with an enormous nominal majority in both Houses found, in the later 1970s, that he had the greatest difficulty in getting his proposals passed. The issue of integrity in government was a recurring refrain throughout the years succeeding Watergate, and a number of public figures were forced from office through the revelation of financial or sexual peccadillos. 'Investigative Journalists' from Maine to California tried to dig into the doings of publicly appointed officials in the hope of unearthing – as Bob Woodward and Carl Bernstein of the *Washington Post* had done[10] – their own Watergate scandal. Finally, in order to prevent future Watergate-style traumas, the American electors voted into office at national, state and local level a series of honest and honourable, but often colourless and unimaginative leaders throughout much of the rest of the 1970s. The times required a rest from the recent upheavals. The Nixon administration, not just because of what it had done in office but because Americans wanted to prevent such things from being done again, played an important part in creating the tone and quality of political life in the years that followed.

The post-Nixon Seventies

The new tone of the post-Nixon Seventies – less confrontation, less public drama, more emphasis on personal integrity and local self-help – was found not just in politics but in many broader currents of national life. No longer were the great issues engaging politicians, columnists, academics, writers and citizens at large the major national and international injustices of the 1960s. Gone now were the colossal military and economic aid to other countries, the huge federal expenditure on space research, the great expansion in schools, highways, and building programmes generally. Now emphasis was on matters more directly affecting the individual: prices at a time of inflation and unemployment; sexual equality in a male-dominated society; the state of the physical environment in a country whose vast resources for the first time looked finite. Even palpable inequities such as racial and sexual discrimination came to be regarded less as national issues than as questions for local and individual action. Tension did arise and demonstrations were held. The busing of children to desegregate schools produced fierce controversy; so did the Bakke case, which was brought (and eventually won) by a white man who objected to being refused admission to a medical school that admitted blacks with lower qualifications. Some of the demands of the women's and gay liberation groups, too, produced powerful support in some quarters and occasional demonstrations were held to display solidarity. By and large, however, the activists of the 1970s were more disposed than their equivalents a decade earlier to fight battles at a local and even personal level. Many of the nation's official leaders, too, stressed how little central government could do and how much self-help could achieve at a time when government budgets had to be severely scrutinized, and the approved rhetoric stressed not how much was being spent but how little. Small, in the words of a book title that became a political slogan, is beautiful. Vast projects and the politics of confrontation might have seemed necessary if the North wanted to desegregate the South, or if a Johnson or a Nixon were to be overthrown as a result of nation-wide popular pressure. But if you wanted to make sure that local air or water was kept clean, or that your local neighbourhood school did not fire homosexual teachers, then less histrionic measures seemed appropriate. The Seventies were more *muted* than the Sixties.

The mood of the Seventies is harder to describe and analyse than that of the Sixties, not only because we are closer to it, but also because its very nature was to eschew the oversimplifications so popular during the earlier period. In the 1960s Americans had often found it easy to define the big issues and to identify their 'goodies' and 'baddies', their causes and solutions; in the 1970s people were more inclined to stress their doubts and their inability to see clearly how best to deal with the problems that faced them. 'Your strength', said President Carter in his Inaugural Address in 1977, so far away in tone from Kennedy's 1961 Inaugural, 'can compensate for my weakness, and your wisdom can help to minimize my mistakes.' Doubt and bafflement were expressed as often as convicton. The USA had come through a series of damaging experiences, and for the first time Americans commonly expressed uncertainty about their nation's capacity to cope adequately with the problems it faced. The old optimism was by no means gone; but on to it had been grafted a mature realization that not all problems could be easily solved, and that some could hardly even be defined with confidence.

These uncertainties helped give the Seventies a character all their own. After the palpably unsuccessful attempt in the 1960s to tackle broad social and international problems, many now turned inward toward a greater commitment to *self*-understanding. As outward certainties seemed shattered, the time seemed ripe for new pathways into inner certainty. One commentator, the historian Christopher Lasch,[11] noted the move from politics to what he called narcissism, a fascination and an unease with self and role, a deep concern with personal and interpersonal performance in the theatre of everyday life. Who am I and what is my relationship with the wider universe? The conundrum was as old as civilization itself, and certainly no novelty to Americans with their penchant for self-definition and self-analysis. But whereas the question had tended to be posed in a social setting in the Sixties, it often took a more individualistic or cosmic form in the Seventies. No longer was the emphasis on 'my' relationship to – or desire to escape from – the black ghetto, the 'totalitarian' campus, the stifling world of bourgeois America; more typical were the bodily preoccupations, a growing vogue for encounter groups, a burgeoning of new religions, a strong emphasis on personal physical, spiritual and psychic health, on knowing your own mind and body, on trusting your own instincts in developing authentic personal relationships.

These themes sounded through the Seventies in many different forms and turned up in much of its popular writing – in sustained pieces like Robert M Pirsig's *Zen and the Art of Motorcycle Maintenance* (1974); in studies of interpersonal relationships like Erving Goffman's *The Presentation of Self in Everyday Life* (1969) and latter-day texts of interpersonal guidance like *Passages, Your Erroneous Zones* and *I'm OK, You're OK*; in semi-mystical works like those of Carlos

Castaneda and in the propaganda literature of popular cults like Scientology or the 'Moonies', and in an endless stream of popular psychology and parapsychology that turned up regularly in the pages of women's magazines as well as on the large and small screen. Some of this was serious, some commercial, most bogus. But by its volume and its popular success it indicated that the search for self-knowledge, one motif of the counter-culture of the Sixties, widely dismissed as an escapist fad in those days, had by the later Seventies all but attained the status of a new conventional wisdom.

There was a similar turn toward subjectivism in the serious literature of the Seventies. This was prefigured by the stress on subjective and confessional forms in the early Sixties and was also fuelled by the profound opposition to the world of public affairs expressed by most major writers during the height of the counter-culture later in that decade. American writing began to realize its historical severance from the modernist era, to search for the 'post-modernist' writing of the late-technetronic age. Saul Bellow, winner of the Nobel Prize for Literature in the Bicentennial year of 1976, explored two generations of writing in *Humboldt's Gift* (1975), comparing Humboldt's Fifties 'modernism' and obsession with historical and political forces with the younger Charlie Citrine's 'comic end-run' and his fascination with a neo-Platonic mysticism. A writing of therapeutic hungers grew; Philip Roth followed *Portnoy's Complaint* with *My Life as a Man* (1974) and *The Professor of Desire* (1977), in which subjective, confessional heroes try to comprehend their inner relation to larger social and historical forces. Works of psychic fantasy flourished, releasing surreal energies and feelings of estrangement, as in Jerzy Kosinski's *Blind Date* (1977) or John Hawkes's *The Passion Artist* (1979). The objective text seemed to dissolve as an imposition on the world; stories frequently took place less in some 'real world' out there than in the functions of the authorial imagination, which followed laws of imaginary possibility rather than of casual probability. 'Post-modernism' became a loose term to cluster together many writers – Hawkes, Kosinski, Robert Coover (*The Public Burning*, 1977), Ronald Sukenick, Donald Barthelme, John Barth (*Letters*, 1979) and Thomas Pynchon, whose *Gravity's Rainbow* (1973) has become seen as the 'post-modern' classic – who questioned the formal authority of text, parodied the traditional securities of art (parody is an important voice of the Seventies, found too in its popular art and film, as in the work of Robert Altman, Woody Allen, and Mel Brooks), or explored a world of psychic anguish. Much of this writing diplays the narcissism, the therapeutic questing, and the doubt about the authenticity of all relations with others that runs through much of the wider culture.

Paradoxically, though, the personal uncertainties, formal insecurities, and self-obsessions so characteristic of serious and popular art in the Seventies reached out toward social and political forms of expression. The Women's Liberation Movement, for example, started out in the Sixties as a series of loosely coalescent groups basing their rhetoric on increasingly militant versions of Betty Friedan (*The Feminine Mystique*, 1963) or Kate Millett (*Sexual Politics*, 1970), modelling their tactics largely on those of black civil rights groups. But in the Seventies, it blossomed into a growing awareness among men and women alike that women had a potential for personal growth and achievement that was part of communal desire yet was denied by the system. Many of the most widely read works of serious fiction produced by women in the Seventies – Erica Jong's *Fear of Flying* (1973), Judith Rossner's *Looking for Mr Goodbar* (1975), Lisa Alther's *Kinflicks*(1976), Sarah Davidson's *Loose Change* (1977), or Marilyn French's *The Women's Room* (1978) – undoubtedly owed part of their impressive sales to the fact that they seemed semi-autobiographical accounts of their authors' often fumbling attempts to come to terms with the hitherto more repressed aspects of womanhood in general and female sexuality in particular. Parallel texts by men – some of Philip Roth's novels, or John Irving's *The World According to Garp* (1978) – looked to the changing psyche of individuals in a world of sexual redefinition. As the Seventies progressed, public acknow-ledgement of female sexuality – and homosexuality – came gradually to be taken for granted in many quarters. It became less common for a man, boasting of his 'conquests', to squirm if a woman mentioned hers. Sexuality in general was accepted more easily in the Seventies than before, and it is almost certain – all the statistics of contraceptive devices, venereal disease, illegitamacies and the rest seem to confirm it, as do the more openly and explicitly sexual books and films of the period – that young unmarried people in the 1970s were more likely to be sexually experienced than in most previous generations. But they were often less brazen about sex than their Sixties equivalents, less inclined to use it as a weapon of shock. The important thing was the authenticity of the experience rather than its public acknowledge-ment. The latter could increasingly be taken for granted, the former never. To many in the 1970s, quality was all.

Indeed, 'quality' and 'authenticity' became principal watchwords of the Seventies, rather as 'relevance' had been in the Sixties. These criteria – personal now rather than social – were applied not only to the processes of personal self-understanding (the central theme of Robert M Pirsig's book), but also to the physical environment within which those processes took place – the air we breathe, the water we drink, the food we eat. Consumer- and environment-protection groups sprang up to monitor these; federal and state governmental agencies were established. Like the quest for self-knowledge, this concern with the quality of the physical environment was not new in America and was certainly not absent in the Sixties, when Ralph Nader launched his tenacious and single-minded attacks on those who produced cars or food or anything else that was dirty or unsafe. But by the Seventies almost everyone – even the big corporations Nader had attacked –

claimed to care about the physical quality of life and the preservation of resources. Moreover, the widespread concern about matters qualitative was accompanied by a new scepticism toward the traditional American tenet that all problems were susceptible to essentially quantitative solutions. It was all very well (said the few in the 1960s and the many in the 1970s) citing facts and figures to prove that the proportion of families below the poverty line had declined from X per cent to Y per cent, that the cost-effectiveness of the US military effort was increasing ('more bangs for a buck') or the drop-out rate in black schools was decreasing. Great new housing schemes had no doubt absorbed a sizeable percentage of the urban homeless and carefully attuned tax policies might well have helped to keep unemployment within politically acceptable limits. But what did these things mean to the texture of life of the individual affected? Phrases like 'the poverty line' or the 'politically acceptable limits' of unemployment, some argued, seemed to suggest a degree of insensitivity at odds with supposedly humanitarian policies. As for the foreign policy of the 1960s, its latter-day critics concentrated on the Vietnam war and felt that the very impersonality with which its prosecution had been analysed and assessed – its initial 'escalation', its 'free-fire zones' and 'body counts', its 'search and destroy missions' and its 'pacification' areas – had reflected a poverty of humanity on the part of those responsible. Numbers, many now argued, had taken the place of people in the thinking of the policy-makers.

The new search for self-knowledge and for a finer quality of physical and spiritual life helped form an America that was less agitated than a decade earlier, more concerned with traditional values, more conservative even. The radicalism of the Sixties came increasingly under question. Egalitarian schooling was criticized by James Coleman and Christopher Jencks, Keynesian economics by Milton Friedman, internationalist and interventionist foreign policies by almost everyone. But the new conservatism had incorporated many of the more radical aspects of the counter-culture of the Sixties, and it is even arguable that the very quiescence of the Seventies was testimony not to the final demise of the counter-culture but to its ultimate if subtle victory. If anything had united the various groups that came together to form the counter-culture of the Sixties (in addition to their opposition to the way things were done by the 'official' culture), it was an insistence that individual self-awareness and community-level participatory democracy were preferable to massive schemes of government-dominated reform, and that qualitative change was better than quantitative. By the later 1970s, these attitudes, diluted and adapted, had found their way to the heart of establishment thinking.

Historians will debate the degree to which the shift in mood in the Seventies was a victory for the counter-culture or evidence of elite America's capacity to absorb its more vociferous critics. On the one hand, there is no doubt that many heterodoxies of the Sixties became the orthodoxies of the late Seventies. On the other, one should not assume that the long hair and jeans, the more open sexuality and the rock music that gradually became almost *de rigueur* ten years later among the nation's elite, represent anything more than the vestigial *folies* of a culture that had by now largely passed into history. Did the counter-culture of the Sixties win or lose? Did it influence the Seventies or was it absorbed by them? No definitive answer has yet emerged among historians. One of the authors has argued elsewhere[12] that the new atmosphere of the 1970s represented a fusion, a new synthesis of the two adversary cultures of the 1960s and that this very process – the integration of two hitherto opposing tendencies – has throughout American history proved to be a characteristic and recurrent pattern. But as the Seventies too pass into the rear-view mirror, new interpretations will doubtless emerge.

Reading America now

Historians often concentrate on the great discontinuities of the past: wars, famines, revolutions, the rise and fall of dynasties and empires. Social scientists, on the other hand, tend to focus on groups of people and their behaviour (often deviant or pathological) at static moments or over brief periods of time. The best historians and social scientists give insights into the workings of a civilization that are comparable to those of a good poet or novelist; but what they rarely do is tell us what most of the people concerned themselves with for most of the time throughout most of history, which is concentrating on the largely unchanging immediacies of life – eating and sleeping, dressing and undressing, travelling to and from work and play, organizing domestic finances, playing with children and chatting to neighbours, rejoicing in health and life, worrying about sickness and death. Thus, it is broadly true, as has been suggested above, that American society was cautiously optimistic in 1960; in a state of almost polarized conflict in 1968; more at peace with itself a decade later. But it is also true that for most individual Americans the texture of life over those twenty years was not dominated by Kennedy's New Frontier, the counter-culture or the new morality of the Carter era, but by the sort of house they lived in and the job they did, the person or people with whom they lived and worked, the local climate, the quality of neighbourhood educational, medical and sporting facilities, the reliability of plumbers and decorators, and the accessibility of friends and family.

What is the relationship between broad themes such as social harmony and discord on the one hand and the millions of more or less unchanging local and personal experiences of life on the other? Did the immediate, daily texture of life as experienced by (say) a black Mississippi sharecropper in 1960, an Iowa farm insurance agent in

1965, a Detroit auto worker in 1970, or a Savannah ice-cream vendor in 1975 conform to the broad pattern of American history that has been outlined? Did the Cuba missile crisis of 1962 or the moon landing of 1969 mean as much to ordinary Americans as the shift from monochrome to colour television or the replacement of stockings by tights? There are no simple answers to these questions, for they presuppose the answer to a more fundamental one: how can we *know* what is or was significant to members of a huge and diverse society? If a man is asked what most concerns him, his answers will depend in part on his perception of whomever does the asking. An official pollster might get the answer 'inflation' or 'race relations': a psychiatrist 'sexual inadequacy' or 'loneliness'. And if an individual reveals different preoccupations, beliefs and values to different investigators, this is true, too, of a society of 200 million people. One historian of modern America, basing his evidence on the statements of politicians, journalists and academics, might cite one set of topics as the nation's principal concerns; another, delving into popular songs, slogans, jokes and television commercials, might find another. The former might judge that America in the Seventies was primarily concerned with such issues as the energy crisis and the weakness of the dollar; the latter might reply that such themes did not get through to most Americans who, unresponsive to the rhetoric of officialdom, continued to be captivated by the attractions of consumerism.

Is it then safer to avoid the larger gestures of history and to concentrate on what can be chronicled with fair certainty: election statistics, trade figures, rates of birth, death and unemployment, the legislative failures and successes of Congress? What about examining the lives of public figures or analysing the functions of the branches of government? There is much to be said for these approaches to history – not because they are safe but because they deal with matters of real importance to society as a whole. Yet a full and rounded picture of American life can only be attempted by a scholar who is prepared to venture into the risky territory of social attitudes and perceptions and to draw inferences from works of the creative and popular imagination as well as from 'factual' sources. The whole story is not available to the historian or anybody else. Nothing short of the total re-enactment of an era could literally be considered the 'whole' story. But it is possible, by attempting to cross-fertilize the chronological perspective of the historian with the insights of social scientists and cultural critics, to recreate and communicate something of the texture of life in the past. A multi-disciplinary approach, one that attempts to incorporate into its purview not only the economic and vital statistics and the sayings and doings of officialdom, but also the informal, off-duty ways in which a culture reveals itself, may be the most dangerous line of approach. But it is surely also the most rewarding.

Notes and references

1. Michael Harrington was to offer a 'radical' exploration of all this in *The Other America*, Macmillan, New York, 1962, and Penguin, Harmondsworth, 1963.
2. Morris Dickstein, *Gates of Eden: American Culture in the Sixties*, Basic Books, New York, 1977, p. 122.
3. Philip Roth, 'Writing American Fiction', *Commentary*, March 1961; reprinted in Roth, *Reading Myself and Others*, Farrar, Strauss & Giroux, New York, 1975; and also in M Bradbury (ed), *The Novel Today*, Fontana, London, 1977.
4. Saul Bellow, 'Some notes on recent American fiction', *Encounter*, 1963; reprinted in M Bradbury (ed), *The Novel Today*, Fontana, London, 1977.
5. Tom Wolfe, 'Seizing the Power', in Tom Wolfe and E W Johnson (eds), *The New Journalism*, Picador, London, 1975, p. 45.
6. Andrew Hacker, *The End of the American Era*, Sidgwick & Jackson, London, 1970, p. 230.
7. Richard Gilman, *The New Republic*, 3 June 1967, 27.
8. John Lahr, *Acting Out America: Essays on Modern Theatre*, Penguin, Harmondsworth, 1972, p. 178.
9. Arthur M Schlesinger, Jr, *The Imperial Presidency*, Houghton Mifflin, Boston, 1973 and Deutsch, London, 1974.
10. Carl Bernstein and Robert Woodward, *All the President's Men*, Simon & Schuster, New York, Secker & Warburg, London, 1974; and *The Final Days*, Avon, New York, Coronet, London, 1977. (*Note*: the authors' names are reversed on some editions.)
11. Christopher Lasch, *The Culture of Narcissism: American Life in an Age of Diminishing Expectations*, Norton, New York, 1978.
12. Daniel Snowman, *Kissing Cousins: An Interpretation of British and American Culture, 1945–75*, Temple Smith, London, 1977. Published in the USA as *Britain and America*, New York U.P., Harper & Row, New York, 1977.

Bibliography

General

The chapter bibliographies that follow give references to selected books and articles bearing upon the subjects of the individual chapters. Many of these, in turn, contain bibliographies of their own which readers will find useful in following up particular topics. But in many cases those requiring further information, particularly factual information, would be well advised to begin by consulting one or more of the standard reference works in the field.

In American History the standard bibliographical aid, which also contains useful advice on methods of research and editing, is Frank Freidel (ed), *Harvard Guide to American History* (rev. edn), 2 vols, Cambridge, Mass., 1974. Volume I lists works according to their generic categories (*e.g.* Biographies, Comprehensive Histories, Historical Poems), while Volume 2 lists them by topics which, in turn, are chronologically arranged (*e.g.* Massachusetts Bay Colony, Compromise of 1850, Post-War Foreign Policy). Also chronological in its approach, and particularly useful for its thumbnail sketches of particular issues and events is Richard B Morris (ed), *Encyclopaedia of American History* (rev. edn), New York, 1970. Part I consists of a basic year-by-year chronology with brief factual descriptions (*e.g.* 1859: John Brown's Raid; 1947: Truman Doctrine), while Part 2 provides topical chronologies (e.g. Territorial Expansion, Population and Immigration, Science and Invention). More comprehensive in its coverage is Louise B Ketz (ed), *Dictionary of American History* (rev edn), 8 vols, New York, 1976, which arranges its entries (*e.g.* Abilene Trail, Canals, Zimmerman Telegram) alphabetically. For biographical information readers should consult Allen Johnson (ed), *Dictionary of American Biography* (rev. edn) 11 vols, New York, 1957. The standard compilation of US statistics is the two-volume bicentennial edition of the *Historical Statistics of the United States*, Washington DC, 1976, published by the US Bureau of the Census, also available in a one-volume version as Ben J Wattenberg, *The Statistical History of the United States: From Colonial Times to the Present*, New York and London, 1976. The most up-to-date and readily-available map collection for American History is Kenneth T Jackson and James Truslow Adams, *Atlas of American History* (rev. edn), New York, 1978.

Of the various histories of American literature, the most detailed and useful is undoubtedly the multi-authored *Literary History of the United States*, (rev. edn), New York and London, 1974, edited by Robert E Spiller, Willard Thorp, Thomas H Johnson, Henry Seidel Canby, Richard M Ludwig and William M Gibson; this is in two volumes, the first a history and the second an admirable bibliography. It can be usefully supplemented with Daniel Hoffman (ed), *Harvard Guide to Contemporary American Writing*, Cambridge Mass., and London, 1979, covering the post-war scene. The best brief history of American literature is Marcus Cunliffe's *The Literature of the United States* (rev. edn), Harmondsworth, 1970. Cunliffe also edited the two handy volumes in the 'Sphere History of Literature in the English Language' devoted to *American Literature to 1900* and *American Literature Since 1900*, London, 1975; also see Robert E Spiller, *The Cycle of American Literature*, New York, 1957. On the American novel, the two main surveys are Richard Chase, *The American Novel and Its Tradition*, Garden City, NY, 1957, and Leslie Fiedler, *Love and Death in the American Novel* (rev. edn), New York, 1966; London, 1970. On poetry, Roy Harvey Pearce's *The Continuity of American Poetry*, Princeton and London, 1961, is sharp and critical; Donald B Stauffer's *A Short History of American Poetry*, New York, 1974, is a ranging survey. On American theatre, the two standard volumes are Arthur H Quinn's *A History of the American Drama from the Beginning to the Civil War*, (2nd edn), New York, 1943, and his *A History of American Drama from the Civil War to the Present Day* (rev. edn), New York, 1964. Main reference works are James D Hart, *The Oxford Companion to American Literature*, (5th edn), Oxford UP, London and New York, 1975, and Malcolm Bradbury, Eric Mottram and Jean Franco (eds), *The Penguin Companion to Literature,* Vol. 3: *American and Latin-American*, Penguin, Harmondsworth, 1971. Invaluable bibliographical and research assistance is found in Lewis Leary, *American Literature*: *A Study and Research Guide*, New York, 1976.

In American Studies generally, a useful general survey, organized according to the main disciplines concerned, from geography to the philosophy, is Dennis Welland (ed), *The United States: A Companion to American Studies*, London, 1974. Also useful, especially from a methodological point of view, are Hennig Cohen (ed), *The American Experience: Approaches to the Study of the United States*, Boston, 1968, and *The American Culture: Approaches to the Study of the United States*, Boston, 1968, which bring together important essays by leading scholars in the subject. Other surveys of central fields that can be mentioned are Oliver W Larkin, *Art in America* (rev. edn), New York, 1960; John T Howard, *Our American Music: A Comprehensive*

History from 1620 to the Present (2nd edn), New York 1966; R Blesh and H Janis, *They All Played Ragtime: The True Story of an American Music,* New York 1950; Paul R Anderson and Max H Fisch, *Philosophy in America, from the Puritans to James* (2nd edn) New York and London, 1965; Merle E Curti, *The Growth of American Thought,* New York, 1943; Russel B Nye, *The Unembarrassed Muse: The Popular Arts in America,* New York, 1970; and F A Ogg and P O Ray, *Introduction to American Government,* New York, 1966.

1. New Founde Land

A useful, paperback documentary source for early exploration is John Conron (ed), *The American Landscape: A Critical Anthology of Prose and Poetry,* Oxford UP, New York and London, 1973. Other basic paperback anthologies are Perry Miller and Thomas H Johnson (eds), *The Puritans: A Sourcebook of their Writings* (2 vols), Harper Torchbooks New York, 1963, generous, with useful editorial material, but largely restricted to the seventeenth century; George F Horner and Robert A Bain (eds), *Colonial and Federalist American Writing,* Odyssey Press, New York, 1966, and Harrison T Meserole (ed), *Seventeeth Century American Poetry,* Norton Library, New York, 1972, admirably complement it. New England's political, legal and constitutional history can be studied in detail in W K Kavenagh (ed), *Foundations of Colonial America: A Documentary History:* Vol. 1, *The North Eastern Colonies,* New York, 1973. Merrill Jensen (ed), *English Historical Documents 9: American Colonial Documents,* London, 1955, extends to social and economic history and embraces the other colonies.

Main works on the discoveries are S E Morison, *The European Discovery of America: The Northern Voyages, A.D. 500–1600,* New York, 1971, an outstanding study by a major maritime historian; D B Quinn, *England and the Discovery of America, 1481–1620,* London, 1974, an authoritative work by a leading British scholar; Howard Mumford Jones, *O Strange New World: American Culture: The Formative Years* London, Chatto & Windus, 1965, which thoroughly ranges from Renaissance myth to the eighteenth century – as does, with more imaginative concerns, John Seelye, *Prophetic Waters: The River in Early American Life and Literature,* New York, 1977, and Edmundo O'Gorman, *The Invention of America,* Bloomington, Indiana, 1961, a striking work by a Mexican scholar.

On Puritan culture, see Perry Miller's early but essential *The New England Mind from Colony to Province,* Cambridge, Mass., 1953, (reprinted 1961), supplemented by the admirable later work of Sacvan Bercovitch in *The Puritan Origins of the American Self,* New Haven, Conn., 1975, and *The American Jeremiad,* Madison, 1978. Bercovitch has also edited *Typology and Early American Literature,* Amherst,

1972, and the stimulating anthology of essays *The American Puritan Imagination*, London, 1974. Another superb general study is Larzer Ziff, *Puritanism in America: New Culture in a New World*, New York, 1973, and E Emerson (ed), *Major Writers of Early American Literature*, Madison, 1972, is a fine collection of critical essays. Other important studies are D B Rutman, *American Puritanism: Faith and Practice*, Philadelphia/New York, 1970; P Boyer and S Nussbaum, *Salem Possessed: The Social Origins of Witchcraft*, Cambridge, Mass., 1974; S C Powell, *Puritan Village: The Formation of a New England Town*, Middletown, Conn., 1963, a definitive study of Sudbury, Mass.; and D E Stannard, *The Puritan Way of Death: A Study in Religion, Culture, and Social Change*, London, 1977.

The best single textbook on colonial history (with extensive bibliography) is R C Simmons, *The American Colonies from Settlement to Independence*, London, 1976; Roger Thompson, *Women in Stuart England and America*, London, 1974, is an exciting comparative study in social history. Henry F May, *The Enlightenment in America*, New York, 1976, is the first serious attempt to define this subject; J P Greene, *The Quest for Power: The Lower house of Assembly in the Southern Royal Colonies, 1689–1776*, Chapel Hill, 1963, is the best study of constitutional conflicts in the colonies (but does not include New England). Bernard Bailyn, *The Origins of American Politics*, New York, 1969, is admirable on the radicalism preceding the American Revolution, reinforcing the important work of Bailyn (ed)., *Pamphlets of the American Revolution, 1750–1776: Vol I, 1750–1765*, Cambridge, Mass., 1965.

2. The first new nation

A Wide-ranging, authoritative survey of the culture and thought of the period is Russel B Nye, *The Cultural Life of the New Nation 1776–1830*, New York and London, 1960. The nature of Republican culture is also the subject of the later chapters of Howard Mumford Jones, *O Strange New World: American Culture: The Formative Years*, New York, 1964; London, 1965. Moses Coit Tyler, *The Literary History of the American Revolution 1763–83* (2 vols), New York, 1897 (reprinted New York, 1957), though partly superseded by modern scholarship, is still an indispensable mine of information. Russel B Nye, *American Literary History 1607–1830*, New York, 1970, is an excellent concise introduction to the main authors and themes. A comprehensive study of the evolution of American literary consciousness is Benjamin T Spencer, *The Quest for Nationality; An American Literary Campaign*, Syracuse, N Y, 1957. Lewis Leary, *Soundings*, Athens, Georgia, 1975, is a stimulating gathering of papers on early American writers, some familiar, others largely forgotten. Robert E Spiller, *The American Literary Revolution 1783–1837*, New York,

1967, is an interesting collection of contemporary materials illustrating the debate concerning American literary independence; other useful collections of historical and literary documents are: Charles L Sandford, *Quest for America 1810–24*, New York, 1964, and Rebecca Grumer, *American Nationalism 1783–1830*, New York, 1971.

Three studies provide differing but representative views of historical approaches to the problem of party conflict after the ratification of the Constitution: James M Banner Jr, *To the Hartford Convention*, New York, 1970, examines New England Federalism in terms of social rather than secessionist factors; Linda K Kerber, *Federalists in Dissent*, Ithaca, N Y, 1970, looks at forms of Federalist opposition; while Richard Buel Jr, *Securing the Revolution*, Ithaca, N Y, 1972, addresses itself to the ways in which party ideologies developed. A good survey of party growth during the Revolution and early years of the Republic is M J Heale, *The Making of American Politics 1750–1850*, London, 1977. Arthur H Shaffer, *The Politics of History*, Chicago, 1975, examines the relationship of the first national historians to concepts of the development of American society; while Perry Miller, *The Life of the Mind in America*, New York, 1965, is particularly valuable for its analysis of religious and legal interpretations of the national experience. Several works are devoted directly and broadly to the form and content of American national outlooks: Merle Curti, *The Roots of American Loyalty*, New York, 1946, is a pioneer study which retains considerable value; also valuable is Clinton Rossiter, *The American Quest 1790–1860*, New York, 1971. Paul C Nagel, *One Nation Indivisible*, New York, 1964, traces the intellectual growth of the idea of Union, while Ernest Lee Tuveson, *Redeemer Nation*, Chicago, 1968, brilliantly explores the role of millenial ideas in advancing the national consciousness of the country.

3.   New England in the nation

In addition to the titles cited in the Notes and references at the end of Chapter 3, students would find it useful to look first at J T Adam's still fresh *New England in the Republic, 1776–1850*, Boston, 1926. On the decline of the first party system, early sectional conflicts and their containment, the reader should consult J M Banner's *To the Hartford Convention*, New York, 1970; Shaw Livermore's *The Twilight of Federalism*, Princeton, 1962; and George Dangerfield's *The Awakening of American Nationalism*, New York, 1965. Walter M Merrill's *Against Wind and Tide*, Cambridge, Mass., 1963, is a sympathetic account of Garrison, one of the most controversial New England reformers; and F O Gattell's *John Gorham Palfrey and the New England Conscience*, Cambridge, Mass., 1963, is an interesting biography of a more conservative but equally humane Bostonian. George H Calcott's *History in the United States, 1800–1860*, Baltimore and London, 1970, is the best introduction to its subject, as is Nancy F Cott's, *The Bonds of Womanhood*, New Haven, 1977; while two studies which synthesize much recent work and methodological developments in their respective areas are Edward Pessen's *Jacksonian America*, Homewood, Ill., 1969, and Peter R Knight's *The Plain People of Boston, 1830–1860*, New York, 1971.

Standard editions for all the main writers in the American Renaissance are now in process, mainly from university presses and under the auspices of the Modern Language Association of America: Ralph Waldo Emerson (the Belknap Press of the Harvard U P); Henry David Thoreau (Princeton U P); Walt Whitman (New York U P); Nathaniel Hawthorne (Ohio State U P); Herman Melville (The Northwestern U P and the Newberry Library) and Emily Dickinson (the Belknap Press of the Harvard U P). Three useful anthologies of Transcendentalist poetry and prose are: George F Whicher (ed), *Poetry of the New England Renaissance 1790–1890*, New York, 1950; Perry Miller (ed), *The American Transcendentalists: Their Prose and Poetry*, New York, 1957, and George Hochfield (ed), *Selected Writings of The American Transcendentalists*, New York, 1966.

The standard critical account of the period is F O Matthiessen, *American Renaissance: Art and Expression in the Age of Emerson and Whitman*, New York, 1941, which may usefully be read with two earlier studies: Lewis Mumford, *The Golden Day; A Study in American Experience and Culture*, New York, 1926, and Van Wyck Brooks, *The Flowering of New England: 1815–1865*, New York, 1936. For an understanding of the various cultural debates and currents of thought, see also Perry Miller, *The Raven and the Whale: The War of Words and Wits in the Era of Poe and Melville*, New York, 1956, and Lawrence Buell, *Literary Transcendentalism: Style and Vision in the American Renaissance*, Ithaca, NY, 1973. A lively, combative account of the inner meanings of the American Renaissance remains D H Lawrence, *Studies in Classic American Literature*, New York, 1923.

Recent scholarship in the period has been prolific. A good general introduction is Harry Levin, *The Power of Blackness*, New York, 1958. The Adamic typology is studied in R W B Lewis, *The American Adam*, Chicago, 1955; the interaction of technology and the frontier in Leo Marx, *The Machine in the Garden*, New York, 1964; the place of folklore and popular tradition in Daniel Hoffman, *Form and Fable in American Fiction*, New York, 1961; the 'subversive' meanings of American literature in Leslie Fiedler, *Love and Death in the American Novel*, New York, 1960; the workings of the symbolic imagination in Charles Feidelson, *Symbolism and American Literature*, Chicago, 1953; and the connections between literature and society in the period in A N Kaul, *The American Vision: Actual and Ideal Society in Nineteenth-Century Fiction*, New Haven, 1963. A study which offers useful discriminations is Marius Bewley, *The Complex Fate*, London, 1952, together with its successor, *The Eccentric Design: Form in the*

Classic American Novel, New York, 1959. Two general studies of American literary tradition are indispensable: Richard Chase, *The American Novel and its tradition*, Garden City, N Y, 1957, and Roy Harvey Pearce, *The Continuity of American Poetry*, Princeton, 1961.

4. The Old South

The fascination which the Old South has held for historians and literary critics alike means that the modern reader is faced with a wealth of material to which he may turn for further study or recreation. The choice of a limited bibliography is, therefore, very difficult; many excellent works have had to be omitted.

General surveys of Southern history whose early chapters cover the period up to the Civil War include Francis Butler Simkins and Charles Pierce Roland, *A History of the South* (4th edn), New York, 1972, an admirable revision and updating of Simkin's standard work, and Monroe Lee Billington, *The American South*, New York, 1971, a comprehensive and up-to-date study of Southern politics, economics and culture. On the period up to 1860, Clement Eaton, *A History of the Old South: The Emergence of a Reluctant Nation* (3rd edn), New York, 1975, is a perceptive, well-written and balanced study. Monroe Lee Billington (ed), *The South: A Central Theme?*, New York, 1969, selects extracts from works on the nature of the South by historians seeking a central theme or explanation of the South's distinctiveness. In similar vein, W J Cash, *The Mind of the South*, New York, 1941, was an early attempt to separate the myth and reality of Southern development; while Charles Eaton, *The Mind of the Old South*, Baton Rouge, 1964, attempts to trace the development of the Southern mind through representative individuals from 1820 to 1860. William R Taylor, *Cavalier and Yankee: The Old South and America National Character*, New York, 1957, investigates the plight of the South within the nation, its search for an historical identity and the resultant historical myths that grew up; and C Vann Woodward, *The Burden of Southern History* (rev. edn), Baton Rouge, 1968, is a collection of essays by an outstanding writer on Southern history, again suggesting explanations for or definitions of the distinctive character of the Southern heritage.

More detailed works on particular periods or aspects of Southern history include the early volumes of the excellent *History of the South* series published by Louisiana State University Press; Vol. I, Wesley Frank Craven, *The Southern Colonies in the Seventeenth Century, 1607–1689*, 1949; Vol. III, John Richard Alden, *The Revolution in the South, 1763–1789*, 1957; Vol. IV, Thomas P Abernethy, *The South in the new Nation, 1789–1819*, 1961; Vol. V, Charles S Sydnor, *The Development of Southern Sectionalism, 1819–1848*, 1948, and Vol. VI,

Avery O Craven, *The Growth of Southern Nationalism, 1848–1861*, 1953. The more recent work by David M Potter, completed and edited by Don E Fehrenbacher, *The Impending Crisis, 1848–1861*, New York, 1976, is a book of impressive length and quality (over 600 pages) offering a fine study of the complex politics and crisis of the 1850s. A balanced and panoramic view of Southern society in the period of immense change and expansion between the adoption of the Federal Constitution and the Civil War is to be found in Clement Eaton, *The Growth of Southern Civilization, 1790–1860*, New York, 1961.

Studies of Southern ante-bellum society include Charles S Sydnor's *Gentlemen Freeholders: Political Practices in Washington's Virginia*, Chapel Hill, 1952, stressing the role and importance of the aristocracy; Frank L Owsley, *Plain Folk of the Old South*, Baton Rouge, 1949, is a useful counterbalance, emphasizing the yeoman influence. The role of the slave and slavery has become very contentious since Urich B Phillips in his *American Negro Slavery*, New York, 1918, and *Life and Labour in the Old South*, Boston, 1929, offered a sympathetic, even sentimental, view of slavery. A much more hostile view appeared in Kenneth M Stampp, *The Peculiar Institution. Slavery in the Ante-Bellum South*, New York, 1956, and Stanley M Elkins, *Slavery: A Problem in American Institutional and Intellectual Life* (3rd edn), Chicago, 1976. Eugene D Genovese, *The Political Economy of Slavery*, New York, 1965, and *Roll Jordan Roll: The World the Slaves Made*, New York, 1974, explains much of the routine life of southern slaves and offers a Marxist view. John W Blassingame, *The Slave Community: Plantation Life in the Antebellum South*, New York, 1972, is thorough, thoughtful and balanced. Robert William Fogel and Stanley L Engerman, *Time on the Cross: The Economics of American Negro Slavery*, Boston, 1974, offered a reappraisal of the viability of slavery based on detailed statistical data incomprehensible to non-specialists, this though now much criticized, has left a permanent mark. Ira Berlin, *Slaves Without Masters: The Free Negro in the Antebellum South*, New York, 1974, is useful on a neglected topic.

No subject in American history has received more extensive treatment than the Civil War, and several good surveys of the rise and fall of the Confederacy exist, including Frank E Vandiver, *Their Tattered Flags: The Epic of the Confederacy*, New York, 1970, a spirited chronological survey; Charles P Roland, *The Confederacy*, Chicago, 1960, Clement Eaton, *History of the Southern Confederacy*, New York, 1954, and Albert D Kirwan, (ed), *The Confederacy A Social and Political History in Documents*, New York, 1959. On the post-war situation, Kenneth M Stampp, *The Era of Reconstruction 1865–1877*, New York, 1965, is an outstanding synthesis of modern writing, while Rembert Patrick, *The Reconstruction of the Nation*, New York, 1967, is a well-balanced and scholarly summary of the same period. Paul H Buck, *The Road to Union 1865–1900*, Boston, 1937, is a beautifully written account which argues that rational integration was more important than divergence in these years.

On the literary front, Mark Twain's *Huckleberry Finn*, 1885, Harriet Beecher Stowe's *Uncle Tom's Cabin*, 1852, and the writings of Edgar Allan Poe are readily available in modern editions; but the works of the majority of the Old South's own writers, including those mentioned in the text, are much less easily obtained. However, libraries may provide copies of William Gilmore Simms's *The Yemassee*, 1835, *Beauchampe*, 1842, and *Woodcraft*, 1854; and of John Pendleton Kennedy's *Swallow Barn*, 1832, and *Horse-shoe Robinson*, 1835.

Sidney Lanier and Henry Timrod were probably the best poets of the Old South. The standard literary history of the Old South is Jay B Hubbells, *The South in American Literature 1607–1900*, Durham, NC, 1954, and Rollin G Osterweiss, *Romanticism and Nationalism in the Old South*, New Haven, Conn., 1949, is a lively account of aspects of the cultural history of the Old South. Louis D Rubin's, *The Writer in the South, Studies in a Literary Community*, Athens, Georgia, 1972, is a fine recent study of the relationship between the South and its writers.

5.   The Frontier West

Though Frederick Jackson Turner was not the first to see the link between the American Frontier West and the growth of a distinctive national culture, his powerful statement of 1893 is the best place to begin a study of it. It has been extensively reprinted, notably in Ray Allen Billington (ed), *The Frontier Thesis: Valid Interpretation of American History?*, New York, 1966, and in George Rogers Taylor (ed), *The Turner Thesis: Concerning the Role of the Frontier in American History* (3rd edn), Lexington, 1972, two valuable anthologies. Billington, while supporting Turner's view, has increasingly attended to the complex factors producing national culture: his latest, most intricate examination is his *America's Frontier Heritage*, New York, 1966. This appears in the valuable series *Histories of the American Frontier*, under Billington's general editorship, notable volumes being Douglas E Leach, *The Northern Colonial Frontier, 1607–1763*, 1966, Kack M Sosin, *The Revolutionary Frontier, 1763–1783*, 1967; Reginald Horsman, *The Frontier in the Formative Years, 1783–1815*, 1970; Rodman Wilson Paul, *Mining Frontiers of the Far West, 1848—1880*, 1963; Oscar O Winther, *The Transportation Frontier: Trans-Mississippi West, 1865–1890*, 1964; and Gilbert C Fite, *The Farmer's Frontier, 1865–1900*, 1966.

Billington also gives a magisterial survey of the entire process of westward movement in his *Westward Expansion* (4th edn), New York, 1974. On this, also see Robert V Hine, *The American West: An*

Interpretative History, Boston, 1973, and R A Burchell (ed), *Westward Expansion*, London, 1974, a collection of documents on the subject. The modern study of towns in the West was begun by Richard C Wade, *The Urban Frontier: The Rise of Western Cities, 1790–1830*, Cambridge, Mass., 1959, which can be supplemented with Robert R Dykstra, *The Cattle Towns*, New York, 1968, and Duane A Smith, *Rocky Mountain Mining Camps: The Urban Frontier*, Bloomington, 1967. One dimension of the culture of the West is explored by Joe B Frantz and Julian E Choate, *The American Cowboy: The Myth and the Reality*, Norman, Oklahoma, 1955, and another by Kent L Steckmesser, *The Western Hero in History and Legend*, Norman, Oklahoma, 1965. The Indian is valuably surveyed in William T Hagan, *American Indians*, Chicago, 1961, while a comparison between the American frontier and frontiers elsewhere is found in Walker D Wyman and Clifton B Kroeber, (eds), *The Frontier in Perspective*, Madison, 1957.

The classic study of the frontier myth in literature and culture is Henry Nash Smith, *Virgin Land: The American West as Symbol and Myth*, Cambridge, Mass., 1950. Lucy L Hazard, *The Frontier in American Literature*, 1927 (2nd edn., New York, 1961), seeks to apply the frontier thesis to nearly all American writing, while Percy H Boynton, *The Rediscovery of the Frontier*, Chicago, 1931, is a useful summary of other books and arguments. But more perceptive is Edwin Fussell, *Frontier: American Literature and the American West*, Princeton, 1965, which concentrates on major nineteenth-century writers; Louis B Wright, *Culture on the Moving Frontier*, Bloomington, 1955; and Hans Galinski, (ed), *The Frontier in American History and Literature*, Frankfurt, 1960. At a more factual level, invaluable material is to be found in Ralph L Husk, *The Literature of the Middle Western Frontier*, (2 vols), New York, 1925; Dorothy Dondore, *The Prairie and the Making of Middle America*, Cedar Rapids, 1926; Mabel Major *et al.*, *Southwest Heritage: A Literary History With Bibliography*, Albuquerque, 1938; Irma K Herron, *The Small Town in American Literature*, 1939 (2nd edn), New York, 1959; and J Frank Dobie, *Guide to the Life and Literature of the Southwest*, Austin, 1943.

Larger questions about the significance of the frontier in American literature are raised by Leo Marx, *The Machine in the Garden: Technology and the Pastoral Ideal in America*, New York, 1964, and Leslie Fiedler, *The Return of the Vanishing American*, London, 1968. Themes in American literature which grow out of the frontier experience are valuably discussed in R W B Lewis, *The American Adam: Innocence, Tragedy, and Tradition in the Nineteenth Century*, Chicago, 1955, and in Tony Tanner, *The Reign of Wonder: Naivety and Reality in American Literature*, Cambridge, England, 1965. Finally, R E Spiller *et al.*, *The Literary History of the United States* (2 vols, 3rd edn), New York, 1963, offers many valuable discussions of the subject, including an entire section (section 6, in volume 2) devoted to the theme.

6. The immigrant experience

The study of American immigration, in all of its variety, has inevitably produced a number of attempts at synthesis. Among the first, and still most readable is Oscar Handlin, *The Uprooted*, Boston, 1951. More recent studies by M A Jones, *American Immigration*, Chicago, 1960, and P A M Taylor, *The Distant Magnet*, London, 1971, usefully survey the whole pattern of immigration.

More detailed monographs worthy of mention are H S Nelli, *The Italians in Chicago, 1880–1930*, New York, 1970, and Oscar Handlin, *Boston's Immigrants: A Study in Acculturation* (rev. edn), Cambridge, Mass., 1959. Among the numerous books on Jewish immigration, see Moses Rischin, *The Promised City: New York's Jews 1870–1914*, Cambridge, Mass., 1962, and Irving Howe, *World of Our Fathers* (British title: *The Immigrant Jews in New York*), London, 1976.

The native response to immigrants is magisterially treated in John Higham, *Strangers in the Land: Patterns of American Nativism, 1860–1925*, (2nd edn), New York, 1963.

The influence of ethnicity, and the prospects of assimilation, have been treated in M Gordon, *Assimilation in American Life*, New York, 1964. The religious dimension is examined by Will Herberg, *Protestant-Catholic-Jew* (rev. edn), Garden City, New York, 1960. Stephen Thernstrom, *The Other Bostonians: Poverty and progress in the American metropolis, 1880–1970*, Cambridge, Mass., 1973, suggests the connections between immigrant and urban life. Among the vast body of periodical literature on immigration, of particular interest is R J R Kennedy, 'Single or triple melting pot? Inter-marriage trends in New Haven, 1870–1940', *American Journal of Sociology*, **49**, 1944, 331–39.

Historians have been much quicker off the mark than literary critics to recognize the importance of immigration as a field of study. This may reflect the prevailing bias and formalism of criticism since the inter-war years. It may also represent a reasoned judgement, not uninfluenced by social factors, as to what actually constitutes the cultural heritage of American letters. Until very recently, immigrants made little contribution to American culture. Theirs was, above all, an instance of regionalism, and it remains true that such a judgement reflects a radical limitation of interest. The rediscovery of ethnicity and the emergence of second- and third-generation immigrant writers may eventually alter this judgement. Until it does, the study of immigrant writing will appeal mainly to sociologists and social historians. There is no satisfactory literary study of the full range of this material, and the few attempts along this line, such as Allen Guttman, *The Jewish Writer in America*, New York, 1971, have not, generally sustained a high level of theoretical interest. Immigrant writing is still marginalized in terms of the accepted canons of American literature; even undoubted masterpieces, such as Henry

Roth's *Call It Sleep*, are little-known. The Jewish 'break-through' in the 1950s has not been followed by a more general reappraisal of the relationship between ethnicity and culture.

A useful approach to the subject may be made through anthologies such as Wayne C Miller, *A Gathering of Ghetto Writers: Irish, Italian, Jewish, Black, Puerto Rican*, New York, 1972. Abraham Chapman, *Jewish-American Literature*, New York, 1974, contains an excellent selection of fiction, poetry, memoirs, and critical appraisals.

7. The black experience

Two excellent collections of documents are Gilbert Osofsky, *The Burden of Race*, New York, 1968, and Bradford Chambers, *Chronicles of Black Protest*, New York, 1968. John Hope Franklin, *From Slavery to Freedom*, New York, 1967, is a scholarly survey; Lerone Bennett, *Before the Mayflower*, Baltimore, 1966, examines black history from a black journalist's viewpoint. Authoritative historical and social studies include Kenneth Stampp, *The Era of Reconstruction*, New York, 1967; John Hope Franklin, *Reconstruction after the Civil War*, Chicago, 1961; C Vann Woodward, *The Strange Career of Jim Crow*, New York, 1955; August Meier, *Negro Thought in America 1880–1915*, Ann Arbor, 1966; Elliot M Rudwick, *Race Riot at East St Louis*, Cleveland, 1966; Dan T Carter, *Scottsboro*, Baton Rouge, 1969; Gilbert Osofsky, *Harlem: The Making of a Ghetto*, New York, 1966; Gunnar Myrdal, *An American Dilemma*, New York, 1944; Kenneth B Clark, *The Dark Ghetto*, London, 1965; E Franklin Frazier, *Black Bourgeoisie*, New York, 1962; Stokely Carmichael and Alex Hamilton, *Black Power*, London, 1968; and C E Lincoln, *Black Muslim*, Boston, 1966.

Principal autobiographies include Frederick Douglass, *Narrative of the Life of Frederick Douglass*, Booker T Washington, *Up from Slavery*, and W E B DuBois, *The Souls of Black Folk*, in *Three Negro Classics*, New York, 1965; Martin Luther King, *Stride Toward Freedom*, New York, 1958; Malcolm X [and Alex Haley], *The Autobiography of Malcolm X*, New York, 1966; Eldridge Cleaver, *Soul on Ice*, London, 1969; George Jackson, *Soledad Brother: The Prison Letters of George Jackson*, New York, 1969; and Angela Davis, *Autobiography*, New York, 1974.

Important biographical studies are Samuel Spencer, *Booker T Washington*, Boston, 1955; Francis Broderick, *W E B DuBois*, Stanford, 1959; Edmund Cronon's life of Garvey, *Black Moses*, Madison, 1955; Sally Belfrage, *Freedom Summer*, London, 1968; Theodore Rosengarten's oral history of a black sharecropper, *All God's Dangers*, New York, 1975; and David L Lewis, *Martin Luther King*, London, 1970.

Among the leading novels by black writers are Charles Chesnutt,

The Marrow of Tradition, Ann Arbor, 1969; Claude McKay, *Banjo*, New York, 1929; Richard Wright, *Native Son*, New York, 1966; Ralph Ellison, *Invisible Man*, New York, 1952; James Baldwin, *Go Tell it on the Mountain*, New York, 1953; John A Williams, *The Man Who Cried I Am*, London, 1968; Ishmael Reed, *Yellow Back Radio Broke Down*, New York, 1972; Toni Morrison, *The Song of Solomon*, New York, 1977; and Alex Haley, *Roots*, New York, 1977.

Useful collections of poetry are James Weldon Johnson, *The Book of American Negro Poetry*, New York, 1922; Dudley Randall, *The Black Poets*, New York, 1971; Clarence Major, *The New Black Poetry*, New York, 1969. Drama collections include Woodie King and Ron Milner (eds), *Black Drama Anthology*, New York, 1971; Ed Bullins, *New Plays for the Black Theatre*, New York, 1969. For particular texts see Ed Bullins, *The Theme of Blackness: The Corner and Other Plays*, New York, 1973; LeRoi Jones, *Dutchman and The Slave*, New York, 1964; and the same author's *The Motion of History and Other Plays*, New York, 1978, published under the name of Amiri Baraka.

For a study of the Negro Renaissance of the 1920s see Nathan Huggins, *Harlem Renaissance*, New York, 1971. The classic statement of its objectives can be found in Alain Locke, *The New Negro*, New York, 1923 (reprinted 1968). For a study of the Second Renaissance see C W E Bigsby, *The Second Black Renaissance*, Westport, Conn., 1980. An account of black writing in the 1930s can be found in James O Young, *Black Writers of the Thirties*, Baton Rouge, 1973, and an analysis of the cultural politics of the twentieth century in Harold Cruse, *The Crisis of the Negro Intellectual*, London, 1969.

8.   The loss of innocence: 1880–1914

There are few general history texts that cover the years 1880–1914. Robert H Wiebe, *The Search for Order, 1877–1920*, New York, 1967, is an excellent study of important themes in the period, and Ray Ginger, *Age of Excess: The United States from 1877–1914*, New York, 1965, is a highly readable account. See also Henry F May, *The End of American Innocence, 1912–1917*, New York, 1959. The impact of industrialism is covered in Thomas C Cochran, *The Age of Enterprise: A Social History of Industrial America*, New York, 1942, and Samuel F Hays, *The Response to Industrialism, 1885–1914*, Chicago, 1957. Both works combine social and economic history. The standard work on cities is Blake McKelvey, *The Urbanization of America 1860–1915*, New Brunswick, 1963; an older study, Arthur M Schlesinger, *The Rise of the City 1878–1898*, New York, 1933, remains a valuable account of rural and urban changes in the late nineteenth century. Richard Hofstadter, *Social Darwinism in American Thought*, Boston, 1955, is the best guide to the American Spencerians, but it should be read in tandem with Sidney Fine, *Laissez-faire and the General Welfare State: A Study of Conflict in American Thought, 1865–1901*, Ann Arbor, 1957, and Charles H Hopkins, *The Rise of the Social Gospel in American Protestantism, 1865–1915*, New Haven, 1940, for a broader picture of the critics of Social Darwinism. The essays edited by H Wayne Morgan, *The Gilded Age*, Syracuse, 1970, present a more constructive view of the period than older critical studies. This is also true of the brilliant essays found in Herbert G Gutman, *Work, Culture and Society in Industrializing America: Essays in American Working-Class and Social History*, New York, 1976. The sections on Populists and Progressives in Richard Hofstadter, *The Age of Reform: from Bryan to F D R*, New York, 1955, offer a stimulating interpretation of the epoch. There is a need for a specific study of the 'New' immigrants, but P A M Taylor, *The Distant Magnet: European Migration to the USA*, and Maldwyn Jones, *Destination America*, London, 1976, provide valuable information on emigrants to America in this period.

The most comprehensive literary history of the period is Jay Martin, *Harvests of Change: American Literature 1865–1914*, Englewood Cliffs, N J, 1967, though this should be read in conjunction with Van Wyck Brooks, *The Confident Years: 1885–1915*, New York, 1952, and Alfred Kazin, *On Native Grounds: An Interpretation of Modern American Prose Literature*, New York, 1942. Equally good, though restricted to the writings of one decade, is Larzer Ziff, *The American 1890s: Life and Times of a Lost Generation*, London, 1967. Of the various studies of Realism and Naturalism, Warner Berthoff, *The Ferment of Realism, 1884–1919*, New York, 1965, and Robert W Schneider, *Five Novelists of the Progressive Era*, New York, 1965, are particularly useful. Though it does not cover the same period as this chapter, George Wickes, *Americans in Paris, 1903–1939*, New York, 1969, is an interesting study of American expatriate writers.

9. The Twenties

Even if the Twenties are no longer regarded as merely a period of fun and frivolity, the decade remains enigmatic. Many issues which have preoccupied scholars over the past twenty years were first highlighted by Henry F May in his lucid article 'Shifting perspectives on the 1920s', *Mississippi Valley Historical Review*, 43, (1956), 405–27. A thorough bibliographical discussion of historical scholarship up to 1965 can be found in Burl Noggle, 'The Twenties: A new historiographical frontier', *Journal of American History*, 53, (1966), 299–314. Some of the best articles on the Twenties have been collected in a volume edited by John Braeman, Robert H Bremner and David Brody, *Change and Continuity in Twentieth Century America: The 1920s*, Columbus, Ohio, 1968. The best general account of the period is still W E Leuchtenberg, *The Perils of Prosperity, 1914–1932*, Chicago,

1958, 1963 and 1973 (a revised version is shortly to be published). Essays on The Great War and the Twenties are collected in Arthur Link (ed), *The Impact of World War I*, New York, 1969.

Contemporary analyses and comments are essential to a sense of the spirit of the Twenties. George Mowry has organized an excellent thematic anthology of contemporary texts, *The Twenties: Fords, Flappers and Fanatics*, Englewood Cliffs, N J, 1963. Some writings of H L Mencken have been collected by Malcolm Moos (ed), *A Carnival of Buncombe*, New York, 1960. Edmund Wilson, *The American Earthquake*, New York, 1958, gives a cultural overview of the Twenties, and *The Shores of Light*, New York, 1952, collects his witty and influential essays and reviews. Malcolm Cowley, *Exile's Return*, New York, 1951 (first publ. 1934), is deservedly the standard memoir of expatriation. Joseph Wood Krutch candidly expressed misgivings about modern values in *The Modern Temper: A Study and A Confession*, New York, 1929, written before the Great Crash.

The traditional view that nothing of significance happened in politics in the Twenties is gradually being eroded. Robert K Murray, *The Politics of Normalcy: Governmental Theory and Practice in the Harding–Coolidge Era*, New York, 1973, condenses and expands his lengthy work on Harding and offers a good and lively interpretation of normalcy. Andrew Sinclair, *The Available Man*, New York and London 1965, paints a redemptive portrait of Harding and shows why his election was more than an accident. David Burner, *The Politics of Provincialism: The Democratic Party in Transition, 1918–32*, New York, 1968, and Samuel Lubell's earlier work *The Future of American Politics*, New York, 1952 analyse the undercurrent of political change that was flowing in the Twenties. The problem of the apparent eclipse of Progressivism was raised by Arthur Link 'What Happened to the Progressive Movement?', *American Historical Review*, **64** (1959), and is examined more deeply in Paul Glad, 'Progressives and the Business Culture of the 1920s', *Journal of American History*, **55** (1966), 75–89, and Don Kirschner, 'Publicity properly applied: The selling of expertise in America, 1900–1929', *American Studies*, **19** (1) (Spring 1978). The cultural richness of the Twenties has been recognized for some time now. Frederick J Hoffman's *The Twenties*, New York, 1955, (rev. ed, 1972), is still probably the best literary critical study of the period, with seven critical essays on central texts at the end of each chapter. Malcolm Bradbury and D Palmer (eds), *The American Novel in the Nineteen Twenties* (Stratford on Avon Studies, Volume 13, London, 1971), is a valuable collection of critical essays on American fiction and society. Daniel Aaron, *Writers on the Left*, Oxford and New York, 1961 (reprinted 1977), is an authoritative study of the radical and proletarian tradition in twentieth-century American literature, offering an illuminating account of the transition from Twenties bohemian radicalism to the Communist party–dominated movement of the thirties. Alfred Kazin's *On Native Grounds*, New

York, 1942, (rev. edn, 1956), is a study of the realist tradition in American fiction, culminating in the 1920s.

F Scott Fitzgerald's witty essays in *The Crack-Up*, Harmondsworth, 1965 (first pub. 1945), analyse the period and Fitzgerald's own role in creating it, while Frederick Lewis Allen, *Only Yesterday*, New York, 1959 (first pub. 1931), offers a lighter contemporary view.

Since the Twenties marked the emergence of modern American criticism, many important studies of the artistic and literary temper were written by critics whose ideas were formed then. Edmund Wilson, *Axel's Castle*, New York, 1931, was written *for* the period as well as about it. Allen Tate, *The Man of Letters in the Modern World*, New York, 1955; Yvor Winters, *In Defense of Reason* (3rd, edn), 1947; Cleanth Brooks, *Modern Poetry and the Tradition*, New York, 1939; John Crowe Ransom, *The World's Body*, Port Washington, New York, 1954 (first pub. 1938); and R P Blackmur, *Form and Value in Modern Poetry*, New York, 1957, are all collections of essays on the modern period by so-called 'New Critics'. The academic, form-orientated New Criticism was shaped both by Twenties literature and by the criticism of T S Eliot, *The Sacred Wood*, 1920, and I A Richards's *The New Criticism*, 1924. C K Stead, *The New Poetic*, London, 1964, and Monroe K Spears, *Dionysius and the City*, New York and London, 1970, offer more evenhanded summaries of Modernism, as do the essays collected in Malcolm Bradbury and James McFarlane (eds),*Modernism*, Harmondsworth, 1976.

Robert and Helyn Lynd's indispensable *Middletown: A Study in American Culture*, New York, 1929, is the classic sociological study of changing values in middle America. *Middletown* is also highly symptomatic of the period it analyses so revealingly.

Many of the divisive issues of the 1920s have, quite rightly, not been studied exclusively in terms of that decade. John Higham, *Strangers in the Land: Patterns of American Nativism*, New Brunswick, N J 1955, includes several excellent chapters analysing the movement for immigration restriction. Joseph Gusfield makes a very telling analysis of the social roots of the prohibition movement in *Symbolic Crusade: Status Politics and the American Temperance Movement*, Urbana and London, 1963. Lawrence Levine, *Defender of the Faith*, New York, 1965, looks at the last decade of William Jennings Bryan's life, and illuminates not only Bryan's career but also the fundamantalist religious controversy.

To understand the economics of the period George Soule, *Prosperity Decade, 1917–1929*, New York, 1947, although over thirty years old, is still very useful. Jim Potter, *The American Economy Between the Wars*, London, 1974, is succinctly written and crammed with important figures. John Kenneth Galbraith, *The Great Crash 1929*, Boston, 1954, is a highly readable book for non-economists. Morrell Heald, 'Business Thought in the Twenties', *American Quarterly*, **13** (1961), 126–39, examines the business creed, and John

William Ward, 'The meaning of Lindbergh's flight', *American Quarterly*, **10** (1958), 3–16, demonstrates how the creed was not held without ambivalence. Labour has frequently been forgotten during this period, But Irving Bernstein's *The Lean Years*, Boston, 1960, gives an excellent account of the eclipse of the labour movement.

William Chafe, *The American Woman: Her Changing Social, Economic, and Political Roles, 1920-1970*, New York, 1972, contradicts the prevalent impression that the role of women improved dramatically during the decade. Paula Fass, *The Damned and the Beautiful*, New York, 1977, although rather too long, is a good examination of the youth culture. The American interpretation of Freud can be found in F H Matthews, 'The Americanization of Sigmund Freud: Adaptations of psychoanalysis before 1917', *Journal of American Studies*, **1** (1) (1967), 39–62, and in Nathan G Hale, Jr, *Freud and the Americans*, Vol. 1 New York, 1971.

In Kevin Brownlow, *The Parade's Gone By*, London, 1968, survivors of Hollywood in the Twenties tell how movies were made and unmade in the studio system. Robert Sklar, *Movie-Made America*, New York, 1975, surveys the interdependence of Hollywood and the rest of American culture. (There is as yet no authoritative critical study of American cinema in the Twenties.)

American art of the 1920s still suffers critically from being seen as a backwater. Harold Rosenberg, *The Tradition of the New*, London, 1970 (first pub. 1961), traces artistic modernism up through the 1950s. Milton W Brown, *The Modern Spirit*, London, 1977, is an illustrated catalogue from the Hayward Gallery which divides the period into tidy 'movements'. Barbara Rose, *American Art Since 1900*, London, 1967, offers a reasonable survey. Bibliographies of black culture and the literature of immigration in the Twenties are found above (Chapters 6 and 7).

10. The Thirties

Among the enormous amount of popular and specialized literature on the New Deal, John Major, *The New Deal*, London, 1968, is a useful annotated anthology of source materials, while Paul K Conkin, *The New Deal*, London, 1968, judiciously analyses the shortcomings of the New Deal. William E Leuchtenburg, *Franklin D Roosevelt and the New Deal, 1932-40*, New York, 1963, remains the best one-volume treatment of the period. J M Burns's excellent *Roosevelt: the Lion and the Fox*, New York, 1956, can be supplemented by Frank Freide's massive biography – 2 volumes to date – *Franklin D Roosevelt*, Boston, 1952–73. Arthur M Schlesinger's first three volumes of the *Age of Roosevelt*: 1. *The Crisis of the Old Order*; 2. *The Coming of the New Deal*; 3. *The Politics of Upheaval*, Boston, 1957–60, are partisan but still a major contribution to the subject. Only slightly less brilliant than *Only Yesterday*, his classic about the 1920s, Frederick Lewis Allen, *Since Yesterday*, New York, 1961, (first pub. 1939) is a witty and evocative portrayal of the social and political events of the time.

William Stott, *Documentary Expression and Thirties America*, New York, 1973, is indispensable and a delight to read. Comparable works of cultural/literary history are Daniel Aaron's study of the influence of radicalism, *Writers on the Left*, New York 1965, and Leo Gurko, *The Angry Decade*, New York, 1968. The last third of Alfred Kazin, *On Native Grounds*, Garden City, NY 1956, is still the best introduction to the Depression novel. Richard H Pells, *Radical Visions and American Dreams*, New York, 1973, is a comprehensive intellectual history with a marvellous bibliography. Pells's excellent discussion of movies can be supplemented by John Baxter, *Hollywood in the Thirties*, London/New York, 1968.

Elegant social and political reportage is to be found in Edmund Wilson *The American Earthquake*, London, 1958, and useful anthologies of Depression materials are Jack Salzman (ed), *Years of Protest*, New York, 1967, and Joseph North (ed), *New Masses: An Anthology of the Rebel Thirties*, New York, 1969. But the authentic voice of Thirties America is clearest in Studs Terkel, *Hard Times*, New York, 1971, and Woody Guthrie's autobiography, *Bound For Glory*, London, 1974.

11. War and cold war

Three highly readable surveys of this period are Eric Goldman, *The Crucial Decade and After: America, 1945-1960*, New York, 1960; Carl N Degler, *Affluence and Anxiety*, Glenview, Ill., 1968; and William E Leuchtenburg, *A Troubled Feast: American Society Since 1945*, Boston, 1973. These can be usefully supplemented by Chester E Eisinger (ed), *The 1940s: Profile of a Nation in Crisis*, New York, 1969, a documents book in the Anchor 'Documents in American Civilization' series.

Wartime strategy is ably discussed in Samuel Eliot Morison, *Strategy and Compromise*, Boston, 1958. Notable among the many studies of post-war American foreign policy are John Spanier, *American Foreign Policy Since World War II*, New York, 1965; Walter La Feber, *America, Russia and the Cold War* (2nd edn), New York, 1968; and Richard M Freeland, *The Truman Doctrine and the Origins of McCarthyism*, New York, 1972. This period has been discussed from 'traditionalist' and 'revisionist' viewpoints; compare, say, Martin F Herz, *Beginnings of the Cold War*, London, 1966, with William Appleman Williams, *The Tragedy of American Diplomacy*, London, 1965. A useful corrective to some of the wilder revisionist claims is Robert Maddox, *The New Left and the Origins of the Cold War*,

Princeton, 1973.

On the politics of Truman, Eisenhower and their times, the best books are Dean Acheson, *Present at the Creation*, New York, 1969; Merle Miller, *Plain Speaking: An Oral Biography of Harry S Truman*, Berkeley, 1974; Robert J Donovan, *Conflict and Crisis: The Presidency of Harry S Truman, 1945-1948*, New York, 1977; Marquis Childs, *Eisenhower: Captive Hero*, New York, 1958; and Emmet John Hughes, *The Ordeal of Power*, New York, 1965. The most comprehensive treatment of economic developments during the period is Harold G Vatter, *The U.S. Economy in the 1950s*, New York, 1963.

America's concern with internal security and Communist subversion is discussed in Alistair Cooke, *A Generation on Trial*, New York, 1950; Edward Shils, *The Torment of Secrecy*, New York, 1956; Richard Rovere, *Senator Joe McCarthy*, New York, 1959; and David Caute, *The Great Fear*, London, 1978. Two useful books dealing with specific cases are John Major, *The Oppenheimer Hearing*, London 1971, and Allan Weinstein, *Perjury: The Hiss–Chambers Case*, New York, 1978. Earl Latham, *The Communist Controversy in Washington: From the New Deal to McCarthy*, Cambridge, Mass., 1966, provides valuable background material and has an admirably level-headed view of the question. On intellectual life in the period, see Richard M Hofstadter, *Anti-Intellectualism in American Life*, London, 1964, and Christopher Lasch, *The Agony of the American Left*, London, 1970. The text of the article refers to many key books in the period – such as J K Galbraith's *The Affluent Society*, Boston, 1958 – which considered larger questions of 'Americanism', of affluence, of homogenization, and of the US role in the modern world.

On the literary scene over this period there are few general studies, though Leslie Fiedler, *Waiting for the End: The American Literary Scene from Hemingway to Baldwin*, London, 1965, is useful, amd Alfred Kazin, *Contemporaries*, London, 1963, and Philip Rahv, *Literature and the Sixth Sense*, London, 1970, are important collections of essays. On post-war fiction, the best book is undoubtedly Tony Tanner, *City of Words: American Fiction, 1950-1970*, London, 1971; but also see Chester E Eisinger, *Fiction of the Forties*, Chicago, 1963; Harry T Moore (ed), *Contemporary American Novelists*, Carbondale, Ill., 1964; and Marcus Klein, *After Alienation: American Novels in Mid-Century*, Cleveland, 1964. For theatre, see Gerald Weales's survey, *American Drama Since World War II*, New York, 1962; Alvin Kernan (ed) *The Modern American Theatre: A Collection of Critical Essays*, Englewood Cliffs, NJ, 1967, is also valuable. On poetry, the key book is M L Rosenthal, *The Modern Poets: A Critical Introduction*, New York, 1960; see also Ralph J Mills, Jr, *Contemporary American Poetry*, New York, 1965, and Eric Homberger, *The Art of the Real*, London, 1977. On the 'beat generation' see Lawrence Lipton, *The Holy Barbarians*, New York, 1959, and Bruce Cook's more recent *The Beat Generation*, New York, 1971.

12. The Sixties and Seventies

A fuller general account of the United States over this period is in Daniel Snowman, *America Since 1920*, London, 1978, and in *Kissing Cousins*, London, 1977 (published in America as *Britain and America*, New York, 1977), where the argument is extended. L S Witten surveys the period in *Cold War America: From Hiroshima to Watergate*, New York, 1974, while Roland Weber (ed), *America in Change: Reflections on the 60s and 70s*, Notre Dame, Ind., 1972, is a useful collection of essays. For a general literary-cultural study of the period, see Morris Dickstein, *Gates of Eden: American Culture in the Sixties*, New York, 1977, an evocative if subjective set of reflections and analyses. An outsider's view of the 1960s is Michael Harrington's exposé of American poverty, *The Other America*, New York, 1962 (repr. Harmondsworth, 1971).

The best books on Kennedy and his times are Theodore C Sorenson, *Kennedy*, New York and London, 1965, and Arthur M Schlesinger, Jr, *A Thousand Days*, London, 1965. Schlesinger's *Robert Kennedy and His Times*, Boston, 1978, adds a sympathetic portrait of 'establishment' liberalism in the mid-1960s. The best insight into Johnson is Doris Kearns, *Lyndon Johnson and the American Dream*, London, 1976, while Johnson's own memoirs appear as *The Vantage Point*, London, 1972. On the counter-culture, see Theodore Roszak's sharp but sentimental *The Making of the Counter-Culture*, New York, 1969; London 1970, and Charles A Reich's unsharp and very sentimental *The Greening of America*, New York, 1970 (repr. Harmondsworth, 1971). For a portrait of the context, Daniel Bell's *The Coming of Post-Industrial Society*, New York, 1973. Among key counter-cultural texts are Alex Haley, *The Autobiography of Malcolm X*, New York, 1965 (repr. Harmondsworth, 1970); Eldridge Cleaver, *Soul on Ice*, New York, 1968; London, 1969; and Betty Friedan, *The Feminine Mystique*, New York, 1963 (repr. Harmondsworth, 1977).

On the literature of the Sixties, see Tony Tanner's excellent study of modern American fiction, *City of Words: American Fiction, 1950-1970*, London, 1971, and Raymond Olderman, *Beyond the Waste Land: The American Novel in the 1960s*, New Haven, Conn., 1972. Poetry is valuably surveyed in M L Rosenthal, *The New Poets: American and British Poetry Since World War II*, New York, 1967, and Eric Homberger, *The Art of the Real*, London, 1977. Theatre is valuably covered in Christopher Bigsby, *Confrontation and Commitment: A Study of Contemporary American Drama, 1959-1966*, Columbia, Missouri, 1967.

Few books have yet been successful in analysing the Seventies, but Christopher Lasch, *The Culture of Narcissism: American Life in an Age of Diminishing Expectations*, New York, 1978, is notable. Watergate afficionados will find volumes by most of the key figures: Richard Nixon's *Memoirs* appeared in 1978 and Henry A Kissinger's

White House Years, in 1979. On the literature of post-modernism, see Jerome Klinkowitz, *Literary Disruptions: The Making of a Post-Contemporary American Fiction*, Urbana, Ill. 1975, and Ihab Hassan, *Paracriticisms: Seven Speculations of the Times*, Chicago, 1975.

Maps

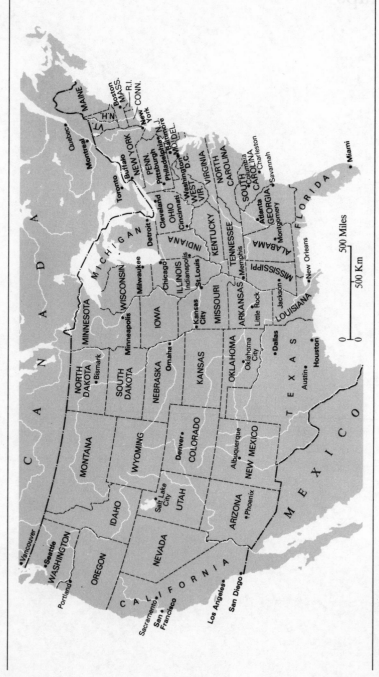

Map 1 The American States

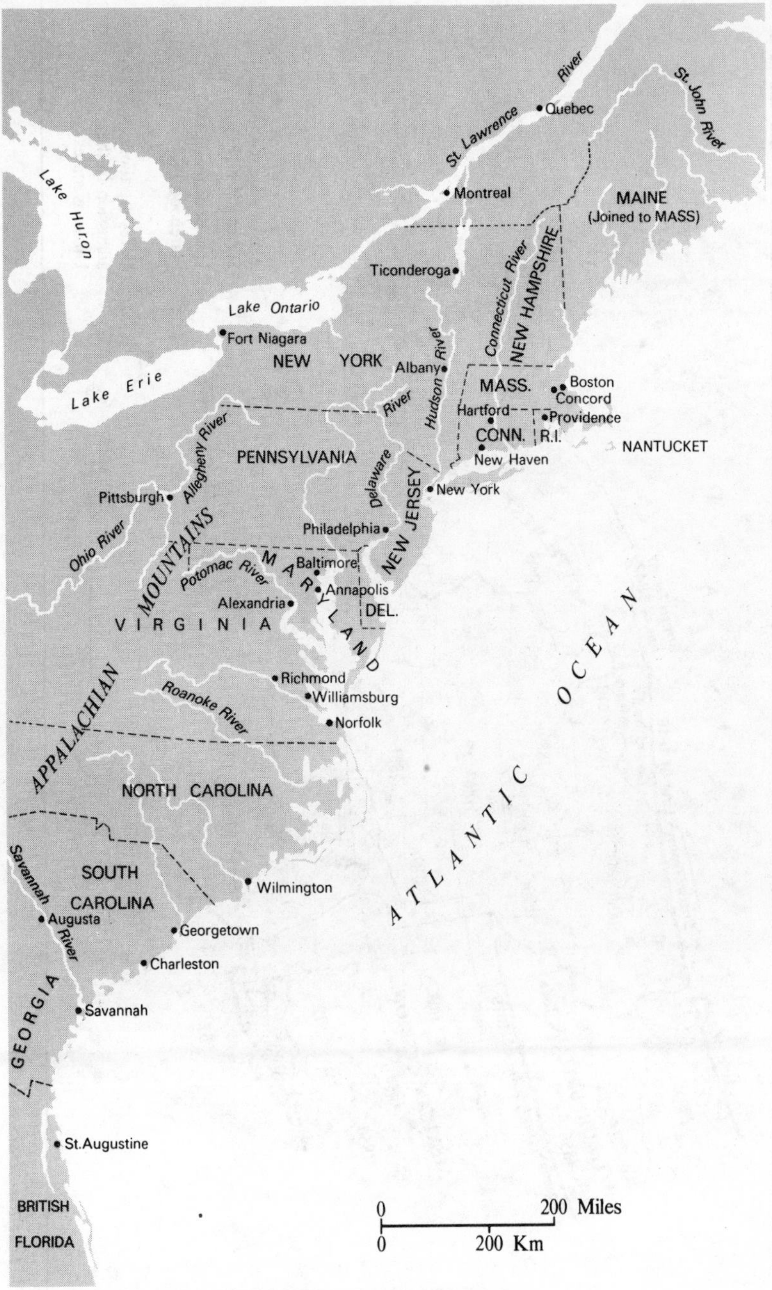

Map 2 *The original thirteen colonies*

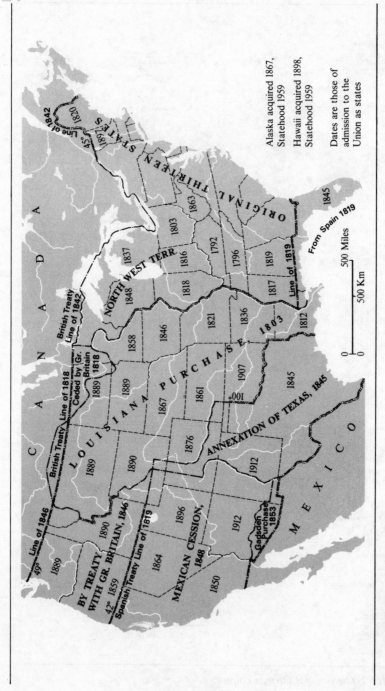

Map 3 Territorial acquisitions

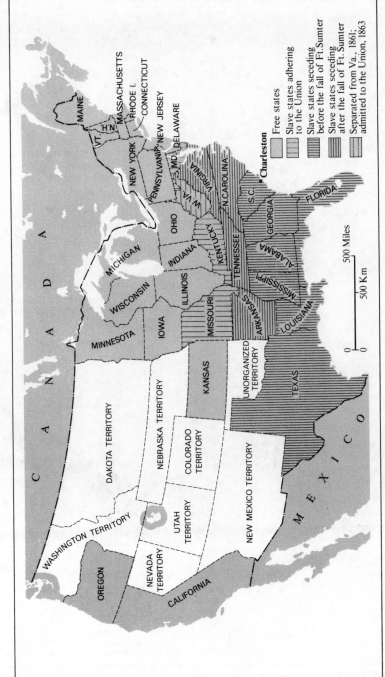

Map 4 *The Civil War*

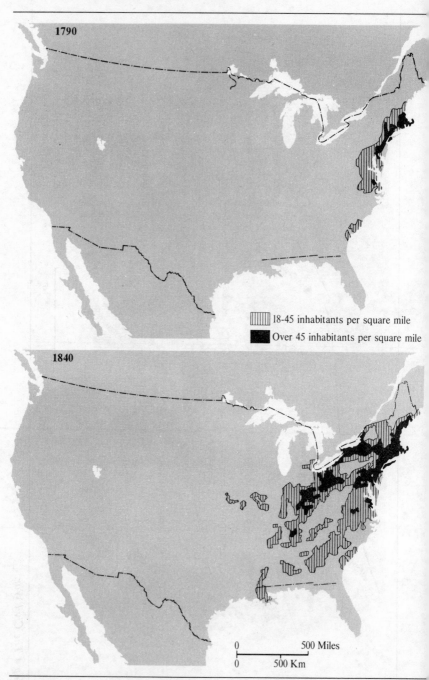

Map 5 *Population expansion, 1790 to 1940*

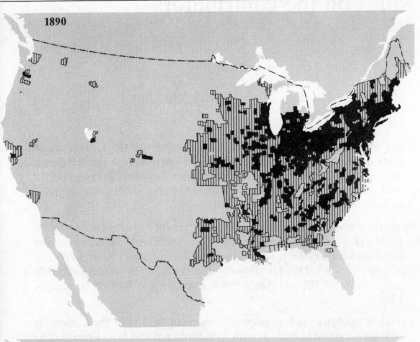

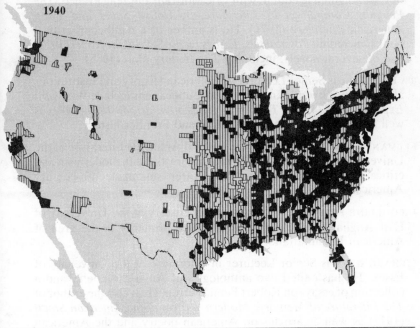

Notes on the contributors

C W E BIGSBY is Reader in American Literature at the University of East Anglia. His publications include *Confrontation and Commitment: A Study of Contemporary American Drama* (1967) and books on Edward Albee, Tom Stoppard, Dada and Surrealism, popular culture and Black American writing.

CHRISTINE BOLT is Reader in American History at the University of Kent. Her publications include *The Antislavery Movement and Reconstruction* (1969); *Victorian Attitudes to Race* (1971); *A History of the U.S.A.* (1974); *Power and Protest in American Life* (co-author, 1980); and *Antislavery, Religion and Reform* (co-editor 1980).

MALCOLM BRADBURY is Professor of American Studies at the University of East Anglia. He edited, with Eric Mottram and Jean Franco, *The Penguin Companion to Literature, 3; United States and Latin American Literature* (1971). He is author of a number of critical books, including *Possibilities: Essays on the State of the Novel* (1972) and of several novels, including *The History Man* (1975).

R A BURCHELL is Senior Lecturer in American History and Institutions at the University of Manchester. His publications include *Westward Expansion* (1974) and *The San Francisco Irish, 1848-1880* (1979) as well as articles on both Immigration and Frontier history.

ELLMAN CRASNOW lectures on English and American Literature at the University of East Anglia. His main interests are in modernism and critical theory, but he has also written on nineteenth-century American literature.

JACQUELINE FEAR lectures in American History at the University of East Anglia. Her research interests are primarily in the area of American Indian affairs.

RICHARD GRAY is Senior Lecturer in Literature at the University of Essex. He has edited two anthologies of American poetry and a collection of essays on Robert Penn Warren. He is also the author of *The Literature of Memory: Modern Writers of the American South* (1977) as well as articles on American poetry and the American South.

PHILIP HAFFENDEN is Reader in American History at the University of Southampton. His publications include *New England in the English Nation, 1689-1713* (1974), as well as essays and articles on colonial North America.

ERIC HOMBERGER. Lecturer in American Literature at the University of East Anglia, is the author of *The Art of the Real* (1977) and other studies of modern English and American literature.

ANDREW HOOK is Bradley Professor of English Literature in the University of Glasgow. His publications include *Scotland and America 1750-1835* (1975) as well as articles on Anglo-American literary relations.

BRIAN LEE is Senior Lecturer and Head of the American Studies Department at the University of Nottingham. His publications include *The Novels of Henry James: A Study of Culture and Consciousness* (1978), as well as numerous articles on a variety of aspects of American literature.

A ROBERT LEE is Lecturer in American Literature and current Chairman of the American Studies committee at the University of Kent. His publications include the Everyman edition of *Moby Dick*, recent articles on Melville, George Eliot, Chester Himes and editorship of *Black Fiction: New Studies in the Black American Novel since 1945*.

HELEN McNEIL lectures on American Literature at the University of East Anglia. She is working on a history of American literature and writes regularly for the *New Statesman*.

PETER MARSHALL is Professor of American History and Institutions in the University of Manchester. His publications are primarily concerned with aspects of Revolutionary and early national history.

EDWARD RANSON lectures in History at the University of Aberdeen. He is the author of various articles on late-nineteenth and early-twentieth-century American military policy.

ROBERT C REINDERS is Senior Lecturer in American History at the University of Nottingham. He was Executive Editor of *The Dictionary of World History* (1973) and is the author of *End of an Era: New Orleans, 1850-1860* (1964), as well as of numerous articles dealing with slavery and the antislavery movement.

DANIEL SNOWMAN has taught Politics and American Studies at the University of Sussex but since 1967 has been a producer of talks and documentaries at the BBC. His publications include *Britain and America: An Interpretation of British and American Culture, 1945 to 1975* (1977) and *America Since 1920* (1978).

HOWARD TEMPERLEY is Editor of the *Journal of American Studies* and Professor of American Studies at the University of East Anglia where he is currently Dean of the School of English and American Studies. His publications include *British Antislavery, 1833-1870* (1972), and articles dealing with various aspects of American and British History.

ROGER THOMPSON is Reader in American History at the University of East Anglia. His publications include *The Golden Door* (1969), *Women in Stuart England and America* (1974) and *Unfit for Modest Ears* (1979).

IAN WALKER is Senior Lecturer in American Literature at the University of Manchester. His research interests are primarily in the earlier part of the nineteenth century.

JOHN WHITE is Lecturer in American History at the University of Hull. His publications include *Slavery in the American South* (1970) (with Ralph Willett), and *Reconstruction after the American Civil War* (1977) as well as articles on American slavery.

RALPH WILLETT is Lecturer in American Literature at the University of Hull. His publications include *Slavery in the American South* (1970) (with John White), and articles on American theatre and popular culture. *The Open Cage*, on American cinema, will be published in 1981.

Index